COUNTER-MEMORIES IN
IRANIAN CINEMA

COUNTER-MEMORIES IN IRANIAN CINEMA

Edited by
Matthias Wittmann and Ute Holl

EDINBURGH
University Press

Edinburgh University Press is one of the leading university presses in the UK.
We publish academic books and journals in our selected subject areas across the
humanities and social sciences, combining cutting-edge scholarship with high editorial
and production values to produce academic works of lasting importance. For more
information visit our website: edinburghuniversitypress.com

© editorial matter and organisation Matthias Wittmann and Ute Holl, 2021, 2023
© the chapters their several authors, 2021

Edinburgh University Press Ltd
The Tun – Holyrood Road
12(2f) Jackson's Entry
Edinburgh EH8 8PJ

First published in hardback by Edinburgh University Press 2021

Typeset in 10/12.5 pt Sabon
by IDSUK (DataConnection) Ltd

A CIP record for this book is available from the British Library

ISBN 978 1 4744 7975 2 (hardback)
ISBN 978 1 4744 7976 9 (paperback)
ISBN 978 1 4744 7977 6 (webready PDF)
ISBN 978 1 4744 7978 3 (epub)

The right of Matthias Wittmann and Ute Holl to be identified as the editors of this
work has been asserted in accordance with the Copyright, Designs and Patents Act
1988, and the Copyright and Related Rights Regulations 2003 (SI No. 2498).

CONTENTS

List of Figures vii
Acknowledgments ix
Notes on Contributors x

    Introduction 1
    Matthias Wittmann and Ute Holl

PART I AN ARCHAEOLOGY OF POSSIBLE FUTURES

1. The Incomplete: Film, Politics, and Remembering the Past 21
   Tara Najd Ahmadi

2. *The Hidden Half*, or the Temporal and Collective Politics of Counter-Memory 31
   Sara Saljoughi

3. Counter-Investigations: On Matchboxes, Black Boxes, and other Forgotten Futures 47
   Chowra Makaremi and Emmanuel Alloa

PART II MATERIAL MATTERS: MEMORY, ACCESSIBILITY, TRANSLATION

4. An Archaeology of Access: Materiality, Historiography, and Iranian Cinema 63
   Blake Atwood

5. Black Seals: Missive from Iran's National Music 85
   Negar Mottahedeh

6. Different Time, Different Space: Filmic Forms of Counter-Memory in Abbas Kiarostami's Koker Trilogy 99
   Ute Holl

PART III   INTERSTICES. NICHES. IMPURE MEMORIES

7. Towards an Impure Memory: An Archaeology of Counter-Memories through Telescoping Lenses 121
   Matthias Wittmann

8. Seeking Love in the Interstices: Acousmatic Listening as Counter-Memory in Abbas Kiarostami's *Shirin* (2008) 146
   Michelle Langford

9. Spiritual Counter-Memories of the War: Mohammad Ali Ahangar's Recent Contributions to the *Sīnemā-ye Defāʿ-ye Moqaddas* 167
   Viktor Ullmann

PART IV   TRANSGENERATIONAL GAPS AND TRANSMISSIONS

10. *Filmfarsi* as Counter-Memory 189
    Pedram Partovi

11. A Shadow for Invisible Films: A Way to Break the Monopoly of Image Production in Iran 216
    Shahram Mokri

12. 'At the End of a Century' (1996) 229
    Bahram Beyzaie (translated by Amir Roshan)

Index 247

FIGURES

1.1	Opening scene with the still image of the girl. (Source: Screen grab from *The Newborns*, 1979)	25
1.2	Zara Khanoom talking to the crowd in front of the University of Tehran's gates. (Source: Screen grab from *The Newborns*, 1979)	27
2.1	Khosrow reading Fereshteh's revealing letter. (Source: Screen grab from *The Hidden Half*, 2001)	32
2.2	Fereshteh's (post-)revolutionary political activism. (Source: Screen grab from *The Hidden Half*, 2001)	33
3.1	The trace of a match that had been scratched. (Source: Screen grab from *Hitch*, 2019)	54
3.2	Wardrobe, full and empty at once. (Source: Screen grab from *Hitch*, 2019)	54
4.1	Audiovisual distortions commence the online version of *The Lor Girl* (1933). Underneath the static, we can see the opening credits	65
4.2	The final musical scene in the digital version of *The Lor Girl* (1933) carries some of the marks of the movie's various material forms, including a large vertical scratch and a watermark for the National Film Archive of Iran	71
5.1	The presence of recording equipment in the *mise-èn-scene* reflexively underscores the status of the film's narrative as mediated by representational technologies. (Source: Screen grabs from *Love Stricken*, 1992)	94

5.2	The natural Parisian garden landscape takes the place of a studio screen, the musicians, in effect, become the after-images of the unveiled European model. (Source: Screen grabs from *Love Stricken*, 1992)	96
6.1	While the path uses tradition to lead the way, the doors are a different matter. (Source: Screen grab from *Where is the Friend's House?*, 1987)	100–101
6.2	Structural memory and zigzagged pathways. (Source: Screen grab from *Where is the Friend's House?*, 1987)	103
7.1	Like emergency rooms, editing rooms are a recurring motif in the history of Iranian cinema. (Source: Screen grab from *May Lady*, 1997)	128
7.2	The protagonist looks at the past as if through the cross-hairs of a telescopic sight. (Source: Screen grab from *Marriage of the Blessed*, 1988)	130
7.3	The ghost of Jamshed, a former journalist who had been 'fished.' (Source: Screen grab from *Fish and Cat*, 2013)	136
7.4	The activities of 'shahīd' Motevaselian are partly hidden behind obstacles blocking the sight. (Source: Screen grab from *Standing in the Dust*, 2016)	138
8.1	Credit sequence depicting scenes from *Khoshrow and Shirin*. (Source: Screen grab from *Shirin*, 2008)	152
8.2	Tears that stream down Golshifteh Farahani's cheek. (Source: Screen grab from *Shirin*, 2008)	162
9.1(a)	The opening scene of *The Scout* . . . (Source: Screen grab from *The Scout*, 1990)	168
9.1(b)	. . . referenced in the beginning of *The Queen*. (Source: Screen grab from *The Queen*, 2012)	168
10.1	Masʿud Dihnamaki's salute to Malik Mutiʿi. (Source: Instagram)	192
10.2	Muhammad ʿAli Fardin (left) in *King of Hearts* and Muhammad Riza Gulzar (right) in *Ice Flower* playing the same role. (Source: Screen grab from Pars Video/TDH Home Entertainment)	202

ACKNOWLEDGMENTS

We would like to thank the Swiss National Science Foundation (SNSF) for supporting our three-year project 'Afterimages of Revolution and War. Trauma- and Memoryscapes in the Post-revolutionary Iranian Cinema' (Basel, Seminar for Media Studies, 2016–19), our graphic designers Caitlin Murphy and Ronny Hunger for the design of our book cover (and conference poster), *Iran Nameh* (especially Gholam Reza Afkhami) for permission to publish Bahram Beyzaie's text, Philip Farah (Beirut/Lisbon) for his critical and meticulous proofreading, Geraldine Lyons for copy-editing the manuscript, Anna Lord for creating the detailed index, and last but not least Gillian Leslie, Fiona Conn, Sam Johnson and Richard Strachan at Edinburgh University Press for their helpful advice, support, and generosity.

CONTRIBUTORS

Emmanuel Alloa is Professor of Aesthetics and Philosophy of Art at the University of Fribourg (Switzerland). His work lies at the intersection of phenomenology, contemporary philosophy, aesthetics, and social theory. He persistently deals with issues around mass violence, testimony, and subjectivation.

Blake Atwood is Associate Professor of Media Studies at the American University of Beirut. He is the author of *Reform Cinema in Iran: Film and Political Change in the Islamic Republic* (Columbia University Press 2016) and *Underground: The Secret Life of Videocassettes in Iran* (The MIT Press, forthcoming).

Ute Holl is Professor of Media Aesthetics at the Seminar for Media Studies (University of Basel). Her principal areas of research are the history of perception and epistemology of audiovisual media, the media history of acoustics and electro-acoustics, as well as experimental and anthropological films.

Michelle Langford is Associate Professor in Film Studies at the University of New South Wales (Sydney, Australia). In her research she focuses on German and Iranian cinema. She is the author of *Allegory in Iranian Cinema: The Aesthetics of Poetry and Resistance* (Bloomsbury 2019). She has also published several articles on Tahmineh Milani, Rakhshan Banietemad, and Sohrab Shahid Saless.

NOTES ON CONTRIBUTORS

Chowra Makaremi is an anthropologist, author and filmmaker. She is Tenured Research Fellow at the National Centre for Scientific Research and teaches at EHESS Graduate Institute in Paris. Since 2019 she has led the ERC programme Off-Site: *Violence, State Formation and Memory Politics: An Off-site Ethnography of Post-revolution Iran*.

Shahram Mokri graduated from the Soura College of Tehran in the field of cinema. *Ashkan, The Fascinating Ring and Other Stories*, his first feature film, made its international debut at the 2009 IFF in Busan. *Fish and Cat* was selected at the 70th Venice International Film Festival and won more than twenty awards worldwide. *Invasion* was selected at the 2017 Berlinale. *Careless Crime*, his latest feature film screened at the 2020 Venice International Film Festival, won the Independent Critics' Award for Original Screenplay. Mokri has also won dozens of awards from festivals in Iran, such as the Tehran Short Film Festival, the Fajr Film Festival, and the Cinema House Film Festival.

Negar Mottahedeh teaches Media Studies in the Program in Literature at Duke University. Her writings on film, social media, and social movements in the Middle East were published by Stanford University Press, Syracuse University Press, Palgrave, Duke University Press, and in several journals and publications such as *WIRED*, *Salon.com*, *The Hill* and *The Observer*. Her work on the global culture of memes and selfies featured at the Victoria and Albert Museum in London, at the Museum of the Moving Image in New York, and at TEDx. Her most recent book is titled *Whisper Tapes: Kate Millett in Iran* (Stanford University Press 2019). She holds a PhD in Comparative Studies in Discourse and Society from the University of Minnesota.

Tara Najd Ahmadi is a scholar and non-fiction filmmaker currently based in Vienna. In 2019 she received her PhD in Visual and Cultural Studies from the University of Rochester, where she was awarded the George Eastman Museum graduate fellowship and the Susan B. Anthony research grant. Najd Ahmadi's film essays have been shown in various venues including the International Short Film Festival Oberhausen and the Edinburgh International Film Festival.

Pedram Partovi is Associate Professor of Islamic History at the American University (Washington, DC). He has written extensively on culture, politics, and society in modern Iran. He recently published a book in Routledge's Iranian Studies series entitled *Popular Iranian Cinema before the Revolution: Family and Nation in Filmfarsi*.

Amir Roshan is a journalist and translator based in Tehran. He is also an alumnus of the Department of Media Studies at the University of Basel. He has translated several articles from Persian to English, and his translations of Persian short stories are currently in publication.

Sara Saljoughi is Assistant Professor of English and Cinema Studies at the University of Toronto. She is the co-editor of *1968 and Global Cinema* (Wayne State University Press 2018). Her essays have appeared in *Camera Obscura*, *Feminist Media Histories*, *Iranian Studies*, *Film Criticism*, and *Film International*.

Viktor Ullmann obtained his MA in Islamic Studies at Freie Universität Berlin, with a thesis focusing on the subversive elements in Iranian children's films from the 1980s. He is currently writing his PhD thesis at the Berlin Graduate School Muslim Cultures and Societies on the staging of Iranian cinema at the Berlin International Film Festival.

Matthias Wittmann is a researcher on media (especially film), curator, and writer. He was Research Associate and Chief Assistant at the Seminar for Media Studies (University of Basel) and Visiting Professor in Vienna. His main areas of research are media mnemographies, transcultural media theory, screenology (3D/360°), and Iranian Cinema, which was explored in the framework of a project ('Afterimages of Revolution and War. Trauma and Memoryscapes in the Post-Revolutionary Cinema') supported by the Swiss National Science Foundation (SNSF). In 2016 he received the Karsten-Witte award for the best scholarly article on film. He has just finished a book about the octopus (*Die Gesellschaft des Tentakels*, 2021) and is currently writing a book on *Martyrographies in Iranian Cinema*.

INTRODUCTION

Matthias Wittmann and Ute Holl

In the year 2014, the *Musée d'Art Moderne de la Ville de Paris* presented an extensive exhibition entitled 'Unedited History. Iran 1960–2014.' It was there that we came across Narmine Sadeg's installation 'Office of Investigation into Diverted Trajectories' (2014), a multimedia interpretation of Farīd ad-Dīn-e 'Aṭṭār's mystical Persian folk tale *The Conference of the Birds (Manṭeq al-ṭaīr)*. 'Attar's allegorical tale on the difficult quest of hundreds of thousands of pilgrim birds for an ideal king – the mythical Persian bird called *Sīmorgh* – ends with the thirty remaining birds having to recognize that the longed-for king is nothing other than the reflection of their own existence: *sī-morgh* also means 'thirty birds' in Persian. Sadeg's installation presents those birds who managed to reach their ideal as dead, stuffed birds, set in a circle. Even if they reached their goal, they are dead by the time they achieved it. This seems to be the fate of mankind too. However, the installation also includes the paths and trajectories of those other birds that were not able to reach their destination. They are sketched on acrylic glass, lined up and suspended on shelves in the background, as if part of an (counter-)archive of lost, deviated, and unrealized paths indicating alternative histories of the present: 'a waiting room of history,'[1] as Dipesh Chakrabarty would say; and the socio-critical writer, teacher, and translator Samad Behrangi (1939–68) would maybe add: *Let's talk about a waiting room for little black fishes.*[2]

As in Narmine Sadeg's installation, and as in any serious historiography, the concern with Iranian history challenges its investigators to search for the archive of the failed or forgotten. What is at stake then is the quest for the crushed and silenced individuals or collectives and the question of representation: how to turn the grand narratives of revolution and war into minor or singular stories and memories of revolt, uprising, refusal, and dissidence?

As the work of Narmine Sadeg demonstrates, the grand narratives themselves are strategies of eliminating the traces of defeated or deviant movements, forces, and projects. And so are historical caesuras, grand events, and the official days of their commemoration, which, in terms of the exhibition's title, 'edit' history. This is also true for the newer and more recent Iranian history. But how could one un-edit the history of Iran between 1960 and 2014? Can we dispense with the term 'revolution' in describing the events of 1978/9? Why should we? And how else can we describe the procedures when, after a period of unyielding social movements and revolts against the injustice of Mohammad Reza Pahlavi's regime, and after the regime had imposed martial law on central cities and the Shah eventually left the country in January 1979, the Ayatollah Khomeini returned from exile and an Islamic Republic was declared on 11 February? These events could be told in political terms, as the long due overthrow of a monarchy which had pompously celebrated its 2,500th anniversary in 1971 while the largest part of the population became increasingly impoverished, eventually demanding participation; or as an effect of economic megalomania, the Pahlavi family investing the fortunes of the oil boom – enabled and supported by the rapidly rising energy consumption of the Western industrial states – to build Tehran as a glittering megacity, investing in real estate speculation and (German and French) nuclear reactors, while few of Iran's towns and most of its villages still had no piped water; it could be told as a moral tale, a cultural resistance against the hegemony of US American cinema, or as a social utopian tale of the exploited, the suppressed working class raging against the arrogant display of capitalistic wealth, struggling for emancipation, with the oil workers as the avant-garde; it could be told as an episode of the Cold War – including the CIA-organized coup to topple Iran's democratically elected prime minister Mohammad Mossadegh in 1953 – and it could also be told in terms of a salvation history, a religious awakening, the departure from Western secularism towards a communal or even communist culture of a Shi'ite Imamate, a movement towards a 'postcolonial contramodernity,'[3] etc.

The films of these years, made before and after the revolution, give diverse, heterogenous, but nevertheless precise accounts of the period. They give voices, bodies, and gestures to peasants and the poor, women and children, to villains, exhausted employees, rebellious students, rural migrant workers, and courageous prostitutes in a Brechtian tradition alike. They show the environments of bourgeois couples as well as of farmers surviving in wastelands or artisan cultures in Tehran's south. While all of these films, as noirs, melodramas, comedies, folk tales, or documentaries, help to understand the events of 1978/9 – or of the later revolts – they defy simple explanation, they opt for ambiguity and paradoxes of history, for the grotesque and the miraculous of its powers, for the singularity of revolts. The films embody the thirty birds that make up the *sī-morgh* as well as the tattered corpses sketched on the sides. They call for the negotiation of historical terms such as revolution or revolt and reconsider the issue of remembering.

When Michel Foucault went to Tehran in the autumn of 1978 as a 'reporter of ideas' for the Italian newspaper *Corriere della Sera*, he rarely spoke of revolution but used the term of uprising (*soulèvement*) instead. His predilection for the term – a matter of constant controversy – was driven by a specific ethical attitude: 'to be respectful when a singularity revolts,' as he wrote in 1979 in his article 'Inutile de se soulever?' ('Useless to revolt?').[4]

Rather than denouncing, yet again, Foucault's enthusiastic endorsement for the Iranian Revolution, it might be more interesting to question the motives and reasons of his enthusiasm. In his book *Foucault and Iran: Islamic Revolution after the Enlightenment*, Behrooz-Ghamari Tabrizi emphasizes the fact that it was primarily the 'constitutive ambivalence' – a term borrowed from Edward Said – of the revolutionary movement which attracted Foucault, since the Western binary model of *secular vs. religious*, or *progressive vs. reactionary*, was no longer useful when speaking in terms of 'revolt' (*soulèvement*) in Iran.[5] Thomas Bauer, Professor of Arabic and Islamic Studies at the University of Münster (Germany), studied the role of ambiguity in past Islamic societies.[6] According to him, Islamic culture for centuries had been characterized by its extremely high degree of tolerance to ambiguity and pluralism while modern and also contemporary fundamentalists of all sides – sides that are mutually related – deny the possibility of coexisting truths and perspectives, conveying totalitarian claims to truth camouflaged as 'alternative truths' into the world. Only authoritarian regimes and ideologies try to make a tabula rasa of the past and to purify memory.

Accepting the gift of pluralism and ambiguity also means accepting the coexistence of many possible *histories of the present*, as Foucault termed it.[7] The notion of counter-memory refers to these possibilities. It maintains that there are memories that are barred from hegemonic history, that have to struggle to enter it at all, but that are, nevertheless, present und produce effects. Such memories have no credibility and no official (technological, medial, social, public, etc.) frame of articulation. For these subjugated memories that have the potential to destabilize official success stories and normative orders of re-membering, Foucault coined the term *counter-memories*, not to be confused with 'counter-revolutionary' memories. They may be understood to complement revolutionary trajectories, albeit with different means. Within the mainstream memories, these memories and their bodies remain invisible, marginalized, subjugated by power effects, epistemic oppression, and knowledge-producing techniques. In his essay, 'Nietzsche, Genealogy, History' (1971), Foucault understood counter-memory as 'a transformation of history into a totally different form of time.'[8] Counter-memories are not negations of memory; their 'counter' operates tactically on many fronts and junctions of power relations, disturbing final meanings, totalitarian conclusions, and the self-evident within the historical perspective. A genealogical perspective views memory – what could be remembered – as a product of power relations. It is not a matter of searching for the origin of remembered experiences, nor of narrating linear developments, but rather of *separating* 'from the contingency that has made us what we are, the possibility of no longer being, doing, or thinking what we are, do, or think,' hence giving a 'new impetus, as far and wide as possible, to the undefined work of freedom,'[9] and one could add: *to the undefined, incomplete, restless work of memory*. Archaeology then, as opposed to hegemonic history, is the method to carve out the 'instances of discourse' and the lines of rupture which produce and shape what we think, say, do, and remember.[10]

A genealogical and archaeological perspective as proposed by Foucault remembers history against the grain, excavating and reactivating silenced experiences and buried struggles. Certainly, counter-memories as insurrections of subjugated knowledge are tactical interventions into the present. It is from the 'here and now' that they produce disruptions, epistemic frictions, tensions between the remembered time and the time of remembering, and make available a multiplicity of possible trajectories as alternative histories of the present. And most importantly, Foucault's claim for a transformation of history into counter-memory, his 'epistemology of resistance,'[11] does not (re)master the past from the sovereign position of a timeless subject or in the name of an established truth – e.g. the truth of an accomplished revolution – but instead renders the present vulnerable to forgotten pasts. If the archive is the 'law of that which can be said,' as Foucault claims in the *Archaeology of Knowledge* (1969),[12] we should then look for counter-memories that do not obey this law while appropriating at the same time the archive and the tools of power in a tactical manner: to re-member the archive. What is interesting for an archaeology of counter-memories, is the locus in which the plurality of resistances and the converging alternative pasts meet. In our case, this place is the material of the Iranian film, as its aesthetic forms are the result of particularly complex power relations, counter-memories, and artistic interventions. An analysis of the tensions underlying cinematic memoryscapes in Iran has to take into consideration the mechanisms of repressing, urging, and searching within the cinematic forms of remembering. For this purpose, we would like to extract and adapt the following questions on the methodology of archaeology from Foucault's book:

> The description of the events of discourse poses this question: how is it that one particular statement (*énoncé*) appeared rather than another? [. . .]; we must grasp the statement in the exact specificity

of its occurrence; determine its conditions of existence, fix at least its limits, establish its correlations with other statements that may be connected with it, and show what other forms of statement it excludes [. . .] we must show why it could not be other than it was, in what respect it is exclusive of any other, how it assumes, in the midst of others and in relation to them, a place that no other could occupy [. . .] A statement (*énoncé*) is linked rather to a 'referential' that is made up not of 'things', 'facts', 'realities', or 'beings', but of laws of possibility, rules of existence for the objects that are named, designated, or described within it, and for the relations that are affirmed or denied in it [. . .] The referential of the statement forms the place, the condition, the field of emergence, the authority to differentiate between individuals or objects, states of things and relations that are brought into play by the statement itself; it defines the possibilities of appearance and delimitation [. . .].[13]

This implies that all approaches which hinge on origins, continuities, and causal relations must be criticized. By contrast, the archaeological approach considers cinematic memoryscapes as a non-linear compaction and layering of different times and competing interests. An archaeologist does not look for a homogeneous space of memory but for ruptures of transmission and gaps, for sudden redistributions and divisions in the field of memory, and thus for entirely new forms of positivity. In Foucault's view, even censorship is not only a power that prohibits and represses sexuality, but it is also a *positive technology* that prescribes, inscribes, and proliferates very specific discourses on sexuality – or meta-discourses on the power of censorship (over sexuality, film distribution, etc.). In other words, *if power always said 'no,' then no one would obey it.*[14]

The 'archive' – as the law of what can be said, as the body and system of rules of formation – also includes non-discursive elements, as Foucault will emphasize at the end of his book: the law of what can be shown and re-membered, the codes of perception, and the enunciative 'fields of memory.'[15] Looking for counter-memories in the history of Iranian cinema does not simply mean to look for alternative memories that resist the main stream of memories and the officially fabricated success stories of revolution, war, and sacred defense. An archaeological perspective that re-members the memoryscapes of post-revolutionary Iranian cinema has to grasp the statements, forms, and procedures in the exact historical specificity of their occurrence, from revolution (1978/9) and wartime (1980–8) across different political periods: the so called 'reconstruction period' under the presidency of Rafsanjani; the Second Khordat reform movement after Khatami's election (1997–2005); the green movement after the re-election of president Ahmadinejad (2009), and Iran's recent 'No Future' movement (Hamid Mohseni) under President

Rohani. This perspective takes into account different generations and transgenerational ruptures, unfinished projects and hidden paths, transcultural exchanges and translations, material histories and cultural heritages, genre histories and transgressions, impure memories and shadows of invisible films, state violence and the insistence of erased memories through multiple layers of memory politics. Of course, public memories do not insist or emerge without specific frameworks and triggering encounters. Many Iranian films – officially approved as well as underground films – enable those encounters and provide frameworks through which people feel empowered or encouraged to participate in struggles of recognition and practices of – collective and individual – remembering. At the site of Iranian cinema, (counter-)memories and (counter-)histories intersect in intricate, ambiguous, and 'multidirectional' ways, as Michael Rothberg would say: 'I suggest that we consider memory as *multidirectional*: as subject to ongoing negotiation, cross-referencing, and borrowing; as productive and not privative.'[16] We are talking about *screens* with many layerings which blur the boundaries between individual and collective memory and which refer to different pasts that are most inadequately structured with chronological 'before/after' dichotomies (before/after 1979 or 1953 or 1905 or . . .). Even though much of what Rothberg writes about multidirectional memories can also claim validity for Iranian memoryscapes, Rothberg underestimates the power of institutions and their contradictions over the structure of memoryscapes.[17] 'Even in the government there isn't a single, fixed point of view; so existing censorship does not necessarily comply with the government's own laws! . . . It is within the gaps between these different points of view, ideologies and "tastes" that we find the space to realize our films,' Rakhshan Banietemad once said in an interview.[18]

What is crucial here is the fact that films not only document ideological trends in line with the interests of dominant institutions (state, church, party, etc.), they can also act as a counterforce, elaborating a counter-history or a counter-analysis of society, as Marc Ferro suggests in *Cinéma et Histoire* (1977). The films discussed in the following all offer access to 'nonvisible zones in the past,'[19] as Ferro would say, zones which are at the same time impossible to remember and impossible to forget. Within the bounds of the past as given by the *institutions of history* (Ferro/Foucault), those zones are not (re-)presentable, not appropriable, and their depiction must often take the form of an enigma for interpretation.

According to Ferro, who considers film as an 'image-object' and proposes a cinematographic reading of history, fiction and non-fiction films can intervene in 'dominant ideological currents' and 'give back to society a history it has been deprived of by the institution of History.'[20] They can arouse a 'new awareness' of overlooked or repressed aspects. Thus, film may be considered as both 'source' and 'agent' of history, shaping 'psycho-socio-historical zones'[21] and sometimes even replacing history itself through imaginative recreation of the past.

Ferro's plea for the value of cinema as counter-history is not in favor of historical revisionism or relativism, nor is he indulging in the game of 'post-truth,' 'anything goes,' or 'alternative truths,' which always demands a superior throne from which a higher truth can be claimed and enforced. Nietzsche's unconventional perspectivism ('There are no facts, only interpretations') is the exact opposite of alternative truths, it is about defending 'true alternatives'[22] as the condition for a more appropriate understanding of objectivity, since his approach has to include experience and the exchange of standpoints (akin to the Soviet montage theory and practice). Ferro's confidence in the laboratory of cinema and the value of the intrinsic 'counter' of history, memory, and society is a plea for a sensitivity that allows us to see and to remember with multiple and different eyes.

An archaeology of counter-memories in Iranian cinema after 1979 is attentive to 'impure,' not 'purified' memoryscapes, to counter-memories that allow eccentric voices and perspectives to interact with mainstream ones, interrogating epistemic exclusions and hegemonies, producing frictions between memory claims and versions of history.

While the revolutionary years of 1978 and 1979 have long been regarded by film scholars as a radical caesura and rupture in transmission, new perspectives are currently emerging, laying the focus on resonances and recursions, reappropriations and refashionings, also across the revolutionary divide. In this respect, it could be useful to recall the ethnological meaning of *memoryscape* (as used by Clifford Geertz among others), a concept that 'refers to a structure of supra-individual commemoration that is both diachronic and synchronic, i.e. consisting of practices and objects that are inherited and through which a connection between generations is established, as well as coexisting simultaneously and functioning as materializations and procedural objectivizations of memory.'[23] The cinematic memoryscapes and after-images studied in this volume are themselves composed of different layers of temporalities and tenses, of latent time forms and moments that insist, from the time before the Iranian Revolution into the period after 1979 and up to the present.

First of all, there is an effort shared by the chapters to bring into play a plurality of histories, theories, and cultures rather than one only, and, accordingly, to be attentive to various forms of remembering and memory. A second issue traversing the chapters is a heightened concern for the barred, the unheard, and the tacit, uncovering symptoms of a counter-memory in the form of aesthetic disturbances and fissures. It is here that, thirdly, the chapters converge in their approach by taking seriously the material side of audiovisual media and their structures of distribution as well as the different forms of official and unofficial media archives. The chapters are connected in the conviction that the 'hidden history' is always visible, audible, tangible, even if symptomatically so. *Screen memories* (Freud) show through hiding and hide through showing. The levels of complexity and stratification of Iranian screen memories call for specific studies. They are multidirectional in manifold, ambiguous ways, consisting of concrete, material fragments that resonate with resistant meanings and point to silenced wounds.

Even though the chapters develop their own, very context-specific notion of counter-memory, they are structured by axes, nodes, and questions that divide the book into four parts: (I) An Archaeology of Possible Futures; (II) Material Matters: Memory, Accessibility, Translation; (III) Interstices. Niches. Impure Memories, and (VI) Transgenerational Gaps and Transmissions.

Part I: An Archaeology of Possible Futures

In the first chapter, 'The Incomplete: Film, Politics, and Remembering the Past,' Tara Najd Ahmadi explores Kianoush Ayari's unfinished documentary *Tāzeh Nafas-hā/The Newborns*, which he shot in the streets of Tehran with a handheld 16 mm camera during the summer of 1979 – shortly after the toppling of the Shah's monarchy. The film documents a unique transitional point, when everything still seemed possible and nothing was yet decided, and thus confronts us with the crucial question: 'What is to be done after the revolution?' Najd Ahmadi takes the open character of the film (which can be felt even today), its unfinished form, and the revolutionary fervor it documents as a starting point for a meticulous close reading that explores the aesthetic qualities of *The Newborns* and sheds light on the emancipatory and resistant potentials that can be found in unfinished projects. With Najd Ahmadi's reading, Ayari's film becomes accessible as a great counter-archive of 'erased history where we can look for the lost pieces of our collective memory' (p. 29)

The incomplete and buried history – mainly of the Marxist revolutionary discourse and left activism in Iran – is also the subject of Sara Saljoughi's contribution *'The Hidden Half*, or the Temporal and Collective Politics of Counter-Memory,' which focuses on Tahmineh Milani's semi-epistolary film *Nīmah-yi Panhān/The Hidden Half* (2001) on the delicate situation of a former activist from the period immediately following the revolution. The protagonist's dissident past, which has been completely hidden from her husband, a prominent judge, 'allegorizes the repression of Marxist revolutionary discourse' (p. 33) before and after 1979. Saljoughi discovers in the film a network of multidirectional, transgenerational, and transtemporal counter-memories and carves out the thread of solidarity which the film forges between different times and generations of women as a basis for a new community. She shows how the film positions the counter-memories at the intersection of class and gender by presenting the intimate sphere of the upper-class couple as a protected space where memories become possible, which in turn transforms the boundaries and possibilities of this very space; and by presenting the 'counter-memory of the revolutionary moment as a critique of the ways in which women's issues were overlooked or marginalized in leftist movements' (p. 41). Saljoughi also undertakes a rehabilitation of the film genre 'melodrama' as a production site of counter-memories, for it was also Milani's use of melodrama elements – a genre that 'has been deemed a "woman's genre" in terms of its aesthetics and mode of address, compared with Iranian art cinema' (p. 42) – that led to the film being marginalized also in the eyes of film scholarship: '"the hidden half" may also be put to work in thinking about the disciplinary practices of Iranian cinema studies' (p. 43).

The third chapter, entitled 'Counter-Investigations: On Matchboxes, Black Boxes, and other Forgotten Futures,' is a conversation between anthropologist and filmmaker Chowra Makaremi and philosopher and image theorist Emmanuel Alloa around *Hitch: An Iranian Story* (2019), Makaremi's internationally acclaimed first documentary feature. Based on a long-running work using auto-fiction and visual anthropology, the movie confronts state violence in post-revolution Iran, documenting a family history of political disappearances and executions in the 1980s, and its memorializing through different frames of denial within the country and in exile. Bodies disappeared, graves and mass graves were destroyed, silence still prevails. To retrieve the facts and the places, one must have access to the archives, but these are missing; one must go back to the places and shoot images, but the access into the country is denied; one must find witnesses ready to speak on their own behalf, but this exposes them to danger and prosecution. One is faced with the challenge of undertaking an archaeology of silenced voices, memory holes, and sealed crypts. What is it that is needed in order to break this silence? '*Hitch* is permanently traversed by this ambivalence between a gaping lack and the almost obtrusive presence of certain material things, which allow to cling to an otherwise erased memory' (p. 52). What the movie 'counter-investigates' is not only 'denial' as a cognitive and emotional experience, but also the complicated and sensitive steps of recollecting a personal story that belongs to a collective history, of digging in films, pictures, and personal archives in order to find some images that help to trace missing memories, forgotten faces, unexplained absences. The conversation between Makaremi and Alloa continues the 'counter-investigations' of the film with other means and further questions circling around a set of crucial concerns: how could silence and symbolic violence be broken? How to loosen the grip of denial and the intimate scratches of power? How can facts be re-established and acts of repair be performed? How can memory holes be filled or at least shaped with appropriate words, images, gestures, concepts, and even mythological narrations from another culture, such as the story of *Antigone*?

PART II: MATERIAL MATTERS: MEMORY, ACCESSIBILITY, TRANSLATION

In 'An Archaeology of Access: Materiality, Historiography, and Iranian Cinema,' Blake Atwood expands the media archaeological approach by delving into the material and immaterial history of *Dukhtar-i Lur/The Lor Girl* (1933), one of the few films from this period that still exists, circulating in different digital resolutions, forms, versions, and rips. With the unprecedented level of digital accessibility of the film (e.g. on video-sharing platforms like YouTube), which contrasts with the decades of inaccessibility, when the National Film Archives carefully protected its original 35 mm format, Atwood's contribution takes the sonic and visual distortions as a starting point to excavate counter-histories of access, distribution, and circulation. In the course of his meticulous, archaeological digging into a profusion of digital and digitized glitches, blips and blurs, (water-)marks, spots, and scratches, and other 'effects of a worn-out videocassette [. . .] fossilized in digital form (p. 65),' Atwood redirects our attention towards a wider network of agents, connections, and coordinates, a network in which the stories of institutions and underground distributions intersect. In this dive through a palimpsest of 'poor images,'[24] as Hito Steyerl would call them, Atwood's chapter unsettles 'the teleological assumptions undergirding the narrative of modernity' and expands the implications of our concept *counter-memory*: 'Just as an individual memory might challenge the master narrative of modernity, so too can the digital version of a film – simultaneously frozen in multiple points of time – expose the shortcomings of an official history' (p. 66).

While Atwood carves out the counter-memories amidst material distortions fossilized in digital form, Negar Mottahedeh in her contribution 'Black Seals: Missive from Iran's National Music,' places the genealogy of counter-memories within a history of exchange between the East and the West. Focusing on *Delshodegān/Love Stricken* (1992), a highly popular Iranian post-revolution fiction film by director Ali Hatami, Mottahedeh's enunciation-oriented investigation tracks down the transcultural exchange nesting in the practices of inscriptive and reproductive technologies. In her chapter, Mottahedeh carves out the layers and levels of Hatami's ambiguous landscape of split enunciations, which undermines its own national statements, illustrating 'how undeniably the nation and its cinema is produced on the grounds of cultural confluences, wedged in the contradictions of a forked tongue' (p. 97). Set in turn-of-the-nineteenth-century Iran, *Love Stricken* 'traces the peregrinations of a group of early twentieth-century musicians to Paris to record traditional music on the newly invented gramophone' (p. 87). While on the surface the film presents characters who find their identity in national and traditional music, on a media-reflexive level it undermines precisely this claimed identity since the music turns out to be a product of cross-cultural influences, studio recordings, enunciative incommensurabilities, and synchronizations of the non-synchronous. Iran finds itself in transit through reproductive technologies and the interplay between self-export and re-import. 'The film's self-reflexive return to the history of the technologies of reproducibility uncovers dormant counter-memories' (p. 97). The more the film explores the past in search of the authentical nation, for a pure and purified self, an auratic 'here and now,' the more ambiguities and hybrid elements become visible and audible, embedded within the film's technologies of representation and enunciative sources. National identity becomes a question of cross-cultural montage.

In 'Different Time, Different Space: Filmic Forms of Counter-Memory in Abbas Kiarotami's Koker Trilogy,' Ute Holl examines Kiarostami's Koker trilogy in terms of historiography, using genealogical procedures. Taking the cue from Nietzsche and Foucault, she argues that memory is a matter of constant translation, negotiating power relations as well as individual forms of resistance and resilience. It is a changing order whose content is shaped according to cultural techniques, discursive formations, and, above all, prevalent media systems. Memories are made of intrinsic connections between people, techniques, and practices; however, these can only be understood in reconstructing a discontinuous set of forces at work. In her contribution, Holl shows how Kiarostami is examining grand metaphors through very material aspects in confronting different cultural techniques of remembering. In negotiating the power inherent in things, such as the door and the pathway, or in the clash of different media, such as scripture and sounds, cinema and television, or in opposing particular spaces such as a stage and a filmset, Kiarostami's films bring out moments where memory as a collective or individual cultural technique falters and fails. In such moments of irritation and disturbances, Kiarostami is on the lookout for situations where memory becomes fuzzy or unreliable and, in collapsing, displays the boundaries of cultural grids at large. In the risky play of shifting identities, spaces, forms of authentication, and even language, a counter-memory makes its sudden appearance and affects what can be remembered, on screen and beyond .

PART III: INTERSTICES. NICHES. IMPURE MEMORIES

In 'Towards an Impure Memory: An Archaeology of Counter-Memories through Telescoping Lenses,' Matthias Wittmann undertakes a re-mapping and a re-examination of selected post-revolutionary Iranian films by using Walter Benjamin's concept of *télescopage* (telescoping) as briefly defined in his *Arcades Project* (1927–40). The '[t]elescoping of the past through the present' as understood by Benjamin locates the possibilities of re-membering particularly in montage techniques, ruptures, and refractions, and not in continuity. Consequently, memories become a product of present constellations, forces, and spatiotemporal overlaps. Departing from the observation that emergency rooms and editing rooms are a recurring motif in the history of Iranian cinema, Wittmann examines through telescoping lenses cinematic trauma- and memoryscapes that *change the law of what can be said, seen, and remembered* (Foucault). These lenses are at the same time intrinsic to the palimpsestic time structures of the examined films, producing ambiguities, collisions, and frictions, herein completely in line with the *principle of heterogeneity* (Foucault). Wittman shows how the post-revolutionary emergency rooms are transformed into editing rooms, from which new instances of enunciations and new grammars of post-traumatic remembering are established. The title 'Towards an Impure Memory' reacts to the attempted 'purification' of Iranian cinema after 1979. A cinema that puts into circulation impure (counter-)memories produces frictions between political promises and social realities, exposing the emptiness and abstractness of the revolutionary semiotics of continuity and purity as put forward by the ideological architects of the Islamic Republic of Iran. The atlas of counter-memories as elaborated in this chapter will also include counter-examples, i.e. purified memories from the 'Sacred Defense cinema,' thereby creating contrasts and demonstrating nuances between different forms of spatiotemporal constellations and tectonics. This archaeology of counter-memories will be undertaken through films from Mohsen Makhmalbaf, Morteza Avini, Ebrahim Hatamikia, Rakhshan Banietemad, Shahram Mokri, and Mohammad Hussein Mahdavian.

In her contribution, 'Seeking Love in the Interstices: Acousmatic Listening as Counter-Memory in Abbas Kiarostami's *Shirin* (2008),' Michelle Langford proposes a new close reading or, better, close listening of Kiarostami's film experiment. As is well known, Kiarostami's adaptation of the classical Persian tale of 'Khosrow and Shirin' – inspired by Nezami's epic poem and its retelling by contemporary Iranian writer Farideh Golbou – completely withholds the images of the story, allowing us instead to watch the faces of 114 actresses – all Iranian except one – as they themselves watch the film that we only experience acousmatically. While Kiarostami's self-reflexive attention to the act of watching has engendered a significant amount of scholarship that focuses largely on questions of vision, gender, and spectatorship, Langford focuses on the off-screen sounds, voices, and music, demonstrating how Kiarostami circumvents the hegemonic privilege of vision, which allows him to completely ignore the censorship guidelines. Langford argues that by rendering the love story acousmatically, Kiarostami makes audible a veritable 'blind spot' in Iranian cinema: romantic love, a figure that has been almost completely effaced in post-revolutionary cinema, returns as a counter-memory, 'one that reactivates the traces of an epic-poetic tradition and in doing so challenges the hegemony of censorship' (p. 147). The counter-memories nest in the 'richly allusive interstitial space between sound and image' (p. 163), encouraging affective listening and giving a sonic body to the woman's desires. Through this affective listening, sonic *mise-en-scène*, and the art of trompe l'oreille the spectator is reoriented towards tantalizing taboos.

Counter-memories can also be tracked down where we least suspect or expect them to be, as Viktor Ullmann shows in his contribution 'Spiritual Counter-Memories of the War: Mohammad Ali Ahangar's Recent Contributions to the *Sīnemā-ye Defāʿ-ye Moqaddas*.' Although liberals are by far the most active group of filmmakers challenging the state's hermeneutical hegemony on the past, recent developments show a small niche of conservative religious films that intend to reinvent the 'Sacred Defense cinema' genre through a counter-reading of the Iran-Iraq War (and its aftermath). These films take their cue not from social criticism, as, for instance, Mohsen Makhmalbaf or even Ebrahim Hatamikia did in the 1980s and 1990s, but – and herein lies their subversive character – from a spiritual approach. The most prolific proponent of this niche is the Abadan-based director Mohammad Ali Ahangar. Starting with his first feature film, *Farzand-e Khāk/Child of Soil* (2008), all his popular works deal with war-induced traumas, re-interrogating the war and its spiritual ramifications for survivors. 'Ahangar paints a decidedly different picture of the war than the official state iconography' (p. 169). Ullmann explores in a sophisticated way the challenge posed by Ahangar's transgressions – especially in two of his later films, *Malakeh/The Queen* (2012) and *Sarv Zīr-e Āb/Cypress Under Water* (2018) – to the genre's discursive boundaries, and that precisely through the production of ghost- and counter-memories. Ullmann's case study is thus about counter-memories that operate from within the hegemonic symbolic order with its religious implications while breaking at the same time 'their mnemonic monopoly' from a spiritual perspective, which does not even shy away from the subject of suicide.

Part IV: Transgenerational Gaps and Transmissions

In his contribution '*Filmfarsi* as Counter-Memory,' Pedram Partovi also deals with the return, or rather the hidden afterlife and survival, of a supposedly disappeared cultural heritage: the passing of actor Nasir Malik Mutiʿi in May 2018 spurred a debate among Iranians about *filmfarsi* ('Persian-film'), the often-derogatory term that critics, industry people, and even fans have used in reference to the Pahlavi-era popular commercial cinema, and its place in 'national culture.' The passing in the year 2000 of another banned *filmfarsi* legend, Muhammad ʿAli Fardin, had invited similar public reactions and similar criticisms of the state media and judiciary for their shameful treatment of a national 'icon.' Partovi's contribution sheds new light on Iranians' 'faulty,' yet shifting, memories of the officially demonized *filmfarsi* since the Islamic Revolution. He argues in his chapter that *filmfarsi* has functioned as a counter-memory, an absent presence in the minds of millions, that decades of imposed forgetting (or imposed memories) did not manage to extinguish, and as a counter-archive of images, sounds, icons, and motives 'that has problematized official ideas of Iranian cinema and national culture both before and after the Islamic Revolution of 1978–9' (p. 189). The afterlife of *filmfarsi* thus functions as an alternative account of the genealogy of the Islamic Revolution and is also a reminder of some sort of 'decadent past,' as Partovi shows in detail with films like Mas'ud Dihnamaki's *Ikhrajiha/The Outcasts* (2007), 'the rather transparent homage' (p. 199) to Iraj Qadiri's *Barzakhiha/The In-betweeners* (1982), whose attempt to pick up the conventions of *filmfarsi* led to the protagonist being banned from all state-run media.

In his chapter 'A Shadow for Invisible Films: A Way to Break the Monopoly of Image Production in Iran,' one of the most internationally acclaimed contemporary Iranian directors, Shahram Mokri, describes from his insider perspective the production conditions, the developments, and the socio-economic context that led to the emergence of a new generation of filmmakers in Iran, generally known as the sixth generation. As someone who studied film and started making films after the year 2000 (1379), at a time when more and more digital video cameras were coming into circulation, Mokri regards this digital revolution as a new opportunity for young filmmakers to challenge and outwit control mechanisms of the authorities who, for this reason, have tried up to the present day to discredit digital filmmaking. In order to show how the digital possibilities brought forth a new generation of filmmakers, Mokri gives novel and highly differentiated insights into the history of the dynamics between economics, technology, and aesthetics in Iran. A wide variety of phenomena is taken into account: from the bureaucratic claims of control over technical equipment (since 1979), the role of video recorders in keeping the visual memory alive, the divisions of the film system – 'cinematic vs. digital division' and what is called the 'Hitchcock/Tarkovsky dichotomy' – up to the generational gaps and conflicts that are also articulated in the use of different film techniques. One section also deals with the so-called 'Khosoulati industry' – a kind of oligarchic system of funding for allegedly independent films. Mokri portrays a nuanced picture of Iran's contemporary film scene and shows how digital film technology has become a tactical tool for shaping and circulating counter-memories. 'This generation has once successfully survived the old and useless rules that were imposed on it and created a new identity for itself despite the shapeless and ever-changing economy in place. This is what makes this generation hopeful that it can break the limitations once again' (p. 228).

In order to offer the reader the widest possible range of positions (and generational perspectives as well), we have decided to include a legendary paper by Bahram Beyzaie. Thanks to the precise translation of Amir Roshan, Beyzaie's article 'At the End of a Century' ('Pas az sad sāl') – written on the occasion of the 100-year anniversary of cinema and first published in Persian in *Iran Nameh*

(1996)[25] – is now accessible to a wider readership. The text is an attempt to give a first-hand account of the visual history of Iranian and Persian culture, from an Iranian filmmaker, dramatist, art historian, director, producer, and scriptwriter whose career stretched over forty-five years and who faced obstacles in filmmaking in both pre- and post-revolutionary Iran. There are various reasons why this article is still relevant, especially in the context of our book. Firstly, there are almost no publications and translations of Beyzaie's writings, neither in German nor in English. Hence, the translation is an attempt to introduce and celebrate one of the most remarkable filmmakers of pre- and post-revolutionary Iranian Cinema. Secondly, many issues raised by Beyzaie in this article are still relevant today, and especially relevant for this book's context. Beyzaie traces back the struggle with censorship and with what he calls 'absolutism' to the cultural history of Iran and Persia. Absolutism according to Beyzaie is not a political system as in the classic definition of political philosophy; it is a worldview which horizontally determines the relation between subjects, and between the subject and him- or herself, what Foucault would call *assujettissement (subjectivation)*. Although cinema is a modern phenomenon, Iran's film industry, like the mural paintings of the medieval period before it, is a victim of the same absolutist control mechanisms and dominant traditional values. '[T]he traditional absolutism has now accepted the image, but more than anything else it has accepted the image of its own victory. [. . .] We have created such an elaborated system which, instead of being at the cinema's disposal, thinks that filmmakers have to be at its service' (p. 241). This is the core thesis of Bezayie's rather pessimistic assessment.

Note on Transliteration

Most of the contributors have applied the Ijmes Transliteration System for Persian. Some of the contributors used a more simplified version or a variant of the table. In themselves, however, the chapters remain coherent and consistently adhere to a system. For almost all the names of renowned authors, filmmakers, film characters, and famous literary works, the common and predominant spelling of the names has been used and the diacritical marks have been dropped.

Notes

1. Dipesh Chakrabarty, *Provincializing Europe. Postcolonial Thought and Historical Difference* (Princeton, NJ: Princeton University Press 2000), p. 9.
2. See his revolutionary childrens's book *The Little Black Fish (Māhī-ye Sīyāh-e Kūchūlū)* from 1974 which was banned in pre-revolutionary Iran.
3. Homi K. Bhabha, *The Location of Culture* (London/New York: Routledge 2004), p. 252.

4. Michel Foucault, 'Useless to Revolt?' (French original in *Le Monde*), in *Essential Works of Foucault 1954–1984*, Vol. 3: Power (New York: The New Press 2000), pp. 449–53, p. 453.
5. Behrooz-Ghamari Tabrizi, *Foucault and Iran: Islamic Revolution after the Enlightenment* (London/Minneapolis: University of Minnesota Press 2016), p. 59.
6. Thomas Bauer, *Die Kultur der Ambiguität. Eine andere Geschichte des Islams* (Berlin: Insel 2011).
7. See Michel Foucault, *Discipline and Punish. The Birth of the Prison* (New York: Random House 1977), p. 31.
8. See Michel Foucault, *Language, Counter-Memory, Practice: Selected Interviews*, ed. Donald Bouchard, trans. Donald Bouchard and Sherry Simon (Ithaca, NY: Cornell University Press 1977), pp. 139–64, p. 160.
9. Michel Foucault, 'What is Enlightenment?,' ed. Paul Rabinow, *The Foucault Reader* (New York: Pantheon Books 1984), pp. 32–50, p. 46.
10. Ibid.
11. José Medina, 'Toward a Foucaultian Epistemology of Resistance: Counter-Memory, Epistemic Friction, and *Guerrilla* Pluralism,' in *Foucault Studies*, No. 12 (2011), pp. 9–35.
12. Foucault, *Archaeology of Knowledge*, trans. A. M. Sheridan Smith (London/New York: Routledge Classics 1989), p. 145.
13. Ibid., pp. 30f., 103.
14. See Michel Foucault, *Dispositive der Macht. Michel Foucault über Sexualität, Wissen und Wahrheit* (Berlin: Merve 1978), pp. 35, 106. (Translation by the authors.)
15. Ibid., pp. 64ff.
16. Michael Rothberg, *Multidirectional Memory. Remembering the Holocaust in the Age of Decolonization* (Stanford, CA: Stanford University Press 2009), p. 3.
17. '[. . .] pursuing memory's multidirectionality encourages us to think of the public sphere as a malleable discursive space in which groups do not simply articulate established positions but actually come into being through their dialogical interactions with others' (ibid., p. 5). It can be assumed that these framework conditions as described by Rothberg will be very difficult to find, and not only in Iran.
18. Rakshan Banietemdad, 'Cinema as a Mirror of the Urban Image,' in Shiva Rhbaran (ed.), *Iranian Cinema Uncensored. Contemporary Film-Makers since the Islamic Revolution* (London/New York: Tauris 2016), pp. 127–46, p. 132.
19. Marc Ferro, *Cinema and History* (Detroit, MI: Wayne State University Press 1988), p. 20.
20. Ibid., pp. 15, 20, 29.
21. Ibid., pp. 12, 83.
22. See Emmanuel Alloa, 'Post-Truth Or: Why Nietzsche is Not Responsible for Trump' (August 2017), https://thephilosophicalsalon.com/post-truth-or-why-nietzsche-is-not-responsible-for-donald-trump/
23. Alexandra Schneider, 'Ta-Ta Ta-Ra Ta-Ta Ra-Ra. 1991 – Kompressionsformate und Memoryscapes,' in Ute Holl and Matthias Wittmann (eds.), *Memoryscapes. Filmformen der Erinnerung* (Zürich/Berlin: Diaphanes 2017), pp. 255–74, p. 258. See also David Middleton and Steven D. Brown, 'Issues in the Socio-Cultural Study

of Memory: Making Memory Matter,' in Jan Valsiner and Alberto Rosa (ed.), *The Cambridge Handbook of Sociocultural Psychology* (Cambridge: Cambridge University Press 2007), pp. 661–77, p. 670.
24. 'The poor image is a copy in motion. Its quality is bad, its resolution substandard. As it accelerates, it deteriorates. It is a ghost of an image, a preview, a thumbnail, an errant idea, an itinerant image distributed for free, squeezed through slow digital connections, compressed, reproduced, ripped, remixed, as well as copied and pasted into other channels of distribution' (Hito Steyerl, 'In Defense of the Poor Image,' in *e-flux*, Vol. 10 (November 2009), https://www.e-flux.com/journal/10/61362/in-defense-of-the-poor-image/).
25. *Iran Nameh*, Vol. 14, No. 3: *Special Issue on Iranian Cinema*.

References

Alloa, Emmanuel, 'Post-Truth Or: Why Nietzsche is Not Responsible for Trump' (August 2017), https://thephilosophicalsalon.com/post-truth-or-why-nietzsche-is-not-responsible-for-donald-trump/

Banietemdad, Rakshan, 'Cinema as a Mirror of the Urban Image,' in Shiva Rahbaran (ed.), *Iranian Cinema Uncensored. Contemporary Film-Makers since the Islamic Revolution* (London/New York: Tauris 2016), pp. 127–46.

Bauer, Thomas, *Die Kultur der Ambiguität. Eine andere Geschichte des Islams* (Berlin: Insel 2011).

Bhabha, Homi K., *The Location of Culture* (London/New York: Routledge 2004).

Chakrabarty, Dipesh, *Provincializing Europe. Postcolonial Thought and Historical Difference* (Princeton, NJ: Princeton University Press 2000).

Ferro, Marc, *Cinema and History* (Detroit, MI: Wayne State University Press 1988).

Foucault, Michel, *Discipline and Punish. The Birth of the Prison* (New York: Random House 1977).

Foucault, Michel, *Language, Counter-Memory, Practice: Selected Interviews*, ed. Donald Bouchard, trans. Donald Bouchard and Sherry Simon (Ithaca, NY: Cornell University Press 1977), pp. 139–64.

Foucault, Michel, *Dispositive der Macht. Michel Foucault über Sexualität, Wissen und Wahrheit* (Berlin: Merve 1978).

Foucault, Michel, 'What is Enlightenment?', *The Foucault Reader*, ed. Paul Rabinow (New York: Pantheon Books 1984), pp. 32–50.

Foucault, *Archaeology of Knowledge*, trans. A. M. Sheridan Smith (London/New York: Routledge Classics 1989).

Foucault, Michel, 'Useless to Revolt?' (French original in *Le Monde*), in *Essential Works of Foucault 1954–1984*, Vol. 3: Power (New York: The New Press 2000), pp. 449–53.

Medina, José, 'Toward a Foucaultian Epistemology of Resistance: Counter-Memory, Epistemic Friction, and *Guerrilla* Pluralism,' in *Foucault Studies*, No. 12 (2011), pp. 9–35.

Middleton, David and Steven D. Brown, 'Issues in the Socio-Cultural Study of Memory: Making Memory Matter,' in Jan Valsiner and Alberto Rosa (eds.), *The Cambridge*

Handbook of Sociocultural Psychology (Cambridge: Cambridge University Press 2007), pp. 661–77.

Rothberg, Michael, *Multidirectional Memory. Remembering the Holocaust in the Age of Decolonization* (Stanford, CA: Stanford University Press 2009).

Schneider, Alexandra, 'Ta-Ta Ta-Ra Ta-Ta Ra-Ra. 1991 – Kompressionsformate und Memoryscapes,' in Ute Holl and Matthias Wittmann (eds.), *Memoryscapes. Filmformen der Erinnerung* (Zürich/Berlin: Diaphanes 2017), pp. 255–74.

Steyerl, Hito, 'In Defense of the Poor Image,' in *e-flux*, Vol. 10 (November 2009), https://www.e-flux.com/journal/10/61362/in-defense-of-the-poor-image/

Tabrizi, Behrooz-Ghamari, *Foucault and Iran: Islamic Revolution after the Enlightenment* (London/Minneapolis: University of Minnesota Press 2016).

PART I

AN ARCHAEOLOGY OF POSSIBLE FUTURES

The history of some is not the history of others.
    Michel Foucault, *Society Must Be Defended* (1975–6)

1. THE INCOMPLETE: FILM, POLITICS, AND REMEMBERING THE PAST

Tara Najd Ahmadi

In the spring and summer of 1979, Iranian filmmaker Kianoush Ayari directed and shot *Tāzeh Nafas-hā/The Newborns* in the streets of Tehran. Recorded with a handheld 16 mm camera, the film documents a transitional point between the Shah's recently toppled aristocratic dictatorship (1941–79) and the implementation of the Islamic Republic that succeeded the 1979 Revolution. This intermediary time was a moment of aesthetic and political liberty, one in which revolutionaries could communicate in public through street theater, meetings, and informal conversations. With its lens turned towards Tehran's crowded streets, the forty-five-minute documentary captures all of the political factions that participated in the 1979 Revolution. In the film, diverse groups of people debate their thoughts, compete over stages and microphones, and, at times, celebrate their victories. The film depicts a utopian freedom, unimaginable for Iranians before or after the revolution.

The Newborns is an unfinished film. By the time the film's rough-cut made it to Channel One, Iran's national television channel, conservative sponsors had already populated the network. As a result, the film never passed the post-production process, as it was not aligned with the organization's new guidelines. In particular, the original sponsors of the film at Channel One were unhappy with the film's inclusion of the crowds depicted on the streets, and although they asked for these scenes to be cut, Ayari refused. Thus, *The Newborns* offers a counter-history, a first-hand account of revolutionary crowds whose existence was forgotten for the past four decades.

Ayari produced *The Newborns* during the short intermediary political moment after the Shah's removal and before Khomeini came to power, a time that reflected a lively and vibrant utopia. The raw-cut footage of the film, which includes music but lacks voice-over narration, was stored at Channel One's archive, and Ayari never had access to it. In my interview with him, he mentions that after Channel One confiscated the film he never knew what happened to the original negatives.[1]

Yet, every once in a while, he saw short parts of the film edited between the works of other filmmakers and broadcast on national television, without crediting him as the filmmaker. During the yearly official anniversary celebrations of the revolution, state-owned television used the shots in various compilations that invoked nostalgic images of the revolution for the broader public.

It was only in 2009 that Ayari gained access to the film, when his friend Pirouz Kalantari encountered a digitized version sold in a small film store on a street in Tehran. Kalantari purchased two copies of the VHS and shared it with Ayari. Ayari was ecstatic that the footage still existed.[2] With Ayari's agreement, the film was transferred to digital format, and uploaded online through unofficial websites. Today the film is accessible on websites such as Ubuweb and Vimeo, where it has had thousands of views.[3] *The Newborns* is an example of numerous unfinished works that have gradually come back to the public's attention decades after their production.

In this chapter, I explore the aesthetic qualities of *The Newborns* to shed light on the emancipatory potential embedded in re-investigating unfinished art projects and films. Because the film remains unfinished – it lacks a voice-over narration, the editing was not finalized, and numerous overexposed and underexposed frames comprise the film – it resists easy conclusions and a sense of resolution. I will explain how this lack of closure in the work can lead to a refreshing openness for its viewers four decades after its production.

The Newborns, in brief, is the story of a wandering camera among revolutionary crowds gathered in the center of Tehran on Enghelab Street (the direct translation in English is Revolution Street). The film's structure is built upon sequences that document the perspectives of various crowds that cannot appear as openly on the streets today: dancers, large circles of people engaged in public political and economic conversations, street performers, drug addicts, and homeless people. In the film, we can see that all of these groups gathered publicly as a result of this *in-between* moment when there was no effective governmental rule.

Some of the crowds that *The Newborns* captures are particularly unique because they presented an urban underclass that resulted from the Shah's 1960s modernization plans.[4] The squatters, slum dwellers, and unskilled workers filmed by Ayari represented the impoverished rural masses who emigrated to Tehran from other regional cities after the Shah's land reform program of 1962.

During these reforms, the government confiscated villagers' lands, causing them to emigrate to cities to look for work. Land reform and subsequent modernization schemes resulted in a profound demographic change throughout the country. With a mass exodus from rural areas, Iran's cities swelled with poor migrants. Asef Bayat explains how this urban underclass played an important role in forming the 1979 Revolution by squatting in abandoned houses or gathering in different areas of the major cities of Iran.[5] The crowds' unpredictable and uncontrollable mode of existence gave them the power to create changes in the city's life despite state disapproval. Therefore, after its establishment, the new government 'cleared' these crowds from the streets by pushing groups such as prostitutes and drug addicts underground. The dominant presence of this urban underclass in *The Newborns* was in harmony with Ayari's broader aesthetics and politics that were cultivated during his early years of filmmaking among the Iranian Free Cinema filmmakers.

Iranian Free Cinema and the 'Imperfect' Form

In 1960 in Tehran, the Eastman Kodak Institute founded what was at the time the Middle East's largest film processing lab.[6] As Iran saw the wider distribution of film and processing products during the 1960s, film became a more accessible medium for various classes, and small groups of young filmmakers formed. The Kodak Institute's main work was processing photos and 8 mm, 16 mm, and 35 mm film negatives. However, 8 mm film could also be processed privately at home, or by sending it outside the country to Germany. This created more freedom in the production of 8 mm film, making it difficult for the Pahlavi state to control and monitor all film production. For this reason, 8 mm film became popular among young Iranian filmmakers, who established an experimental cinema collective – Free Cinema (*Sinamā-ye Āzad*).

These young filmmakers collaborated on innovative film projects, funded their own productions, and organized their own festivals, and they soon expanded their activities to different cities in Iran. Their collaboration was fueled, in part, by the disconnect between the common commercial filmmaking practices at the time, generally known as *filmfarsi*, and the Hollywood cinema available through television channels. One of the young filmmakers who worked with Free Cinema was Ayari, who was a native of Ahwaz. A city situated in the south of Iran, Ahwaz was one of the important places in which Free Cinema filmmakers were active, and 8 mm film was highly popular among them.[7] Free Cinema's main goal was to stay away from any form of capitalistic or dominant forms that ruled the commercial world of film distribution. The young filmmakers of Free Cinema wanted to remove all the barriers that distanced the masses from the cinema.

Scholars have written extensively about the influence of Europe and North America on Iranian cinema since its first arrival into the nation, particularly about the fascination of the late Qajar kings (1789–1925) and the Pahlavis with Western cinema and their effort to import it into Iran. Yet scholarship has overlooked these more marginal forms of filmmaking within the country, particularly in how they connected to global interventions in the cinematic world during the Cold War, including the international move towards the creation of a *third cinema*. Influenced by the Cuban Revolution (1959), the Vietnamese victory over the French and U.S. (1954 and 1975), and Algerian independence in the late 1960s and early 1970s, third-world intellectuals called for a 'tricontinental revolution.'[8] Ho Chi Minh, Che Guevara, and Frantz Fanon served as ideological inspirations for the movement, all of whom called for justice against oppressive and imperialist forces. The third-world film ideology was reflected in a series of important writings, including Cuban Julio García Espinosa's 1969 essay *For an Imperfect Cinema*. In his text, Espinosa advocated for 'low' forms of production and asserted that the mere act of communication via cinema was more important than the quality of the final product. He argued that a cinema committed to creating change must inevitably be imperfect, from low-quality productions to incomplete products. Espinosa explained that 'imperfect cinema' would put an end to the modern Christian tradition that gave primacy to a so-called 'suffering' artist, or the idea that the 'neurotic artist's' work only gained value and authenticity from suffering for perfection.[9]

The third cinema theories influenced a variety of groups and filmmakers around the world, including the members of the Free Cinema, who started creating works that were highly radical both in form and content. As a result, Free Cinema filmmakers participated in more experimental and short film festivals in Europe during the early 1970s.[10] By seeing works from other filmmakers who shared similar revolutionary sensibilities, they connected themselves to a global range of artworks. Developments in the Free Cinema movement were screened in theaters across the country. It was within this context that *The Newborns* came to life.

THE NEWBORNS, A HISTORIC DOCUMENT

The Newborns starts with a controversial scene that depicts a young girl standing in downtown Tehran, holding a red book by Fatah, an armed revolutionary group in Palestine. At first, it may seem atypical that a child is advertising a guerilla act. But after the viewer's initial shock subsides, they can see the image as a demonstration of the international revolutionary solidarity that was common across the Middle East, especially among the revolutionary left. The film's pre-title, *Summer of 1979, in Today's Tehran (Tābestāne 1357, dar Tehrāne Emrūz)*, appears letter by letter on the frozen image of the girl. The words are

Figure 1.1 Opening scene with the still image of the girl. (Source: Screen grab from *The Newborns*, 1979).

in the bold font 'titr' that was used in newspaper headlines reporting important revolutionary news at the time. Both the progressive appearance of the title on the screen and the transition from a still photo to moving images reflect the cultural and political change in a revolutionary society. The opening scene highlights the act of writing, the practice of creating, and the work of naming.

Additionally, the pre-title offers the viewer a simultaneous glimpse into two distinct eras: the summer of 1979 and 'today's' Tehran. It was as if Ayari was aware that the film would not be viewed in 1979, so he dated and titled the film in a way that depicts both the summer during which it was shot and the Tehran of today's audience. The use of two time tenses, 'that summer, in this city' highlights changes in the city's life over time, until today. The child's face in the background also symbolizes an unknown future, a 'yet to come' in the summer of 1979. The opening scene's incorporation of the still image implies the adaptation and reversal of a commonly employed filmmaking technique: that of freezing a moving image. A famous example of this image is the end sequence of French filmmaker François Truffaut's *The 400 Blows* (1959), in which Truffaut freezes the end of the film on the image of a boy, Antoine Doinel. In doing so, Truffaut leaves the boy's story open-ended, framing him in a permanently irresolvable uncertainty. French New Wave cinema had an oversized influence on Iranian filmmakers; thus, we can imagine that the opening sequence of *The Newborns* can be an homage to the famous ending of *400 Blows*. Doinel's movement ends when he encounters the ocean, which he had always dreamed of seeing. Conversely, the girl in *The Newborns* stands within a revolutionary ocean of people. If Doinel has doubts when he confronts the ocean, the child in *The Newborns* is inevitably subsumed in that ocean. Both children, however, have emotionless expressions on their faces. They are startled as they encounter the scale of what they see and stare with open mouths.

The Lack of Narration

Towards the end of *The Newborns*, a woman is shown speaking to a crowd gathered outside the University of Tehran, on Enghelab Street. As she speaks, she condemns the cooperation between the United States and Israeli governments in the occupation of Palestine. The woman, Zahra Khanoom (Zahra Yaghoubi), had been a well-known prostitute and madam in downtown Tehran before the revolution. Despite her checkered past, during the short period of state-less freedom, Zahra Khanoom transformed into a vocal public figure. Her elevated position in front of a large number of men who stare silently at her with fascination and confusion demonstrates the dynamism of this transitory period, evincing the way that society became more tolerant of what had been previously morally unacceptable. The camera shows medium-close-up shots of Zahra's face and hands while she professes her anti-imperialist speech. After a long take of her speech, the audio is bleeped out. Because of the general incompletion of the film, it is unclear whether this is the result of technical difficulties or if Ayari censored her cursing. After a second of pause, the soundtrack of the film plays underneath the footage of her speech, connecting Zahra to the other revolutionaries in the film through a musical theme.

When Zahra talks about imperialist powers, her sentences often do not make much sense. Fascinated by the crowds, excited by her temporary power to captivate a large number of people, she stands on a pedestal to give a speech, but she is incoherent. She shouts and names things: Israel, America, Palestine, freedom, imperialism, enemy, us the people. Her statements lack clear and logical connections. Zahra's breathlessness in this scene is a microcosm of the film's speechless life.

The lack of narration to connect the visuals in *The Newborns* creates an opportunity for approximating oneself to the characters on the screen without the mediation of the voice-over. In fact, if Ahmad Rasoulzadeh, the narrator whose name appears in the first title of the film, had actually narrated *The Newborns*, our understanding of the film would be very different. But Ayari deliberately kept Rasoulzadeh's name at the beginning of the film. His goal was

Figure 1.2 Zara Khanoom talking to the crowd in front of the University of Tehran's gates. (Source: Screen grab from *The Newborns*, 1979).

to publicize the fact that the film was censored upfront, and to let the audience know that what they see is an incomplete film.

During my interview with Ayari, he mentions that some have suggested that he should just take out the narrator's name from the beginning of the film. This way 'no one will know that it is incomplete,' and thus he could circulate it widely again. But Ayari disagrees with this approach, asserting that 'I want the film to be known as incomplete and I don't want to hide the fact that it is censored. I think my audience will still want to see the film even though it is incomplete.'[11]

'WHAT IS TO BE DONE' WITH THE UNFINISHED?

In her study of the politics of *why* and *how* artworks were rendered incomplete during revolutionary periods, particularly the French Revolution, Linda Nochlin situates the production of incomplete works within their historical context. Nochlin ascribes a revolutionary potential to unfinished works of art produced during the French Revolution. She analyzes the representation of ruins and fragments in French revolutionary artwork and argues that these ruins are signs of the transition towards modernity because they were created in opposition to French society's traditional definition of art. In fact, the French Revolution galvanized the eighteenth-century discourse that later considered fragments as positive rather than negative tropes. For French revolutionary artists, fragments and ruins did not symbolize nostalgia for the past. Instead, they became signs of political commitment, for they pulverized the perceived notions of repressive traditions. In other words, artistic fragments during revolutionary eras can be signs of a rebellion against tradition and a message for future generations.[12]

Additionally, Walter Benjamin looks to history and remembering as a way to complete what is left incomplete.[13] In other words, Benjamin addresses the incompleteness of the history of class struggle and considers *re-membering* an act of justice towards the past. Projects that are forcibly interrupted gesture towards the historic moment that compelled their incompletion, and also point to our responsibility towards relating this history. Benjamin wrote extensively on the importance of continuity in history, and the necessity of studying history's failures from the perspectives of the oppressed. As an example, he describes Paul Klee's 1920 print, *The Angel of History* (*Angelus Novus*, 1920), in which the angel's face is turned towards the past and attempts to make a 'whole' of what has been smashed through history. But he cannot awaken the dead as he wishes because a storm named 'progress' propels him into the future.[14]

Influenced by Trotsky, Benjamin resisted the imperialist notions of progress and modernity, and associated them with Fascism.[15] Trotsky's writings and Benjamin's pessimistic views towards modernity formed a theory put into practice by the Iranian revolutionaries during the 1970s. The people's rejection of the Pahlavis' U.S.-led modernization agenda as well as the unjust distribution of wealth in the country led to the denunciation of a regime in the 1970s.[16] To Benjamin, the path to a radical transformation of society was not the further acceleration of progress, but instead a rejection of its entire framework. Here, too, I argue that to understand the films and artworks produced in this period, we have to understand the part of the revolution that was an attempt to stand outside the Western paradigm of progress.

For Benjamin, it is not the machine's movement forward that must be taken into account. He writes: 'Some in the progressive left believe that Marx says that revolutions are the locomotive of world history. But perhaps it is quite otherwise. Perhaps revolutions are an attempt by the passengers on this train – namely the human race – to activate the emergency brake.'[17] In fact, for Benjamin it is the interruption caused by the individuals inside the train that is a critical revolutionary moment. Benjamin considers this tension as an inherent quality of revolution and the humanizing dimension of a mechanism that is supposed to push society forward through the history.[18] This pause is a sign of the individual's resistance to the norms; here also, Ayari's incomplete film and his persistence in maintaining the current status, rather than modifying it for viewing, highlights a tension inherent in suspended and incomplete projects made during revolutionary times, and as Benjamin writes it brings ethics to society's forward movement, humanizes it, and creates moments of critical thinking.

When we exhume these unfinished or unseen films from decades of existence in the world of perceived failure, they take on a ghostly appearance in search of a viewer. They offer a great archive of the erased history where we can look for the lost pieces of our collective memory. By drawing attention to the wounds on their body, these films inevitably invite their audience to look at the quality of incompletion as a possibility for continuing what was left aside. Each time that it is projected on the screen or viewed on a monitor, it teases and laughs at our notion of complete, failed, and forgotten.

Notes

1. Kianoush Ayari, phone interview by the author, 29 February 2019.
2. Roozbeh Sadr Ara, 'The Formation of Urban Documentary Cinema in Iran,' *Hamshahri Magazin*, Vol. 35 (October 2009), p. 79.
3. Ibid., p. 78.
4. Asef Bayat, *Street Politics: Poor People's Movements in Iran* (New York: Columbia University Press 1997), p. 29.
5. The new urban poor came with what Bayat calls 'ingenious methods,' such as engaging in noisy demonstrations, breaking the water pipes to direct it to the areas in which they stayed, and stealing electricity from the main city lines (ibid., p. 86).
6. Mohammad Sina, 'A Review of Iran's Documentary Cinema,' *Farabi Journal*, No. 59–60, p. 132.
7. Ibid., p. 143.
8. Anthony R. Guneratne and Wimal Dissanayake (eds.), *Rethinking Third Cinema* (New York: Routledge 2003), p. 55.
9. Julio García Espinosa, 'For an Imperfect Cinema,' trans. Julianne Burton, Jump Cut, No. 20 (May 1979), pp. 24–6.
10. For more information on this, see Basir Nasibi, *Ten Years of Iran's Free Cinema* (in Persian) (Saarbrücken: Cinema-ye-Azad 1994).
11. Ayari, interview by the author.
12. Linda Nochlin, *The Body In Pieces: The Fragment as a Metaphor of Modernity* (London: Thames & Hudson 2001), p. 8.
13. It is the importance of the historic validity of an event that Walter Benjamin highlights when writing on the necessity of revisiting the past as an inevitable path towards winning the fight against the Fascist German state. For Benjamin, studying the historic moment goes hand in hand with fighting the enemy and the ruling class. See, Michael Löwy, *Fire Alarm: Reading Walter Benjamin's 'On the Concept of History'* (London/New York: Verso 2006), p. 25.
14. Walter Benjamin, *Illuminations* (New York: Schocken Books 2007), p. 257.
15. As Michael Löwy writes, many of Benjamin's texts suggest a correspondence between modernity, or progress, and a hellish damnation (Löwy, *Fire Alarm*, p. 59).

16. In fact, many revolutions that fought against networks of power and exploitation in colonized countries such as Algeria and Indochina were moments when the colonized resistance responded to the exploitation of the colonizer under the name of progress and modernity.
17. Löwy, *Fire Alarm*, p. 67.
18. In 'On The Concept of History,' Benjamin describes a chess machine that always wins against its opponent only because a hunchback is hiding inside the machine. The hunchback is the soul of the machine who controls the mechanical movements and pauses, just as the train's travelers have the power to create a pause in its forward movement (see ibid., p. 26).

References

Bayat, Asef, *Street Politics: Poor People's Movements in Iran* (New York: Columbia University Press 1997).

Benjamin, Walter, 'Theses on the Philosophy of History,' in *Illuminations*, trans. Harry Zohn, edited and with an introduction by Hannah Arendt (New York: Schocken Books 2007), pp. 253–64.

Espinosa, Julio García, 'For an Imperfect Cinema,' trans. Julianne Burton, *Jump Cut*, No. 20 (May 1979), pp. 24–6.

Guneratne, Anthony R. and Wimal Dissanayake (eds.), *Rethinking the Third Cinema* (New York: Routledge 2003).

Löwy, Michael, *Fire Alarm: Reading Walter Benjamin's 'On the Concept of History'* (London/New York: Verso 2006).

Nasibi, Basir, *Ten Years of Iran's Free Cinema* (in Persian) (Saarbrücken: Cinema-ye-Azad 1994).

Nochlin, Linda, *The Body in Pieces: The Fragment as a Metaphor of Modernity* (London: Thames & Hudson 2001).

Sadr Ara, Roozbeh, 'The Formation of Urban Documentary Cinema in Iran' (in Persian), *Hamshahri* Magazin, No. 35 (October 2009), p. 79.

Sina, Mohammad, 'A Review of Iran's Documentary Cinema' (in Persian), *Farabi Journal*, No. 59–60 (July 2006).

2. *THE HIDDEN HALF*, OR THE TEMPORAL AND COLLECTIVE POLITICS OF COUNTER-MEMORY

Sara Saljoughi

The opening credits of Tahmineh Milani's *Nīmah-yi Panhān/The Hidden Half* (2001), show the title of the film written over the lead character Fereshteh's back. In the freeze frame, she is turned away from the camera, wearing all black. Fereshteh's obscured identity signals the expansive meaning of 'half' in the film's title. What is hidden in Fereshteh's identity is the half of her story she has not yet told. But what also remains hidden, the film suggests, is the repressed history of the revolutionary struggle leading to and following the 1979 Revolution. Women and their experiences of this concealed history constitute the other hidden half conjured by the film. *The Hidden Half* brings this history to the fore through telling women's stories. In doing so, it proposes the notions of counter-history and collectivity as inextricable political projects. The film presents Fereshteh's account of an ignored, repressed, or forgotten history as an act that makes it possible to uncover and articulate further narratives. Fereshteh's forgotten story can be seen as a counter-memory of subjugated knowledge: a practice of remembering that for Foucault allows subversion and resistance to come to the fore. The notion of counter-memory is central to the structure of the film as it reveals the marginality of women in public processes of remembering. It is also a method through which the film presents a notion of temporality created from multiple moments of resistance. These occur in the acts of remembering, writing, narrating, and imaging. The film's elaboration of counter-memory is immanent to its own status as a marginalized object that commands a counter-history of Iranian national cinema.

Figure 2.1 Khosrow reading Fereshteh's revealing letter. (Source: Screen grab from *The Hidden Half*, 2001).

The Hidden Half is a semi-epistolary narrative that recounts the experiences of Fereshteh, a former activist in the period immediately following the revolution. When Fereshteh, who is now an upper-middle-class housewife, learns that her husband Khosrow, a prominent judge, will be reviewing the appeal of a woman sentenced to death for her political activities, Fereshteh writes a letter to her husband revealing for the first time her own political past.

It is only within the confines of marriage – a legally sanctioned relation, that the memory of a woman's revolutionary past can be narrated. An important part of Fereshteh's political life includes a romance with an older, married intellectual named Roozbeh Javid. The inclusion of this element adds further complexity to the revelations and their impact on Fereshteh's marriage. As Khosrow reads the text of Fereshteh's letter, the film uses flashbacks to narrate the events of Fereshteh's life. Her hope is that by revealing her past, she can urge Khosrow to see the similarities between his wife and the prisoner, and therefore listen attentively to and judge her appeal fairly. By visualizing his wife in the position of political activist (and a communist, at that), her husband is forced, however unconsciously, to humanize a prisoner whose case he has prejudged without hearing. Fereshteh anticipates this possibility, which emerges from her confidence that he is a 'good man,' and it motivates her intervention.

Figure 2.2 Fereshteh's (post-)revolutionary political activism. (Source: Screen grab from *The Hidden Half*, 2001).

The repression of political action in the early days of the revolutionary period is remembered in the context of the repression of political action in the present reality of the Islamic Republic of Iran (IRI). Fereshteh's revolutionary past, which has been completely hidden from her husband, allegorizes the repression of Marxist revolutionary discourse from the project of national consolidation after the establishment of the IRI. What her husband doesn't know is that Fereshteh herself narrowly escaped imprisonment and execution for her anti-state activities. Her counter-memory of the revolutionary moment forges a thread of continuity between the two periods, creating a multidimensional and non-teleological sense of temporality as well as solidarity between the two women. The political prisoner has been accused of subversion in the earliest period of the IRI. From Fereshteh's perspective, this makes her far from anonymous but rather easily imagined as one of her comrades from that period. Fereshteh's act of remembering, then, which she must recall in order to 'image' this woman as a comrade, also creates a sort of personal counter-memory wherein her own past becomes linked to this woman's present. The essay explores the ways in which Fereshteh's counter-memory enlists the attention of the regime (via her husband) in noting her opposition to a homogenized and sanitized version of the past. Her past leftist activism has to be hidden in order to protect the elite position she enjoys as the wife of a top-ranking judge. It is thus through revising the intimate space of marriage that the politics of remembering the past are transformed. Finally, the essay analyzes the repercussions of this practice of counter-memory towards the establishment of new collectivities, here represented primarily by Fereshteh relinquishing a protected position in order to align herself with another woman.

Milani's film was released in the middle of the presidential term of Mohammad Khatami, whose reform politics had the effect of loosening restrictions on cultural production.[1] Despite Khatami's period in power coinciding with a marked shift in film production (along with worldwide recognition of post-revolutionary Iranian cinema), Milani was nonetheless arrested for making *The Hidden Half*, a film that speaks openly about political resistance. Milani was held in prison on charges of using art against the regime. Of particular issue was an interview she gave after the film was released, in which she stated that many friends and colleagues were arrested by the regime for revolutionary activities.[2] The film had passed inspection by censors but drew attention after being released, presumably because the film's narration of the revolutionary struggle challenges the regime's own narrative.

In using the terms 'counter-memory' and 'counter-history' to discuss *The Hidden Half*, I draw on a Foucaultian concept of memory as a practice that always emerges in relation to power.[3] This context of power relations, José Medina notes, 'places practices of remembering and forgetting [...] in such a way that possibilities of resistance and subversion are brought to the fore.'[4] Medina argues that if we interrogate practices of remembering we learn 'the multiplicity of trajectories that converge in the epistemic negotiations in which memories are formed or deformed, maintained alive or killed.'[5] The matrix of power that Fereshteh's narrative addresses is both diegetic and extra-diegetic. Within the film, it is unambiguously Khosrow's profession as a judge that marks Fereshteh's disclosure as a political practice with subversion as her intention. Without this intimate and direct link to state power, the laying bare of Fereshteh's past is an issue of marital trustworthiness that is of no consequence in public terms. Yet Khosrow's profession is less relevant when we consider *The Hidden Half* as a cultural object that resuscitates memories that have been killed, i.e. the left's memory of the revolution. In other words, even if the narration of the past had no diegetic consequence for the fate of the political prisoner, its extra-diegetic context is one in which to speak of *this* memory of the revolution is to challenge the story that the IRI tells about itself.

To speak, however, of Foucault's notion of counter-history as it is discussed in the context of 'race war' in *Society Must be Defended* would take us far afield from this chapter's focus on *The Hidden Half*. Yet it is necessary to say a few words here about the stakes of discussing Milani's film as an example of counter-history. On the one hand, we might say that the film, which provides a leftist account of the revolutionary era from the perspective of a woman, indeed presents the 'discourse of those who have no glory.'[6] In the official history of the Islamic Republic of Iran, this is a perspective that is not merely marginalized, but indeed criminalized, as represented by the anonymous woman prisoner. To be identified with anti-state revolutionary action remains an act of treason regardless of the time of its discovery. On a minor scale, the film's revelation of the 'hidden half' of Fereshteh within the intimate space of her marriage also allows the emergence of something that has been absent, thereby contributing to the mise en abyme structure of the concept of 'the hidden half' as it is operative within the film. In conceiving the 'hidden half' more broadly, we must keep in mind how the history of the Iranian Revolution has been written in disciplinary terms. In the Anglo-American academy, the history of the Iranian Revolution has largely been written by what Naghmeh Sohrabi calls the left historiography, a generation of exiled scholars who identify as the defeated of the revolutionary struggle.[7] Much of what we know to be the historiography of the revolution emphasizes and brings to the fore what has been absent in official discourses of the IRI. Yet, as Behrouz Ghamari-Tabrizi notes, the meaning of the revolution remains a contested field, making narratives such as the fictional one offered by Fereshteh crucial in the process of writing Iranian history.[8] *The Hidden Half* emerges from within Iran and thus it occupies a rather strange position as a national cultural product that operates against the interests of the state. It is this duality of speaking the discourse of the exiled left historiography from within the state that makes Milani's project antagonistic to the IRI.

What is crucial here in my discussion of the film as counter-history is the ways in which it prompts a more complex notion of temporality by linking Fereshteh's past political activities with the present situation of the prisoner facing the death penalty. A form of counter-history emerges in this reading of the film, where I privilege the film's ability to perform one of the key facets of counter-history, its 'multi-agential account of social struggles.'[9] The temporal linkages between the two earlier periods of Iranian history (the Mossadegh era and the revolutionary period) with the present illuminates changing positions and modes of agency. Fereshteh's shifting form of agency is one view into a decades-long social struggle in Iran; as the narrative progressives, multiple viewpoints and experiences unfold to tell a complex story about power, resistance, and subversion.

Covering the immediate post-revolutionary moment, the *Hidden Half* highlights the potential and excitement of those first days of an Iran free of the monarchy. Fereshteh is active in a communist group, diligently reading revolutionary texts, attending meetings, and participating in organized actions. This period is remembered with fondness and, more importantly, as core to Fereshteh's sense of self, which in the present moment of the diegesis has been completely obscured. The critique embedded in the portrayal of these periods laments the fecund period of hope following the revolution. What is clear in the film's representation is the felt sense, on the side of the left, that there exists agency to radically change society. Some twenty years later, the effects of the Islamic Republic's restructuring of Iranian society have become deeply entrenched. Fereshteh is a symbol of this lost utopian past, for she has completely eradicated any trace of it in her present life. When she learns of the anonymous woman prisoner, however, Fereshteh's attention is turned away from the demands of the present (childcare, household management) to the memory of her repressed past. Her act of intervention renews for her the hopeful quality of that earlier period. Through Fereshteh and her narration, the film highlights the differences between the two periods. At the same time, it forges a link between the two by way of Fereshteh's involvement in political action and the woman awaiting her appeal trial in prison.

A Private Marriage Made Public

The division between the public and private spheres of life in Iran is widely commented upon by scholars.[10] Social life in Iran has traditionally been organized through a division between the private and public spheres of life. The private connotes that which is inside and is the realm of the inner self, whereas the public connotes the outside and is where the outer self appears. Maintaining this dichotomy is integral to social mores related to propriety and dignity. Of key importance in this relation is the idea of protecting the inner self or that which is inside, intimate, and private. This disposition to the social is articulated at various scales of social interaction, from the conversational practice of *ta'āruf*, which one could argue conceals desires and proclivities, to the prevalence of structures such as the walled garden, a conspicuous architectural practice that enacts the division of private and public spatially.[11]

In *The Hidden Half*, Milani frames Fereshteh's life to illustrate the deep integration of these inside/outside values. Fereshteh has maintained this division to a radical degree wherein even her husband is not privy to what she admits is her true inner self – her political convictions, her history, her desires and anxieties. The fact that Khosrow doesn't know her true identity suggests that there is something placed between private and public, and it is her marriage that marks that intermediary zone. The film will exploit this position in order to show the ramifications of breaking the division between private and public. Milani brilliantly uses the institution of marriage to crystallize the intricate relation between private and public. Within the safety of marriage, a publicly valued but ultimately private relation (with its own legal privileges), Fereshteh is able to narrate a counter-memory that threatens the official history of the state. Against the voluminous backdrop of public monuments of memory (such as murals commemorating Iran-Iraq War martyrs), Fereshteh's narrative deftly challenges the official position that women have not made private and public sacrifices in the nation's recent political history.

While the marriage, as concept and as plot device, is pivotal to what the film has to say about the private and public, the film's visual formal strategies work to reinforce these ideas. For example, late in the film a long shot shows Fereshteh emerging from the locked door to her building. We see her from the perspective of Rastegar, the regime agent who haunted Fereshteh throughout her youth and who now, unbeknownst to her, works with her husband. Her identity, the inner fabric of her personal life, is shielded by this door, which reveals nothing of the interior when opened, and whose dimensions shroud Fereshteh with a degree of concealment that is protective. From Rastegar's point of view across the street the door emphasizes the ways in which Fereshteh has indeed been able to hide her identity. The sudden discovery, on Rastegar's part, that his boss is married to Fereshteh also shows how well the division between private and public is maintained. Khosrow might be in daily contact with Rastegar, even traveling together for work, but that does not guarantee the intimacy of friendship. Finally, that this particular shot and framing of Fereshteh occurs late in the film suggests that despite the narrative that we have just learned, we might still be on the outside, as Rastegar is, and that there is more protecting Fereshteh's inner self than we can imagine.

The film's narrative uses the politics of concealment and modesty to emphasize Fereshteh's 'public' remembering as transgressive. The privacy of marriage mutates the private/public dynamic because Fereshteh's husband is a judge and therefore functions in the text as a symbol of the regime, making Fereshteh's narration of this history neither entirely private nor immediately public. The nature of her narration differs from a private conversation between husband and wife. When Fereshteh narrates her personal history to Khosrow, she does so as his wife, but also as a member of the public addressing a representative of the state.

Fereshteh's marriage to Khosrow functions to provide a formal outlet for Fereshteh's confession, which would not be heard or legible otherwise. This emphasizes that the private sphere is the realm of counter-memory, which is impossible to articulate in the public sphere. The narration of the letter she has written to him makes up most of the film's runtime, putting it in the company of other epistolary Iranian films such as Rakhshan Banietemad's *The May Lady/Banu-e Ordibehesht* (1998). On a superficial level, the epistolary film is a cinematic convention that has been especially useful for depicting desire and heterosexual relationships in post-revolutionary Iranian cinema.[12] It establishes intimacy and contact without showing any physical expressions of love and sexual desire. In Milani's use of the epistolary as the primary means through which Fereshteh's husband learns of her past, however, the director takes advantage of the convention to represent an unrepresentable past of political activism. While Fereshteh's narration of the revolutionary events provides an account of her participation, the epistolary mode of the narration effectively puts the imaging of these events as emerging from her husband. As Khosrow reads Fereshteh's account, the film frames him as though he imagines the events that she describes. The camera shows him in close-up, giving us a tangible sense of his imagining of these events. The visual representation of the revolutionary events, therefore, is structured as Khosrow's imagination. In this sense, Fereshteh is able to speak through her husband, for not only is he fluent in the institutional language of the Iranian state but he is one of its representatives. By speaking to him, she speaks to the legal system of the state. This illuminates Fereshteh's very different position from the anonymous female prisoner, who has no such representative. Thus, Fereshteh's marriage gives her a status that removes her from what might be called a subaltern position, and gives her, by proxy of her husband, the ability to speak both for herself and for the prisoner.[13]

There is also, of course, a utopian dimension to the film's epistolary mode. By setting up Khosrow's 'imaging' of the Iranian Revolution through the flashbacks, the film forces a public reckoning with the hidden past. This analysis relies on Khosrow's symbolic presence as a representative of the regime. But he is not any representative. It is important that Milani sets him up as a judge who will specifically have the power to determine the life of a political prisoner. He could have been a 'softer' representative of the government, but instead his position as one who determines whether political dissidence is punishable by death gives the flashback a particularly important function in the text. It becomes a way of exposing to the hegemonic that which it has actively repressed. In her reading of Milani's films, Michelle Langford argues that the 'Fereshteh trilogy functions in precisely this way, seeking to critique a patriarchal and ideological system through an examination of how that system deeply affects the intimate spheres of home and family in Iran.'[14] For Langford this influence of the 'system' on the home is suggested through the character of Khosrow, for '[I]t is through Khosrow, who represents both the domestic realm of the family and the broader institution of "the law", that the film expresses a hope that the law may one day be capable of paying more attention to the needs of women.'[15] By allowing Khosrow to 'see' the repressed past that has been present before him (an act that, according to Langford, makes him a co-narrator), the film makes Fereshteh's history speak directly to power. In doing so, the film makes a bold and hopeful gesture in the name of uncovering silenced memories.

That this happens within the structure of a marriage is doubly important. It suggests, in rather explicit ways, that despite being in a loving and seemingly harmonious marriage, there is a way in which the woman as wife remains a kind of blank figure whose specificity matters less than her fulfillment of her wifely duties. For example, in the first few minutes of the film we see Khosrow ask Fereshteh to pack his bags and her response suggests this is a normal duty of hers, in addition to cooking, cleaning, offering him tea, fetching the children, overseeing their work, feeding them, liaising with the school (when the teacher calls), and so on. But it seems that it was not necessary for Fereshteh to be known, in her singularity, for this harmony to emerge and take shape. When Khosrow and Fereshteh met, he was unaware of her political activities and thus of the majority of her life. In fact, this implies that things are so harmonious because Fereshteh's identity becomes a kind of tabula rasa for the life of the husband and the family (and in some ways, for the nation, given that Khosrow is its representative).

Through the marriage, however, Fereshteh does assume an identity – that of the wife of a prominent judge. The importance of this identity is twofold. Firstly, it is what allows her to conceal her activist past. It is not simply that she has kept her story private, but that her status as a regime insider gives her a degree of protection from any allegation of such a past. Indeed, we see this early in Khosrow's courting of Fereshteh, where he draws on personal connections to allow her to re-enroll at the university. The public meaning of her private relationship disallows a leftist, revolutionary past. Secondly, Fereshteh's usurpation of the social status of her marriage is where her agency emerges in the present. She catapults herself out of this protected category by revealing her affiliations and in doing so shatters the regime's mythology of its pure power, namely that it has cleaned its house of dissidents. In sum, Fereshteh's revelation undoes the concealing work performed by her marriage. And in risking her sanctioned position, she opens the possibility of forging solidarity and new forms of collectivity.

Solidarity, or Three Women

The Hidden Half begins with the premise of empathy and solidarity as given forms of relation among the women in the film. When Fereshteh learns her husband will be traveling to Shiraz to hear the imprisoned woman's trial, she does not need much detail to feel a sense of responsibility in her role as the judge's spouse. In other words, she is predisposed to feeling a sense of comradeship with this stranger for she imagines the imprisoned woman's circumstances as a fate that might have been her own. When Fereshteh tells Khosrow she is concerned for the woman, he is not convinced. Rather, he tells Fereshteh 'not everyone is pure and good like you.' The film, however, sets up spectators to question this notion of purity, by giving us Fereshteh's perspective on what awaits the woman prisoner.

The line of political struggle from Fereshteh to the anonymous woman expands late in the film to include the Mossadegh period's struggle against the Pahlavi monarchy and Western imperialism. In a confrontation with Javid's wife, Afarin, Fereshteh learns that she bears a striking physical resemblance to Javid's first love, Mahmonir, a young woman who was a pro-Mossadegh activist murdered during the uprisings. The young woman was a committed political activist, much like Fereshteh, and in Afarin's telling of the story Javid has continually been in search of this lost love. Through this revelation, women's participation across mid- to late twentieth-century Iranian struggles is connected. Structurally, the film's narrative shows the different ways in which women's experiences constitute the hidden half no matter the political context: the Mossadegh activist is dead and gone, Fereshteh's story is hidden, and the contemporary political prisoner is anonymous.

The film draws on these three women to show, in different ways, the damage done by concealment and silence. From the perspective of her public life, Fereshteh is the hegemonic standard of the ideal Iranian wife and mother. This is the condition that makes it possible for her individual story of resistance to emerge. But Fereshteh's protected position, by way of marriage, and her cultivated image as a 'good,' pious woman also makes it clear that the possibilities of bringing marginalized histories to light are limited for most women. She tells the story that the anonymous woman cannot.

The political prisoner remains anonymous throughout the film. We do not see her face, learn her name, or the details of her case. She assumes a generic quality that gives the film a device for a broader allegorical statement about the multiplicity of such cases in Iran. She is one of many and leaving her story vague illustrates the impossibility of her counter-memory ever coming to light. Despite the fact that the court will hear the political prisoner's appeal, her narrative will not necessarily change her fate. The story of political dissent in contemporary Iran is always already apprehended and judged by the legal system. It is this grim reality in which Fereshteh wants to intervene by telling her husband her own story. The forum of her memories and his private act of reading will beget closer attention and empathy than the system of justice that the prisoner faces. Fereshteh knows the limitations of a legal system that is designed to punish those who resist.

Like Fereshteh, we do not learn much about Mahmonir, Javid's first love, throughout the film. She constitutes the 'hidden half' of Javid's relationship to Fereshteh, for it is her resemblance to the dead lover that constitutes Javid's attraction to Fereshteh. She is also the 'hidden half' of Javid's marriage to Afarin, for he has spent a lifetime desirous of the long-lost lover. More importantly, however, Afarin is presented as yet another woman who has been silenced and marginalized, despite her elite class status.

Afarin speaks with a stutter and she conveys this to Fereshteh as the reason for her reticence to speak around someone as articulate and committed as Fereshteh. Although she is pivotal to the plot (and the reason Fereshteh stops seeing Javid), she only has one significant scene in which she reveals her personal history to Fereshteh privately. She narrates a trajectory of her life that makes her speech disability central to how she and others – most importantly Javid – view her. The character's stutter gives the script another angle from which to show stories that might be omitted from official discourse. We come to this position from Afarin's own admission that her condition prevents her from readily speaking. This reticence materializes in the *mise-en-scène* of her narration scene. When she begins telling Fereshteh the climax of her story – the 1953 coup that ousted Mossadegh – her back is entirely to the camera as she tells the story. The effect is a reduction in our ability to fully comprehend her narration. At the same time, Milani employs a highly melodramatic musical track to heighten the drama of the story. The music is so loud and dissonant that it, along with the visual composition of the sequence, has the effect of drowning out Afarin's words. This emphasizes that when women do speak, they are not always heard, and that there are elements that obscure and marginalize their words and experiences.

Though it is not the focus of the film, we can also read Fereshteh's counter-memory of the revolutionary moment as a critique of the ways in which women's issues were overlooked or marginalized in leftist movements. Through Fereshteh's trajectory, we see that within leftist groups there was little concern for issues of social reproduction that were particularly relevant to women. As many Iranian feminist historians have noted, women's issues were completely peripheral to the agendas of various revolutionary group.[16] This is alluded to in one of the café scenes, when Fereshteh asks her group leader about love and marriage. Fereshteh's questions emerge from the mind of an impressionistic young person who seeks advice on how to live from everyone she encounters, whether that is her dogmatic comrades or the arrogant Javid. She recognizes a gulf between different desires and plans. Though she may be part of a revolutionary scene, she is also inundated with messages that universally assume that 'good' young women marry. In an effort to save herself from political imprisonment, she chooses to marry Khosrow and live her life cloaked in a kind of anonymity. Here, it is impossible to ignore how all the periods depicted in the film suggest that the fate of women is determined by their private relationships and through reliance on a degree of protection emerging from the decisions of men.

The links created in the film between the present, the early days following the revolution, and the Mossadegh area suggest a temporal continuity in the struggle against pure forms of power by the state. While the threat of incarceration and death are clear in each period, the film is especially interested in the question of history, memory, and the way those forces of power impinge on women's stories. What the film tries to suggest is indeed a Foucaultian idea about what happens when that which has been silenced emerges from the margins or is recognized as giving structure to how history is narrated. The film has a lack of narrative closure. We do not learn the stakes of Fereshteh's confession, for herself, or for the political prisoner. On the one hand, we can analyze this as the film's skepticism about the degree to which the private can impact the public. In other words, the agency of private revelations seems limited in its capacity to create change. On the other hand, the film shows how radically the sharing of hidden or repressed memories alters relationships and worldviews. Furthermore, they prompt people in very different positions of power to create new relationships, showing how the struggle against pure power is waged on many different fronts.

Counter-Histories of Iranian Cinema

While Milani is a well-known filmmaker – her earlier film *Daw Zan/Two Women* (1999) in particular has received a great deal of attention – in general her films have not gained the kind of critical attention bestowed upon her male contemporaries. This is not especially unusual, particularly in the Iranian context where despite the increase of women in film production following the revolution, they are still a minority when it comes to prominent directors. One of the reasons for the relative exclusion of Milani from discussions of Iranian art cinema has to do with the aesthetics of melodrama, which evoke none of the landscapes and pace that foreign audiences have come to expect from Iranian filmmakers. *The Hidden Half* can be considered as part of a loose trilogy with Milani's films *Two Women* and *Vakonesh Panjom/The Fifth Reaction* (2003), all of which feature a lead character named Fereshteh. The emphasis on Fereshteh's internal turmoil set against the backdrop of the revolution and its aftermath is strikingly dissonant from Iranian art cinema's avoidance of both these matters and character development.

It is worth considering the ways in which melodrama has been deemed a 'woman's genre' in terms of its aesthetics and mode of address, compared with Iranian art cinema. The soundtracks to melodramatic films are often saccharine, cuing emotional responses rather than allowing spectators to notice and reflect on their responses. In *The Hidden Half*, acting is directed for full emotional impact, particularly in the many scenes that involve an outpouring of emotional revelations. Other elements of the *mise-en-scène*, such as the types of objects selected and displayed, follow the 'excessive' qualities of melodrama. The café in which Fereshteh and her comrades meet, for example, is not only draped with posters of Che Guevara and Ho Chi Minh, but the camera abruptly turns to these images in the midst of a discussion on revolutionary politics, lingering there for longer than expected. The spectator is thus again cued to the significance of the setting, which can be considered an excessive aesthetics as compared with one where these images would be retained as part of the background not as the explicit focus of any shots. All of this is clearly in contrast with the long takes and general neo-realist aesthetic of Iranian art cinema, which largely eschews extra-diegetic sound and other features in the aesthetics of melodrama. These fundamental differences have affected the reception of melodrama and other popular Iranian cinema.

In one of the few scholarly analyses of *The Hidden Half*, Michelle Langford uses the notion of 'practical melodrama' to discuss the production of pathos in the film and what that affords in terms of revealing the complexities of the private/public dichotomy in Iran.[17] By invoking melodrama as the genre best suited to exploring issues central to the women's movement in Iran, Langford draws on germinal film studies debates on rethinking melodrama in order to argue against the omission of the popular in most studies of Iranian cinema. While the present chapter does not specifically pursue the question of melodrama, I wish to draw on Langford's intervention to investigate the dearth of scholarship on Milani's film and how 'the hidden half' may also be put to work in thinking about the disciplinary practices of Iranian cinema studies.

Milani's relative marginality in the scholarly literature on Iranian cinema suggests that any discussion of a counter-history in this field must also question positivist approaches to the history of Iranian cinema. In the case of *The Hidden Half*, the dominant historical narrative of the IRI and the positivist approaches to Iranian film history become entangled like strange bedfellows. The representation of the revolution in *The Hidden Half* stands out as singular in a body of films in which this monumental event has scarcely been portrayed.[18] Because this history has been repressed in favor of a narrative that consolidates the epistemological regime of the Islamic Republic, its representation on screen is a limitation few directors have overcome. Milani's contributions to a counter-history of the Iranian Revolution are thus profound, particularly given the ways in which her films deviate from their contemporaries in terms of an explicit focus on the political. While filmmakers such as Kiarostami have been accused of evading the political, Milani's political feminist cinema has been ignored in scholarly debates.[19] This can be attributed, in part, to art cinema's currency on the global film market. Indeed, in the formation of Iranian cinema studies as an area of scholarly research, there appears an implicit link between a film's recognition and exposure (particularly by foreign audiences) and its representation in the scholarly literature. Art cinema emerges in this scholarly context as national cinema by definition, given that it is most often what is distributed internationally.[20] This trend has started to decline, as evidenced by recent publications on popular cinema and earlier periods of Iranian cinema.[21] But contemporary popular cinema remains marginal and, in this respect, *The Hidden Half* counters notions of Iranian film history as written in the international scholarly literature. By drawing attention to films that have not received much scholarly attention – which is different from critical or mainstream attention – we can begin to analyze the lacunae in our disciplinary discourse.

In conclusion, *The Hidden Half* tells a complex story about the role of memory in the politics of counter-history. One of the major contributions the film makes to our understanding of Iranian cinema is through its laying bare the kinds of filmmaking that are valued in how we write cinematic history. Despite its singularity as a state-funded film addressing the left history of the revolution and depicting the revolutionary struggle, it has not gained much traction in the scholarship on Iranian literature. At the same time, the film's story points to the ways in which crucial histories of political action remain obscured and repressed. Through Fereshteh's chronicle of her political activism, the film suggests that to speak and write counter-memory allows new forms of solidarity and collectivity to emerge. When Fereshteh shares her personal story with her husband, she does so in order to intervene in another woman's future – to possibly save her from a death sentence for her political activities against the state. Counter-memory thus functions in the film as the very source for the radical alteration of the political present.

Notes

1. On the relationship of Khatami's regime to cinema, see Blake Atwood, *Reform Cinema in Iran: Film and Political Change in the Islamic Republic* (New York: Columbia University Press 2016).
2. Dana Harris, 'Biz Rallies around Iranian Helmer,' in *Variety*, Vol. 384, No. 12 (5–11 November 2001), p. 6; Steve Ross, 'Thorn in their Side,' in *The Guardian*, 2 November 2001, https://www.theguardian.com/film/2001/nov/02/filmcensorship.artsfeatures (accessed 15 October 2020).
3. See also Marc Ferro, 'Film: A Counter-Analysis of Society,' in *Cinema and History*, trans. Naomi Greene (Detroit, MI: Wayne State University Press 1988), p. 23.
4. José Medina, 'Towards a Foucaultian Epistemology of Resistance: Counter-Memory, Epistemic Friction, and Guerilla Pluralism,' in *Foucault Studies*, No. 12 (2011), pp. 9–35, p. 10.
5. Ibid., p. 10.
6. Michel Foucault, *Society Must be Defended* (New York: Picador 2003), p. 70.
7. See Naghmeh Sohrabi, 'The "Problem-Space" of the Historiography of the Iranian Revolution,' in *History Compass*, Vol. 16, No. 11 (November 2018), n.p.
8. Behrouz Ghamari-Tabrizi, 'Revisiting Foucault in Iran: A Response,' in *Jadaliyya* (25 April 25 2017), https://www.jadaliyya.com/Details/34232. He notes, however, that the history of the Revolution, unlike other revolutions, was written by the defeated, not the winners.
9. Gabriel Rockhill, 'Foucault, Genealogy, Counter-History,' *Theory and Event*, Vol. 23, No. 1 (January 2020), pp. 88–119, p. 108.
10. There is a significant literature on the notion of the public and private split in Iranian studies. For works relevant to the current topic, see Roxanne Varzi, *Warring Souls: Youth, Media, and Martyrdom in Post-Revolutionary Iran* (Durham, NC: Duke University Press 2006) and Hamid Naficy, 'Veiled Voice and Vision in Iranian Cinema: The Evolution of Rakhshan Banietemad's Films,' in *Social Research*, Vol. 67, No. 2 (Summer 2000), p. 559–76.
11. Farzaneh Milani, *Veils and Words: The Emerging Voices of Iranian Women Writers* (Syracuse, NY: Syracuse University Press 1992).

12. See for example the discussion of Rakhshan Banietemad's films in Gönül Dönmez-Colin, *Women, Islam, and Cinema* (London: Reaktion 2004).
13. I use subaltern here to refer to the ways in which those without access to the language of institutions require a representative to speak on their behalf – Gayatri Chakravorty Spivak, 'Can the Subaltern Speak?,' in Cary Nelson and Lawrence Grossberg (eds.), *Marxism and the Interpretation of Culture* (London: Macmillan 1988), pp. 271–313.
14. Michelle Langford, 'Practical Melodrama: From Recognition to Action in Tahmineh Milani's Fereshteh Trilogy,' in *Screen*, Vol. 51, No.4 (Winter 2010), pp. 341–64.
15. Ibid., p. 352.
16. See Haideh Moghissi, *Populism and Feminism in Iran: Women's Struggle in a Male Defined Revolutionary Moment* (London: Palgrave 1996); Parvin Paidar, *Women and the Political Process in Twentieth-Century Iran* (Cambridge: Cambridge University Press 1995); Eliz Sanasarian, *The Women's Rights Movement in Iran: Mutiny, Appeasement, and Repression from 1900 to Khomeini* (New York: Praeger 1982).
17. Langford, 'Practical Melodrama,' pp. 343–5.
18. In this respect, the Iranian Revolution is rather unique compared to other world historical events that have been routinely depicted on film.
19. See Azadeh Farahmand, 'Perspectives on Recent (International Acclaim for) Iranian Cinema,' in Richard Tapper (ed.), *New Iranian Cinema: Politics, Representation and Identity* (London: I.B. Tauris 2002).
20. Andrew Higson, 'The Concept of National Cinema,' *Screen*, Vol. 30, No. 4 (Autumn 1989), pp. 36–47.
21. Pedram Partovi, *Popular Iranian Cinema Before the Revolution: Family and Nation in Filmfarsi* (New York: Routledge 2017) and Golbarg Rekabtalaei, *Iranian Cosmopolitanism: A Cinematic History* (Cambridge: Cambridge University Press 2019).

References

Atwood, Blake, *Reform Cinema in Iran: Film and Political Change in the Islamic Republic* (New York: Columbia University Press 2016).

Dönmez-Colin, Gönül, *Women, Islam, and Cinema* (London: Reaktion 2004).

Farahmand, Azadeh. 'Perspectives on Recent (International Acclaim for) Iranian Cinema,' in Richard Tapper (ed.), *New Iranian Cinema: Politics, Representation and Identity* (London: I.B. Tauris 2002).

Ferro, Marc, 'Film: A Counter-Analysis of Society,' in *Cinema and History*, trans. Naomi Greene (Detroit, MI: Wayne State University Press 1988).

Foucault, Michel, *Society Must be Defended: Lectures at the Collège de France, 1975–1976*, trans. David Macey. ed. Mauro Bertani and Alessandro Fontana (New York: Picador 2003).

Ghamari-Tabrizi, Behrouz, 'Revisiting Foucault in Iran: A Response,' in *Jadaliyya* (25 April 2017), https://www.jadaliyya.com/Details/34232

Harris, Dana, 'Biz Rallies around Iranian Helmer,' *Variety*, Vol. 384, No. 12 (5–11 November 2001).

Higson, Andrew, 'The Concept of National Cinema,' *Screen*, Vol. 30, No. 4 (Autumn 1989), pp. 36–47.

Langford, Michelle, 'Practical Melodrama: From Recognition to Action in Tahmineh Milani's Fereshteh Trilogy,' *Screen*, Vol. 51, No. 4 (Winter 2010), pp. 341–64.

Medina, José, 'Towards a Foucaultian Epistemology of Resistance: Counter-Memory, Epistemic Friction, and *Guerilla* Pluralism,' in *Foucault Studies*, No. 12 (2011), pp. 9–35.

Milani, Farzaneh, *Veils and Words: The Emerging Voices of Iranian Women Writers* (Syracuse, NY: Syracuse University Press 1992).

Moghissi, Haideh, *Populism and Feminism in Iran: Women's Struggle in a Male Defined Revolutionary Moment* (London: Palgrave 1996).

Naficy, Hamid, 'Veiled Voice and Vision in Iranian Cinema: The Evolution of Rakhshan Banietemad's Films,' *Social Research*, Vol. 67, No. 2 (Summer 2000), pp. 559–76.

Paidar, Parvin, *Women and the Political Process in Twentieth-Century Iran* (Cambridge: Cambridge University Press 1995).

Partovi, Pedram, *Popular Iranian Cinema before the Revolution: Family and Nation in Filmfarsi* (New York: Routledge 2017).

Rekabtalaei, Golbarg, *Iranian Cosmopolitanism: A Cinematic History* (Cambridge: Cambridge University Press 2019).

Rockhill, Gabriel, 'Foucault, Genealogy, Counter-History,' in *Theory and Event*, Vol. 23, No. 1 (January 2020), pp. 85–119.

Ross, Steve, 'Thorn in their Side,' *The Guardian*, 2 November 2001, https://www.theguardian.com/film/2001/nov/02/filmcensorship.artsfeatures

Sanasarian, Eliz, *The Women's Rights Movement in Iran: Mutiny, Appeasement, and Repression from 1900 to Khomeini* (New York: Praeger 1982).

Sohrabi, Naghmeh, 'The "Problem-Space" of the Historiography of the 1979 Iranian Revolution,' *History Compass*, Vol. 16, No. 11 (November 2018).

Spivak, Gayatri Chakravorty, 'Can the Subaltern Speak?,' in Cary Nelson and Lawrence Grossberg (eds.), *Marxism and the Interpretation of Culture* (London: Macmillan 1988), pp. 271–313.

Varzi, Roxanne, *Warring Souls: Youth, Media, and Martyrdom in Post-Revolutionary Iran*, (Durham, NC: Duke University Press 2006).

3. COUNTER-INVESTIGATIONS. ON MATCHBOXES, BLACK BOXES, AND OTHER FORGOTTEN FUTURES

Chowra Makaremi and Emmanuel Alloa

Chowra Makaremi, you are a social anthropologist, known for decisive research on migratory confinement policies in Europe, as well as for an ongoing study on post-revolutionary violence in Iran. *Hitch* (2019) is your first film. While in other works of yours, you describe your method as ethnographical, at the beginning of *Hitch*, you compare your work to that of an archaeologist. Could you elaborate on that? Why do you think the comparison with archaeology is more appropriate than that with the work of, say, an ethnographer or of a historian?

This comparison slowly emerged throughout the process of filmmaking. My first question was: how to tell a story of violence in a way that makes denial, and the texture of violence as a lived experience, tangible? Massacres are stories full of secrets: they remain a secret of the power (but not *too* secret, otherwise there wouldn't be fear or terror), and they outlive as family secrets. These two dimensions are linked, which is why I work on the articulation of the political and the intimate. And I look at things from this angle because I feel that the long-lasting effects of violence, as an instrument of silencing and social-political engineering, precisely reside in this articulation. What is the relationship to archaeology? It's about secret and absence. The past is conveyed to us in an encrypted way. It is covered by layers of dust brought about by the passing of years. Under the dust, what remains are objects in which some information is encoded: at one point, the narration that conveys memories from one generation to the other has stopped, or that thread has been lost. Contrary to history or ethnography, which rely very much on the 'truth' of the witness (the oral or written testimony), I feel that archaeology's departure point is the absence of the witness-narrator, beyond repair. This absence is not a shortage, but an epistemic premise.

My film talks about the massacre of people who have been turned into disappeared: there will never be a witness of this process. There can be survivors of violence, very rare people who witnessed the massacres, but there is no witness to disappearance. Yet how can we talk about this? How can we relate to this process and to the ones who have been through this process? I don't know if this question or this search are legitimate, feasible, or even 'sane' (and in the movie, I share this interrogation with the viewer), but it has been one aspect of resistance against state violence: a political resistance that roots deep into our affects. As such it deserves to be documented. But how to document it and to film it? In order to find an answer, the first thing I did is to go to Périgord, at my brother's place, where there is a cupboard where all the objects that remain from my mother are kept. For three days, I stayed in a room with the cupboard, a camera, and some lights. It was a bet, an experience, almost a magical thinking: I didn't go through the few newspapers and books trying to gather information, but I filmed and photographed the objects because I wanted to find out their secret. I believed there was a secret, I believed I could find something although I didn't know what. It was beyond any kind of rational investigation. If I had found nothing, then I would probably not have made a movie. But I found a trace. Not on the spot, but later on, when I watched my rushes. My mother was a collector: she had collections of matchboxes and watches. The close-up on a matchbox was showing the trace of a match that had been scratched. Behind this scratch there was the gesture, and the hand of the person who did it. And there was my mother, or the closest I ever get to her actual presence. I had filmed the matchbox with a slow (trembling) traveling, and maybe this is what revealed the gesture behind the scratch: I wonder if I would have seen it if the image was static. In any case, I had found where to start from, and the notion of 'trace' became the red thread in making the movie. I would be collecting traces, as both remains and clues – as signs of the passing of time, and as what has not been destroyed after all this time. Some time later, I heard an archaeologist talking on the radio about the magic of her work: she said that behind a sculpture or a writing, there was a gesture, and behind the gesture, there was the presence of a person who had lived sometimes dozens of thousands of years ago. This presence is all the more magical that absence is the departure point of archaeology. What methodology do we invent to unearth the past in the absence of witnesses and human narratives?

So really, the comparison with archaeology emerged through research and filming. It imposed itself and acquired yet another dimension when I was confronted to the destruction of my aunt's grave. My aunt was executed in the early 1980s, and the last trace of the movie was due to be her grave, which had a long and telling story. But two years after I started working on the film, I was towards the end of the editing process when this grave, along with other graves of people executed in the 1980s, was suddenly destroyed. It happened at once, without warning. Now these graves and the remains of the executees are under a road: people who 'existed' as dead for decades have been turned into disappeared. We know they are here, under urban constructions, but there is no trace of them and no way to mark their place in today's public space. The process of their death, burial, and profanation is a public secret that lies in the hand of archaeological investigation now. In the film, I worked with satellite imagery in order to touch on this archaeological truth of violence.

I understand there's a truly forensic dimension to your archaeology, since it's about re-establishing the facts about what really happened. But I also sense there's something more to your endeavor: you want to undo the symbolic violence, which consists in the deliberate negation of the crimes. You mention the politics of disappearance, and maybe you had in mind the parallels of South America's *desaparecidos*, although it seems to me there's also a decisive difference: while the military regimes in Chile and Argentina deliberately left the families in the dark about whether their abducted kin was dead or alive, and thus impeding even the beginning of a work of mourning, in the case of your mother and aunt and of all the other thousands of uncounted executed opponents, the exerted symbolic difference is the reverse. You seem to imply that this time, the relatives knew where the graves were, and regularly gathered there (the victims 'existed' as dead, as you say). Only now, this deliberate and successive removal of traces, hidden behind alleged requirements of urbanization, aims at impeding the work of mourning that had been taken place for years, thus creating a twice-behaved forced disappearance. Would you state that your film operates on both levels, both in seeking to re-establish the facts as well as in performing an act of repair? Do you think that, in the event that one day, the perpetrators will have managed to remove all the traces of what happened, a film like yours can become a virtual site of remembrance?

The film is definitely a response to the violence of denialism. The 'politics of disappearance' in Iran was quite messy. The suppression of opponents was systematic and it was a state politics, but it took various forms. The bodies of the executed were sometimes given back to their families, and sometimes not. Sometimes the marking of graves was allowed and sometimes not. There were families who never knew the fate of their disappeared relatives, as in the case of the South American *desaparecidos*, but they were a minority. Thousands of executed prisoners disappeared – although their families were informed of their execution – and did not have a proper grave site: some are in the infamous Khavaran mass grave on the outskirts of Tehran. Other times, the authorities gave back the bodies, all the while forbidding their burial: they had to be buried in the family private yard. Some bodies were not given back but were 'properly' buried by the authorities in a cemetery. For the latter, one can never be sure whether the burial did actually take place or not. In my mother's case for instance, word was given out that several hundred killed prisoners were supposedly buried in individual graves over one single night, which is practically very difficult. The local population believes that the prisoners were likely buried in an unknown mass grave, and that new stones with their names were put on older graves in the cemetery. This is what my grandmother implies in the film when she talks about that woman who asks her in the cemetery: 'when you put your daughter in the grave, didn't you notice someone else was buried there?'

We don't know if my mother's remains are actually under the grave that holds her name. We don't know if my aunt gave birth or not before she was executed (she was pregnant). So even when there is a grave site – which isn't always the case – there are many unsolved questions that belong to the field of forensic expertise, which is out of reach in the current situation. I'm giving these details to illustrate how difficult it is to draw lines between 'proper dead' and disappearance. It is more of a twilight zone. The victim 'exists' but this existence is fragile and difficult to establish. Their non-existence is equally difficult to establish; they have been stolen from our episteme of truth, based on fact-finding. The body is there, but maybe not, or the body is there but can be displaced suddenly, or the grave can be covered-up without explanation . . .

The question of disappearance is tricky for two reasons at least. First of all, the notion of 'enforced disappearance' is a technique of state repression that has been defined in international human rights as a specific form of crime.[1] If the situation doesn't fit the legal definition, you won't call it 'disappearance.' Secondly, this definition was forged and established itself through collective mobilizations: it is a legal characterization (of a crime) that opens the path for judiciary action, since it enables the relatives of a disappeared person to file a lawsuit. This judiciary struggle was based on a brilliant and inspiring argumentation that reverted states' erasures of their crimes as a crime in itself (through the concept of 'enforced disappearance'). But the problem with legal weapons is that they drag you into a process of characterization of events, which means tracking the exact correspondence between what took place and the elements of the crime as defined by the law. How do you characterize the crimes? Do these elements actually meet the required definitions? The reality I've tried to track in the movie only partly belongs to (and meets) these definitions.

As far as I remember, I have read lawyers trying to establish that the 1988 massacre could qualify as 'crime against humanity,' because it met the legal definition. In the early 2000s, when I started to investigate more about this past, no historical narrative was available but there were a few articles debating legal issues of whether or not 1988 was a crime against humanity. The narrative of what happened was conveyed through these legal discussions. There is something truly biased about this: the frames we created to grasp reality actually move us away from the events in their material, messy, contradictory stuff. If we debate legal characterization before we write history; if we write history through human rights concerns then we risk 'losing' the memory of the events. This impression, which is my first adult-contact with this past, is the actual incentive of the movie: what is the lived reality behind what we call 'a crime against humanity'? How can we talk about these facts when we are not focused on 'proving' that they fit such and such definition? How can I tell this story of violence when I am not trying to establish a human rights abuse? These are the reasons why, for my own record, I related to the movie project as a 'counter-investigation': not an independent investigation, but the contrary of an investigation, e.g. a quest for truth that is epistemically different from investigative fact-finding.

To go back to your questions, this is a reason why my film is rather weak at establishing facts. Fortunately, there are other initiatives that have established the facts of state crimes during the 1980s in Iran, among which well-documented human rights reports and a people's tribunal held in 2012. For a decade now, a small community has been working on the Iranian 1980s with a legal perspective inspired by transitional justice (the paradox being that transition is not even remotely at sight, but this is another topic). Especially, a documentary movie called *Those Who Said No*[2] was shot during the 2012 people's tribunal. This film, widely distributed on TV, was more efficient than the legal initiative (the people's tribunal) in showing state violence, which is a vivid proof that human rights and legal arenas should not be considered as hegemonic sites of truth-telling. In our contemporary imaginaries, the only arenas of truth are the courts and UN or international forums. But isn't this delusional? These arenas are the most important ones if you want judgment, sanction, and official establishment of responsibility. But if you want acknowledgment, publicity, recognition, then there are other places to invest, and other episteme to explore. I believe cinema is the most powerful of them. This is why the end of *Hitch* takes place in an alternate reality that exists in cinema alone. The plot doesn't unravel in France, or in Iran, but literarily *in* the movie. So yes, the movie becomes a site of memory.

Indeed, and in this respect, *Hitch* is not only the result of a 'counter-investigation,' as you call it, but perfectly matches this idea of an atopic, ever-moving 'memoryscape.' A central element of the film is this wardrobe your father has been carrying around since in exile, and where some of your mother's personal belongings are kept, as if in a small museum of things. Towards the end of the film, this wardrobe – full and empty at once – even embarks on an imaginary journey. As if mirroring its title, *Hitch* is permanently traversed by

this ambivalence between a gaping lack and the almost obtrusive presence of certain material things, which allow to cling to an otherwise erased memory. I imagine that especially in your own case, these material things operate as transitional objects of sorts, that allow you to find your way back to buried early childhood memories or even to events before your birth. But there's also the risk, as one scene with your father in front of that wardrobe beautifully exemplifies, of fetishizing these objects and thus embalming them into a museal past. Your film thus raises the issue of the 'uses' of memory, against their potential sacralization. It is a literally striking moment, when you – somehow forcing your father's hand – talk him into taking a matchbox out of the memorial wardrobe and try to light it. As your father had warned you: the phosphorous material doesn't catch fire, after so many years. I wanted to ask you to say a bit more about that scene. Had you anticipated that moment? Was there a form of disenchantment or was there also something liberating about it?

I prepared the scene, but I did not expect this outcome. My discussion with my father is obviously staged (we sit on the floor side by side close to the wardrobe – I chose the frame). I am not filming here, as is the case earlier in the movie when I talk with my father in the car, or when I collect my grandmother's memories. Georgi Lazarevski, the chief operator who did the photography, works a lot for feature films: the temporality of the shooting was quite slow and self-conscious, very different from the sometimes-chaotic scenes I shot in Iran. Before the shooting, I talked with my father about what I wanted to do, and we watched together some documentary movies (like for instance movies by Claudio Pazienza and Avi Mograbi) that give a sense of the layers of reality I was interested in. I told you previously about the trace on the matchbox, and how it was a trigger that helped me find a path for the movie's 'quest.' But I knew that I didn't want these questions about traces and presence to be told by a voice-over on the images of the matchbox for instance. I had to find a language. I think that what I did (probably inspired by a touch of clown I see both in Pazienza and Mograbi, who are otherwise very different) – was to throw myself in and stage encounters with my father and my brother, around one specific object: the matchbox, the wine yard. Before I worked on *Hitch*, I edited a short video called *Antigone 88* shot in Iran in 2007. The story of Antigone is not only about her obsession to bury her brother Polynice, it is also about the opposition between one brother (Eteocles) who is glorified as a hero, and the other who is let without burial. This echoes strongly the Iranian context in 1988, when the public space was overwhelmed with monuments and paintings celebrating the hundreds of thousands of martyrs of the war, while at the same time mass graves were dug in secret for political opponents. In *Hitch*, when I talk with my father (and my brother), I am wearing a long red dress and I am confronting them about how to live with this past. I am almost playing the *Antigone*; I am, at least, performing a stereotyped image of what they see in me when they think I am too much attached to digging out the past. We had these debates for many years while I was working on my grandfather's notebook, shooting in Iran, etc. I tried to raise these questions in front of the camera but they wouldn't go there. In a way I understand them, because since I was the director working with a team and with control over the editing, the game was not fair. It would have been an asymmetric re-enactment of the old argument we were having over and over for years: them saying I was trapped in the past, and me saying that it was political research. My dress was a reminder of this argument, and a way to bring back in the movie this tension (this relation to the past seen as dissident).

So I am sitting by my father's side, and I talk to him about the matchbox. But the way he touches the matchbox awakens a familiar feeling that I share with him: these objects have become relics. I know that I am touching a sensible nerve because my father is a firm atheist; so of course he disagrees with me. This irritates me: this is why I challenge him to burn a match. It is not an allegory or something I ever thought about before; it just came during the shooting. I am irritated and I want to push him. So what happened is that as soon as we sat together by the wardrobe and touch the objects, a very old tension came back: the tension linked to the sacralization of memory and its suffocating effect. It was not prepared; I suddenly felt the urge to push my father and provoke him. To be honest, I didn't care very much about cracking the match (lighting it, or spoiling it): I wanted to make my point and to show that these are indeed relics, no matter how atheist their curator is. If my father was right, if there was no sacralization as he pretended, then he could endure the destruction of the matches, and all this would be filmed. It was no longer a discussion between two adults on traces and memory, as I maybe anticipated it, but a childish confrontation. I found myself dragged into this because of the way we touched and looked at the objects. It was bodily. And the climax of the scene is in the body as well. My father firmly denies the sacred nature of these objects, but while he is saying these words, he picks up very carefully every little piece of wood and dust of phosphorous from the cracked match, to put it back in the box. Here again the gesture gives us access to a sea of thoughts and emotions. During the screenings, people laugh at this point. I like this laugher: you laugh because the tension resolves in a comic ending, but at the same time, you feel the love and respect of this man for his 'disappeared wife' and the experience of loss. I don't see which words, and how words could convey what this gesture shows. I like the idea to tell the history of violence in Iran through the picking up of a cracked match. Then you know why you are making a movie.

This scene has changed something in our conversation with my father, since I was able, at the very end of the shooting process, to hold the camera and film

Figure 3.1 The trace of a match that had been scratched. (Source: Screen grab from *Hitch*, 2019).

Figure 3.2 Wardrobe, full and empty at once. (Source: Screen grab from *Hitch*, 2019).

him (it is actually our first scene in the movie, when we talk in the car, but it is the last scene I shot). I could not do this first: I needed the mediation of the chief operator and the staging. In a way, the making of the movie was also the trajectory of our dialogue.

I think you are stressing something very important here: traumas, whether personal or collective, can never be addressed frontally, they need to be circumvented, and lateral entry points need to be found so as to approximate them. I find it telling that in this long and often disheartening process, which took you years and wasn't always easily accepted by all your family members, since it meant reopening many wounds, you took detours through objects (like the matchbox) but sometimes also through stories from completely different contexts (such as the figure of Antigone). Why use a Greek drama to explain an Iranian tragedy? The only explanation I have is that this detour through another cultural context is the only way to approximate what is otherwise too intimately close. But it also made me think that it sometimes happens the other way round. For some strange coincidence, in another important classical Greek tragedy by Aeschylus (*The Persians*) which has the Greek-Persian Wars as its background, the Athenians are forced into taking the point of the view of the Persian women who mourn their own dead just as they do. It is as if the request for burial suddenly opened up something like a universal anthropological fact which goes beyond political disagreements. Hence this paradoxical claim by the Iranian authorities that make use of some alleged rule in the Shari'a about the right to unearth the graves after thirty years and to build a road above the burial sites of those that were seen as political enemies.

For me, Antigone was the first entry point into the political dimension of my personal experience: it was a confirmation that kinship and a stubborn attachment to the right to mourn were forces of resistance and opposition – and had always been such forces. Shi'a tradition offers many references to family loyalty and mourning as political forces (Shi'ism itself can be read as a memory of the vanquished), and the art of the *ta'ziyeh* as a traditional street theater recounting the Shi'a dramas may have offered interesting comparisons and references. The Persian epopee of the *Book of the Kings* (*Shāhnāmeh*) is also very rich with stories of loss and resistance. But to tell the truth, I chose Antigone because my cultural references are foremost Western, since I grew up in France. I understand Antigone better than *ta'ziyeh* and the *Shāhnāmeh*. The film doesn't focus on how it was to grow up in exile, the double belonging, etc., but exile is a component of the story I tell. The fact that the story of the Iranian revolution and its tragic aftermath is told by mixing cultural references and languages bespeaks the political experience and effects of state violence: it was an exclusionary violence, meant for purging the new post-revolutionary nation from all that did not fit the narrative of the Islamic revolution. In reaction, counter-memories like the ones gathered in *Hitch* tell the story from the point of view of the 'remnants' of the nation. This is why my father's testimony on the radio in 1988, right after the massacres, is important when the journalist asks him at the end: 'Do you still want to go back to Iran?' – 'Every morning,

I open my eyes and I dream I am in Iran. I am doing all this for my country,' he answers. The relation between inside and outside is an important element of narration (inside/outside the house in Iran; inside/outside Iran) and is reminded by the well-known expression of 'red line' (*khate qermez*), e.g. the unspoken frontier that has been internalized by all Iranians, about the subjects that shall remain untouched if you want to stay safe. In regards to the memory of state violence in the 1980s, which is an ultimate red line, the frontier that excludes us passes over us. This tension is also present in the movie through the question of language and translation. In an earlier version, my grandfather's testimony was read in French; then I decided to read it in Persian and it required quite a long work of deciphering, and getting into it. As I say in the film, after translating my grandfather's memoirs, in 2010, I had a dream in which I fluently conversed in Persian: the language I spoke exactly when I came in France at six, and that I have lost and regained through the years but not with the fluency that I had at the time (my 'native' language now being French). This fluent knowledge of Persian is somewhere in me, since I can hear it in my dream. Finding fluency again in Persian and connecting to this layer through the reading out loud of my grandfather's testimony for the movie's voice-over was another practice of archaeology.

Let me return for a moment to this transcultural play of references. In the Greek tragedy which inspired you to make your first video in 2007 about these events, *Antigone*, there's not only the tension between generations (Antigone and her uncle Creon) but also within a generation, between Antigone and her sister Ismene who tries convincing her she should abandon her impossible quest and look towards a pacified future. Besides the impactful scene with your father in front of the wardrobe, there's the other scene you just mentioned, that in the vineyards, with your brother. While sharing a common story, your brother has decided to take a different stance about the events. Towards dusk, bathed by a warm light of the ending day, you are sitting on a hill in Southern France, where your brother has settled and where he grows his Shiraz wine, which connects him to your family's city but also to Rumi's love for inebriants which so much frighten the rigorists of all kinds. Yet he inverts George Santayana's famous saying, and claims: those who only remember the past are doomed to repeat it infinitely. His digging the earth is not that of the archaeologist but that of the wine grower. Your choice was another one. In what respect do you remain inexorably bound to this archaeological endeavor, even beyond *Hitch*, also in your current vast project on an *Off-Site* Memory of Violence?

Santayana says, 'Those who forget the past are doomed to repeat it,' which speaks to our generation. In 2009, I remember Iranian friends being literarily stunned by the nature and scope of the repression after the uprisings: people didn't suspect the state of being capable of torturing people in special detention centers, of killing protesters and making them disappear. As a consequence of the silence surrounding what happened in the 1980s, people ignored what the state was capable of. Forgetting distorted the range of possibilities, and in 2009, the civil society suffered greatly of the gap between its representation of the state, and the real practices and culture of terror. This is why a genealogical approach to state violence is necessary and empowering. Much work remains to be done in this field, and I am still digging into this subject, working with counter-archives where documentation and fact-finding is difficult.

In the film, the scene you are referring to is part of an ongoing conversation with my brother. When I was filming the objects in the wardrobe, my brother told me: 'I believe that what you are doing is impossible.' Beyond individual choices of engaging or not with a painful past, he is convinced that the memory work cannot be done by our generation (we don't have the tools, the legitimacy, and we are not in the right position). It is a strategic stand. When I asked him if I could film him and our conversation, he refused. But eventually, during the shooting, he accepted this one shot, one evening when he came back from work. The editing of this scene was difficult because the length of a silence or a choice in the sequencing could break the balance and undermine his position. On the contrary, I wanted his position to be as strong as possible, as is the case in reality, because this pragmatic outlook is the 'as default' position that best fits the intellectual and moral frames of our liberal societies. He is convinced he is right, and I am also almost convinced he is right. However, I am working with what little remains in me that cannot surrender to this reasonable stance. Doing justice to this alternative, strong position, that says 'just break out' was a way to welcome at the heart of the movie something that potentially threatened the whole enterprise and make it fall apart from inside. Some people came to see me after the movie to tell me 'I think your brother is right.' I wanted the film to mirror this tension to the point of rupture. I do not share much personal emotion in the movie, but I wanted this discomfort and trouble to be felt in a very structural way.

What you are stressing here is the crucial importance of editing in documentary practices at large. For some reason, as opposed to fiction cinema, documentary film is still all too often associated with either a documentation of the facts or as a militant form of intervention, but in point of truth, *Hitch*, and the various stages of its post-production process, reveals the role of a critical editing. Your choice of making your brother's position as strong as possible, as opposed to your own, places you on the side of a politics of dialectical montage, in line with Walter Benjamin's conception of historical images. The same goes for the fact that you included a shot where your father explains why anything related to the political opposition still generates such heated reactions today, as the

subsequent Iraq-Iran War and the attitude of some of these oppositional groups throws its shadow back on the first years of the revolution too. For sure, *Hitch* is distrustful of any oversimplification, and permanently faces the spectator with this tension between a personal inquiry and a transindividual quest for historical truth, between an archaeology of past facts and a screening of current political violence. It seems to me that, through this dialectical montage, you want to insist on how certain forces are still at work, as radical thanatopolitics, where the living are governed through the dead, but also elicit possible triggers of resistance, finding hope in the acts of those who have preceded us. How can there be an uprising today, against injustice and oblivion? In a passage from *The Spirit of Utopia*, which for some obscure reason was not included in the English translation, Ernst Bloch writes the following: 'What happened only ever happened half, and the strength that allowed it to happen, which expressed itself insufficiently, continues to work in us and continues to shine on all of this half-one, still under way, on all this futurity in our back.'[3] Do these lines speak to you, as they do to me?

Very much so. The film starts with footage archives from an unfinished documentary movie shot in the summer of 1979 in the streets of Tehran: *Tāzeh Nafas-hā (The Newborns)* by Kianoush Ayari. These images are like a time capsule giving us access to the emotions, hopes, sounds, and colors of the revolution – something ephemeral that was very soon covered up by political anxieties, turmoil, and betrayals. At the time, people had no idea of how things would turn out; the moments they were going through were just promises of a new beginning (the title of Ayari's documentary) and the collective adventure was yet to come. Retrospectively, nothing came but a tremendous disappointment experienced through tragedies of war and political violence. This moment of beginning and hope in the future, experienced at the time as a premise of what was to come, *was* the revolutionary moment itself actually. It is what remains today, through archival fragments. The film starts from these fragments because I wanted to root the story in these political emotions the way a writer soaks her pen in an inkwell.

The film looks at history through family genealogy: what was handed over from my mother to me through the medium of my grandfather writing down the events in a notebook. However, along this fruitful branch of the tree, there is an aborted branch that counts as much for me: it is the story of my aunt Fataneh, who did not have any child. We are not sure actually, since she may have given birth before she was executed. It is not likely, but it is not impossible ... it is still a question mark. The fact is that no one carries on today the memory of this woman's hopes and fights and dreams for the future. The film's 'quest,' if there is any, is about reconnecting with what has been aborted there – crushed by a violence that is busy erasing its own traces. It is not only about finding ways to trace the state crimes. It is also about getting in touch with what has been erased through these killings: ideas, ideals, dreams, hopes, utopias, illusions, promises . . . these young revolutionaries (many, many of whom died childless, and were actually almost kids themselves, in their late teens or early twenties) – these revolutionaries were not as much living in the present as they were oriented towards the future. This future that never existed (the future of the revolution) is their legacy to us: it is not a political program but a way of being in the world with the belief that things can be changed, that it is 'worth the uprising.' Foucault, in response to the critics against his enthusiasm for the Iranian revolution – and mainly his lack of lucidity about the kind of political force and program incarnated by the Iranian clergy – wrote a last article on the subject in early 1980, titled 'Useless to Revolt?' ('Inutile de se soulever?').[4] This question sums up what, in a revolution, goes beyond the weighing of what has been lost against what has been gained. This is where the film starts from, and also where it ends, when the original music in the last scene fades away to give place to an archive sound playing the hymn of the 1979 Revolution. This song is very significant and was used through time as a symbol of hope for change: its cover was the hymn of Mir-Hosein Musavī's presidential campaign in 2009.[5] At the end of the journey, we didn't take any significant step towards justice or truth, but the archaeological work led us to a layer where we can listen to the sound of the revolution and hear the emotions that triggered it.

Chowra Makaremi, thank you for your time and for this inspiring dialogue.

Notes

1. Key milestones are the 1992 Declaration on the Protection of All Persons from Enforced Disappearance, the 1994 Inter-American Convention on Forced Disappearance of Persons, and the 2006 International Convention for the Protection of All Persons from Enforced Disappearance.
2. By Nima Sarvestani (Sweden, Germany, Nimafilm, Ma.ja.de. Filmproduktion, SVT, DR TV and ZDF, 89 min. 2014).
3. Ernst Bloch, *Der Geist der Utopie*, trans. E. A. (Munich-Leipzig: Duncker & Humblot 1918), p. 335.
4. Michel Foucault, 'Inutile de se soulever?', *Le Monde*, 11–12 May 1979, pp. 1–2 ('Useless to Revolt?', in James Fabion (ed.), *Essential Works of Foucault: Power* (London: Penguin 2000), pp. 449–53.)
5. Mir-Hosein Musavī was a reformist candidate raising high hopes for democratic changes during the 2009 presidential elections, which were eventually rigged in favor of the incumbent conservative president Mahmud Ahmadinejād. This sparked nationwide protests that turned into a movement against the Iranian government and supreme leader. Mir-Hosein Musavī served as prime minister during

the Iran-Iraq War and was in charge at the time of the 1988 massacres. After Ali Khāmenehī became supreme leader in 1989, Musavi retired from political life for twenty years, before leading Iran's reformist movement in 2009. He was arrested during the post-election protests and has been under house arrest for more than a decade.

PART II

MATERIAL MATTERS: MEMORY, ACCESSIBILITY, TRANSLATION

The class struggle is a fight for the crude and material things without which no refined and spiritual things could exist.
>Walter Benjamin, 'On the Concept of History' (1940)

4. AN ARCHAEOLOGY OF ACCESS: MATERIALITY, HISTORIOGRAPHY, AND IRANIAN CINEMA

Blake Atwood

In 2016 I visited Tehran's Cinema Museum and wandered through its carefully planned corridors as they opened up to large exhibition halls. I made my way through an assemblage of movie posters, ephemera, and old film equipment before descending a narrow staircase and entering a dark room. A painting by Jafar Tejaratchi – illuminated only by a small lamp above its frame – depicted a rambunctious outdoor movie theater from the early twentieth century. Behind me, several rows of chairs sat facing a small screen. Although a clunky old film projector stood at the back of the room, black-and-white images were projected silently onto the screen from a digital device hanging above the chairs. As I slipped into an empty row, I immediately recognized the scene from *Dukhtar-i Lur*/*The Lor Girl* (1933). Described in promotional materials at the time of its release as 'the first ever Persian-language sound film and musical,' *The Lor Girl* has achieved a prominent place in the history of Iran's national cinema, despite the fact that it was produced entirely in Bombay as a collaboration between an Iranian expat, Abdolhossein Sepanta, and an Indian Parsi filmmaker, Ardeshir Irani. Given its significance to the institutional history of Iranian cinema, it made sense that *The Lor Girl* would be among the few moving images shown in the viewing room of the country's only film museum.

As I watched the familiar scenes, I marveled at the film's crisp sounds and sharp images. The high-quality digital copy that was projected in the Cinema Museum was much clearer than the version I had seen many times before. Beginning in the early 2010s, the study of Iranian cinema benefitted a great deal when anonymous users began uploading old Iranian movies onto video-sharing platforms like YouTube.[1] Yet the sound and image quality of these copies varies a great deal. The digital version of *The Lor Girl* that has circulated online since 2012 tests the patience of even its most devoted fans. It is replete with washed out images, distortions, and warbled sounds. At certain points, it is barely legible. I had always assumed that the YouTube version's poor quality had meant that the celluloid film itself had deteriorated beyond repair. We often uncritically accept the poor image as par for the course when attempting to access old, obscure films. However, my chance encounter with *The Lor Girl* at the Cinema Museum challenged my assumptions about the film and raised questions about its history of access.

Seeing the high-resolution version of *The Lor Girl* at the Cinema Museum was thus cause to revisit the online version that I had grown to love. *The Lor Girl* – as the first Persian-language talkie – opens in anticipation of its sound. What must it have sounded like to hear Persian emanating from the screen for the first time? This is a question that contemporary scholars of Iranian cinema might ask as they settle in to watch the film online, perhaps for the first time. Yet the online version of *The Lor Girl* falters in its first note. As a silent title frame gives way to the film's first sound, a storm of black-and-white pixels invades the screen and the long-awaited first musical note is stretched to the edge of shrill. Moments later, the same thing happens again: visual static and warped sounds overtake the frame, this time interrupting the film for almost two seconds. Such glitches continue to punctuate the digital version of *The Lor Girl*, becoming part of the experience of watching it online.

As I would later realize, embedded in these glitches is a history of access that challenges the traditional historiography of Iranian cinema. Of course, such distortions are not necessarily surprising when it comes to accessing media. Copying, transferring, and converting all leave their marks on a medium's material. These visual and audio signs become hardwired into the medium itself – clues left behind from the processes of distribution and circulation that determine everyday media use.

The blips and blurs that I described above are not a celluloid film's nitrate deterioration nor the low resolution of a digital rip; rather they are the marks left behind when a videocassette's engineering has been exceeded, when constant use and reuse have worn down the delicate magnetic ribbon. Thus, the online version of *The Lor Girl* was created not from a film copy but from a well-worn videocassette. The various material forms that have housed *The Lor Girl* direct us to questions about how people have accessed the film over the last seventy years. Although we have an impressive body of scholarly work that situates *The Lor Girl* in the context of its original production and distribution in the early 1930s, we do not yet have accounts of its long history of access.

AN ARCHAEOLOGY OF ACCESS

Figure 4.1 Audiovisual distortions commence the online version of *The Lor Girl* (1933). Underneath the static, we can see the opening credits.

In this chapter, I ask what it would mean to take these audiovisual distortions seriously. How do we make sense of the effects of a worn-out videocassette, which have now been fossilized in digital form? How might the distortions that have become part of the online version of *The Lor Girl* challenge the traditional story of Iranian cinema? In order to answer these questions, I turn to media archaeology as a critical methodology. As Jussi Parikka explains, 'Media archaeology sees media culture as sedimented and layered, a fold of time and materiality where the past might be suddenly discovered anew.'[2] The online version of *The Lor Girl* – which many scholars have recently found their way to on YouTube and other video-sharing platforms – resulted from different media technologies over time, as the movie was relocated from celluloid film to analog cassette and then to digital file. Its audiovisual distortions are the materialization of the layering of these different media technologies and the practices that have formed around them.

Unpacking these layers allows us to challenge grand narratives. Essential to such grand narratives is the 'from . . . to' motif in many of the histories of cinema, which often favor linear development such as the move from early to narrative cinema or the transformation from silent to sound film. Drawing on media archeological approaches, Thomas Elsaesser has shown the shortcomings of such 'from ... to ...' histories, arguing that in almost every instance they have proven wrong.³ Such histories are, of course, legion in the historiography of Iranian cinema. After all, much of the scholarship is premised on the transformation *from* a pre-revolutionary commercial cinema *to* post-revolutionary 'Islamicate' cinema. As Elsaesser and others argue, attention to the material conditions of media allows entirely new conceptions of historical time, wherein history is not necessarily teleological.

This perspective is especially pressing when it comes to *The Lor Girl*. At the time of its release, the film was advertised in Iranian publications with the alternative title *Iran of Yesterday and Iran of Today*.⁴ Such a title almost demands that the film be considered through the prism of 'from ... to ...' that Elsaesser warns against. And yet the layered and sedimented digital version points us to a very different understanding of *The Lor Girl* – perhaps contrary to the content of the film itself. Indeed, the history made visible in the digital *Lor Girl*'s audiovisual distortions is not linear or teleological but rather convoluted and even unwelcome.

By thinking through the materiality of the digital version of *The Lor Girl*, we might also expand what we understand *counter-memory* to mean. After all, Foucault understood counter-memory as 'a transformation of history into a totally different form of time.'⁵ This definition shares in the critiques of genealogy and teleology that power media archaeology. Of course, the work that the online version of *The Lor Girl* performs is different than the individual memories that Foucault imagined when he wrote of counter-memory. Yet the digital *Lor Girl* is about collective memory. As we will see, the digital version remembers screenings and movie theaters; the underground network forged through the circulation of videocassettes; and the likes, shares, and anonymous uploads of online communities. It recalls its own history of access. Unsanctioned and unofficial, it is an archive unto itself, storing and attesting to an account of Iranian cinema that is radically different than the one we're familiar with. It pushes back against the stories of success that typically adorn the history of Iranian cinema, and instead directs us to the failures of technology, of state policy, and of cinema itself. Imagining these failures runs contrary to the cognitive framework of modernity, in which assessments like improvement, progress, and growth are the only marks of success. Just as an individual memory might challenge the master narrative of modernity, so too can the digital version of a film – simultaneously frozen in multiple points of time – expose the shortcomings of an official history. Perhaps most radically of all, to analyze the online version of *The Lor Girl* in light of counter-memory is also to declare this 1933 film alive and well, part of now and the future.

In what follows, I perform an archaeology of access. I excavate the distortions in the digital version of *The Lor Girl* to try to understand how they ended up there in the first place. I examine what these blips and blurs tell us about the life of the film once it was removed from Iranian movie houses in 1933. I argue that the digital version of *The Lor Girl*, by redirecting our attention to videocassettes and film archives, begins to unsettle the teleological assumptions undergirding the narrative of modernity that anchor so much of the work on Iranian cinema. Such an analysis also demands that we take questions of access, distribution, and circulation seriously in order to challenge our existing canons.[6]

The first *Lor Girl*

As one of the few extant examples of filmmaking from this period, *The Lor Girl* has attracted a great deal of scholarly attention, especially over the last decade. Relatively little filmmaking occurred in Iran until after World War II.[7] Given the small number of films produced in that early period and the even smaller number of films that have been preserved, *The Lor Girl* has become central to many comprehensive accounts of the history of Iranian cinema. Such accounts regale *The Lor Girl* as a film of many firsts – the first sound film, one of the first narrative films, the first co-production, and a prototype for the conventions of later commercial films. Indeed, in many accounts of Iranian cinema, *The Lor Girl* doesn't simply fit into what we know about the larger patterns of Iranian cinema; it is the genesis of that narrative.

'The first ever Persian-language sound film and musical' has offered scholars the perfect symphony of technological, political, and cultural progress. The film's plot celebrates the modernization efforts of Reza Shah Pahlavi, who ruled over Iran between 1925 and 1941. *The Lor Girl* – or *Iran of Yesterday and Iran of Today* – tells the story of Jafar, a Qajar government official, who is sent to Khuzestan in western Iran to settle the tribes in the years following World War I. This is a lawless Iran – the Iran of yesterday referenced in the title. At a roadside inn along the way, he meets Golnar, a woman who is being held captive by a group of bandits there. They fall in love, and after Golnar cleverly outsmarts her captors, they escape to Bombay. In India they lead modern lives among railroads, skyscrapers, and all of the affordances of British imperialism. Adorned in modern European attire, he reads the newspaper while she plays a few notes on the piano. When word arrives that the Qajar monarchy has been overthrown and replaced with Reza Shah's new dynasty, they determine that Iran is now modern, and they happily decide to return. This is the Iran of today in the title.

The film's plot thus lends itself to a reading of nationalistic progress, which has been the predominant lens through which scholars have understood the film. As Golbarg Rekabtalaei has shown, this understanding of *The Lor Girl* can be traced back to its critical reception at the time of its initial release. A growing cohort of professional film critics praised the film for its portrayal of Iran's modernizing efforts and its growing Westernization. One such reviewer described the audience's euphoric reaction when Jafar and Golnar decide to return to Iran at the end of the film: 'patriots ... applauded, cheered, and whistled out of joy.' According to the reviewer, the audience's enthusiastic response shook the movie theater.[8] Such an animated response also alerts us to the ways in which the film – from its very first exhibitions in Iran – became subsumed into a nationalist discourse that denied the film its transnational origins.[9] Despite the fact that the film had been produced by the Imperial Film Company of Bombay in India, for critics and audiences the film became strictly about Iran's national story of modernization.

Given the original reception of the film, it is not surprising that subsequent scholarship on *The Lor Girl* in both English and Persian has emphasized the film as uncritically emblematic of Iranian nationalism and modernity, especially at the time of its release. Hamid Naficy's authoritative four-volume *A Social History of Iranian Cinema* embodies these themes and is representative of the now-enshrined account of Iranian film history as a 'microphysics of both national cinema and modernity.'[10] *The Lor Girl* figures prominently in the first volume, in which Naficy positions the film as part of a transitional cinema that 'helped create a new, modern national identity.'[11] Such an understanding of the film has inspired other scholars, as well. Laudan Nooshin, for example, argues that through its soundtrack *The Lor Girl* advances a vision of Iranian nationalism that is 'modern, Persian-centric, and Western-facing.'[12]

Even as scholars have pushed back against the nationalistic lens that has determined much of *The Lor Girl*'s critical and scholarly reception, they have found the rubric of modernity productive in their evaluation of the film. Laura Fish, for example, has shown that the scholarship on *The Lor Girl* has tended to overlook Parsi Indian contributions to the film's production. Because the film was shot and produced entirely in Bombay, its production depended on relatively few Iranian actors or laborers – a fact that most scholars acknowledge but do not allow to inform their analyses. Fish decenters this perspective and acknowledges the film's site of production by offering an examination of what she calls the 'Bombay interlude,' or the montage of images of the modern Bombay cityscape that appears when Jafar and Golnar arrive to the city. Fish argues that Golnar and Jafar are made modern by their experiences in Bombay and 'can only return to Iran once it has achieved the same level of modernity that they have experienced in India.'[13] In this scheme, the film both valorizes Iran's modernizing efforts under Reza Shah but also provides Parsi Bombay as a model of modernity.

Control over technology is also central to how recent scholarship has triangulated modernity, cinema, and *The Lor Girl*. Indeed, *The Lor Girl* did more than just represent Reza Shah's modernization efforts. As a feature-length sound film, it was also a technological achievement unto itself. As Jalal Omid has suggested, *The Lor Girl* originally included a scene in which Jafar and Gonar tour the Imperial Film Company, thus positioning the production of the film itself as a modern marvel.[14] In particular, given the centrality of sound technology to the experience of watching *The Lor Girl*, scholars have pored over what the film's sounds might have meant to audiences at the time and what they signify to the larger story of Iranian cinema. Naficy, for example, argues that that the institutionalization of sound disciplined audiences by silencing them. This new form of spectatorship was, according to Naficy, 'another step in their becoming modern.'[15] Meanwhile, Claire Cooley has shown that the film sonically produced 'bourgeois gender norms in colonial Bombay and modernizing Iran.'[16] She shows that sound technology actually precluded certain gendered possibilities, insisting on demure, modest womanhood as the only possibility for a modern Golnar. Such an analysis attunes us to the ways in which the sounds of *The Lor Girl* intersected with gendered notions of modernity.

As we can see, *The Lor Girl* has been the subject of a considerable amount of scholarly attention over the last decade. This growing body of scholarship has illuminated the film's investment in paradigms like modernity and nationalism; the exciting possibilities and troubling foreclosures that come with sound technology; and the transnational circuits of production that made the film possible. Despite their variant – and sometimes even divergent – conclusions, these works are joined together in their commitment to understanding how *The Lor Girl* contributed to the development of Iranian cinema. Whether scholars situate *The Lor Girl* as an essential moment in Iranian national cinema or within a global circuit of which Iran was a part, they acknowledge the film as concurrent with the debates about modernity and nation that were taking place at the time of the film's production and exhibition in the 1930s. Indeed, these interpretations also disclose a scholarly disposition to this film in particular and to cinema as whole. All of these accounts attempt to understand the film in light of its context. What can *The Lor Girl* tell us about Iranian (or Indian) modernization and nationalism, and what in turn can the social, political, and technological conditions of the 1930s tell us about *The Lor Girl*?

As Bruno Latour reminds us, however, context is tricky business. 'Context stinks!' he once wrote.[17] Elaborating on his ideas, Rita Felski argues that 'the difficulty of context-talk is not just a bias towards historical origins but also in its ways of conceiving agency and causality.'[18] Although context is at the heart of cultural studies, the push and pull between text and context often diminishes a wider network of agents, relationships, and coordinates through which we might appreciate a film like *The Lor Girl*. The 'text' that interests me – the online version of *The Lor Girl* – is situated in a larger constellation of actors, objects, and connections, of which the 1933 film version is just one part. As we will see, to study such a text requires a very different approach than scholars of *The Lor Girl* have thus far attempted.

The Material Lor Girl

My approach to *The Lor Girl* attends to the long life of the movie rather than just one version of it. I am not particularly interested in what it can tell us about 1930s Iran or about one moment in the development of Iranian cinema. To be sure, these are valuable ways to think about the film – and I have learned a lot from the works I cite above. But as scholars, if we are going to continue writing about *The Lor Girl*, we need a new vocabulary and, indeed, an entirely new way of positioning ourselves vis-à-vis the movie. In what follows, I am more interested in what the movie – as it has occupied a range of material forms since the early 1930s – can tell us about how to study Iranian cinema. Thus, my approach does not *fast-forward* through the distortions in the digital version of *The Lor Girl* but rather *pauses* on these glitches and reflects on what they tell us about Iranian cinema's relationship to materiality, access, and distribution. How do we write these issues into our accounts of Iranian cinema? The online version of *The Lor Girl* seems the perfect object through which to experiment with some of these ideas. As some scholars claim, the 1933 film helped initiate industrialized filmmaking in Iran in the 1930s,[19] and yet the movie has also lived a dynamic life since then.

Before beginning my analysis, I want to press upon two caveats with respect to my approach here. First, I am not proposing a rigorous study of the provenance of *The Lor Girl* film reel since its original exhibition in 1933. In the section that follows, I will probably raise more questions than I answer about how the movie has been converted, distributed, and transmitted over the last seventy years. Despite my best efforts, I know very little about the mechanisms and labor that supported the conversion of *The Lor Girl* from celluloid film to videocassette to digital file. Secondly, I do not subscribe to the purist line of thinking in film studies that claims that scholars must view films in their original format in order to study or write about them.[20] On the contrary, as much as I am trying to shift the conversation by looking at the digital version of *The Lor Girl*, I believe that any viewership – no matter how formal or informal – can yield rigorous analysis of a particular film. In other words, as much as I want to insist on the digital version of *The Lor Girl*, I do not believe it can only be studied as such.

Let us begin not with the start but rather the end – with the digital *Lor Girl*'s last scene. Jafar returns to the couple's palatial home in Bombay to the sounds of Golnar playing the piano. He ascends a large, ornate staircase as cheerful notes fill the air. A thin horizontal line of black-and-white pixels travels the screen. Jafar enters the piano room and commends Golnar on learning to play so well. Small white grain spots occasionally dust the frame. Jafar suggests that Golnar play the song he taught her yesterday. She agrees but only if he'll sing along. As she begins to play, a large white scratch mark hits like lightening over her head.

With his hand casually resting on the piano, Jafar launches into the song, whose lyrics vaunt Iranian land and the spirt of Iranians – the smooth tenor of his voice impossible to ignore. Each refrain is punctuated with 'dowrah-yi Pahlavi' or 'the Pahlavi era,' a reference to Reza Shah Pahlavi's monarchy. As he sings, the sound becomes detached from the image, and his final hand gesture occurs several seconds after we have heard the ultimate 'dowrah-yi Pahlavi.' A black frame transitions to the conversation between Golnar and Jafar as they decide it is finally time to return back to Iran. Throughout the scene, a watermark sits in the bottom-right corner that reads *Fīlmkhānah-yi Millī-yi Īrān* or the National Film Archive of Iran.

The scene that I have just described embodies what we know about *The Lor Girl*. We can only imagine the delight that Iranian audiences felt in 1933 when they heard such a patriotic song emanating from the screen. We can easily see how the song showcased sound film technology at the service of the nation state, even modeling a new modern identity for its viewers. But how do we account for the other details that I have described, which are no less a part of the digital version of *The Lor Girl*? We can see how the musical performance affirms our

Figure 4.2 The final musical scene in the digital version of *The Lor Girl* (1933) carries some of the marks of the movie's various material forms, including a large vertical scratch and a watermark for the National Film Archive of Iran.

traditional accounts of Iranian cinema as the story of Iranian national modernity. But, in that case, what do the VHS tracking, film decay, and sound distortions reveal? I argue that these sights and sounds – embedded, preserved, and fossilized – point us to a material history of *The Lor Girl* that operates at a different pace than the usual tempo of Iranian film history. If traditional accounts of Iranian cinema valorize its successes, its progress, and its victories, then the material history of *The Lor Girl* tracks its failures: the failure of technology; the failure of policy; and the failure of access. In this vision of Iranian cinema, such failures do not exist instead of the successes, but rather alongside and on top of them.

These modes – failing, succeeding, progress, stasis – exist simultaneously in the online version of *The Lor Girl*. To return to the language of media archaeology, such moments are 'layered and sedimented.'[21] Extending this idea, the spots, glitches, and grains that I described above are, in fact, reminders of the movie's material life as they exist in a single frame. Lucas Hilderbrand suggests that every medium 'has a specific aesthetic of failure.'[22] In the digital version of *The Lor Girl*, we see the failures of two different storage technologies: celluloid film and the videocassette.

For celluloid film, technological failure can be found in organic shapes: the soft curve of a scratch, specks of dust, or splotches of decay. A good example of this film damage is the vertical line that appears over Golnar's head as she plays the piano. This mark is likely the result of a scratch on the negative itself. Or, we might return to the grainy spots that pepper the scene: the now fossilized specks of dust that occupied the film negative at a particular moment in time. These marks may be the result of mishandling or poor storage conditions, but they are also simply a matter of time. Celluloid film was not designed to last forever. Pops, washouts, and sparkles have thus become par for the course when accessing old films, and this fact is seared into the online version of *The Lor Girl* on YouTube.

The marks of damaged celluloid film in the digital *Lor Girl* exist simultaneously with another set of visual cues. Videocassette technology has also left behind traces of its mechanical processes, including storage, duplication, and exhibition. These are the geometric shapes in the scene I described above: bars, pixels, lines, and stretches. We might, for example, consider the noise bar that travels the screen as Jafar returns home. Throughout the scene, we also find evidence of dropout, or instances in which absent visual information creates the illusion of white specks – often small tight squares, in contrast to the granular dust on film. When it comes to home video technology, these glitches and distortions are a result of magnetic degeneration, which occurs when the engineering of the videocassette has been exceeded. Indeed, just like the filmic distortions, these video flares are marks of excess. The irony of these video glitches is that videocassettes were intended as a technology of copying that would allow people to record, watch, and re-watch television. And yet every duplication also results in a degree of deterioration. Over time, the degeneration of the videocassette's delicate magnetic ribbon accumulates and manifests in the audiovisual distortions that we see in the last scene of *The Lor Girl*. Not every videocassette will bear the traces of its excesses; only the most worn, the most loved, the most used.

I linger on these audiovisual distortions because they index *The Lor Girl*'s multiple materialities. In other words, these clues remind us that *The Lor Girl* existed on film and on video before its current digital shape. Indeed, these brief interruptions are not interruptions at all; instead, they are testaments to the ways in which people and institutions have preserved, distributed, and accessed the movie over the last seven decades. These efforts, too, are part of the history of *The Lor Girl* as it has come to exist on YouTube and other video-sharing platforms. In light of this, we might ask what kinds of technological and institutional forces have shaped the materiality of *The Lor Girl* at various points in history. What kinds of power have shaped the various marks that adorn the online video?

I argue that if we endeavor to answer such questions about the marks and glitches in the digital *Lor Girl*, we need to look to the 1980s rather than the 1930s. In the 1980s, the materiality of cinema was changing drastically in Iran – as in other places. Specifically, new playback technologies like videocassettes reconfigured people's everyday relationship to cinema by transforming the movies from ephemeral sights and sounds to objects that could be touched, traded, and purchased. Meanwhile, the Islamic Republic's growing institutional and legal frameworks sought to consolidate the new government's political power by establishing control over the distribution, exhibition, and preservation of films.

In the late 1970s and early 1980s, negotiations over Iranian cinema played out in the most material ways. This was a time when movie theaters burned to the ground, film reels were set ablaze, and hard, plastic cassettes circulated underground through a vast informal infrastructure that supplied millions of people with movies on video. While we have many accounts of the 1970s and 1980s as a time of ideological and aesthetic transformation of Iranian cinema, we know far less about the material forces that shaped cinema culture at that time. As we will see, the online version of *The Lor Girl*, perhaps unexpectedly, embodies those forces.

Accessing *The Lor Girl*

To think through *The Lor Girl* in its material forms requires that we first locate it. In the summer of 2016, I toured *Fīlmkhānah-yi Millī-yi Īrān* or the National Film Archive of Iran (NFAI). The impressive facilities featured large storage vaults for film negatives and positives, an auditorium-style viewing room, and sophisticated labs for developing, preserving, and restoring film. The tour included a stop in a carpeted room filled with shelves of videocassettes. Unlike the film reels earlier in the tour, the videocassettes were within reach, and I delighted in browsing them. Most of the cassettes were copies, housed in familiar but generic sleeves that read the likes of Fuji, JVC, and Sony, along with a handwritten label on the side identifying the movie. In this room, I saw a copy of *The Lor Girl*. I ran my index finger over the label as I sounded out the title. Just steps away – a few meters really – another version of the movie existed in the NFAI building. The original 35 mm film of *The Lor Girl* was locked away in a climate-controlled chamber, protected from browsing, viewing, and handling. The national archives thus house at least two version of *The Lor Girl*, each in a unique material form: one constituted of a plastic shell, magnetic ribbon, and metal screws, the other made of flexible nitrocellulose film with sprocket holes for a projector and a quad track with the sounds.

Just as both versions exist in the NFAI holdings, so too do both material forms occupy the digital copy of the movie. As I suggested above, many of the marks that we can see in the online version of the *The Lor Girl*, including scratches and grains of dust, refer us back to the movie's original 35 mm film form. The only known copy of the 35 mm film is held by the NFAI.[23] According to one employee at NFAI, the family of Reza Damavandi deposited the film to the archives in 1989.[24] Damavandi had worked for the Imperial Film Company that produced *The Lor Girl*, and he was also the husband of Ruhangiz Saminezhad, who played the role of Golnar. While usually the NFAI pays for acquisitions like *The Lor Girl*, the Damavandi family chose to donate the film to the archives for free. However, the presence of *The Lor Girl* on 35 mm at NFAI does not necessarily mean that it is readily accessible. On the contrary, given the significance and rarity of this particular film, archive officials do not allow anyone to view or handle the original film.

The inaccessibility of *The Lor Girl* film at NFAI echoes a familiar tension within the discourse on audiovisual archives. As Rick Prelinger argues, traditional film archives are premised on 'two missions, preservation and access.' However, of these two missions, archivists have 'tended to privilege preservation.'[25] Prelinger suggests a variety of material, financial, and legal reasons that archivists prioritize preservation over access.[26] According to NFAI officials, *The Lor Girl* remains inaccessible for material reasons: loading the original 35 mm film into a projector is simply too demanding on this old, delicate, and valuable holding. As a result, at the time of the film's acquisition and per NFAI procedure, archivists derived two positive duplicates and one negative. NFAI also converted the film to video, so that scholars could watch and study it as part of Iranian national cinema. At the time, the telecine process was housed off site at the Farabi Cinema Foundation (*Bunyād-i Sinīmā-yi Fārābī*). The conversion of *The Lor Girl* to video thus took place in its facilities in 1989.[27]

Ultimately, the inaccessibility of *The Lor Girl* on film in NFAI exists alongside the inaccessibility of many other Iranian films. In fact, it demonstrates that not all inacessibilities are created equal. As Caroline Frick reminds us, 'The preservation of so-called national or state heritage is not, and never has been, a neutral concept, although it is presented as such by politicians, the press, intellectuals, and archivists.'[28] To return to *The Lor Girl*, its safe preservation on 35 mm film matters, even if it is not easily accessible to the public. Around the same time that NFAI acquired *The Lor Girl* – one of its most valuable holdings – the newly established Ministry of Culture and Islamic Guidance (MCIG) set thousands of Iranian films reels on fire, including many originals. Proximity is important here. The NFAI is housed in the same building in Tehran as the MCIG. So while *The Lor Girl* was swiftly and efficiently ushered into protective custody, thousands of other films burned in the courtyard of the same building. Which films to burn, and which to save?

The burning of thousands of Pahlavi-era Iranian films in 1985, known in Persian as *fīlmsūzān*, was a remarkable event, even if it has not been well documented in popular and scholarly sources. The decision to destroy film reels grew out of the MCIG's increasingly rigid oversight over cinema in the mid-1980s. In February 1985, at the order of Fakhreddin Anvar, the newly appointed Deputy for Cinematic Affairs within the MCIG, agents raided dozens of film production and distribution companies with the mission of collecting unpermitted films. According to reports, 140 truckloads of 35 mm film reels were brought to the courtyards of the MCIG and other governmental buildings. After a week-long inspection of the films, arrests were made, but the unpermitted reels themselves were left to the elements. Sun and moisture damaged many of them beyond repair. Eventually, the films were set on fire and destroyed forever. It is impossible to know exactly how many films were destroyed in these burnings. Experts estimate between 3,000–5,000 reels.[29] How many of those were original film negatives remains unclear. But NFAI officials have claimed that a significant number of films from the Pahlavi era have been lost forever.[30]

How might we understand the preservation of *The Lor Girl* – also a Pahlavi-era film – in the context of these acts of destruction? As Frick argues, preservation 'should be viewed as discourse or as socially structured practice' rather than the 'natural, logical' order of things.[31] With this in mind, the decision to preserve *The Lor Girl* film was the result of multiple political and cultural forces rather than simply the obvious choice. To a certain extent, the film's preservation operates in the same nationalist framework we already know the film to exist in. After all, an archive that institutionalizes Iranian national cinema would prioritize *The Lor Girl*, because – as we saw above – it so easily speaks to the development of Iranian cinema and its entanglements with nationalism and modernity. And yet to fully appreciate the meaning of such an act of preservation, we need also to consider what has been excluded from the archive – or destroyed before it could get there. Indeed, the preservation of *The Lor Girl* is as much about what has been saved as what has been destroyed. Its preservation matters because, as we saw, not all films have been preserved equally and in fact some have been actively destroyed.

All of these material forces – from the preservation of the original film to the destruction of thousands of other reels – are embodied in the digital version of *The Lor Girl*. The scratches, dust, and decay that have become emblazoned in the online version of *The Lor Girl* clearly direct us to a vault in the National Film Archive of Iran. But that vault is not simply a neutral repository for cultural artifacts. Rather it represents a process of inclusion and exclusion, of preservation and destruction. Indeed, *The Lor Girl*'s deposit at the national archives coincided with the violent obliteration of many other Iranian films at the hands of the state. Thus, the film marks on the digital video lead us not only to the moment of *The Lor Girl*'s preservation in the 1980s but also to the larger processes that were determining what constitutes national heritage worth saving at the time, when the Islamic Republic was radically reimagining what cinema should be. Thus, the presence of the film textures in the digital *Lor Girl* serves as an invitation to reflect on what is absent from the archive and the political forces that created those absences – especially the decision to burn many Iranian film reels in the 1980s. Meanwhile, a second layer of marks in the digital *Lor Girl* leads us to a simultaneous process of underground copying and distributing rare Iranian films on videocassette by non-state actors.

Throughout the YouTube version of *The Lor Girl*, static, noise bars, and jitters draw our attention to the videocassette from which the digital file was created. Sometimes these marks sit uncomfortably on the frame, a nuisance or annoyance that we try to overlook in order to follow the love story between Jafar and Golnar. At other times, though, the distortions of analog video technology overpower the scene, impossible to ignore, disrupting the film's linearity. For example, in a crucial scene early in the movie, Golnar performs a love song as she discovers that Jafar has been ambushed by Qoli Khan, the tribal leader who is also holding her captive. In the build up to that scene, small pixels begin appearing on the image; the density of these white spots increases with every second to the point of filling the screen. The image begins to skew before losing its vertical stability and traveling up the screen. Finally, the sounds of voices warp into long, stretched notes while thick horizontal blocks of white pixels completely obscure our view. The image tries to stabilize: the black-and-white figures return to the screen for just a moment before silence and white noise win out once again. Then, the movie swiftly resumes clearer than ever with Golnar sitting in a courtyard preparing to sing.

Of course, the videocassette distortions on the digital version of *The Lor Girl* come as no surprise. We know that NFAI employees converted the 35 mm film to videocassette in the 1980s in order to give scholars access to the film.

The *Fīlmkhānah-yi Millī-yi Īrān* (NFAI) watermark in the bottom-right corner of the movie assures us that the video version was produced by the national archives. And yet, as I will show, the video marks in the digital *Lor Girl* also direct us to a history of access outside of the NFAI and specifically to an underground system of distribution that ran contrary to the very official channels of access represented by the NFAI and its neighbor the MCIG. The kind of distortions that I just described exceed the normal wear and tear of a videocassette. In other words, the videocassette marks in the online version of *The Lor Girl* do not simply memorialize an institutional copy of a movie that is occasionally accessed by scholars; instead, they point to a videocassette that has been taped over, watched and re-watched, duplicated, passed around, shared, and traded.

In order to account for such a videocassette, we need to situate the video copy of *The Lor Girl* in a larger set of policies determining access to cinema at the time. In the 1980s, in addition to burning Iranian film reels, the MCIG issued another radical policy that shaped how people distributed and accessed movies: a wholescale ban on home video technology. Between 1983 and 1994, the personal use of videocassettes, video players, and camcorders was forbidden in Iran. As I have argued elsewhere, the video ban did very little to curtail the proliferation of videocassettes in the country. Instead, it drove them underground, where a vast, informal network or video distribution developed, providing millions of Iranians with access to movies that were unsanctioned by the state. This underground network, which continued the momentum of the legal distribution of videocassettes before the ban, supplied a wide range of international cinema, including Hollywood blockbusters, European arthouse films, Indian musicals, and Iranian movies from before the revolution. At the heart of this system was the video dealer, who secretly delivered videocassettes to people's homes, usually in a large nondescript briefcase.[32] At first glance the video of *The Lor Girl* in the NFAI would appear to have little to do with this underground world of videocassettes. After all, institutions like the NFAI were exempt from the video ban, which is how archivists were able to create a copy of *The Lor Girl* in the first place. And yet the extreme video distortions tell us that the story of *The Lor Girl* videocassette does not end in the archives.

The significant video decay in the online version of *The Lor Girl* suggests that the movie also circulated through the underground video infrastructure that I described above. The exact way in which *The Lor Girl* entered this informal economy is less clear, but the frequency and degree of video distortions signal one of the hallmark features of underground video distribution in Iran. The videocassettes that moved through this informal circuit bore witness to their own underground distribution and access through the marks of their deterioration. Hilderbrand calls this phenomenon 'bootleg's aesthetic of access.'[33]

Because the circulation of movies on video was illegal, it formed around certain practices that were particularly demanding on the videocassette's engineering. Unable to import new video equipment, the informal laborers involved in the underground circulation of videocassettes had a limited stock of supplies with which to operate. As a result, they capitalized on the videocassette's most inherent quality: the ability to copy, duplicate, and re-copy. In other words, movies on video were taped over one another on the same videocassette again and again. This was largely a rental market, so having the ability to introduce new content for consumers was prioritized. In this way, the same videocassette could be profited off many times over. However, the continual process of duplication that sustained the underground network also wore down the delicate technical mechanisms in the country's underground videocassettes. With every duplication or copy-over, the audiovisual quality degenerated. These deteriorations were preserved, reproduced, and magnified each time. An accumulation of video use, access, and duplication has been memorialized in the digital version of *The Lor Girl* through its glitches.

Thus, the audiovisual distortions in the digital version of *The Lor Girl* remind us that the movie not only existed on videocassette but also circulated through the underground video network. Over the last several years, I have been conducting oral history interviews in order to learn more about the mechanisms that fueled this informal system. Surprisingly, *The Lor Girl* came up often in my interviews. Art school students remembered working with specialized video dealers to secure a copy, or film buffs recalled their delight at discovering the first Persian-language talkie. When I set out to learn more about a black market for videocassettes in Iran in the 1980s and 1990s, I never expected that a film from 1933 would feature so prominently in my interviews. To me, the film had always seemed innocuous – even if it was sometimes problematic in representations. I discovered, however, that while the film itself did little to challenge the Islamic Republic's new system of control at the time, its *access* did.

During our discussions, my interlocutors occasionally mentioned a film critic who was renowned for his large collection of movies on video. Unlike most people who rented videos or purchased a select few, this particular cinephile had amassed a huge collection of videocassettes – everything from the mainstream to the obscure, the popular to the niche. The crown jewel of his collection was a rare copy of *The Lor Girl*. He was arrested in 2001 and charged with distributing unpermitted videocassettes – a charge that he denies to this day. His video collection was confiscated, and he was held in jail for many months. Eventually, he was released on bail and then fled the country. Such a story shows how the underground video infrastructure was anything but neutral. Instead, it was a highly politicized system that was always already in opposition to the state and its systems of control. As we can see, the stakes of access outside of an institutional framework like the NFAI were quite high. The friction between everyday people's desire for access to cinema and the state's attempts to control that access has been made material in the video decay that is now visible in the digital *Lor Girl*. Those marks attest to a time when ordinary users took advantage of a consumer technology in order to access media outside of state control. Exaggerated pixels, distorted sounds, and obtrusive noise bars signal technical failures within the videocassette but also the political and cultural failures of media in the Islamic Republic.

Canons, Cults, and Conclusions

By excavating video decay, nitrate degradation, pixels, scratches, and dust now fossilized in digital form, I have performed an archaeology of access on the online version of *The Lor Girl*. Such an archaeology of access yields a material history in which media are not simply modes of transmission but also physical objects that must be handled, preserved, and destroyed. This work is important because the digital file – now available to stream and download – has flattened the vertical, material layers of history into an immaterial format. Performing an archaeology of access thus involves freeing those layers. As Parikka writes, media archaeology proposes that 'you start in the middle – from the entanglement of past and present, and accept the complexity this decision brings with it to any analysis of modern media culture.'[34] The various blips and blurs in the digital *Lor Girl* are a place where past technologies such as film and videocassette meet the technological present through a digital file. Part of this encounter is preserved through the failings of technology itself, through audiovisual distortions – deterioration and decay – that remind us that media can't always keep up with the demands and desires of their users. However, that is only part of the story. At the same time that these marks preserve a material history of *The Lor Girl*, the mechanisms of digital compression also obscure the technologies, policies, and institutions that have determined access to the movie since 1933. Because of this flattening or compression, it is tempting to view the digital *Lor Girl* as an unmediated representation of the original film and the period in which it was produced. But what new things do we learn if we acknowledge the digital file as an accumulation of attempts to access the film rather than simply viewing it as the film itself?

Attention to the glitches in the digital version of *The Lor Girl* has brought us to some unexpected places, including to the courtyard of the MCIG where thousands of Iranian film reels were burned and to an underground world where videocassettes were secretly passed and traded off book and out of sight. The material history of *The Lor Girl* that emerges from the audiovisual distortions embedded in the digital file tells us very little about the original film itself. Instead, it teaches us about the institutions, technologies, and processes that have structured access to Iranian cinema, especially in the 1980s and 1990s. Such a history takes failure as its starting point by acknowledging the scratches, decay, and distortions that mark nearly every second of the digital file. According to Jennifer Gabrys, technological failures are 'fossils of forgotten dreams' and 'the residue of collapsed utopias.'[35] She argues that it is only by acknowledging such failures we might 'move beyond those more "totalizing" aspects of technology, such as progress, teleological reasoning, or the heroism of invention.'[36] I propose that archaeologies of access might mobilize new temporalities for the study of Iranian cinema. The material history of *The Lor Girl* that I sketched out in this chapter is one small case study, but it directs us to a much bigger question. What time continuums outside of modernity, progress, and success might be available to us as scholars of Iranian cinema?

In the same vein, keeping track of the question of access within this material history has serious implications for the scholarship we produce. As we saw at the beginning of this chapter, the last decade has witnessed an explosion of research on *The Lor Girl*. In fact, as Babak Tabarraee claims, '*The Lor Girl*'s continuous commemoration by the scholars of Iranian cinema outside Iran also makes it an object of transnational academic cult fandom.'[37] Why do we have so many studies of *The Lor Girl* when so many other Iranian films have gone unexamined? The academic fandom that Tabarraee describes is no doubt tied to the sudden accessibility of the movie on YouTube and other video-sharing sites. As we saw, this open accessibility is in contrast to the relative inaccessibility to the film in the National Film Archive of Iran. At the same time, I believe that the issue of access is Iranian film studies' dirty little secret. The kinds of histories we have of Iranian cinema are very much structured by the access that scholars have had to specific films at certain times. This is especially true to those of us who live and write outside of Iran. Yet very rarely do we acknowledge how we happened upon a particular film, and even more rarely do we reflect on the powers, institutions, and practices that have made that access possible.[38] In this chapter, lingering on the various marks on the digital *Lor Girl* – rather than looking over them – has also served as a call to think more critically about how access to certain films has conditioned the kinds of canons that exist in the history of Iranian cinema.

Notes

1. For more on the circulation of Iranian cinema on YouTube, see Laura Fish, 'Remixing Vulgarity: Reinterpreting the Legacy of Popular Iranian Cinema,' *The Velvet Light Trap*, Vol. 85 (Spring 2020), pp. 53–64 and *Arisen from the Grave: Collecting and Distributing Mid-Century Iranian Popular Cinema*, PhD dissertation (University of Texas at Austin 2019).
2. Jussi Parikka, *What is Media Archeology?* (Cambridge: Polity, 2012), p. 2.
3. Thomas Elsaesser, 'The New Film History as Media Archeology,' *Cinémas*, Vol. 14, Nos. 2–3 (Spring 2004), pp. 75–117.

4. Golbarg Rekabtalaei, *Iranian Cosmopolitanism: A Cinematic History* (Cambridge: Cambridge University Press 2019), p. 104.
5. Michel Foucault, *Language, Counter-memory, Practice: Selected Essays and Interviews*, trans. Donald F. Bouchard and Sherry Simon (Ithaca, NY: Cornell University Press 1977), p. 160.
6. My ideas in this chapter have been shaped by other efforts to understand the ways in which distribution and access have shaped mid-century Iranian cinema, especially work by Kaveh Askari. For more, see Kaveh Askari, 'An Afterlife for Junk Prints: Serials and Other "Classics" in Late-1920s Tehran,' in *Silent Cinema and the Politics of Space*, eds. Jennifer M. Bean, Anupama Kapse, and Laura Horak (Bloomington: Indiana University Press 2014), pp. 99–120, and Kaveh Askari, 'Eastern Boys and Failed Heroes: Iranian Cinema in the World's Orbit,' in *Cinema Journal*, Vol. 57, No. 3 (Spring 2018), pp. 29–53.
7. Musa Khamushi, 'Causes of the Production Discontinuance of Iranian Films during 1937–1948,' in *Quarterly Review of Film and Video*, Vol. 37, No. 2 (2020), pp. 167–79.
8. Rekabtalaei, *Iranian Cosmopolitanism*, p. 108.
9. Ibid., p. 109–10.
10. Hamid Naficy, *A Social History of Iranian Cinema, Vol. 1: The Artisnal Era, 1897–1941* (Durham, NC: Duke University Press 2011), p. 2.
11. Ibid., p. 196.
12. Laudan Nooshin, 'Windows onto Other Worlds: Music and the Negotiation of Otherness in Iranian Cinema,' in *Music and the Moving Image*, Vol. 12, No. 3 (Fall 2019), p. 34.
13. Laura Fish, 'The Bombay Interlude: Parsi Transnational Aspirations in the First Persian Sound Film,' in *Transnational Cinemas*, Vol. 9, No. 2 (2018), p. 209.
14. Jamal Omid, *Tārīkh-i sīnamā-yi Īrān, 1279–1375* [The History of Iranian Cinema, 1900–1995] (Tehran: Entesharāt-e Rowzāneh 1995), p. 66.
15. Naficy, *A Social History of Iranian Cinema*, Vol. 1, p. 230.
16. Claire Cooley, 'The "Problem of Respectable Ladies Joining Films": Industrial Traffic, Female Stardom and the First Talkies in Bombay and Tehran,' in *Industrial Networks and Cinemas of India: Shooting Stars, Shifting Geographies and Multiplying Media*, eds. Monika Mehta and Madhuja Mukherjee (London: Routledge, 2020), pp. 35–47.
17. Bruno Latour, *Reassembling the Social: An Introduction to Actor-Network-Theory* (Oxford: Oxford University Press 2005), p. 148.
18. Rita Felski, *The Limits of Critique* (Chicago: University of Chicago Press 2015), p. 162.
19. Naficy, *A Social History of Iranian Cinema*, Vol. 1, pp. 197–275. See also Pedram Partovi, *Popular Iranian Cinema before the Revolution* (New York: Routledge 2017), p. 36. Partovi argues that sound films like *The Lor Girl* helped transform cinema in Iran from 'a high culture event or mere curiosity' into a dynamic part of everyday life. He also credits *The Lor Girl* with helping to initiate the 'first formal regime of governmental regulation for cinema operations and film screenings . . . in January 1936.'
20. Caetlin Benson-Allott has highlighted the irony of this kind of insistance, nothing that 'only "film studies" continues to insist on the primacy of the cinematic experiences,

and we do so in spite of our own video-enabled research and pedagogy.' In particular, she references a series of debates that have taken place within the Society for Cinema and Media Studies about the role of video in film studies classrooms. An underlying assumption in these debates is film scholars and students should analyze a particular movie through its original medium. According to this logic, a film must be seen on film. For more, see Caetlin Benson-Allott, *Killer Tapes and Shattered Screens: Video Spectatorship from VHS to File Sharing* (Berkeley: University of California Press 2013), p. 7, and 'Statement on the Use of Video in Classroom,' in *Cinema Journal*, Vol. 30, No. 4 (Summer 1991), pp. 3–6.
21. Parikka, *What is Media Archeology?*, p. 2.
22. Lucas Hilderbrand, *Inherent Vice: Bootleg Histories of Videotape and Copyright* (Durham, NC: Duke University Press 2009), p. 13.
23. Abbas Baharloo, 'Dukhtar-i Lur' [The Lor Girl], in *Dānishnāmah Īrānzamīn* [Encyclopedia of Greater Iran], http://portal.nlai.ir/EI/Wiki%20Pages/%D8%AF%D8%AE%D8%AA%D8%B1%20%D9%84%D8%B1.aspx (accessed 15 October 2020).
24. Interview with NFAI official, 10 June 2020.
25. Rick Prelinger, 'Archives and Access in the 21st Century,' in *Cinema Journal*, Vol. 46, No. 3 (Spring 2007), pp. 114–18, p. 114.
26. Prelinger is particularly interested in the legal ramifications of open access to audiovisual archives. Often, archive holdings are protected by copyright. As he writes, 'Many moving image archives held materials covertly, without explicit authorization, again making access to materials risky.' For more, see Prelinger, 'Archives and Access in the 21st Century,' p. 114.
27. Interview with NFAI official, 16 June 2020.
28. Caroline Frick, *Saving Cinema: The Politics of Preservation* (New York: Oxford University Press 2010), p. 19.
29. Samaneh Farahani, 'Nigātīv-hā'i kih sukhtand: nigāhī bih ijrā-yi ṭarḥ-i jamʿāvarī-yi fīlm-hā-yi khārijī' [The Negatives that Were Burned: A Look at the Implementation of the Plan to Collect Foreign Films], *Shahr-i Kitāb* 6 (January 2018), pp. 70–2.
30. Hamid Naficy, *A Social History of Iranian Cinema, Vol. 3: The Islamicate Period, 1978–1984* (Durham: Duke University Press 2012), p. 82.
31. Frick, *Saving Cinema*, p. 13.
32. Blake Atwood, 'The Little Devil Comes Home: Video, the State, and Amateur Cinema,' in *Film History*, Vol. 30, No. 1 (Spring 2018), pp. 138–67.
33. Hilderbrand, *Inherent Vice*, p. 6.
34. Parikka, *What is Media Archeology?*, p. 5.
35. Jennifer Gabrys, *Digital Rubbish: A Natural History of Electronics* (Ann Arbor: University of Michigan Press 2011), p. 106.
36. Ibid.
37. Babak Tabarraee, 'Iranian Cult Cinema,' in *The Routledge Companion to Cult Cinema*, eds. Ernest Mathijs and Jamie Sexton (London: Routledge 2019), p. 99.
38. Some notable exceptions are Azadeh Farahmand, 'Disentangling the International Film Festival Circuit: Genre and Iranian Cinema,' in *Global Art Cinema: New Theories and Histories*, eds. Rosalind Galt and Karl Schoonover (New York: Oxford University Press 2010), pp. 413–42, and Fish, *Arisen from the Grave*.

References

Askari, Kaveh, 'An Afterlife for Junk Prints: Serials and Other "Classics" in Late-1920s Tehran,' in Jennifer M. Bean, Anupama Kapse, and Laura Horak (eds.), *Silent Cinema and the Politics of Space* (Bloomington: Indiana University Press 2014), pp. 99–120.

Askari, Kaveh, 'Eastern Boys and Failed Heroes: Iranian Cinema in the World's Orbit,' in *Cinema Journal*, Vol. 57, No. 3 (Spring 2018), pp. 29–53.

Atwood, Blake, 'The Little Devil Comes Home: Video, the State, and Amateur Cinema,' in *Film History*, Vol. 30, No. 1 (Spring 2018), pp. 138–67.

Baharloo, Abbas, 'Dukhtar-i Lur' [The Lor Girl], in *Dānishnāmah Īrānzamīn* [Encyclopedia of Greater Iran], http://portal.nlai.ir/EI/Wiki%20Pages/%D8%AF%D8%AE%D8%AA%D8%B1%20%D9%84%D8%B1.aspx (accessed 15 October 2020).

Benson-Allott, Caetlin, *Killer Tapes and Shattered Screens: Video Spectatorship from VHS to File Sharing* (Berkeley: University of California Press 2013).

Benson-Allott, Caetlin, 'Statement on the Use of Video in Classroom,' in *Cinema Journal*, Vol. 30, No. 4 (Summer 1991), pp. 3–6.

Cooley, Claire, 'The "Problem of Respectable Ladies Joining Films": Industrial Traffic, Female Stardom and the First Talkies in Bombay and Tehran,' in Monika Mehta and Madhuja Mukherjee (eds.), *Industrial Networks and Cinemas of India: Shooting Stars, Shifting Geographies and Multiplying Media* (London: Routledge 2020), pp. 35–47.

Elsaesser, Thomas, 'The New Film History as Media Archeology,' in *Cinémas*, Vol. 14, Nos. 2–3 (Spring 2004), pp. 75–117.

Farahani, Samaneh, 'Nigātīv-hā'i kih sukhtand: nigāhī bih ijrā-yi tarḥ-i jam'āvarī-yi fīlm-hā-yi khārijī' [The Negatives that Were Burned: A Look at the Implementation of the Plan to Collect Foreign Films], in *Shahr-i Kitāb*, Vol. 6 (January 2018), pp. 70–2.

Farahmand, Azadeh, 'Disentangling the International Film Festival Circuit: Genre and Iranian Cinema,' in Rosalind Galt and Karl Schoonover (eds.), *Global Art Cinema: New Theories and Histories* (New York: Oxford University Press 2010), pp. 413–42.

Felski, Rita, *The Limits of Critique* (Chicago: University of Chicago Press 2015).

Fish, Laura, *Arisen from the Grave: Collecting and Distributing Mid-Century Iranian Popular Cinema*, PhD dissertation (University of Texas at Austin 2019).

Fish, Laura, 'The Bombay Interlude: Parsi Transnational Aspirations in the First Persian Sound Film,' in *Transnational Cinemas*, Vol. 9, No. 2 (2018).

Fish, Laura, 'Remixing Vulgarity: Reinterpreting the Legacy of Popular Iranian Cinema,' in *The Velvet Light Trap*, Vol. 85 (Spring 2020), pp. 53–64.

Foucault, Michel, *Language, Counter-memory, Practice: Selected Essays and Interviews*, trans. Donald F. Bouchard and Sherry Simon (Ithaca, NY: Cornell University Press 1977).

Frick, Caroline, *Saving Cinema: The Politics of Preservation* (New York: Oxford University Press 2010).

Gabrys, Jennifer, *Digital Rubbish: A Natural History of Electronics* (Ann Arbor: University of Michigan Press 2011).

Hilderbrand, Lucas, *Inherent Vice: Bootleg Histories of Videotape and Copyright* (Durham, NC: Duke University Press 2009).

Khamushi, Musa, 'Causes of the Production Discontinuance of Iranian Films during 1937–1948,' in *Quarterly Review of Film and Video*, Vol. 37, No. 2 (2020), pp. 167–79.

Latour, Bruno, *Reassembling the Social: An Introduction to Actor-Network-Theory* (Oxford: Oxford University Press 2005).

Naficy, Hamid, *A Social History of Iranian Cinema, Vol. 1: The Artisnal Era, 1897–1941* (Durham, NC: Duke University Press 2011).

Naficy, Hamid, *A Social History of Iranian Cinema, Vol. 3: The Islamicate Period, 1978–1984* (Durham, NC: Duke University Press 2012).

Nooshin, Laudan, 'Windows onto Other Worlds: Music and the Negotiation of Otherness in Iranian Cinema,' in *Music and the Moving Image*, Vol. 12, No. 3 (Fall 2019).

Omid, Jamal, *Tārīkh-i sīnamā-yi Īrān, 1279–1375* [The History of Iranian Cinema, 1900–1995] (Tehran: Enteshārāt-e Rowzāneh 1995).

Parikka, Jussi, *What is Media Archeology?* (Cambridge: Polity 2012).

Partovi, Pedram, *Popular Iranian Cinema before the Revolution* (New York: Routledge 2017).

Prelinger, Rick, 'Archives and Access in the 21st Century,' in *Cinema Journal*, Vol. 46, No. 3 (Spring 2007), pp. 114–18.

Rekabtalaei, Golbarg, *Iranian Cosmopolitanism: A Cinematic History* (Cambridge: Cambridge University Press, 2019).

Tabarraee, Babak, 'Iranian Cult Cinema,' in Ernest Mathijs and Jamie Sexton (eds.), *The Routledge Companion to Cult Cinema* (London: Routledge 2019), pp. 98–104.

5. BLACK SEALS: MISSIVE FROM IRAN'S NATIONAL MUSIC

Negar Mottahedeh

> The cathedral leaves its locale to be received in the studio of a lover of art; the choral production, performed in an auditorium or in the open air, resounds in the drawing room.
>
> Walter Benjamin, *The Work of Art in the Age of Mechanical Reproduction* (1936)

> Ultimately the phonograph records are not artworks but the black seals on the missives that are rushing towards us from all sides in the traffic with technology; missives whose formulations capture the sounds of creation, the first and the last sounds, judgment upon life and message about that which may come thereafter.
>
> Theodor W. Adorno, *The Form of the Phonograph Record* (1934)

This piece briefly traces the introduction of visual and aural representational technologies to Iran. It places the genealogy of these technologies within a history of exchange between the East and the West. Focusing on *Love Stricken/ Delshodegān* (1992) a highly popular Iranian post-revolution fiction film by director Ali Hatami, this piece maintains that the historical exchange nests in the practices of inscriptive technologies, and as such continues to affect their modes of enunciation over time, charging the language of representation with ambiguity. It thus attempts to chart the ambiguities that surface in close readings of the film's thematic contents and the organization of the film's discourse.

Ali Hatami was one of Iran's most prolific contemporary filmmakers until his untimely death at the age of fifty-two in 1996. Lauded as the master poet of Iranian cinema, the overwhelming popularity of his work for the screen in Iran has been noted for its heavy emphasis on dialogue and for its rich poetic language and composition. Although involved in the film industry before the Iranian Revolution, Hatami's work after the revolution is known for introducing new innovations in what he has referred to as, 'the historical genre.' In 1982 Hatami made *Hāji Wāshington*, a film about the tribulations of the Persian ambassador to the United States during the reign of the monarch Nasir al-Din Shah Qajar (r. 1848–96). Two years later, in 1984, Hatami made *Kamāl al-Mulk*, a fictional film about the famous nineteenth-century Iranian painter in the court of Nasir al-Din Shah. Made in 1990, *Mādar/Mother*, is one of Hatami's best-known films in the West. It excavates the buried histories of forced Westernization under Reza Shah Pahlavi (r. 1925–41). Hatami's *Love Stricken* (sometimes rendered in English also as *The Enamored*, or *Haunted by Love*), produced two years after *Mādar*, follows a group of Iranian musicians who travel to Europe to record traditional music on the early gramophone. The film is set during the rule of Ahmad Shah Qajar (r. 1909–25). According to Hatami, although the film is about the processes involved in the recording of music, 'the specific historical figures' associated with the recording of traditional music are unimportant to the film itself. Hatami's aim in *Love Stricken* was to create characters that had no other identity except one that is associated with music. More than a documentary about the nation's past, the film is a fictionalized reflection on the inscription and standardization of traditional music. As such, the film deals with the *longue durée* of contingencies that have surrounded and continue to inform the historical inscription of 'the national' in representational technologies. The nation's past and present are coeval in *Love Stricken* and, as such, interact in representational form. This insight is borne out in Hatami's discussion of the choices he made in directing the film: 'I thought it would be interesting to show that early sound recording devices are curiosities not only for the contemporary audience of the film, but for my characters as well.'[1] Fictional characters on the screen and audience members present before the screen are seen as inhabiting synchronous positions vis-à-vis mediating technologies – technologies that simultaneously plot the course of the narrative on screen and, too, constitute and represent the nation's identity, past, and present.

This temporal confluence is used as a means to resist and upend the determining marks of standardization, which, put more forthrightly, is the stamp of the imperial domination of Hollywood globally. The 'all-time' of musical history in *Love Stricken* is in this way brought into a messianic and revolutionary confrontation with the dominant force that standardizes vision and hearing. This intervention in cultural practices identifies precisely the site of struggle for Hatami, a struggle that he also sees as any national cinema's struggle against the homogenization of the medium of film itself. In order to confront the domination of Hollywood, *Love Stricken* embraces the 'messianic all-time' of music, its recording, representation, and reception. Grounded in this redemptive temporal confluence, the film sees itself as confronting the imperial effects of cinematic standardization.

In my reading, Hatami's emphasis on the processes of production underscores the significance of cinema's own productive technologies and the most obvious technological fork in film, namely that which separates the visual from the aural. Hatami's focus on the international history of cinema and on the processes of national production, by contrast, underscores the importance of that history to his project, emphasizing the international alongside the uniquely – and he insists, national – engagement with the mediating technologies. In light of this, the focus of my analysis of *Love Stricken*, will be a close reading of the meanings, messages, and contradictions forwarded on two tracks, sound and image. I insist on upholding the contradictions that arise within a secondary forking as well, namely those produced through the alternative positioning of the film narrative on the one hand and of enunciation on the other, as they refer to what is emphatically national. True, my approach abandons the hermeneutics of reading film as narrative, but it allows for a reflection on the enactive sites of culture in which the utopian image of the nation is produced.

Preoccupied with the processes involved in the production and inscription of sound and of national representation, *Love Stricken* repeatedly reflects on its own processes of production, that is, on what Christian Metz refers to as 'filmic enunciation.'[2] I will attempt to show the ways in which enunciation, as the landscape that inscribes the topography of film production and the unconscious site of the national address, self-reflexively reveals the very things that upend the messages and meanings produced by the film's own narrative statements. In reading *Love Stricken*, then, I will discuss the ways in which narrative statements regarding the identity of the nation, the nation's history, and its representation, are time and again contradicted by the histories and identities embedded within the film's representational technologies and enunciative sources.

Love Stricken (1992)

Based in turn-of-the-century Iran, *Love Stricken* traces the peregrinations of a group of early twentieth-century musicians to Paris to record traditional music on the newly invented gramophone. Historical in its leanings, the film narrative is preoccupied with the processes involved in the production of musical instruments and of sound recordings. This preoccupation with production and inscription consistently reflects on the film's own processes. Thus, the issue of production, national and aural, is clearly one of the concepts that the film offers up for analysis. *Love Stricken*'s narrative spans the period under the reign of Ahmad Shah, who ruled Iran during the revolutionary riots of 1909, riots that ultimately established a constitutional monarchy in Iran. While the film itself is emphatically ahistorical in its choice of characters and in its representation of historical events, it may be important to remark that the period in which the narrative is set is one of enormous turmoil in which Iran suffered a sad fate in the hands of an incompetent young monarch unable to resist European domination. The latter is a point left unacknowledged in the film narrative, which anachronistically overturns the conventional cultural hierarchies buried in the history of the film's own technologies and instead sets Iran's contemporary post-1979 moral economy in parity with the Western technological, economic, and political superiority at the turn of the twentieth century.

The World

In the film, the young monarch, Ahmad Shah, is approached by one of his foreign advisors to assemble a traditional group of musicians to go to France to record music on new foreign equipment. In effect the musicians are to do what many did in this period, which is to traverse the space separating Tehran and Paris to bring back to Iran the product of a national modernity. The film's thematic preoccupation with the history of sound recording in the Iranian constitutional era thus self-reflexively recalls the historical role played by the gramophone as studio sound displaced live musicians with sound that was pre-recorded on a wax plate abroad. Inscribing the passage of time, the phonograph needle and reproducer would become catalysts for the reinscription of spaces, simultaneously destabilizing in this singular move the traditional boundaries that were demarcated by sexual difference, demarcated, that is, by veils and walls.

The historian Farhang Rijai observes that three early ventures to London, Paris, and Tiblisi by leading Iranian musicians were made to pursue the foreign 'Gramophone Company's' objective to record Iranian sound on a new invention. Admittedly a slight groove in the otherwise extensive chronicle of sound recording, these traversals in space came towards the end of a civil war in Iran in which the nation's past, its history, became the primary loci of struggles over the constitution of the nation's modern identity.[3] The constitutionalists would in this struggle eventually take over Tehran, depose the Shah, and execute some of the anti-constitutionalists. The temporal configuration that conditions Hatami's historical film suggests that these events both precede and follow the film's narrative setting. In the film, the present is a time out of time, a past-future conjunction that as 'all-time' is associated with a messianic resurrection scheduled for the Day of Judgment.

Love Stricken opens with a close-up shot of the interior of a mechanical music box, decorated on the exterior with a clock. Ahmad Shah stands next to the music box, enjoying the 'voix celeste.' Seated outside the royal palace, after an abrupt transition to the subsequent scene, Ahmad Shah expresses his desire for the world to be a music box 'in which every voice is the sound of music and every conversation a song.' His minister informs him that a Monsieur Joli, a foreigner with a plan for recording music, has asked permission to gain audience with the Shah. As the modern monarch rides his bicycle in the park surrounding the royal palace conversing with the foreigner, in scene 3, he agrees to Monsieur Joli's plan to gather up and record the sound of the traditional Iranian musicians abroad. Together, these three scenes locate the historical, technological, and affective contexts for the national inscription of traditional music on the phonograph record. What is important to note is that 'the idea' of the phonograph is introduced in the film narrative, after the Shah has expressed his musical vision for the world. In the film, the monarch's enjoyment of the music box is given as the motivating force behind the introduction of recorded music to Iran. Against the historical claims made about the forced commercialization of sound recording by the foreign 'Gramophone Company,' the film formulates a historically motivated *national* rationale for the importation of recorded sound. In this way, the film's opening sequence adjusts the sight lines of its audience to provide an altered perspective on modern national history from the perspective of the revolutionary present and a different look at the formation of Iranian identity in relation to it. In the film, the music box – a measure of temporality associated with its adorning clock – provides the genealogical ground, as well as the technological motivation, for the production of mechanized sound in Iran. The young monarch's desire is set up by the film to charge the technology that will etch the groove of Iranian sound on a foreign wax plate. The Shah's imaginary world, like the world of the film, situates the nation, a uniquely modern world, envisioned, mediated, and produced by mechanized music and song.

Production

The scene that bears the overtures of the film, doubly emphasizes the issue of production, this time national, artisanal, and technological. The scene depicts an old craftsman working on various parts of a new type of *tar*, a traditional Iranian string instrument made out of wood. In close-ups and medium shots of the craftsman and the parts of the instrument that he is working on, the camera focuses on the steps involved in giving shape to the wood as the craftsman sands it, glues the parts of the instrument together, and finally polishes and strings the *tar*. Non-diegetic string music plays over this scene and rhythmically ushers the coming-into-being of a new instrument that advances innovations in Iranian traditional music. The overture, customarily a self-reflexive sequence in which films reflect on the means of their own coming into being, introduces *Love Stricken*'s actors, its film crew, and its director by name. As these credits roll, *Love Stricken* simultaneously catalogs the investment that the film has in interrogating the genealogy of an aural medium – a medium that comes to function as a mediator of national tradition. The credits roll as the old craftsman works on the tar. The craftsmen who produce the world of the film (the crew) and those artists who have been called to produce what will represent the nation to the world are introduced together in text and image form. Together these productive forces come to fulfill the young monarch's vision of a world imbued with song and music. In accenting the processes of manufacturing, both visually and textually, the overture doubly signals the film's interest in processes of production. This emphasis not only posits Iran's musical history as a subject of cinematic reflection, but also the film's reflection on itself as a produced object. That is to say, *Love Stricken*, as a film made in an isolationist period in Iran's post-revolutionary history about 'a moment' in the history of national representation, also shows itself interested in interrogating the mediating processes by which any representation of nationhood comes into being.

What can be said about the genesis of the modern nation? What grounds this history and what motivates its evolution? What mediates the nation's constitution? What impact does foreign influence have on the nation's evolution? The emphasis on the processes of production in the opening sequences of the film pressures the historical context for the inscription of national representations and the influences of such representational technologies in the making of modern Iran and in crafting its identity. What marks and tempers national identity in this process of mediation?

The juxtaposition of innovations in traditional and modern musical technologies in the image track and the non-diegetic sound of studio-recorded string music on the overture sets the foundation for the questions that become fundamental for the film itself. The simultaneity of the two representations produces an analogic relationship between transformations in traditional representational media (*tar* music) in Iran and the technological innovations in (studio) sound recording associated with *farang* (Europe) in the film. Although the two innovations are posited as equally new, modern, and progressive in the film's overture, the juxtaposition of studio sound and the visual attention to the process involved in the production of the traditional string instrument, split between the sound and the image track, reflexively recalls the historical role played by the gramophone as it displaced live musicians (who, we should remember, were artisans not unlike the film's craftsman) with recorded film sound in the early years of film production everywhere. Thus the film seems to mourn an auratic national loss, while celebrating the gramophone's reproducible sound – a celebration of a medium that was responsible for so many cultural and technological innovations, including sound films, which, far from being 'talkies,' were more like primitive musicals, not unlike *Love Stricken* itself.

Testing

The scene in which the musicians are introduced opens to a group of four musicians testing the *tar* assembled in the course of the overture. The music is diegetic in this scene, emphasizing by contrast the use of non-diegetic studio music we hear in the scene set up in the overture. The *mise-en-scène* is structured as if on the set of a photo studio. In the scene, the musicians are framed by two landscape paintings and white pillars. Left over from the days of the *Daguerreotype*, when it was necessary for the photographic subject to lean and stand still during a twenty- to thirty-minute minute exposure time of 'inorganic immobility,' such painted British garden backdrops would consistently frame photographs taken during the nineteenth century in Iran.

Love Stricken's gesture of framing within the film frame suggests the film's self-reflexivity. As such, the scene provides an overdetermined enunciative site that simultaneously ties the film to the early history of photography and the camera's historical relation to the introduction of film technology to Iran. This scene, in which traditional live musicians play a newly invented national instrument against a photo-studio landscape, reflects on the genealogy of representational arts and their relation to the history of national modernity. In this genealogy, photography provides the earliest images of the encounter between machine and man.[4] This scene, representing the musicians testing the new *tar* in *Love Stricken*, suggests that advancement in aural representative forms follows innovations in the visual arts. Historically speaking, in other words, the national subject has already traversed his/her groundedness in a specific geographic environment and interior landscape with the invention of the camera (referenced by the studio landscape), at the very moment when national sound loses its auratic context.

The European garden landscape that is represented in the photo-studio screen in this early scene provides the backdrop for the reproducibility of the national subject in effigy. The film foregrounds in this way the logic of transformation and the reconstitution of selves in and through the representational technologies of film. The subjects of the camera, in this scene, are transformed and transported into other settings through the process of mediation: Iranian men, playing traditional instruments, sit against the backdrop of a European landscape and are transformed by that context.

The film narrative also comes with a warning against the Western values as embedded in standardized representational strategies. In the scene in which the drummer converses with his wife and his mother about going to *farang*, the drummer's wife asks if *farang* is the same place she has seen in the *Shahr-i farang* (literally, 'Europe City,' a popular peepshow in Iran that projected fantastic images of Europe), where the mosques have towers, she says, instead of domes? Inquiring about the distance of *farang* from Tehran, she says that she's seen the *farangi* women in the *Shahr-i farang*. She describes their perfumes and clothes and remarks that they look just like dolls and warns her husband not to let them 'get into his frame' (*narand to jeldet!*, i.e. 'don't fall for them'). Predictably, it is precisely these women that enter and disrupt the seams of the filmic frame as the musicians start recording their nationalist music on wax abroad.

The scene that follows opens with a long shot of a European cityscape in which European men in top hats and suits walk arm in arm with European women in Victorian garments, bonnets, umbrellas, and white gloves. This scene, which represents the arrival of the musicians in Europe, also marks, by contrast, the nineteenth-century freedom of heterosexual exchange in the West. Repeated scenes such as this reveal a stark contrast between Iranian women who walk around Tehran covered by the veil and the unveiled women who the musicians encounter as they traverse the Parisian city streets, instruments in hand. This scene from the musicians' traversal of the Paris streets recalls eighteenth- and nineteenth-century travelogue entries by Iranian voyagers to the West, who describe Europe in terms of the status of European women and the public display of heterosexuality.

Missive 1

In *Love Stricken*, the scene signifying the musicians' arrival in Europe by staging a heterosocial *mise-en-scène* is taken in long shot. As such it comments on the film's preceding scenes. In its juxtaposition of cultural differences (between the travelers and the Europeans), the film articulates its own struggle to find a representational grammar in keeping with Iran's post-revolutionary modesty laws. On the level of the film narrative, these juxtapositions compare the moral superiority of an imagined 'uncontaminated' and chaste Islamic culture of the contemporary moment to a generalized sense of European moral laxity.

Maintaining a short lens, the scene in *Love Stricken* anachronistically shows itself critical of European heterosociality and thus eludes censorship in the Islamic Republic. But this self-consciously anachronistic overture to the post-revolutionary theocracy's sensibilities is merely a precursor to the actual site of recording, where the film's argument regarding the production of modern national identity, and the function of representation in this context, is forged. The gramophone, identified by the film as the historical site for the construction and inscription of a modern Iranian identity, becomes the focal point of this articulation. The musicians' arrival at the Parisian studio foregrounds the film's emphatic preoccupation with the enunciative site of this national identity: as if obsessed with its displacement of the book as sole chronicle of national history and identity, the film repeatedly returns to the question and the role of representational culture and technology in relation to it. In this scene, the presence of recording equipment in the *mise-èn-scene* reflexively and deliberately underscores the status of the film's narrative as mediated by representational technologies.

In the lead-up to this scene, the musicians walk out of the Pension de Paris to traverse the city in their stroll towards the recording studio. At the entrance, the English sign 'Recording Studios' signals the Persian tongue's indifference to the specificity of *farang*, as if to say, 'The other speaks in a foreign tongue, and we do not care if it is English or French.' Indoors, the next scene is set in the recording studio and emphasizes the status of recorded diegetic and non-diegetic sound as fundamental to the modern constitution of national identity through cinematic technologies. In this scene, as musicians set up and as the recording begins, what we hear on the soundtrack is diegetic sound. In other words, the music that we, as the audience, hear is coming from the instruments the musicians are actually playing within the visual frame. There is a sound synchronicity with the instruments we see played on screen.

As the singing begins, however, there is a cutaway to outside scenes, and the musicians start their stroll along the Parisian city streets once again. The sound we hear over the outdoor scene is studio recorded sound and it is non-diegetic; that is, no instrument is shown to be playing the musical score. Studio-recorded music continues to play the score we heard the musicians play in the studio but the musicians now merely stroll and look about the Parisian city streets. What we hear as the scene returns to the recording studio is a continuation of this non-diegetic studio recorded musical score. The soundtrack no longer synchronizes with the instruments we see the musicians playing. The music that played outside wanders into the studio and plays independently of the musicians' movements. Indeed what seems to have taken place in the musicians' traversal of the city on the visual track is so disruptive to the process of the recording that the drummer stops playing the score and starts wandering about the recording studio to satisfy his curiosity about the recording process itself.

What is marring the otherwise seamless montage is that the process of narrative construction – that process involved in the construction of a national identity through the film's mediating technologies – seems to be unsettling the synchronous harmony between sound and image. It is as if what takes place on the street – namely, the heterosocial visual exchange in the foreign sites and the non-diegetic Iranian sound that accompanies the musicians' traversal of the foreign city – is now being brought back into the studio and recorded along with the national music. This, indeed, is the message that is scopically mediated through the recording tube as the audience duplicates the drummer's gaze peering into the tube to see the needle inscribing the sights of Paris and the sound of Iran on wax.

Figure 5.1 The presence of recording equipment in the *mise-èn-scene* reflexively underscores the status of the film's narrative as mediated by representational technologies. (Source: Screen grabs from *Love Stricken*, 1992).

This slippage on wax is the enunciative backdrop to an ironically patriotic lyric poem that is sung into the gramophone. The repeated refrain in this poem identifies the singers as 'the enamored' worshippers of neither East nor West (one of the slogans of the revolutionary years) and the lovers of the beloved nation, rendered symbolically by the iconography of the lion and the crowning sun – the century-old symbol of Iran.

Missive 2

In a subsequent scene in which the musicians regroup to play the same piece of music in a park, the question of enunciation is underscored anew. Here the scopic and the aural become incommensurable and non-synchronous, once again. Set outdoors, the scene opens to a shot of a photographer and his female model. The model poses before the camera in the manner typical of late nineteenth-century *carte de visite* studio poses; that is, set against the backdrop of a European garden landscape. In this session, however, the conventional painted studio backdrop is absent. Contrasting with the early scene in which the musicians tested the new *tar* against the painted European landscape, the natural Parisian garden landscape takes the place of a studio screen. The oddity of playing out the scene of portrait photography outdoors is here underscored by the conversation that follows between photographer and model, where at the end of the session the model asks in French if they are going to do it again and he answers, 'Yes, tomorrow, if the weather is good.' The exchange between the photographer and his model emphasizes the history of early photo-technology, which depended on the predictability of light available only indoors – in other words, only in studio spaces.

The presence of the camera, in this first shot, alerts the film's audience to the status of its own vision as mediated and does so by foregrounding the technology that enables the images its audience sees on screen. With this emphasis on the mediating role of the camera, the musicians, in effect, become the after-images of the unveiled European model who, earlier in the sequence, is captured by a camera that reflexively stands within the narrative for the film's own camera.

As after-images of the unveiled European model, the musicians, representative of Iran abroad, forcefully wedge the question of national identity and cultural difference into an open ambivalence. While in the earlier scenes of the musicians' arrival the camera kept its distance from the staging of heterosexuality on the Paris streets, thus asserting the superiority of Iran's contemporary values, this scene situates both Europe and Iran within the same frame and simultaneously framed by the same lens. This comparative lens, now more ambivalent than that used to stage the musicians' arrival, asks where contemporary Iran stands in relation to Europe past and present. Given Iran's dependence

Figure 5.2 The natural Parisian garden landscape takes the place of a studio screen; the musicians, in effect, become the after-images of the unveiled European model. (Source: Screen grabs from *Love Stricken*, 1992).

on mediating technologies that share an international history, how is the nation able to claim national purity in representation?

The status of sound becomes as important as the status of the visual in the film's response.

Missive 3

As the musicians start their practice, it becomes quite clear that the music that we are hearing is a studio recording played over the outdoor landscape. What has happened to the national music is precisely what should have happened, but did not, to the photographer's session. Studio sound plays outdoors, and the outdoors becomes the site of *carte de visite* poses. In this way, the film reiterates the non-synchronicity of the scopic and aural. This enunciative incommensurability pressures the issue of national identity by mapping the production of national identity onto traversals in space, where what is being inscribed as modern Iran is externalized and then reconstructed and internalized on the backdrop of an intimate visual exchange between the European gaze eastward and the westward gaze of Iranian travelers in Europe.

Love Stricken foregrounds what Iranian films from the earliest post-revolutionary years demonstrated repeatedly in the form of a quiet political protest on the level of enunciation. Like many of its contemporaries, the film appears on the narrative level to comply with the demands put on the film and media industry to construct a national culture that shows Iran as critical of Western influence. It represents the national lifestyle as 'traditional,' Shi'ite, and 'pure,' even if anachronistically. The film's self-reflexive return to the history of the technologies of reproducibility uncovers dormant counter-memories, however, undoing any claim to a purified selfhood in national representation. Self-reflexive, *Love Stricken*'s government-compliant narrative unfolds on a contestatory landscape of enunciation that illustrates how undeniably the nation and its cinema is produced on the grounds of cultural confluences, wedged in the contradictions of a forked tongue.

Notes

1. Omid Rawhani, 'Ali Hatami: Kargardan-e Delshodegan, Man Ghali Mibafam,' in *Film: Mah Nameh-ye Sinema*, Vol. 2 (1999), pp. 541–5, p. 544.
2. One could think of enunciation as the organizing 'source' of the film narrative. See Christian Metz, *Impersonal Enunciation, or the Place of Film* (New York: Columbia University Press 2016). For Hatami the specificity of cultural difference was to be inscribed within the source and process of production of the film itself. Metz articulates this more precisely, as the site of cinematic enunciation, where narrative meaning is produced, patterned, and organized. According to Hatami, for Iranian cinema to be national, this process of ordering and patterning would have to signal

the national difference: 'I cannot tell an Iranian story on the patterns and production processes of the West. What I mean is, I have seen musicals or films about music in European and global cinemas and I have seen many of them and with a great deal of attention. But what I am attempting to do, and this is where my efforts have converged in the last years, is to realize a language, a style, a production process that arrives through the clarity of Persian speech and Persian storytelling' (Rawhani, 'Ali Hatami,' p. 545). What Hatami means in referring to speech and narration is not dialogue precisely. National difference in his film must be conditioned by the specificity of 'technique' and 'style.' Thus national difference for Hatami is the difference that emerges not out of a difference in content and dialogue so much as in the determined ordering of undetermined elements – enunciation, more specifically (Thomas Elsaesser, 'From Sign to Mind: A General Introduction,' in *The Film Spectator: From Sign to Mind*, ed. Warren Buckland (Amsterdam: Amsterdam University Press 1995), pp. 9–17, p. 12). John Mowitt's important intervention on the role of enunciation, as that which joins text to industry in cinema, fleshes out this very cursory discussion of the unconscious site of national address in my own work. See John Mowitt, *Re-Takes: Postcoloniality and Foreign Film Languages* (Minneapolis: University of Minnesota Press 2005).
3. Mohamad Tavakoli-Targhi, *Refashioning Iran: Orientalism, Occidentalism, and Historiography* (Hampshire and New York: Palgrave Macmillan 2001), p. 142.
4. See Walter Benjamin, *The Arcades Project. Konvolute J*, ed. Rolf Tiedemann, trans. Howard Eiland and Kevin McLaughlin (Cambridge, MA: Harvard University Press, Belknap Press 1999), p. 678.

Bibliography

Benjamin, Walter, *The Arcades Project. Konvolute J*, ed. Rolf Tiedemann, trans. Howard Eiland and Kevin McLaughlin (Cambridge, MA: Harvard University Press, Belknap Press 1999).

Elsaesser, Thomas, 'From Sign to Mind: A General Introduction,' in Warren Buckland (ed.), *The Film Spectator: From Sign to Mind* (Amsterdam: Amsterdam University Press 1995), pp. 9–17.

Metz, Christian, *Impersonal Enunciation, or the Place of Film* (New York City: Columbia University Press 2016).

Mowitt, John, *Re-Takes: Postcoloniality and Foreign Film Languages* (Minneapolis: University of Minnesota Press 2005).

Rawhani, Omid, 'Ali Hatami: Kargardan-e Delshodegan, Man Ghali Mibafam,' in *Film: Mah Nameh-ye Sinema*, Vol. 2 (1999), pp. 541–5.

Rijai'i, Farhang, *Ganji Sukhtih: Pajuheshi dar Musighiye Ahdi Qajar* (Tehran: Shirkatih Ahya-yi Kitab 1994).

Tavakoli-Targhi, Mohamad, *Refashioning Iran: Orientalism, Occidentalism, and Historiography* (Hampshire and New York: Palgrave Macmillan 2001).

6. DIFFERENT TIME, DIFFERENT SPACE: FILMIC FORMS OF COUNTER-MEMORY IN ABBAS KIAROSTAMI'S KOKER TRILOGY

Ute Holl

METAPHORS AND MATERIALITIES

Abbas Kiarostami's film *Khāne-ye dūst kojāst?/Where is the Friend's House?* (1987) is structured by two grand metaphors of memory: the pathway and the door. The schoolboy Ahmad, who desperately needs to find his friend living in a mountain village nearby, can run up a zigzagged path without hesitating to ask for the way, because the path itself is a materialized and practical, even if tacit, form of social memory. As past actions made present, the path connects to the boy's body in transferring the information it contains about how to reach the friend's village right into Ahmad's movements.[1] Saving and suspending the knowledge of direction and place, the pathway liberates the physical energies of the boy, who can follow his goal running fast, oblivious to any spatial orientation. Information about the route itself can thus be neglected or forgotten.[2] The path, then, as infrastructure, is a cultural, collective, and transparent dispositive of memory,[3] an unconscious form in terms of psychoanalysis. It is connecting to the physical body and remains a structural form of memory without a subject, subjecting everybody.

The specific door, however, which marks the friend's house and distinguishes it from all other houses in the village, poses an altogether different problem and brings the swift movements of the boy to a sudden halt. To find the door, a singular and explicit form of memory is needed, a specific description which demands an individual form of remembering and the participation of other subjects. Singular traces and fragments of knowledge have to be assembled. As in the account of Simonides of Keos, the legendary founder of mnemo-techniques, this particular form of remembering relates space and rhetoric, or space and description. Locating the friend's house makes is necessary to communicate in words and gestures. In the Iranian village of Poshteh, where the friend lives, there is no general numbering of streets or houses, no general technique or code of identifying and addressing a person and thus making him or her a subject.[4] The little boy therefore needs to resort to individual descriptions of the door: apparently it is blue, as some say, but to the dismay of the little searcher many of the doors in Poshteh are blue; they are semi-industrially made, even if they are distinguished by individual marks of climate and usage. The boy has to resort to the friend's family name, which seems to be equally widespread, as are schoolboys' crimson trousers, which initially promise to be a possible trace to the friend's whereabouts. While the path uses tradition to lead the way, the doors are a different matter. They force Ahmad to ask others in order to recollect a memory that was once supposed to be collective and has now faded away and vanished.

Kiarostami's film *Where is the Friend's House?* – as his famous Koker trilogy, including *Zendegī Va Dīgar Hitch*/*Life and Nothing More* (1992) and *Zīr-e Derakhtān-e Zeytūn*/*Through the Olive Trees* (1994), as a whole – confronts collective and culturally stable forms of implicit and tacit memory on the one hand, with forms of remembering that do not have a steadfast institutional or cultural framing on the other. These films do not simply opt for the values of a stable collective memory. On the contrary, they show that culturally stern structures of memory can inhibit curiosity, initiative, and, as in the case of *Khāne-ye*

DIFFERENT TIME, DIFFERENT SPACE

Figure 6.1 (a–c) While the path uses tradition to lead the way, the doors are a different matter. (Source: Screen grab from *Where is the Friend's House?*, 1987).

dūst kojāst?, even acts of sincere friendship. Cultural memory guarantees that as long as one follows the trodden path one is connected to a past operating in the present. But while the path provides implicit knowledge, it also conveys how difficult it is to get off the beaten track, to rid oneself of the forces of memory and culture, to include who has been tacitly excluded, for instance, because there is no path to his doorstep and, thus, as a lady says in the last film of the trilogy, 'we don't have an address anymore.' Kiarostami's films focus on moments where memory as a collective or individual cultural technique falters and fails, where it is disturbed or becomes fuzzy and unreliable and where its collapsing undermines culture as a whole. Indeed, Kiarostami's films intentionally produce such moments of imploding memory.

In his considerate portraits of the villagers, the film shows how forces of the past and those of the present are in constant battle, visible in faces, gestures, movements. Rather than delivering accounts of events or morality tales, the film observes the forces at work in people's behavior, actions, and reactions. Kiarostami's aesthetics therefore acquire a status of being neither documentary nor fictitious but in search of a new approach to reality altogether. On the one hand, there is a focus on the materiality of things, at the same time, the filming and editing work is done with stern abstractions. Already the vivid title of the first Koker film is not a quotation taken from the young protagonist, but from a poem by Sohrab Sepehri: 'Address.' Sepehri's poetry, due to his concern with Japanese art, relies on strictly formal composing. Sepehri's poem indicates a path in this way: 'Before you get to the garden tree / there's a garden lane / more green than god's dream.'[5]

Instead of adapting either documentary or fictional forms, Kiarostami's films meticulously examine the strategies of constructing reality or fiction. These strategies are traced and marked in the worlds before the camera as well as in the camera work or editing. One of Kiarostami's own strategies to escape the blunt difference between fiction and document is to formally open his scenes towards the incidental, the aleatoric, the contingent, and unplanned.[6] In this way, the structural memory of the many zigzagged pathways in his films is shown as inscribed on the surface of his protagonists' bodies: sweating, smiling, blushing.[7]

On the other hand, Kiarostami observes how his actors and actresses – professionals or amateurs – oscillate between presence and performance, between the memory of a script and the memory of the body. In this way, the films form a strong opposition against all aesthetics of representation in favor of making present, presentation. With this strategy, Kiarostami is able to challenge and change the relation of power, narration, and memory in cinema.[8] Thus, his films counter memory in its basic structures.

While the search for the friend's house will turn out to be unsuccessful, the film *Where is the Friend's House?* itself turns into a negotiation of doors and the knowledge attached to them. Old, handcrafted doors, retaining and displaying the Persian art of woodcarving, *Monabat-Kāry*, are opposed to new industrially made doors about to be exchanged for the village's old doors, which, in turn, as the vendor of the new doors alleges, are traded to Teheran's

DIFFERENT TIME, DIFFERENT SPACE

Figure 6.2 Structural memory and zigzagged pathways. (Source: Screen grab from *Where is the Friend's House?*, 1987).

museums as memorabilia. The old carpenter and doormaker of Poshteh, who insists in helping the boy in his search, explains that the old doors are singularly beautiful, even in their process of aging and decay, in their cracks and fissures. They indicate individual houses and are themselves a cross-generational form of memory. Their material matters and it marks their singularity. In fact, the singularly beautiful images of the film underline that memory only exists if attached to material things and practices. In its singular images, the film's memory turns self-reflexive.

The new steel-doors, as their vendor maintains, are supposed to last for a lifetime. Some of the elderly men, hanging out in front of the village shop, refuse to buy and object that they know what a door is. But what is a lifetime? Already, their own concepts of education and respect prove to be obsolescent, customs are turning into fading memories. The film, however, does not mourn the decay of these customs, instead showing that this form of embodied tradition is largely based on simple force: Ahmad's grandfather insists that giving the young a good spanking at intervals will teach them to remember manners and obedience and turn them into good citizens. The film in its logic and aesthetics – cast, shooting, editing, sound dramaturgy, and the sparely used music – is exactly the reversal of this force, even if maintaining the idea of a bodily memory.

While showing two opposing techniques of social memory, general pathways, and particular doors, Kiarostami's film negotiates transitions of memory techniques. The film may point to an impending loss of cultural knowledge, heritage, and history; however, it is also concerned with the difficulty of getting rid of those structures that impede the young to invent their own ways. Thus, we are reminded that the first image of the film *Where is the Friend's House?* had, in fact, been an extended shot on the door and doorknob of the village classroom. Here, yet another basic form of mnemo-technique is taught: the boys – and obviously boys only – learn to read and write. Scripture – according to Plato the poison of memory and of the truth of the spoken word, and according to Jacques Derrida its disavowed basis,[9] – opens up a new culture for the boys, unknown to their parents and grandparents. In learning to read letters, they unlearn to read doors. Kiarostami keeps this in balance with emancipation: schooling should liberate the boys from agricultural or artisan work, or household errands, which their elders expect of them. On the other hand, the film unmistakably shows the disciplinary measures involved: the boys have to sit still, write onto prefabricated lines, into notebooks that all look alike, causing the initial trouble of the confounded exercise books. Finally, the cultural techniques of reading and writing not only install a new form of memory, but also a new staff of authorities, blind to experiences that escape symbolization in letters.

The film *Where is the Friend's House?* was made between a series of documentaries on schoolchildren and education, dealing with forms of disciplinary measures and initiation into society at large. These films are touching in that they document the psychological and physical force of educational measures, as well as the utter incomprehension of the adult world towards serious thoughts and considerations of children. Addressing the issue of memory, the Koker trilogy takes seriously what philosopher Friedrich Nietzsche discovered about the implementation of memory:

> Indeed, there is perhaps nothing more fearful and more terrible in the entire prehistory of human beings than the technique for developing his memory. 'We burn something in so that it remains in the memory. Only something which never ceases to cause pain remains in the memory' – that is a leading principle of the most ancient (unfortunately also the longest) psychology on earth. We might even say that everywhere on earth nowadays where there is still solemnity, seriousness, mystery, and gloomy colours in the lives of men and people, something of that terror continues its work [. . .].[10]

While for Nietzsche an enhancement of memory through bodily pain seems inescapable, *Where is the Friend's House?* keeps negotiating the issue. It confronts memory and materiality, and unconscious structures of memory and conscious forms of remembering, but it also poses broader questions:

where is my people's knowledge stored? How is it imprinted or otherwise 'burned in'? Which are the media that form a people's memory, implicitly or explicitly? What kind of materials and practices are involved? In what way is memory connected to media of communication – words, letters, books, pathways, or doors and their carvings. And eventually, how does the memory of cinema interfere?

Media and Memory

Memory is composed of a material complex as well as of discursive systems, signs, practices, action, and behavior. It is neither just technical hardware, nor just infrastructure or procedural rules, but the interlacing of all. Memory is not a stable order of data, as computers, hard-drives, or, in fact, memory sticks might suggest. Much rather, memory is a changing order that forms its content according to historical media as well as cultural techniques and discursive formations. Memories are composed of an intrinsic connection between people, techniques, and practices.

Cinema's memory differs from radio's memory or, in fact, from the computer's and the internet's knotted pathways of remembering. Kiarostami addresses this in the last image of the film *Where is the Friend's House?* While the schoolteacher accepts and appreciates the homework in the exercise books, giving his signature, the boys hold their breath, knowing that the identical handwriting might reveal their deceit. And while the audience – especially those slow in deciphering Arabic letters or in reading Farsi – sees the writing but never really learns what exactly it is about, we all perceive, with a bit of sentiment, the dried flower in the friend's exercise book, a flower that the boy had been given by the old carpenter in Poshteh. This image is proof to a silent alliance between cinema's memory and those visual, tangible, and highly affective experiences that cannot be captured in written words. Cinema can remember what writing cannot: visual forms and figures as well as sounds and noises that literature would have to transfer into symbolic orders to store them. But this is not a one-directional path. In remembering, societies or individuals, communicating through media, mechanical, electronical, or other, may also re-configure memory. This is the precondition of all experience.[11]

The second film of the trilogy, *Life and Nothing More*, will center around the television and its net of global broadcasting as a medium of forgetting one's present. In the third film finally, *Through the Olive Trees*, cinema itself is examined as a means of producing and reconfiguring memory and memories. Media and memory then are at the core of the trilogy's considerations. It is through this conjunction that Kiarostami addresses the difficulties of cultural and political change in Iranian society. His films are not simply documents of

Iranian history, but much rather negotiate the basic problems of all historiography, namely the question of memory and its reconfiguration of events: 'To be sure, the truths of memory are often in tension with the truths of history.'[12] The cinema of Kiarostami counters conventional structures of memory in confronting documentary forms with images and sounds, movements and voices that transcend expected orders of behavior. A memory based in practices and behavior of course counters a revolution that, although prepared by electronic media, claims to act in the name of scripture.

The virtue of Kiarostami's cinema is then that it defies representation and makes cinema a case of life and death. In a conversation with Jean-Luc Nancy Kiarostami states:

> I can't bear narrative cinema. I leave the theater. The more it engages in storytelling and the better it does it, the greater my resistance to it. The only way to envision a new cinema is to have more regard for the spectator's role. It's necessary to envision an unfinished and incomplete cinema so that the spectator can intervene and fill the void, the lacks.[13]

The second part of Koker trilogy, *Life and Nothing More*, is paradigmatic in this reference to discontinuities, missing links, cracks, and fissures. And it makes sure that these aesthetics of discontinuity and intermittence are intrinsic to cinema – and opposed to television. Analog television, with its continuous flow of signals, is adequate for covering news and disaster in a mode of presence.[14] Thereby, television replaces all experience of contiguousness (including, as Jean-Luc Nancy reminds us, the haptic quality of film as a small skin, a *pellicule*[15]). With its scanning mode of observations taken with utmost immediacy – and, sometimes, indiscretion – then transmitted over long distances, television creates a paradoxical form of vicinity. It represents the immediate. In addition, television in the strict sense does not have a memory. The signals can be kept in constant transition, recording them is an additional feature which is unnecessary for broadcasting the images.[16]

In the film *Life and Nothing More*, the two grand paradigms of the first film, pathway and door, are replaced in more than one sense: firstly, the landscapes and buildings of the Gilan region are destroyed by the huge earthquake of 1990, pathways and doors were missing and literally being replaced. Secondly, the new film had to position itself against the excitement and voyeurism of ubiquitous television images. Therefore, doors and paths were replaced with visual iterations of gazes and frames. Thirdly, in its recursions and iterations, the cinematic form itself serves as a mnemo-basis, a structure for Kiarostami's personal memories of his instant trip to the sites of destruction:

'In June 1990, an earthquake of catastrophic proportions jolted Northern Iran, killing tens of thousands of people and causing unbelievable damage. Immediately I decided to make my way to the vicinity of Koker, a village where four years earlier I had shot *Where is my Friend's House?* My concern was to find out the fate of the two young actors who played in the film but I failed to locate them. However, there was so much else to see . . . .'[17]

While Kiarostami did travel to the Gilan region, where his family came from, right after hearing of the disaster, and while he did take one of his sons to relocate, retrieve, and literally remember the cast of his first film, he did not shoot *Life and Nothing More* at the time but went back five and then eleven months after the earthquake to restage what he had witnessed or remembered of it: 'it was all a reconstruction, although it looked like a documentary.'[18] What the film shows is what Kiarostami remembers to have remembered – probably based on written notes and photographs – and then recast into filmic forms. Cinematic memory in its characteristics, the recording and montage of images and sounds, thus forms memories that are neither real nor fictitious.

It is central to the notion of medially reconfiguring the forms of memory that we do not confound reconstruction with representation. In fact, the two notions mark the opposite sides of mnemo-technical interventions. Reconstructions actually mark alienated and abstract forms in order to expose the difference between – probably – traumatic and irrepresentable incidents and their cinematic restaging. Representation on the other hand deletes or denies this difference. Cinema has to find its own form of distancing and alienation, lack or fissure, not only in order to avoid sensationalism, reporter's voyeurism, and false solicitousness, but to point towards the traces of the event. The traces are distinguished from immediate experience according to the memory form of cinema. In this process, the filmed layers of events and memories start shifting.

The film *Life and Nothing More* begins with music from the off, obviously broadcast by another medium, either radio or television, eventually interrupted by a female's voice addressing the audiences – the diegetic ones in the film, as well as us, the cinema's audience, far away from the site of the catastrophe and very distant in time – on behalf of the Red Halfmoon, to propose measures of support for children who have lost parents and homes. All the while, the first image, a shot through the window of a toll booth on the highway, shows the windows of customer's cars, intermittently stopping and moving on, and in the background, more booths and more car windows passing by, forming a strange mis en abyme of gazes. Dynamically, the cars' window frames are jerking by, intermittently, just like single frames in front of a projection machine. This opening shot also points to the fact that cinema, as opposed to television coverage and electronic images, prompts the audience to consider the *hors-champ*, the off-space, that film implies but does not show. The alter ego of the director in the film and his fictional son, Puya, travel through the landscapes as in a camera obscura, looking out to all sides to see jammed roads, destroyed houses, and desperate people, all of it framed by the cars' windows. The false immediacy television tends to suggest in its shots from the scenes of destruction is here intentionally alienated by the form of framing as a remediation of the gaze.

This cinematic framing and fragmenting of the gaze is augmented in an extended sequence – ten minutes into the film – of traveling through a tunnel. In the dark, the sleeping boy in the back of the car is, again intermittently, illuminated. While he sleeps or daydreams, only the noise of cars passing by is audible. In this second Koker film, it is mostly the sound that disturbs the imaginary closure of the scenes. This becomes very obvious after the cut which ends the tunnel sequence, suggesting that the car has apparently already reached the mountainous region of Gilan. While the two travelers drive though a city of ruins and rubble, passed workforces clearing up the space, a strange sound montage is heard from the off, mixing a singing voice, transmitted through a megaphone, resembling a muezzin's, albeit sounding like a pop song, with the rhythmical sound of shoveling, as well as strange noises of voices seemingly played backwards. This montage does not really match what is shown in the image and it remains undecidable whether it comes from the environment, the car's radio, or from the imagination and nightmares of the sleeping boy. It is in these frames of multiple references that a subject or an 'author' of the remembrances shifts. Moreover, the difference between perception, or the direct filming of a situation, and memories, reconstruction of former impressions, are indistinguishable. Sounds and images could be the memories of people outside or the travelers in the car, who are shocked by sights and sounds of destruction. Traumatic incidents that cannot be adequately remembered are thus condensed into a cinematic tableau of different time-layers, which radically escapes filmic conventions of representation. Instead, it presents – indeed, it makes present – the situation as a tableau constructing memory against the grain of single impressions and in terms of a compressed time. Thus, the extended overture of the film proposes a third form of highly artificial reconstruction of a disastrous reality.

Only when father and son leave the highway and enter a zigzagged path with an uncertain ending do they encounter singular people with singular objects carried on their shoulders as if to mock the perception in Platon's cave. Here, however, it is not the objects nor ideas that matter but the carrying bodies as Kiarostami's film depicts them in their ascents on zigzagged streets and paths. The man who had played the old carpenter in *Where is the Friend's House?* incidentally shows up carrying a urinal, recalling Duchamp and surreal invectives against representation, complaining that cinema's temporal strategies of making people look older than they are actually compromise all concepts of time and, thus, of memory. He, too, is inserted into a time of crisis, condensed according to the cinema.

All the witnesses from along the road will stick their heads into the car window and deliver their accounts of events. The film becomes a protocol of injured and hurt bodies. The witnesses complain and mourn, the physicality of their reports is more important that the descriptions of the earthquake itself. Against this physicality, an abstraction is brought into position. The framing of their heads separates them from the surrounding reality, and the role of the witness is underscored as never being immediate but always mediated and remediated to, exactly, create authenticity according to a medium involved; in this case, the cinema. In assembling various forms and sources of information which he had collected during his first trip, Kiarostami abandons the position of a metaphysical, a historian's subject of remembering. While assembling stories of the earthquake's disaster, the film also assembles a discourse of memory as a whole. In this, he leaves the construction of memory to the spectators.

Following Friedrich Nietzsche's concept of analyzing history in reconstructing a discontinuous set of forces instead of assuming a continuous evolutionary development discovered in figures and facts, Michel Foucault listed a set of procedures to ensure the safeguarding of true historical events. These are set against the metaphysical abstraction of a universal truth that, according to Nietzsche, needs itself to be deciphered as a result of violent claims and battles in the past. The notion of truth had only been turned into a universal entity through practical and hands-on procedures or authentification, or, as Foucault puts it, through 'the long baking process of history.'[19] Instead of assuming a single origin of a presumed development in history, Nietzsche and, in fact, Foucault encourage historians to watch out for vast numbers of accounts and numberless beginnings, going back into the ramifications of historical data and documents as a genealogist would. Historiography then should examine evidence like archaeologists do if they study 'passing events in their proper dispersion.'[20] Historians should insist on the 'heterogeneity'[21] of phenomena, where the antiquarian's history imagines a consistency of facts and events. The 'gray, meticulous and patiently documentary'[22] work of genealogists then consists in reconstructing forces and media, bodies and passions at work in history.[23] In focusing on the body, as 'the inscribed surface of events,'[24] taking sentiments and passions, as well as fear and violence, seriously as symptoms of historical power relations, this Foucauldian genealogy refrains from the assumption of a subject of metahistorical knowledge, and prompts us to look out for 'the reversal of a relationship of forces'[25] and most of all for the 'transformation of history into a totally different form of time.'[26] It is this procedure that Foucault calls the construction of a counter-memory. And it is extraordinarily surprising how much his description corresponds to how cinematically based historiography operates: recording heterogenous materials, things, architectures, light, and sounds as well as actions, bodies, or voices as forms of enunciation; blending and relating different places and times, confusing the identities of actors, actresses, and their roles in scanning their features in close-ups, for instance. Cinema, more than the static images of photography, can register physical symptoms of historical antagonistic forces as they inscribe themselves onto faces and surfaces of the body. However, the parallels between a genealogist's model of history and cinema may seem less surprising if we keep in sight that Nietzsche wrote the relevant texts in this respect exactly at the time when chrono-photography took over proofs and evidences on the fields of psychiatry, physiology, and criminology, experiments from which cinema as a cultural technique and as an entertainment industry eventually emerged. Foucault, quoting from 'Twilight of the Idols,' reminds us that Nietzsche at the time tended to merge 'historical and physiological' arguments.[27]

Two aspects are important for the analysis of cinematic formations of a counter-memory: the turning of historical perception away from events, decisions, or battles towards forces at work in human and non-human relations; and, secondly, the establishing of a different time form. This is exactly what the many layers of Kiarostami's film in its images and framings, sounds and voices, accounts and silences achieve: they form a time structure that is neither in synch with immediate documentary filming of witnesses and disastrous sights, nor is it a fictitious narration. The bodies of the actors and actresses, their movements and voices, and even the filmmaker's attention towards their thirst and their need to urinate, as Jean-Luc Nancy underlines in his essay on the Koker trilogy, *The Evidence of Film*, counters conventional models of what historical facts are composed of. Filmic memory informs memories differently. Finally, Kiarostami in his film collects evidence not in reorganizing what he found on his first excursion, but in picturing 'passing events in their proper dispersion.'[28] The memory of cinema, not the memory of single protagonists is at work in the film.

In this respect, the metaphorical image, which Jean-Luc Nancy sees 'at the center of the film'[29] – a washed-out color print of an elderly peasant, sitting at his table with his tea glass, plate and pipe, *chopoq* – is probably less emblematic for the film's memory discourse than Nancy wishes it to be. This poster, pasted across a crack in a partially destroyed house, the fissure crossing both poster and wall, rather points to the basic cinematic aesthetics of voids in or in-between images than to a forgotten lore or, as Alberto Elena supposes, 'the image of a picture torn by a great crack in the wall of one of the damaged houses, serves as a last powerful symbol of the stubborn fortitude of the villagers.'[30] In fact, Kiarostami had attached the poster, of which thousands were distributed in the villages in the 1980s, to the cracked wall during his filming of the 'reconstruction' of memories, and had himself meticulously applied the fissure to the image.[31] The fissure is therefore less a reminder of natural forces than emblematic for interventions of the cinema and film directors.

DIFFERENT TIME, DIFFERENT SPACE

Cinema's memory in the Koker trilogy is exposed as the invisible operative moment of images perceived only as blind spot, or in contrast to other media. Kiarostami deploys the issue of the ubiquitous television and in this case the news of the World Cup soccer games to point out the structure of a memory formed by multiple media, print, radio, or television, but obviously dominated by television. As such it pervades Iranian culture, at the same time connecting it to global communication. When father and son pick up another boy on the road to Koker – who reminds them that he had also had a part in the school scenes of *Where is the Friends' House?* – their conversation is constantly disturbed by a confusion of the reports on the earthquake, which the fictitious film director had asked for – 'Tell us what happened!' – and those of the match between Brazil and Scotland – 'Scotland scored first.' The title of the film itself is also connected to the issue of television. In a conversation with a young man who is busy installing an antenna on the side of the road, the film director asks him if he thought it proper to watch a soccer game in a time of mourning. The man answers: 'To tell the truth, I am also in mourning. I have lost my sister and three cousins. But what can we do? The cup takes place every four years. We can't miss it. Life goes on.' Kiarostami's very cinematic intervention here is to address global communication while it is interrupted, the antenna in construction, the transmission malfunctioning, the people camping outside hoping for the broadcast to take place. His images and sounds focus on the discontinuity and, exactly, the gap between ongoing life and an endless television broadcast that covers it. In this, Kiarostami's admiration for the people in despair has been mistaken for a call to confidence and perseverance. The films propose much rather an essay on a society's self-reflexion with the help of cinema and its aesthetics of discontinuity.[32]

MASQUERADES AND SIMULATION

The impact of cinema itself on the construction of memory is the issue of the last of the Koker films, *Through the Olive Trees*, in its self-reflexive turns and double and triple masquerades in the mis en scènes. Pretending to be a documentation of the making of a feature film, every shot in *Through the Olive Trees* is meticulously framed, propped, and enacted and as carefully staged as a theater play. Then again, many protagonists speak right across the theatrical fourth wall into the camera, irritating the diegetic illusion.

What might seem to be a play with reality is, however, a serious game: part two and three of the trilogy are concerned with the question of how media, and specifically cinema, might provide a form of memory for an inconceivable and inexpressible disaster, the earthquake that caused between 35,000 and 50,000 deaths and left an estimated number of between 60,000–100,000 people injured. Instead of providing a coherent form of institutional or ritual mourning as a collectively solid form of memory, the films attempt to open access for all to sincere mourning and, at the same time, invent a different conception of life in its fragility.

The film begins with unfurling the relentless power relations that any feature film shoot implies: the casting of young girls, who admire the director, the transformation of environments into credible filmsets with props and technical paraphernalia, the clearing of the space from people that normally inhabit it, giving actresses and actors false names and finally forcing them to wear costumes they don't like and to say lines that do not match their sentiments to the world, to each other, and towards their self-image and -esteem. On the other hand, the film invests all its possible art and technology into creating an unmediated relation to the environment, things, and people, focusing on the material reality of walls, flowers, or naked feet.

Through the Olive Trees takes up the case of a young man, Hossein, whom the fictious director in *Life and Nothing More* had interviewed about his wedding. Hossein maintains to have married his bride right after the earthquake, although he claims to have lost sixty-five of his friends and family, explaining that he had taken the advantage of the moment and the chaos to outplay family customs and to accomplish facts. However, and this had found the approval of the director, he had taken care of his wife and found a house for them to live in against all odds. This is one of rare moments in *Life and Nothing More* where Kiarostami had the seemingly documentary soundtrack covered with music, Antonio Vivaldi's solemn *Concert for Two Horns*, thus overtly and obviously drawing on feature film conventions.

That same scene is restaged in *Through the Olive Trees*, at the bottom of the same staircase of the same house, with the fictious director of the former film, played by Farhad Kheradmand, delivering the same lines, directed by another actor acting as director, Mohammad Ali Keshavarz, in place of Abbas Kiarostami's directing in *Life and Nothing More*, surrounded by a bored film team that in the former film we had not seen. Actually, to augment confusion, the scene is restaged and re-enacted in two versions, first with a young man playing Hossein, who turns out to have a speech impediment, and then by the actor, or amateur player, Hossein Rezai, who had played Hossein in *Life and Nothing More*, now pretending to play himself. In a series of takes, he enters the frame again and again, carrying a sack of plaster or explaining his marriage procedure, exactly as in the 'original' scene, which, as we meanwhile know, was in fact a postponed reconstruction of events remembered in another medium. Foucault's advice for a genealogist's research – to 'push the masquerade to its limits'[33] in order to erase the idea of origin and understand the cultural fabrications of identities, or rather their constitutive fragility, as well as the 'baking' of an absolute truth – is here projected onto cinematic strategies of producing impressions of truthful memories. In playing with masquerades, Kiarostami teaches his audience how authenticity is made in cinema, but at the same time he provokes emotions and reactions that might stand in for 'life and nothing more.'

In the course of filming, another level of narration is introduced. It turns out that Hossein, who also performs as assistant and caterer on the set, had been trying to court the actress of the protagonist Tahereh, also named Tahereh, outside of the set, against her and her family's will, and the project failed with the earthquake and the death of Tahereh's parents. All this caused Hossein, as he says, to mistake the tremors' origin as caused by his own heart beating. The long account of Hossein's, telling 'the director' about his failed courtship, seems unstaged, real, and sincere. But when he remembers his last encounter with the girl and her grandmother at the village's cemetery, something extraordinary happens: the film cuts into a flashback, music and sounds announcing the transition to a different time and place. The most conventional form indicating remembrance in terms of cinematic fiction, the flashback, now seems overtly staged and an obvious simulation of a filmic return to the past. Also, it crosses out the false immediacy of the former confession. In the cinematically framed past, then, we see Hossein, following him closely trailing the grandmother in a path though the olive trees, again failing in his proposal. Lost in the olive grove he stumbles into another filmset, which we only see from the outside, technicians and crew, but the sound indicates that we have arrived in (a restaging of) a scene from the film *Life and Nothing More*. From then on, the circular movements of endless repetitions of takes on the set, so similar to each other as to make us doubt that they were not simply copied in the lab, and constant refererences to corresponding scenes in former films make it impossible for the spectator to organize his memories in the time and reality loops of scenes. Even Mrs. Shivas's clapperboard, covering the whole field of the image and pushing the audience into the crew's perspective of watching rushes, only multiplies the levels of recognition and remembering. Caught in the film as if in a Möbius-strip of memory, spectators hope for the redemptive order 'cut!' from the director. But the cuts only add further levels of re-enactment and repetition.

These entanglements and shifts of identities as well as places, times, and tenses, which are so easy for the cinema to engender, are altogether impossible to reproduce in words. Helplessly, one is tempted to revert to punctuation marks: 'Hossein,' 'he,' 'himself,' or [the actor]. Writing has to settle for a certain general description, while film can picture people and things in their individual particularity. Film forms of referencing use indexical traits and traces of materialities to produce identity in terms of photographic media. On the other hand, editing and montage are able to link images across the logics of time and space to produce non-linear, condensed, and contradictory tenses and places. In cinema, therefore, the two models of memory, pathway and door keep returning: the unconscious memory of the pathway in the continuous movement of photographic images, which our perception follows automatically; and the particular and discontinuous nexus produced in montage, a form or narration which has often been compared to a corridor with many possible doors to choose from. This includes the exit via gap or void.

Through the perception of gaps and voids, through intentional disturbances such as discontinuities, asynchronous sounds, or the confusion of on-set and off-set relations, can the mediality of the medium come into view of the spectators. In pointing to the construction of truth and reality in film, cinematic memory, as an operation of organizing memories in their plural, can be analyzed as contingent and subjected to transformation. Kiarostami's intentional disorganization of any stable basis for remembering past events then turns the spectator's attention towards the tacit order of collective memory, has him stumble across what was thought to be pencil's nature. Kiarostami's films denaturalize the laws and logics of memory. In this, Kiarostami's cinema is blowing the cover of cinematic evidence as such and countering its culture, as Nancy writes: 'Cinema (and with it television, video, and photography: in Kiarostami's films they play a part that is not accidental) makes evident a conspicuous form of the world, a form or a sense.'[34] This destabilization of social, mental, and political certitude, usually secured and safeguarded by institutions of the trust in records and archives, must be understood as the effort of genealogical research into a history that negotiates life without the warrant of vitalism: 'the true historical sense confirms our existence among countless lost events, without a landmark or a point of reference.'[35]

Memory is not content, but a structure, and this structure not only changes with different media but also with the use of a medium and the disorganization of its orders. In Chris Marker's *Sans Soleil*, the female narrator reads from the letters of a fictitious cameraman Sandor Krasna: 'He wrote me: I will have spent my life trying to understand the function of remembering, which is not the opposite of forgetting, but rather its lining. We do not remember, we rewrite memory much as history is rewritten.' And he adds a question that may also have been the outset for Kiarostami's Koker studies: 'How can one remember thirst?' If memory is a matter of translation, it is also a matter of leaving somethings untranslatable, in the realm of the unnoticed, the unperceived, in lacks, breaks, and fissures.

Notes

1. Cf. Richard Terdiman, *Present Past: Modernity and the Memory Crisis* (Ithaca, NY: Cornell University Press 1993).
2. Cf. Elena Esposito, *La memoria sociale. Mezzi per comunicare e modi di dimenticare* (Roma-Bari: Laterza 2001).
3. Cf. even if the latter is subdivided into communicative, cultural, and political memories according to the structure of their transference, as in Jan Assmann, 'Globalization,

Universalism, and the Erosion of Cultural Memory,' in *Memory in a Global Age. Discourses, Practices and Trajectories*, eds. A. Assmann and S. Conrad (New York: Palgrave Macmillan Memory Studies 2010), pp. 121–37.
4. Cf. Bernhard Siegert, '(Not) in Place. The Grid, or, Cultural Techniques of Ruling Spaces,' in B. Siegert, *Cultural Techniques, Grids, Filters, Doors and Other Articulations of the Real* (New York: Fordham University Press 2015), pp. 97–120.
5. Sohrab Sepehri, 'Where is the House of the Friend?,' in Sohrab Sepehri, *A Selection of Poems from the Eight Book* (Bloomington, IN: Balboa Press 2013), p. 131. It was the French distributor that opted for '*My* Friend's House,' German and some English translators followed. Hence the variations of the title, *the* or *my* friend's house.
6. Cf. Ute Holl, 'Mit ohne Ordnung. Kontingenzproduktion als Strategie des Dokumentarischen (zum Beispiel Abbas Kiarostami),' in Sichtbar machen. Politiken des Dokumentarfilms, eds. Elisabeth Büttner et. al. (Ed.)(Berlin: Vorwerk 8 [Texte zum Dokumentarfilm]), pp. 111–30.
7. I thank Matthias Wittmann for reminding me of the vast literature on the figuration of zigzagged paths in the iconography of Persian miniatures. Kirarostami himself, however, in his dialogue with Jean-Luc Nancy Kiarostami, states that 'I've never really felt close to Persian miniature painting.' 'Abbas Kiarostami, Jean-Luc Nancy in Conversation,' in Jean-Luc Nancy, *Abbas Kiarostami. The Evidence of Film* (Bruxelles: Yves Gevaert Éditeur 2001), pp. 80–95, p. 80. Of course, that does not mean that he is not working within a cultural heritage and, thus, cultural memory.
8. Cf. Alberto Elena, *The Cinema of Abbas Kiarostami* (London: Iran Heritage Foundation 2005), p. 72f.
9. Cf. Jacques Derrida, *Of Grammatology* (Baltimore, MD: The Johns Hopkins University Press 1997).
10. Friedrich Nietzsche, *On the Genealogy of Morals. A Polemical Tract*, trans. Ian Johnston (Arlington, VA: Richer Resources Publications 2005), p. 45.
11. Cf. Walter Benjamin, 'Experience and Poverty,' first published in *Die Welt im Wort* (Prague, December 1933), in Walter Benjamin, Selected Writings Volume 2: 1927–1934 (Cambridge, MA and London: The Belknap Press of Harvard University Press 1999), pp. 731–6.
12. Michael Rothberg, *Multidirectional Memory. Remembering the Holocaust in the Age of Decolonization* (Stanford, CA: Stanford University Press 2009), p. 14.
13. 'Abbas Kiarostami, Jean-Luc Nancy in Conversation,' in Jean-Luc Nancy, *Abbas Kiarostami. The Evidence of Film* (Bruxelles: Yves Gevaert Éditeur 2001), pp. 80–95, p. 88.
14. Cf. Gilles Deleuze, *Cinema 2: Time Image* (Minneapolis: Minnesota University Press 1989): 'The fundamental idea is that, already in television, there is no space or image either, but only electronic lines: "the fundamental concept in television is time" (Nam June Paik, interview with Fargier, *Cahiers du cinema*, no. 299, avril 1979)' (p. 331, fn8).
15. Jean-Luc Nancy, 'Evidence du film. Abbas Kiarostami,' in Jean-Luc Nancy, *Abbas Kiarostami. The Evidence of Film* (Bruxelles: Yves Gevaert Éditeur 2001), pp. 9–79, p. 46.

16. Cf. Mary Ann Doane, 'Information, Crisis, Catastrophe,' in *Logics of Television. Essays in Cultural Criticism*, ed. Patricia Mellencamp (Bloomington: Indiana University Press 1990), pp. 222–39. Doane in fact turns the argument around in analyzing that television needs the interruptions of catastrophe and crisis in order to make sense of the permanent flow of information: 'There is a very striking sense in which televisual catastrophe conforms to the definition offered by catastrophe theory whereby catastrophe represents discontinuity in an otherwise continuous system' (p. 232).
17. Kiarostami in the press book distributed by the Farabi Cinema Foundation, quoted according to Elena, *The Cinema of Abbas Kiarostami*, p. 92.
18. From an interview with Laurence Giavarini and Thierry Jousse, quoted according to Elena, *The Cinema of Abbas Kiarostami*, p. 94.
19. Michel Foucault, 'Nietzsche, Genealogy, History,' in Michel Foucault, Language, Counter-Memory, Practice: Selected Essays and Interviews (Ithaca, NY: Cornell University Press 1980), pp. 139–64, p. 144.
20. Ibid., p. 146.
21. Ibid., p. 147.
22. Ibid., p. 139.
23. Ibid., p. 144.
24. Ibid., p. 148.
25. Ibid., p. 154.
26. Ibid., p. 160.
27. Ibid., p. 156.
28. Ibid., p. 146.
29. Jean Luc Nancy, *The Evidence of Film*, p. 62.
30. Alberto Elena, *The Cinema of Abbas Kiarostami*, p. 99.
31. Cf. 'Abbas Kiarostami and Jean Luc Nancy in Conversation,' in Jean Luc Nancy, *The Evidence of Film*, p. 82.
32. Cf. the critical reception of the film in Iran, documented and commented on by Elena, *The Cinema of Abbas Kiarostami*, p. 103ff.
33. Foucault, 'Nietzsche, Genealogy, History,' p. 161.
34. Nancy, *The Evidence of Film*, p. 12.
35. Foucault, 'Nietzsche, Genealogy, History,' p. 155.

References

Assmann, Jan, 'Globalization, Universalism, and the Erosion of Cultural Memory,' in A. Assmann and S. Conrad (eds.), *Memory in a Global Age. Discourses, Practices and Trajectories* (New York: Palgrave Macmillan Memory Studies 2010), pp. 121–37.
Benjamin, Walter, 'Experience and Poverty,' first published in *Die Welt im Wort* (Prague, December 1933), in Walter Benjamin, *Selected Writings Volume 2: 1927–1934* (Cambridge, MA and London: The Belknap Press of Harvard University Press 1999), pp. 731–6.
Deleuze, Gilles, *Cinema 2: Time Image* (Minneapolis: Minnesota University Press 1989).
Derrida, Jacques, *Of Grammatology* (Baltimore, MD: The Johns Hopkins University Press 1997).

Doane, Mary Ann, 'Information, Crisis, Catastrophe,' in Patricia Mellencamp (ed.), *Logics of Television. Essays in Cultural Criticism* (Bloomington: Indiana University Press 1990), pp. 222–39.

Elena, Alberto, *The Cinema of Abbas Kiarostami* (London: Iran Heritage Foundation 2005).

Esposito, Elena, *La memoria sociale. Mezzi per comunicare e modi di dimenticare* (Roma-Bari: Laterza 2001).

Foucault, Michel, 'Nietzsche, Genealogy, History,' in Michel Foucault, *Language, Counter-Memory, Practice: Selected Essays and Interviews* (Ithaca, NY: Cornell University Press 1980).

Holl, Ute, 'Mit ohne Ordnung. Kontingenzproduktion als Strategie des Dokumentarischen (zum Beispiel Abbas Kiarostami),' in Elisabeth Büttner et al. (eds.), *Sichtbar machen. Politiken des Dokumentarfilms* (Berlin: Vorwerk 8 [Texte zum Dokumentarfilm]).

Nancy, Jean-Luc, *Abbas Kiarostami. The Evidence of Film* (Bruxelles: Yves Gevaert Éditeur 2001).

Nietzsche, Friedrich, *On the Genealogy of Morals. A Polemical Tract*, trans. Ian Johnston (Arlington, VA: Richer Resources Publications 2005).

Rothberg, Michael, *Multidirectional Memory. Remembering the Holocaust in the Age of Decolonization* (Stanford, CA: Stanford University Press 2009).

Sepehri, Sohrab, 'Where is the House of the Friend?,' in Sohrab Sepehri, *A Selection of Poems from the Eight Book* (Bloomington, IN: Balboa Press 2013).

Siegert, Bernhard, '(Not) in Place. The Grid, or, Cultural Techniques of Ruling Spaces,' in B. Siegert, *Cultural Techniques, Grids, Filters, Doors and Other Articulations of the Real* (New York: Fordham University Press 2015), pp. 97–120.

Terdiman, Richard, *Present Past: Modernity and the Memory Crisis* (Ithaca, NY: Cornell University Press 1993).

PART III

INTERSTICES. NICHES. IMPURE MEMORIES

[. . .] it is within these contradictions and gaps that the roots of alternative thinking are formed.

Rakhshan Banietemad, Cinema as a Mirror of
the Urban Image (Interview, 2015)

7. TOWARDS AN IMPURE MEMORY: AN ARCHAEOLOGY OF COUNTER-MEMORIES THROUGH TELESCOPING LENSES

Matthias Wittmann

EMERGENCY ROOM

In *Censoring an Iranian Love Story* (2009), Shahriar Mandanipour's meta-novel on the creation of a love story under conditions of censorship, Mandanipour rehearses a series of reflections on the meaning of the *emergency room* in Iranian everyday life:

> Hospital emergency rooms in Iran are places that perhaps even the art of cinema cannot justly portray. For you to have some concept of an Iranian emergency room, let me say only that the annual average number of people killed in road accidents in Iran is ten times greater than the number of Americans killed to date in the second war with Iraq. Therefore, as Sara and Dara sit in that hospital, the doors to the emergency room constantly open, and the casualties of highways, freeways, and streets, and the casualties of hundreds of other locations and accidents, are rushed in.[1]

And, one might add, car or motorcycle crashes and post-accident emergency rooms also constitute a long-standing *topos* in the history of Iranian cinema – *nota bene*, before and after the revolution of 1979. Be it allegorically or realistically, they show up in films as different as Masoud Kimiai's *Qeysar/Caesar* (1969), where the first scene after the credit sequence (designed by Abbas Kiarostami and Amir Naderi) begins with a close-up of the emergency lights and the sound of a rescue vehicle; or Ebrahim Hatamikia's first feature film *Hawiyat/Identity* (1986), where the main character of the film is a hooligan biker who loses his memory after an accident and assumes the identity of a *basījī*; or Bahram Beyzaie's *Mosāferān/Travellers* (1992), where the protagonist (Shahin Alizadeh) announces at the very beginning that they will all die in a car accident on the way to Teheran; or Parviz Shabazi's *Nafas-e 'amīq/Deep Breath* (2003), at the end of which the urban slackers die in a car accident. What seems to resonate in this last scene is the same daring lust for life that ends up killing the already-stabbed *lūṭī*, Reḍā, on his motorbike, to the sounds of Farhad Mehrad's famous song *Mard-e tanhā*, at the end of Masoud Kimiai's *Reżā Motorī/Reza Motorcyclist* (1970).

Needless to say, the list could be extended indefinitely. For my purposes here, I would particularly highlight Mohsen Makhmalbaf's *'Arūsy-e khubān/Marriage of the Blessed* (1988), produced towards the end of the First Gulf War, which throws us immediately and literally head first in the midst of a hospital scene: we follow the point of view of a nurse pushing a trolley with food and medical instruments through a corridor until he kicks open the door of a room full of traumatized war victims. In terms of expressivity, this madhouse packed with social symptoms and hysterias could very well be compared with Sam Fuller's *Shock Corridor* (1963). The legend of the sacred martyrs – together with the cult of pain, the pathos of sacrifice, and the ideology of suffering – returns here in the form of caricature and farce. What we are confronted with are shell-shocked soldiers, 'living martyrs' as they were called: furiously gesticulating bodies, stammering and crying, which repeatedly re-enact war situations and radio communication scenes. Fragments of memory keep surging in flash frames showing trenches, tanks, bazookas, aerial bombings, bodies torn to pieces, explosions, and martyrs' bandanas. The above-mentioned film by Hatamikia, namely *Identity*, designs the exact opposite of this shattered personality: after a process of inner purification, the main character, who initially suffered from memory loss, removes the face bandages – as we know it from (neo-)noir films like *Dark Passage* (1947, Delmer Daves), *Johnny Got his Gun* (1971, Dalton Trumbo), *La Jetée* (1962, Chris Marker), or *Suture* (1993, Scott McGehee) – to uncover a new Shi'a face. We have a final healing of all wounds and stitches, and a protagonist who is ready to adopt an exemplary *basījī* identity.

While Hatamikia brings out an immaculate, unbroken subjectivity from revolution and war, Makhmalbaf sketches a fragmented and stuttering sensorium. The film puts the focus on a traumatized photographer in shock, not only because of the war itself, but also because of the emptied, unredeemed promises of the Islamic Revolution. The highly experimental mnemography presents the revolutionary subjects as not at all healthy and in harmony with themselves. On the contrary, by means of montage-cataracts,[2] they are exhibited as sick and shattered, dissociated by post-revolutionary phantom pains, memory flashes, and delirious-hallucinatory superimpositions, which conflate past and present, revolution and war: typewriter sounds turn into machine gun salvos, bureaucratic state apparatuses into war machines, patients' crutches into weapons for the *sacred defense*.

The assault of war technology on the senses is conveyed through the montage technology of film. At the same time, though, another crisis of perception is addressed, one that has to do with the revolutionary iconoclasm and the general project of re-educating the senses, as detailed by Negar Mottahedeh: '[. . .] the post-revolutionary film industry was charged with re-educating the national sensorium and inscribing a new national subject-spectator severed from dominant cinema's formal systems of looking.'[3] The demand after the revolution for a re-education of perception and a transformation of the former culture of the spectacle, which was attributed to the Shah's regime, into a culture committed to Islamic values was carried out against a background of numerous catastrophic *ruptures in the continuity of transmission* (Yerushalmi) and *metamorphoses in the field of perception* (Virilio), and these were conditioned as much by war as by cinema.[4]

In Makhmalbaf's film, the violence of montage technology is a 'displaced allegory' – as Mottahedeh would call it: a 'second-level message'[5] – which affects the cinematic form, and not so much the narration. Mottahedeh uses the concept of allegory in the sense of Frederic Jameson who considers it in his political film aesthetic as a structural split or wound in the representation, articulating an absent cause, a political unconscious: '[. . .] allegory means imperfect representation or the failure of representation [. . .] [I]t always breaks down.'[6] The trauma conveyed by the montage techniques can also be considered as a kind of meta-wound: it is not simply a matter of subjectivity traumatized by shell-shock and war, but one that is also scattered and torn apart by various frames, tropes, semantic networks, and 'resources for negotiating life and (re)making the self,'[7] as will be discussed below.

Makhmalbaf's film deals with phenomena like PTSD (post-traumatic stress disorder) and *depreshen (afsordegi)* – shell-shock and trauma. As Orkideh Behrouzan has pointed out in her book *Prozak Diaries* (2016), in a culture where many other discourses had currency, it was not at all common nor self-evident to resort to psychoanalytical and neuropathological concepts and frameworks in order to find individual truth and retrospective meaning, cope with wounds and loss, articulate – even create – subjective experiences. '*Marriage of the Blessed* was among the earliest artistic expressions of PTSD. More narratives emerged over the following decade.'[8] As Behrouzan has shown, it was only in the late 1980s that a psychiatric discourse – between psychopharmacology and psychoanalysis – was introduced into the Iranian cultural sphere, to be followed in the 1990s by 'depreshen talk': 'By the end of the 1990s, a Persian psychiatric vernacular had emerged in society: *afsordegi* (depression), *depreshen, dep zadan* (becoming depressed), *toromā* (trauma), *esteress* (stress), *bish-fa'āli* (hyperactivity in children), and the Persianized catch-all term for antidepressants, *Prozāk*.'[9] It is crucial that not only new terms have found their way into everyday language, but that the population – across all social strata – was confronted with both traditional and modern 'modes of self-recognition,'[10] grammars of re-membering, and registers for interpreting emotional experiences. One could also speak of *double binds* (Bateson[11]) and of different ways of claiming access to one's true self. A true self which sees itself fragmented into different bits. Illness, grief, loss, lament, mourning, or happiness are formed at the site of interference between 'contradictory or mutually exclusive imperatives' that shaped the different generations.[12] The psychiatric subjectivity began to compete with other subjectivities that were forged by 'distinct and incommensurable imaginations, vocabularies, values, and visual imageries':[13] martyrographies, gendered ways of witnessing, Zoroastrian heritage, the Shi'a ethos and mourning culture, Sufi mystical foundations of memoryscapes (also as a counter-ideology), and other ritualized traditions of memory. One could therefore speak of a structural meta-trauma arising from the frictions and incommensurabilities between medico-cultural, psychoanalytical, religious, and other traditional narratives that offer articulatory structures for the unsayable wound, the non-narratable, that which defies the symbolic order – what since Pierre Janet (1859–1947) in Europe is considered as an essential characteristic of trauma. Nevertheless, the Western paradigm 'trauma' is not sufficient to cover what Behrouzan calls 'ruptures':

> Rupture allows for the complexity of historical conditions and their emotional afterlife, as well as for the new cultural forms they generate. It also allows the conceptual capacity to convey the infusion, diffusion, and multiplicity of experiences across generations. My focus, thus, is not on the events per se, but on the consequent burden of remembering their residues that are bound to be overlooked by institutionalized memory – in other words, on their assimilation and inscription into the present and its cultural or artistic forms.[14]

The filmic procedures are part of those artistic forms. Although in dialogue with medicine, psychiatry, Shi'ism, and other interrelated cultural discourses, they created their own trauma- and memoryscapes, which in turn became a shared memory and shaped the collective and individual forms of memory. It is remarkable that Makhmalbaf uses the 'emergency room' as a (counter-) dispositif to develop a critique of institutionalized memory, a kind of counter-memory, which is primarily produced by means of filmic montage. The emergency room is transformed into an editing room, from which a new instance of post-traumatic and post-revolutionary enunciation and a new point of re-membering is established.

If the archive is the 'law of that which can be said,' as Foucault claims in the *Archaeology of Knowledge*,[15] then Makhmalbaf's memoryscapes can be considered as an attempt to use montage techniques as a subversive device, through which he seeks to rewrite the grammar of archiving – i.e. the order of what can be seen, said, and remembered. The emblematic emergency room serves here as a laboratory of time, space, and perception, of fractures and deformations, in which new zones of emergence – regarding historic references, subject positions, and points of re-membering – are created.

Editing Room

Like emergency rooms, editing rooms are a recurring motif in the history of Iranian cinema, especially after the revolution. Let us recall Bahram Beyzaie's thriller *Shāyad Vaqtī Digar/Maybe Some Other Time* (1987), which starts in the editing room: the male protagonist Modabber (Siamak Atlassi), an average middle-class resident of Teheran, is working on the dubbing of a documentary on air pollution in his city. While working on sound-image relations – specifically on a traffic jam sequence – he believes he sees his wife Kian (Susan Taslimi) sitting in a car next to another man. The sequence is replayed over and over again, and the past re-examined thoroughly, also outside the editing room. This comes to a climax when one day, in an antiques shop, the different layers of reality swirl in a hallucinatory outburst. It turns out ultimately that Kian has a twin sister who was given away after birth and who grew up in a totally different environment. What the protagonist thus progressively uncovers is an alternative forgotten history, comparable to the counter-memories that reveal the hidden, (counter-)revolutionary activities of Fereshteh (Niki Karimi) in Tahmineh Milani's *Nīmah-yi Panhān/The Hidden Half* (2001, see Chapter 2 in this book).

A totally different point of re-membering qua point of editing can be found in Morteza Avini's *Haqiqat/Truth* (1980–1) and *Revāyat-e Fath/Chronicles of Victory/Narration of Triumph* (1985–8). A theoretician and practitioner of Islamic cinema and one of the most prominent documentary filmmakers of the 'Sacred Defense cinema' (*Sinemā-ye Defā'-ye moqaddas*), Avini was very much influenced by Martin Heidegger, or, rather, by Ahmad Fardid's reading and interpretation of Heidegger. It is the same Fardid who developed the term and concept *gharbzadegi* (*westoxification*), a term that became popular through its appropriation by Jalal al-Ahmad (1923–69). As Behrouzan has shown, even psychoanalysis has been considered as a kind of westoxification: 'After the 1979 Revolution, Freud's name would be removed from public media and print for years.'[16] As a committed Islamic and genuine post-revolutionary filmmaker,

Avini did not engineer a psychoanalytical subject, but a 'sacred subjectivity,' as Hamid Naficy would call it.[17]

Chronicles of Victory – financed by the state television network Voice and Vision – is a series of more than sixty episodes that Avini shot with his film team Jihad Television (first on 16 mm, then on video). In these episodes, he developed a kind of martyrography of the war between Iran and Iraq (1980–8). The events at the front are staged as *lines of faith*, *illumination* and *return to nature*, also in the sense of a return to a pre-modern Islam, to a collective identity of Shi'a martyrs in line with the Karbala paradigm, i.e. the will to die for the cause.[18] The episodes operate with a romanticized temporality qua circularity where the future promises the return to a happier past. The sacralized depiction of life at the front, of combat operations and the preparations preceding them emphasize the fighter's collective identity as set against the westernized modern subjectivity. The soldiers and the *basīj* volunteers are shown in their collective daily activities (cooking, praying, etc.) and during the ritual preparations for battle – i.e. for the crossing to the world of martyrs – and this is supplemented with religious chanting and Avini's voice-over narration which, like a religious sermon, makes frequent allusions to Shi'a martyrdom and mythology.

Remarkable in the context of my argumentation are the recurring scenes in which Avini stages himself as a kind of master of narration and enunciation at the editing table, suturing modern technology with pre-modern ideology, binding the fighting subjects, the cinematography, and the audience to a collective identity and testimony. In his essays and articles, later published as a book under the title of *Magic Mirror* (Vols. I–III, 1998/9) Avini even refers to Marshall McLuhan's dictum from *Understanding Media* (1964): 'The medium is the message.'[19] If the media dominate our ontology and if the message of Western media consists in spreading a capitalist temporality, the Islamic technician had to master the medium in line with the values of Islam. In order to produce a cinema capable of reflecting the reality of the revolution and the war, Avini argued, filmmakers needed to create a new form. And indeed, his *Chronicles of Victory*, in particular, played a crucial role in the building of the Islamic Republic's national identity and in what could be called with Mohammad Tavakoli-Targhi its 'clerico-engineering.'

> Together with the Islamic revolutionary commitment to the building of a divinely inspired society, the operational concepts from the field of engineering provided the foundation for an epistemic shift from an organic and curative to a synthetic and constructional conception of politics, religion, and culture. As a result of this shift, the rhetoric of engineering became increasingly hegemonic, influencing the conceptualization, description, and explanation of religion and politics in post-revolutionary

Iran [. . .] [I]nvolving 'geometry of politics' (*hindisah-i siyasi*), 'geometry of governance' (*hindisah-i hukumat*), and 'geometry of political competition' (*hindisah-i riqabat-i siyasi*).[20]

The engineering of the soul in the Islamic Republic – the divine geometry of politics – also used a rhetoric of *purification* (*pāksazi*), as a systematic response to the Western cultural invasion. Impurity, admixture, hybridity, and ambiguity were condemned as heretical, even though structures of ambiguity are part as well of the history of Islam itself, as Thomas Bauer has shown in his book on the Islamic culture of ambiguity.[21] Be that as it may, ambiguity always remains suspicious in totalitarian systems.

The *clerico-engineering* also tried to purify memory by creating a continuous past, a history of improvement and redemption, and a great, unifying collective memory, stretching the present times back to Karbala and the origins of Shi'a. The Shah's regime before the revolution tried to create another historical continuity, by prohibiting all criticism of the officially fabricated success story called 'industrialization,' 'secularization,' and 'modernization.' Part of this banned criticism were also resistant forms of an 'unofficial, popular civil religion,' as Pedram Partovi has shown convincingly in his book *Popular Iranian Cinema before the Revolution*.[22]

Impure Memory

Towards an Impure Memory does not refer to André Bazin's notion of the *impure (mixed) ontology of cinema*,[23] on account of the mixing of different art forms (theater, literature, etc.) that it entails, but it reacts to the attempted 'purification' of Iranian cinema after 1979. A cinema that puts into circulation impure (counter-)memories produces frictions between political promises and social realities, exposing the emptiness and abstractness of the revolutionary semiotics of purity put forward by the ideological architects of the Islamic Republic of Iran. This brings me to a third example of a film scene taking place in an editing room, which can be seen as a counterpoint to the clerico-engineering described above.

In her self-reflexive meta-film *Banu-ye Ordibehesht/May Lady* (1997), Rakhshan Banietemad addresses the problem of representation – especially the representation of female agency, subjectivity, and desire – in the framework of a fiction movie about documentary filmmaking. It is the story of Forugh Kia (Minoo Farshchi), a forty-two-year-old female documentary film director, who is a divorced single mother. She has a liaison with a man to whom she is not married and lives with her almost adult son who behaves like a jealous lover. Worthy of mention, she is starting a film project about an exemplary mother in Iranian society. The problem: during her research, she is confronted with such

Figure 7.1 Like emergency rooms, editing rooms are a recurring motif in the history of Iranian cinema. (Source: Screen grab from *May Lady*, 1997).

a diversity of single mothers from different social classes that she increasingly finds herself incapable to decide who the exemplary mother would be. Crucial is the scene in the editing room, wherein the protagonist Forugh is getting completely drowned in a plethora of collected interviews, portrait photos, and documentary snippets. This is Banietemad's way to deal with a crucial ethical dilemma of ethno-sociography, under ideological restrictions aiming at permanently forming, reforming and standardizing the 'imaginary relationship of individuals to their real conditions'[24] (Louis Althusser).

It is precisely this failure of representation, the incommensurability of individual lives, and the impossibility of a uniform memory, that Banietemad's documentary and feature films consistently address, challenging totalizing categories such as, for example, the broad category of *mustaz'afin*. 'Interestingly the term *mustaz'afin* entered Khomeini's discourse only during the height of the revolution, when he used it merely to repudiate the communists and attempted to offer an alternative (Islamic) and non-communist conceptualization of the poor, the lower-classes.'[25] How to keep in touch with multiple layers of society? What does it mean to pick up one individual case, one case study, and transform it into a category, an exemplary case for society, while thousands of other singularities are dismissed? How can one avoid transforming the act of photography or the gesture of filming into an act of symbolic violence through representation and purification, cutting off all the other conflicting realities and possible worlds?

TÉLESCOPAGE

In the following, I would like to expose and discuss several examples of what I call 'impure memory,' as a more specific cultural form of the notion of 'counter-memory.' Since impure memories relate as well to collapses and accidents within continuous time structures (i.e. within the propagandistic success stories), providing a non-stoic, broken, and unaccomplished image of subjectivity as well as an inconsistent affective framework, I will use a model from Walter Benjamin as a supplement: his concept of *télescopage* (telescoping) as briefly defined in his *Arcades Project* (1927–40). According to this notion, the past is considered as a phenomenon that could only be known and illuminated through a constellation of events – including medial events – from the present. The '[t]elescoping of the past through the present'[26] is a technique of re-membering and of collective recollection that locates the possibilities of remembering particularly in montage techniques and refraction, and not in continuity. Consequently, memory becomes a product of present constellations, refractions, and forces. It is remarkable that telescoping does not only refer to collision in an optical sense – to the optical device *telescopium* (far-seeing), which uses multiple (refracting) lenses and reflecting mirrors – but also to collision in the sense of accident (*accidents télescopiques*), hence to a post-traumatic constellation: squeezed wagons, telescoped into one another. This brings us back to the starting point of this chapter, the *emergency room* and the question of rupture, of accident within continuity. Lastly, telescoping can also be related to the 'telescopic violence of the road': the assaults on the 'security of vision' caused by the speed a passenger experiences when sitting in a vehicle, as described by Paul Virilio:

> [...] the term 'télescopage' [...] is itself composed of two meanings: 'examine what is at a distance' *[télescope]* and 'mix indiscriminately' *[télescoper]*. The optical illusion of the telescope consists of approaching what is distant in order to examine it, and that of the automobile of mixing indiscriminately what is close and what is distant. This accelerated traversal is linked, therefore, with a certain problem of perception; the course becomes an excessive joining of what is distant with what is close, and the function of high-speed vehicles consists less in transporting the passenger than in causing physical reality to slide by, that is, to modify as with various lenses the surfaces of visual experience.[27]

Thus, the term telescoping is related to intricate spatiotemporal collisions and collapses, locating the possibilities of remembering not in linearity and continuity, but rather in rupture, caesura, and above all, in montage. The atlas of counter-memories as elaborated in this chapter will occasionally also include counter-examples, i.e. purified memories from the 'Sacred Defense cinema' that do not correspond exactly to 'telescopings' in Benjamin's sense and have the function of demonstrating nuances between different forms of spatiotemporal constellations and tectonics.

SCRATCHING THE PAST OR ONLY IDEOLOGIES TURN THE PAST INTO *TABULA RASA*

The first example is once again taken from Mohsen Makhmalbaf's 'anti-Sacred Defense' movie *Marriage of the Blessed*, which transformed the perspective on revolutionary subjectivity. As we shall see, however, the 'Sacred Defense' scheme did not really disappear, but merely shifted to another level.

At the beginning of the film, Haji (Ebrahim Abadi) – this is the name of the photographer – is picked up from the hospital in a Mercedes. Through the windscreen and the Mercedes star he sees the slogans and the graffiti lingering on the street walls. These date back from the time of the revolution and remind the photographer of its unredeemed promises: 'We will drag all capitalists to the court of justice (Imam Khomeini)' or, in a more war-romantic vein, 'Volunteer combatant, a lion in battlefields, a victim in town.'[28] The protagonist looks at the past as if through the cross-hairs of a telescopic sight.

Figure 7.2 The protagonist looks at the past as if through the cross-hairs of a telescopic sight. (Source: Screen grab from *Marriage of the Blessed*, 1988).

A similar construction can be discerned, when the photographer – through the optical finder of his intra-diegetic camera – not only sees the social misery of present conditions, but also demonstrations and protests from the past, for example banners showing Islamic theologians of liberation such as Ali Shariʿati. It is as if his memories from the time of the revolution start superimposing through the camera lens like hallucinatory visions. They turn into insisting parasitic images. Here, the photographer uses his camera not only to take photos but also as a means to cancel reality; by repeatedly pressing the camera's shutter release button, he tries to erase the haunting images and scratch the empty promises in order to create the conditions for a new societal ideal.

The constructions in both scenes are without any doubt remarkable, as if the past could only be re-exposed, retroactively elucidated from the standpoint of a specific 'here and now.' Nevertheless, I would like to argue that Makhmalbaf's construction is a *telescoping of the past through the present* (Benjamin) only at first glance. What appears to be a re-evaluation of the events of the revolution through the after-images of the war, and conversely those of the war through the after-images of the revolution, is basically carried by an iconoclastic longing for a return to a purified self. As a former pro-Islamic activist, whose first movies were shown in prisons and mosques as re-education films in the service of revolutionary values, Makhmalbaf is still trapped in a Manichean logic and binary opposition between reality and ideal, and is still driven by a revolutionary iconoclasm, i.e. a new iconography that again tries to scratch out all the wrong trajectories of the past. Thus, Makhmalbaf is not really searching for alternative *pasts of the present* (Foucault), which, not least due to his own revolutionary fervour, were overlooked. He still measures the present against the ideal of his past and believes not only in the arrival of radical social change, but also in what Shariʿati would call *bāzgasht be Khīshtan (return to the self)*. In other words, he is still committed to a religious political ethics and to the *shahādat*: 'a return to this self by exposing thoughts and ideas that had been figuratively "hidden" from [. . .] collective memory. At the same time, in a recursive gesture, the *shahīd* was to be understood as the self to which the return (*bāzgasht*) was directed. In this vein, Shariʿati's *shahīd* chooses to die.'[29]

Makhmalbaf's photographer does not choose death, the extinction of his physical body, but he becomes a living martyr. He does not testify to his faith through stoicism, quietism, and death-defying courage (like one character from an early Hatamikia film) but retains this still existing faith in a possible purity – an anti-imperialist return to a purified self – through disruptions, refractions, ruptures, symptoms, which from that time on were encapsulated in the label PTSD. In this respect and on a meta-level, the film is actually about impure memories (more or less consciously); the cinematically negotiated phenomena – *toromā, depreshen/ afsordegi*, or *āsib-e ruhi/ejtemā'i* (psychological and social pathologies) – can be deciphered as a battleground for competing imperatives and changing frameworks:

Marxist, Sufi, Shi'a, psychiatry, biomedicine, and other public discourses. Haji is burnt (*sukhteh*) and he keeps on burning like an open wound (*zakhm*), longing for purification and for an (impossible) return to a lost self that never existed in a pure form.

Embodied Counter-Memory

The next instance of counter-memory is from *Gilāneh* (2004), a film co-written and co-directed by Rakhshan Banietemad and Mohsen Abdolvahab, which constellates the end of the First Gulf War (1988) and the beginning of the Third Gulf War (2003) in an elaborate way, also involving television images used as *screen memories* (Freud[30]). The film blends the (war) times with one another so that one war covers (screens) the other one, producing echoes and correspondences across time. It is quite remarkable that in the same year in which *Gilāneh* was released, Bahman Ghobadi's *Lākposhtha ham parvāz mikonand/Turtles can Fly* also came out – another film that is set on the eve of the US invasion of Iraq, this time in the Kurdish refugee camp on the Iraqi-Turkish border.

Gilāneh is not only a village in Gilan (Iran), it is also the name of a widowed mother (Fatemeh Motamed-Arya), who has to send her son Ismael (Bahram Radan) to the war between Iran and Iraq. '*Gilāneh* evokes a particularly matriotic concept of *vatan* [homeland] [. . .].'[31] While the first half of the film takes place at the end of the Iran-Iraq War, the second half is set fifteen years later, on the day the United States began bombing Baghdad (20 March 2003). Thus, we are confronted with a telescoping of the wounds from the Iran-Iraq War into the social conditions of a present that stands again on the threshold of war. Tired from life and far away from her daughter Maygol (Baran Kosari) who lives with her husband and child in Teheran, Gilāneh continues to take care of her bedridden, chemically wounded son. As the transition between the first and second half of the film is particularly significant, it will be recalled here in the very vivid description by Michelle Langford:

> Black screen, indistinct voices, the sound of laboured breathing. Cut to the image of a young man, Ismael (Bahram Radan), his body writhing uncontrollably, overtaken by a sudden violent seizure. An old woman, Gilāneh, Ismael's mother, rushes to his side to comfort him and to protect his body from further injury, but she is herself struck with such force by Ismael's flailing arm that she is propelled out of the shot. The camera remains steady, forcing the viewer to witness the trauma of this convulsing body. Undaunted by the injury inflicted on her own head, Gilāneh struggles to lift her son back onto the bed from which he had fallen during the seizure. Unblinkingly, the camera observes the heaviness of his dead weight as she wraps her arms around his body, hugging him tightly and

proceeds to heave this awkward and helpless body with all her might, with every ounce of strength left in her own stooped body, weakened by age. Her pain is palpable, but her commitment to her son's care is greater than any pain she could possibly endure. In the next shot, we see her hobbling out into the cool dawn air to wash his soiled clothes. Life goes on.[32]

Remarkable is the way in which this scene deals with Ismael's body gestures as a kind of battlefield of struggling forces and imperatives. To put it in the form of a question: what language is the body of Ismael re-membering? Not only do we see heavy convulsions, but also a living martyr who is beating his chest. As is well known, chest-beating [*sinah zani*] is part of the Shi'ite mourning ceremonies, *mātam*, performed during Muharram together with self-flagellation [*zanjir zani*]. I would like to consider the ritual of chest-beating as a 'technique of the body' as conceived by Marcel Mauss in 1934.

> By this expression I mean the ways in which from society to society men know how to use their bodies [. . .] These 'habits' do not just vary with individuals and their imitations, they vary especially between societies, educations, proprieties and fashions, prestiges [. . .] I call technique an action which is effective and traditional (and you will see that in this it is no different from a magical, religious or symbolic action).[33]

Thus, we have different registers to interpret Ismael's drumming on the chest: quite pragmatically and soberly considered, it is a desperate attempt on his part to catch his breath anew and keep himself alive. At the same time, it is a physical reaction that has been culturally ingrained into his body, a symbolic action that establishes an imaginary relationship to the real conditions.

Banietemad presents a very institution-oriented perspective on body memory. Just as there seems to be no individual memory, no outside to the collectively shared and standardized screen memories shown on TV, the convulsions of the injured and traumatized body are also articulated within normative patterns of behavior. The code for post-heroic behavior becomes a hysterical parody of the tragic governmental instrumentalization of the body. At the same time, and this should not be underestimated, the chest-beating can be interpreted as an instance of counter-memory: an expression of a body memory passed on from generation to generation, referring back to a pre-revolutionary ritual that was part of a resistant popular civil religion quite opposed to any official state religious code. As Pedram Partovi has convincingly shown, popular Iranian cinema before 1979 was full of forms that appropriated the resistant codes of civil street religion and theatrical performances.[34] Seen in this way, Ismael's convulsing body becomes a body of flickering meanings and polysemic ambiguities between official memory and counter-memory, individual and collective memory. Counter-memory is also the capacity to see in a thing what it is not, to see it other than it is, in order to break through the symbolic order. Banietemad's art of ambiguity proposes both, an archaeological and genealogical perspective on bodily gestures that have conflicting histories and refer to a present that is not at ease with itself. The chest-beating refers on the one hand to state repression and the disciplining of the body and, on the other hand, to a virtual revolution that is yet to come. It is in these moments that Banietemad's art of constructing subversive allegories becomes visible, revealing the differences between totalizing nation-building allegories and disjunctive, dialectical allegories. While the former do not tolerate ambiguities, Banietemad's *Gilāneh* consists of concrete, material fragments that resonate with resistant meanings and, as Langford emphasizes, point to the nation's wounds, 'rather than effacing them through the discourse of martyrology.'[35]

Ghost Dance or Time is Out of Joint

In his internationally acclaimed, time-looped one-long-take-horror-film *Māhi va Gorbeh/Fish and Cat* (2013), Shahram Mokri created very different procedures to generate resonances, interferences, and time overlaps in order to let counter-memories emerge.

The film is a unique combination of everyday realism and surrealism, and it is precisely in this (sur-)realism that the younger Teheran middle class rediscovered a certain attitude towards life laden with concrete fears and existential anxieties. Like hardly any other film, *Fish and Cat* was deciphered by this audience – not least on social media platforms – in terms of socio-political implications and socio-critical subtexts. I would like to highlight one of these layers. To cut a potentially endless story short, we experience in the film the appropriation of a public space, a lakeside, by a community of young campers who transform this space into a resistant heterotopia, a counter-public sphere, an underground scene. At the same time, this closed community is highly porous, vulnerable to forgotten, insisting pasts, to what Nicolas Abraham and Maria Torok call a 'crypt.' In his foreword to Torok and Abraham's *The Wolf Man's Magic Word: A Cryptonymy* (1976), Jacques Derrida points out that 'crypt' – as a transphenomenological concept for 'displacement' – does not follow the topography of the individual unconscious. As an 'effect of impossible or refused mourning,' the incorporated crypt is also part of a transgenerationally shared public structure and a secret interior to this structure.[36] This secret interior is at the same time external to the interior. Thus, it is a structural void, a *hermetically sealed space*, yet shared by everybody, and passed from generation to generation through a code that preserves the secret, safeguards this inner space, by encrypting it along a transgenerational line of muting. It is the incorporation of a structural void that keeps the hidden dead alive. The Self becomes a 'cemetery guard': 'The crypt is enclosed within the self, but as a foreign place, prohibited, excluded. The self is not the proprietor of what he is guarding.'[37]

A crypt is a traumatic scene, built on violence, and passed on as a sealed space that produces ghost effects. It is the incorporation of a transphenomenal, transgenerational X, an empty space, which – like a post-hypnotic suggestion – gives birth to phantoms. Those phantoms are invisible hands that reach out not from one's own unconscious, but from another person's, they are 'heterocryptic,'[38] and only kept alive through this transmission.

There are countless crypts and heterocryptic structures interwoven in Mokri's film, which uses the technique of spatial circling, chain linking and temporal looping to produce ghosts and overlaps between spatialized times. In addition, the intended heterotopology is thwarted by a generational conflict, which also finds its spatial expression here:

> There are two groups of people. On one side there are the Ghosts, the Cats, the Hunters, with dirty looks and unpleasant faces, in the shelter of the forest. On the other side, there are the Fishes: polite and innocent, like happy and hopeful kids, busy with their kites, in the shelter of the lake [. . .] The Hunters have their own regrets too. Unlike these youths, the Fishes, the Hunters' relationships have not been free [. . .] The Hunters belong to another generation.[39]

What connects and separates the worlds, ensures continuity, draws borders and crosses them, is the perpetual traveling of the camera. The space is opened up and fragmented as well in the interplay of *cadre* and *cache*, with a camera that returns over and over again to the same locations, and by doing so, transforming them into time forks where the spatiotemporal looped trajectories of the characters intersect. What is called 'flashback' or 'flashforward' in conventional films is replaced here by a spatial constellation, interlocking times through the continuity of the strolling camera, which simultaneously reveals and conceals what apparently takes place or has taken place or will take place. The time is 'out of joint,' 'out of order,' 'disadjusted,' one could say with Jacques Derrida (quoting Shakespeare's *Hamlet*) – '*ana-chronique*.'[40] At the same time, it seems that the disparate times and the different generational visions are held together – conjoined – by a very powerful and diabolic mechanism that keeps the characters trapped in loops, introducing delays, preventing encounters, and creating stagnation that suspends temporality, as in a condition of permanent drunkenness. The effect is one of suspension of temporality. We are thus dealing with a mythological time structure: a machine 'for the obliteration of time' as Claude Lévi-Strauss would say, a machine that 'immobilizes passing time,' transforming the diachronic totality (of watching a movie or listening to music) into 'a synchronic totality, enclosed within itself.'[41] The time in question is one that maintains homogeneity, while at the same time asserting the immutability of class structures in society.

However, there are also ghosts that actually disrupt and disturb this spatio-temporal order of immutability. The opening text insert of the film does not only tell us that the film is inspired by a real-life backwoods restaurant that served human flesh in Northern Iran, but also that the case fell into oblivion, 'similar to other stories about murder and bloodshed . . . .' There are many of these hidden in the mythological time structure of the film, untold or half-told or insisting stories of political dissidence and violence – like the shooting of Neda Agha-Soltan – that overlap in its folded structure, haunting the characters like ghosts that nest in the holes of memory. There is even a real ghost called Jamshid, a former journalist, whom we see for eight minutes in the film (1:42:00–1:50:00), communicating with the present through an interpreter girl, Nadia, a kind of medium, and through a voice recorder held by a reporter. The appearance of the ghost (long raincoat, long shawl) is a traceable marker, especially for the Iranian audience, pointing back to those more than eighty intellectuals (writers, translators, poets, political activists; among others, Dariush Forouhar and his wife Parvaneh Eskandari Forouhar) who were victims of the so-called 'Chain Murders of Iran' (*qatlhā-ye zanjīrehī*): a series of murders from 1988 to 1998 carried out by internal agents of the government. The fact that more and more critical intellectuals, like fish coming to the surface, dared to express their opinions on public media became an opportunity to 'fish them out.'

Figure 7.3 The ghost of Jamshed, a former journalist who had been 'fished.' (Source: Screen grab from *Fish and Cat*, 2013).

I want to argue that in Mokri's film the telescoping structure of memory that we have dealt with so far is transformed into a structure of interconnected, overlapping loops. Hunters, fish, and ghosts are altogether fenced in by memory snatchers. How does the absence of bodies and traces imprison our memories? What the movie investigates are chained circles of forgetting, denial, and silence built around sealed holes of memory and vanished bodies, crypts, and wounds, haunted by ghosts of history in search of a connection, a moment in time, and a witness ready to speak in their names.

Screen Memories or a *Télescopage* that is Not One

As a kind of counter-example to the counter-memories presented so far, I would like to briefly discuss a film that can be considered as a representative of some recent attempts to refashion and rebrand the 'Sacred Defense cinema' genre. I am drawing on Mohammad Hussein Mahdavian's *Istādeh dar Ghobār/Standing in the Dust* (2016), a biopic and docudrama about the Revolutionary Guard commander Ahmad Motevaselian, who disappeared in 1982 in Lebanon along with three other Iranians. The fact that he disappeared made him a role model in martyrdom and a privileged subject of cinematic martyrography. *Standing in the Dust* won several prices: the Crystal Simorgh for best film at the 34th Fajr Film Festival and the award for best film at the 14th International Resistance Film Festival in Teheran, a festival organized annually during the 'Sacred Defense Week' to commemorate the Iran-Iraq War. Indeed, in terms of technical and aesthetic standards, the film can be considered as highly sophisticated and cleverly made. We are dealing with an aesthetics that is based on a restless, shaky camera, with allegedly arbitrary movements, pretending to follow the characters (while in fact it is the other way around) – a kind of 'direct cinema'-mimicry, I would say, that one can also find in some films by Olivier Assayas. Especially noteworthy is the artful and tricky narrative perspective, which is at the same time the site of re-membering. The film makes use of what can be called 'lip-synching': a technique for matching the lip movements of a speaking or singing person with pre-recordings, a strategy that one can also find in films like Harald Bergmann's *Brinkmann's Rage* (2006) or Peter Middleton's and James Spinney's *Notes on Blindness* (2016).

Telling the story of the commander from his childhood days until his disappearance, the film can be considered as a 'docudrama.' The actors' voices are replaced by voice-overs from family members, friends, and, in some rare instances, by real audio clips of Motevaselian's speeches. There are also eyewitness depictions from other commanders, including Mohammad Ebrahim Hemmat, killed in Operation Kheibar, the 1984 offensive in the southern marshes, during which the Iraqis made heavy use of chemical weapons, and Mohsen Vezvaie, killed in the 1982 Operation Beit ol-Moqaddas as part of the liberation of Khorramshahr. The film makes every effort to strive for authenticity by trans-visualizing the oral eye-witness reports with ostensible accuracy.

The terms 'bearing witness' and 'testimony' are crucial in this respect, since the Islamic term *shahīd* – often translated as *martyr* – derives from the Quranic Arabic word for *witness*, as is also the case in Greek, where *martus* – the root word for *martyr* – means: 'the one who bears witness.' Accordingly, the film puts the viewer in a cleverly constructed position of an eye witness, or alternatively ear witness, of the past. This access to the past is also reinforced through a constant tele-lens perspective on past events from the present site of re-membering. In this way, the spectator is able to see these events like a witness having 'first-hand' access through a spyglass perspective that creates an intense and intimate relationship of co-belonging between past and present, akin to a continuous transgenerational broadcasting. At the same time, this constructed witness viewpoint is kept at a mystifying distance: events, especially the activities of 'shahīd' Motevaselian, are partly hidden behind obstacles blocking the sight, thereby elevating the moments in question to a mystical sphere full of details to be added by the spectator's imagination.

The events are simultaneously 'here and now' and 'there and then,' and the aura of the *shahīd* is generated through establishing transgenerational contact and withdrawing it at the same time. Nevertheless, the whole device remains for the sake of continuity between past and present; and in this sense it is the exact

Figure 7.4 The activities of 'shahīd' Motevaselian are partly hidden behind obstacles blocking the sight. (Source: Screen grab from *Standing in the Dust*, 2016).

opposite of what Benjamin conceives as *télescopage*, which never assumes a continuous timeline between past and present but the force of ceaseless change: many pasts and many presents. Decisive for Benjamin is the moment (*Jetzt-Zeit*; *Jetzt der Erkennbarkeit*) and its retroactive force calling into question the historical narrative of the victorious. 'The class struggle,' writes Benjamin in his 'Theses on The Philosophy of History' (often also referred to as 'On the Concept of History'), 'is a fight for the crude and material things without which no refined and spiritual things could exist.'[42] The class struggle involves not only the labor and pain of the oppressed, but also the force of dialectical critique, which calls into question the memory created by the oppressor. As Derrida would say: 'simultaneity is the myth of a total reading or description, promoted to the status of a regulatory ideal.'[43] *Standing in the Dust* maintains exactly this simultaneity and continuity between past and present, reality and ideology, fact and fiction. This 'total recall' covers the harsh realities with revolutionary rhetorics and semiotics, avoiding frictions between political promises and social realities, upholding a revolution without revolutionaries: a permanent completed revolution, abounding in realized ideals that prevent the development of what can be called with Solanas and Getino a 'liberated personality.'[44]

Viewed in this light, the film could be related to many (post-)classical films from the 'Sacred Defense' repertoire such as Ebrahim Hatamikia's *Az Karkheh tā Rāin/From Karkheh to Rhine* (1992), a film about a *basījī* suffering from leukaemia who is treated in a clinic on the Rhine. The protagonist's war memories are constructed as homogeneous spaces that are continuously connected to the present. This is particularly evident in the scene in which Hatamikia also attempts an alleged telescoping: the terminally ill protagonist is pushed into the MRI scanner tube and hears the drumming of the machine, which blends with the remembered chest-beating on the battlefield of war. Before he passes away towards the end of the movie, the patient lying in his sickbed starts to beat his chest rhythmically with his fist, while remembering heroic actions from the gas-infested battlefield and listening to the screams of his newborn baby, played for him by his wife from a tape recorder, thereby fueling emotions even more as it also evokes Khomeini's messages and sermons, which also circulated on tapes during the revolution. At stake is the question of intergenerational transmission – broadcasting – of Islamic identity. Incidentally, we also see these iconic audio cassettes in the opening credits of *Standing in the Dust*, this time with the voices of Motevaselian and his contemporaries.

In the year 2016, when *Standing in the Dust* was released and awarded prizes, another archive was made available to the Iranian public, an archive that pointed to an alternative post-revolutionary history of the present, consisting of counter-memories that unmasked and debunked the memories of *Standing in the Dust* as *screen memories* in the literal sense: as memories that show (screen) something by covering (screening) something else. In that same year indeed, the 'Montazeri audio tapes' were made public on the latter's official website, run by his family and followers, documenting a meeting Montazeri held in 1988 with judiciary officials involved in the mass executions during that period. On these audio tapes one can hear Montazeri criticizing the 'death commission' and declaring that this state crime discredits the entire judicial system of the Islamic Republic. The release of this audio recording from nearly three decades before not only reopened old wounds, but also made the present vulnerable to forgotten pasts.

Counter-memories have the potential to destabilize the homogeneous memory, whether in politics or aesthetics. They emphasize what Foucault calls the *principle of heterogeneity* [. . .]: 'The history of some is not the history of others [. . .] What looks like right, law, or obligation from the point of view of power looks like the abuse of power, violence, and exaction when it is seen from the viewpoint of the new discourse.'[45] It is precisely this principle of heterogeneity that is being challenged anew nowadays against the background of the coronavirus pandemic:

> The regime in Iran has taken the opportunity provided by this political environment to connect the current coronavirus pandemic to the memories and experiences of past national traumas in the hope of positioning all these crises on a single ideological arc that spans the lifetime of the Islamic Republic, right up to the present. This ideological work is manifested particularly in the transposition of iconographic motifs from the time of the Iran-Iraq War (1980–1988) to the current pandemic, such as passing under the Quran, an act that in state propaganda is inextricably associated with marching to the war front [. . .] By framing the current crisis in the context of previous struggles, the government creates a unifying narrative of resistance that traverses space and time.[46]

One poster even shows Morteza Avini, who died in 1993 in a landmine explosion, looking through the viewfinder of his camera as if witnessing the current events surrounding the coronavirus and reporting on the heroic struggle of the sacred health defenders from the beyond of an (idyllic) past. Thus, we have here a telescoping with a reversed sign: the present time is seen through a past projecting the same struggle, the same trenches and 'chronicles of victory' again and again on completely different conditions. The telescopings, counter-memories, and impure memories described in this chapter work exactly against this grain: they do not use the post-catastrophic collapse of space and time to transcend these dimensions and negate change in the name of a completed revolution, but they intervene and work from an emergency room that has its exact place in the now, avoiding any simultaneity between past and present, re-opening archives of lost, deviated traces, as part of an unfinished revolution. *Simultaneity is the myth of a total reading* (Derrida).

Notes

1. Shahriar Mandanipour, *Censoring an Iranian Love Story* (New York: Vintage Books 2009), p. 114.
2. See Siegfried Kracauer, *History. The Last Things Before the Last* (Princeton, NJ: Princeton University Press 2013), p. 167.
3. Negar Mottahedeh, *Displaced Allegories. Post-Revolutionary Iranian Cinema* (Durham, NC and London: Duke University Press 2008), p. 56.
4. It is known that Makhmalbaf, himself a fervent supporter of the Islamic Revolution, actively advocated at first such a sensorial re-education program. His first films were shown in mosques and prisons, and before the revolution he was himself imprisoned as a pro-Islamist activist for having attacked a policeman with a knife. He then became a state filmmaker only to turn later on into a critical dissident.
5. Mottahedeh, *Displaced Allegories*, p. 3.
6. Fredric Jameson, 'Interview with Sara Danius and Stefan Jonsson,' in *Jameson on Jameson: Conversations on Cultural Marxism*, ed. Ian Bichana (Durham, NC: Duke University Press, 2007), p. 169.
7. Orkideh Behrouzan, *Prozak Diaries. Psychiatry and Generational Memory in Iran* (Stanford, CA: Stanford University Press 2016), p. 33.
8. Ibid., p. 183.
9. Ibid., p. 21.
10. Ibid., p. 99.
11. Ibid., p. 27.
12. Ibid.
13. Ibid., p. 30.
14. Ibid.
15. Michel Foucault, *Archaeology of Knowledge*, trans. A. M. Sheridan Smith (London and New York: Routledge Classics 1989), p. 145.
16. Behrouzan, *Prozak Diaries*, p. 38.
17. Hamid Naficy, *A Social History of Iranian Cinema, Vol. 4: The Globalizing Era 1984–2010* (Durham, NC and London: Duke University Press 2012), p. 12ff.
18. The Shi'a pilgrimage site of Karbala – a stretch of desert originally – represents the site of a martyrdom that occurred in the year 680, when Imam Hussein, the grandson of the Prophet Mohammad, and his supporters sacrificed their lives in battle with the Omayyad caliph Yazid I and his soldiers. The events in question are historically attested to a certain extent only and were expanded mythopoetically to include loyalty, betrayal, the motive of the fall, and an ultimate martyrdom, namely of Hussein himself. The so-called 'Karbala paradigm,' or rather Karbala doctrine, became the prevailing matrix of remembrance through which the Shi'a architects of the theocracy fused the revolution and the religious war into a continuum and established a logical connection between them. In line with Hayden White's distinction between elementary forms of history writing, one can associate

the Karbala narrative with the form of tragedy: it acquires its meaning through the representation of a terrible past with the aim of preventing its return in the future. This master narrative has also been a component in several sub-genres within the 'sacred defense cinema'. See Hayden White, *Metahistory. The Historical Imagination in Nineteenth-Century Europe* (Baltimore, MD and London: Johns Hopkins University Press 1973), p. 9.
19. See Kaveh Abbasian, 'The Iran-Iraq War and the Sacred Defence Cinema' (lecture given on 16 February), in *Journal of the Iran Society*, Vol. 2, No. 16 (September 2017), pp. 34–40, p. 36.
20. Mohamad Tavakoli-Targhi, 'The Emergence of *Clerico-Engineering* as a Form of Governance in Iran,' in *Iran Nameh*, Vol. 27, Nos. 2–3 (2012), p. 14f.
21. Thomas Bauer, *Die Kultur der Ambiguität. Eine andere Geschichte des Islams* (Berlin: Insel 2011).
22. Pedram Partovi, *Popular Iranian Cinema before the Revolution* (London and New York: Routledge 2017), p. 21.
23. André Bazin, 'In Defense of Mixed Cinema,' in André Bazin, *What is Cinema?* Essays selected and translated by Hugh Gray (Berkeley, Los Angeles and London: University of California Press 2005), pp. 53–75.
24. 'Ideology represents the imaginary relationship of individuals to their real conditions of existence' – Louis Althusser, 'Ideology and Ideological State Apparatuses,' in Louis Althusser, Lenin and Philosophy and other Essays (New York: Monthly Review Press 2001), pp. 121–76.
25. Asef Bayat, *Street Politics. Poor People's Movements in Iran* (New York: Columbia University Press 1997), p. 43.
26. Walter Benjamin, *The Arcades Project*, trans. Howard Eiland and Kevin McLaughlin (Cambridge, MA and London: Harvard University Press 1999), p. 471.
27. Paul Virilio, *Negative Horizon. An Essay in Dromoscopy* (London and New York: Continuum 2005), pp. 106, 112f.
28. The translations are taken directly from the film's official subtitles.
29. Arash Davari, 'A Return to Which Self?: Ali Shari'ati and Frantz Fanon on the Political Ethics of Insurrectionary Violence,' in *Comparative Studies of South Asia, Africa and the Middle East*, Vol. 34, No. 1 (2014), pp. 86–105, p. 89.
30. See Sigmund Freud, 'Screen Memories,' in *Standard Edition*, Vol. 3 (London: Hogarth Press 1953ff.), pp. 301–22.
31. Michelle Langford, *Allegory in Iranian Cinema. The Aesthetics of Poetry and Resistance* (London and New York: Bloomsbury Academic 2019), p. 170.
32. Ibid., p. 169.
33. Marcel Mauss, 'Techniques of the Body,' in *Economy and Society*, Vol. 2, No. 1 (1973), pp. 70–88.
34. See note 22 above.
35. Langford, *Allegory in Iranian Cinema*, p. 191.
36. Jacques Derrida, 'Fors: The Anglish Words of Nicolas Abraham and Maria Torok' (Foreword), in Nicolas Abraham and Maria Torok, *The Wolf Man's Magic Word: A Cryptonymy*, trans. Nicholas Rand (Minneapolis: University of Minnesota Press 1985), pp. xi–xlviii, p. xxi.

37. Ibid., pp. xiv, xxxv.
38. Ibid., p. xxxi.
39. Majid Eslami, 'The Lake against the Forest.' Unpublished manuscript based on a talk that was given by Majid Eslami at the 2016 Basel conference Image under Construction. Revolution of Forms in Iranian Cinema before and after 1979.
40. Jacques Derrida, *Specters of Marx. The State of the Debt, the Work of Mourning and the New International* (New York and London: Routledge 2006), pp. 20, 25.
41. Claude Lévi-Strauss, *Mythologica I: The Raw and the Cooked* (New York: Harper & Row 1969), p. 16.
42. Walter Benjamin, 'On the Concept of History,' in Selected Writings 4, eds. Howard Eiland and Michael W. Jennings (Cambridge, MA: Belknap Press of Harvard University Press 2003), p. 391.
43. Jacques Derrida, 'Force and Signification,' in *Writing and Difference*, trans. Alan Bass (London: RKP 1978), p. 24.
44. Fernando Solanas and Octavio Getino, 'Toward a Third Cinema,' in *Cinéaste*, Vol. 4, No. 3: Latin American Militant Cinema (Winter 1970–1), pp. 1–10, p. 3.
45. Michel Foucault, *Society Must Be Defended* (New York: Picador 2003), pp. 69ff.
46. Kevin L. Schwart and Olmo Gölz, 'Going to War with the Coronavirus and Maintaining the State of Resistance in Iran,' in Merik – Middle East Research and Information Project (2020), https://merip.org/2020/09/going-to-war-with-the-coronavirus-and-maintaining-the-state-of-resistance-in-iran/?fbclid=IwAR0M5fRDFJcxfEEO75cfkf-tTv8y3cQtwTgEA-bLqUTp9R1cRvV_Rl8boI4 (last accessed 15 October 2020).

References

Abbasian, Kaveh, 'The Iran-Iraq War and the Sacred Defence Cinema' (lecture given on 16 February), in *Journal of the Iran Society*, Vol. 2, No. 16 (September 2017).

Althusser, Louis, 'Ideology and Ideological State Apparatuses,' in Louis Althusser, *Lenin and Philosophy and other Essays* (New York: Monthly Review Press 2001).

Bauer, Thomas, *Die Kultur der Ambiguität. Eine andere Geschichte des Islams* (Berlin: Insel 2011).

Bayat, Asef, *Street Politics. Poor People's Movements in Iran* (New York: Columbia University Press 1997).

Bazin, André, 'In Defense of Mixed Cinema,' in André Bazin, *What is Cinema?* Essays selected and translated by Hugh Gray (Berkeley, Los Angeles and London: University of California Press 2005).

Behrouzan, Orkideh, *Prozak Diaries. Psychiatry and Generational Memory in Iran* (Stanford, CA: Stanford University Press 2016).

Benjamin, Walter, *The Arcades Project*, trans. Howard Eiland and Kevin McLaughlin (Cambridge, MA and London: Harvard University Press 1999).

Benjamin, Walter, 'On the Concept of History,' in *Selected Writings 4*, eds. Howard Eiland and Michael W. Jennings (Cambridge, MA: Belknap Press of Harvard University Press 2003).

Davari, Arash, 'A Return to Which Self?: Ali Shari'ati and Frantz Fanon on the Political Ethics of Insurrectionary Violence,' in *Comparative Studies of South Asia, Africa and the Middle East*, Vol. 34, No. 1 (2014), pp. 86–105.

Derrida, Jacques, 'Force and Signification,' in *Writing and Difference*, trans. Alan Bass (London: RKP 1978).

Derrida, Jacques, 'Fors: The Anglish Words of Nicolas Abraham and Maria Torok' (Foreword), in Nicolas Abraham and Maria Torok, *The Wolf Man's Magic Word: A Cryptonymy*, trans. Nicholas Rand (Minneapolis: University of Minnesota Press 1985), pp. xi–xlviii, p. xxi.

Derrida, Jacques, *Specters of Marx. The State of the Debt, the Work of Mourning and the New International* (New York and London: Routledge 2006), pp. 20, 25.

Eslami, Majid, 'The Lake against the Forest.' Unpublished manuscript based on a talk that was given by Majid Eslami at the 2016 Basel conference Image under Construction. Revolution of Forms in Iranian Cinema before and after 1979.

Foucault, Michel, *Archaeology of Knowledge*, trans. A. M. Sheridan Smith (London and New York: Routledge Classics 1989).

Foucault, Michel, *Society Must Be Defended* (New York: Picador 2003).

Freud, Sigmund, 'Screen Memories,' in *Standard Edition*, Vol. 3 (London: Hogarth Press 1953ff.), pp. 301–22.

Jameson, Fredric, 'Interview with Sara Danius and Stefan Jonsson,' in Ian Bichana (ed.), *Jameson on Jameson: Conversations on Cultural Marxism* (Durham, NC: Duke University Press, 2007).

Kracauer, Siegfried, *History. The Last Things Before the Last* (Princeton, NJ: Princeton University Press 2013).

Langford, Michelle, *Allegory in Iranian Cinema. The Aesthetics of Poetry and Resistance* (London and New York: Bloomsbury Academic 2019).

Lévi-Strauss, Claude, *Mythologica I: The Raw and the Cooked* (New York: Harper & Row 1969).

Mandanipour, Shahriar, *Censoring an Iranian Love Story* (New York: Vintage Books 2009).

Mauss, Marcel, 'Techniques of the Body,' in *Economy and Society*, Vol. 2, No. 1 (1973), pp. 70–88.

Mottahedeh, Negar, *Displaced Allegories. Post-Revolutionary Iranian Cinema* (Durham, NC and London: Duke University Press 2008).

Naficy, Hamid, *Social History of Iranian Cinema, Vol. 4: The Globalizing Era 1984–2010* (Durham, NC and London: Duke University Press 2012).

Partovi, Pedram, *Popular Iranian Cinema before the Revolution* (London and New York: Routledge 2017), p. 21.

Schwart, Kevin L. and Olmo Gölz, 'Going to War with the Coronavirus and Maintaining the State of Resistance in Iran,' in Merik – Middle East Research and Information Project (2020), https://merip.org/2020/09/going-to-war-with-the-coronavirus-and-maintaining-the-state-of-resistance-in-iran/?fbclid=IwAR0M5fRDFJcxfEEO75cfkf-tTv8y3cQtwTgEA-bLqUTp9R1cRvV_Rl8boI4 (last accessed 15 October 2020).

Solanas, Fernando and Octavio Getino, 'Toward a Third Cinema,' in *Cinéaste*, Vol. 4, No. 3: Latin American Militant Cinema (Winter 1970–1), pp. 1–10.

Tavakoli-Targhi Mohamad, 'The Emergence of *Clerico-Engineering* as a Form of Governance in Iran,' in *Iran Nameh*, Vol. 27, Nos. 2–3 (2012).

Virilio, Paul, *Negative Horizon. An Essay in Dromoscopy* (London and New York: Continuum 2005).

White, Hayden, *Metahistory. The Historical Imagination in Nineteenth-Century Europe* (Baltimore, MD and London: Johns Hopkins University Press 1973).

8. SEEKING LOVE IN THE INTERSTICES: ACOUSMATIC LISTENING AS COUNTER-MEMORY IN ABBAS KIAROSTAMI'S *SHIRIN* (2008)

Michelle Langford

Abbas Kiarostami's 2008 film *Shirin* adopted a novel approach to fictional feature filmmaking. While the film ostensibly tells the classic Persian tale of 'Khosrow and Shirin,' inspired by Nezami Ganjavi's epic poem, it withholds any vision of this story from view. Instead, for the duration of the film's ninety minutes, the camera is trained on the faces of 109 actresses – all Iranian except one – as they are seated in a cinema apparently watching a film.[1] We experience this 'film-within-a-film,' which never existed as such, only acousmatically through dialogue, music, and sound effects that emanate from the interstices of the off-screen space. Throughout the film, the faces of the actresses on screen seem to cue us to the emotional undulations of the story. I say 'seem to' for the accompanying love story of Khosrow and Shirin was only decided upon after the visuals had been filmed. The actresses were simply asked to think of something sad, like a melodramatic movie, while the crew created lighting effects to mimic light being reflected onto their faces from a cinema screen. The only stimuli were a few dots that the crew moved around behind the camera, providing something for their eyes to track. It was Kiarostami who later invested these visible expressions with meaning in the editing process, choosing shots that would correspond with the various affects generated by the soundtrack.

Understandably, Kiarostami's visual concentration on the act of spectatorship has engendered a significant amount of scholarship that focuses largely on questions of vision, gender, and spectatorship. Scholars, such as Sara Saljoughi have productively analyzed how the female spectators pictured within Kiarostami's film return a female gaze that has largely been absent from Iranian cinema in the post-revolutionary era.[2] Similarly, Asbjørn Grønstadt has argued that the dominance of the close-up of female faces allows the women's on-screen gazes to connect with our own, and that the film's 'convoluted interaction of gazes generates [. . .] a *cinema of ethical intimacy*, an existential space of spectatorial emancipation and optic communality.'[3] This scholarly emphasis on the visual aspects of the film has perhaps been 'directed' by Kiarostami himself, for in interview, he once said of the film '[t]he story was not important to me [. . .] I believe if you dare let go of the story, you will come across a new thing which is the Cinema itself. In fact, I suggest you let go of the story and just keep your eyes on the screen.'[4]

Without taking my eyes from the screen entirely, I propose to take into account not only the age-old story of embattled love told in *Shirin*, but to pay attention to the off-screen sounds, voices, and music that tell tales of passionate love in a realm that is always withheld, hidden from view. While Kiarostami's aim may well have been to call upon viewers to pay attention to the screen, at the same time I think his film strategically counters this hegemonic privileging of vision. Indeed, the first words of the film, spoken by the title character Shirin implore us to listen: 'Listen to me sisters. It is time for my story now.' This, and the dominant role played by the female voice throughout the film, suggests that we should not simply take Kiarostami at his word. We should instead heed the words of the female narrator. I argue that the film may well inspire in its viewers another posture – a casting down of our eyes and an opening of our ears so that we may hear the story a of passionate love that has long been forbidden from Iran's cinema screens. Perhaps Kiarostami's film even encourages us to take part in the practice of *falgoosh*, an active listening-in on the conversations of strangers in order to interpret in them some omen: good or bad.[5] I ask, what can this listening in on the story of Khosrow and Shirin tell us about the place of love in Iranian cinema? I argue that by rendering the love story acousmatically, in the sense theorized by Michel Chion,[6] Kiarostami makes audible a veritable 'blind spot' in post-revolutionary Iranian cinema, which has, with few exceptions, largely effaced the very topic of earthly and erotic love, a topic that has been central to Persian poetry and literature across the ages. In this context, therefore, *Shirin* performs an act of counter-memory, one that reactivates the traces of an epic-poetic tradition and in doing so challenges the hegemony of censorship. *Shirin* does this – as others have already pointed out – by challenging the hegemony of patriarchal vision through the film's emphasis on female spectatorship, but, beyond this, I assert that Kiarostami's film also challenges the hegemony of vision itself by activating the female voice in such a way that she is able to both voice and embody her own desires. In order to pursue this line of inquiry, we must open our ears, but before doing so, let's consider the place of worldly love and eroticism in post-revolutionary Iranian cinema.

Love in Post-Revolutionary Iranian Cinema

In post-revolutionary Iranian cinema, overt depictions of physical love and desire have been few and far between. Iran's strict censorship regulations limit the ways in which loving, intimate relationships between men and women may be presented. In the wake of the revolution, the Ministry of Culture and Islamic Guidance introduced a long list of prohibitions that would inadvertently curtail the treatment of love and eroticism in film. Under the regulations, filmmakers are prevented from depicting women in tight or revealing clothing or showing physical contact between unrelated men and women. Even the exchange of desiring gazes and amorous dialogue risks crossing a red line.[7] Indeed, the removal of any hint of erotic love from the screen was central to the task of 'purging' and 'purifying' the film industry after the revolution so that it could be made 'modest' and brought into line with the values of the new nation. In part, this was to counter the perceived 'amorality' and sexual explicitness of the commercial cinema of the pre-revolutionary period. However, despite this imposition of modesty, love and intimacy have not remained entirely absent from the screen, for, as I have argued elsewhere, Iranian filmmakers have found ways of indirectly suggesting moments of tenderness, intimacy, and even eroticism through allusion, metaphor, allegory, and other forms of suggestive imagery.[8] Where male-female intimacy occurs, it is typically relegated to the off-screen space, left aside to be conjured up in the mind of the viewer. As we will see, in *Shirin* Kiarostami has prioritized this off-screen space, requiring a very active engagement by the spectator whose sensorium is split between seeing and hearing.

Despite the various prohibitions of censorship, however, Iranian films are not entirely bereft of sensuality. The kinds of directly erotic 'visual pleasures' associated with Hollywood-style filmmaking are displaced into other kinds of affective registers, including the acousmatic register employed in *Shirin*. Beyond the various displacements of eroticism from the visual realm, some filmmakers have drawn inspiration from Persian poetry in their search for ways of creatively dealing with romantic love. Indeed, as Shahla Haeri has argued, despite a legal discourse that would forbid such material from the screen 'the "erotic" discourse that is ever so subtly embedded in Persian poetry and popular culture' has thrived 'below the surface.'[9] In *Shirin*, Kiarostami appears to have done exactly that.

During the years of the Iran-Iraq War (1980–8), Iranian films remained relatively austere, but in the years that followed filmmakers turned to lighter subjects, including love and relationships. The rise of female-centered melodramatic films in the 1990s is clear evidence of this, although just like the prototypical love stories of Persian literature, in such films love tends to be figured in unfulfilling and often tragic terms.[10] One early attempt to break the taboo against love was Mohsen Makhmalbaf's highly poetic *Nobat-e 'Asheghī/A Time for Love* (1991), which was premiered at the 1991 Fajr Film Festival along with a number of other films about love. As Atwood has shown, Makhmalbaf's film, which included an allusive 'sex scene,' became a trigger-point for heated debates among politicians, intellectuals, the public, and the clerical establishment about the role of cinema in society. What many viewers regarded as a fairly obvious reference to adulterous sexual relations generated something of a moral panic among conservatives over this infiltration of 'cheap love' into the film industry.[11] Discourses around cinema since the establishment of the Islamic Republic had been founded on the 'injection theory,' a theory based on the assumption that film has the power to 'inject' potentially undesirable attitudes into its spectators. It is largely the injection theory that is used to justify stringent censorship, for viewers must be protected from dangerous images and ideas.[12] Thus, the film's supposed representation of earthly love, rather than spiritual love, posed a threat to the moral fabric of the nation. However, as Atwood highlights, Islamic scholar Abdolkarim Soroush, who undertook a close analysis of the film, was the first to consider the film's romantic qualities in terms of spiritual or mystical love, a 'reading' that was further expounded by Makhmalbaf himself in an essay collection he published in 1993.[13] In response to the public's outrage over the 'sex scene,' Makhmalbaf maintained that the 'film never consummates' the affair between the married woman and her lover, also emphasizing that the treatment of love remains 'within the realm of mysticism.'[14] While there may be a degree of sleight of hand at work in Makhmalbaf's mystical reading, designed to throw critics off the scent of other possible intentions, according to Atwood, the debates about the film's treatment of love are evidence not only of the film's textual openness that allowed for multiple interpretations, they also revealed something important about the kind of 'viewing practices that were developing in the Islamic Republic at the time and that encouraged viewers to find meaning in codes and allegories.' 'In such a sense,' continues Atwood, 'the "sex scene" in *Time of Love* becomes a fulfilment of some viewers' desires rather than simply a strategy on the part of the director.'[15] Such an argument might appear to reverse the 'injection theory' by granting viewers interpretive power over the images. Although they approach the question of love and desire in Iranian cinema from different perspectives, both Atwood and Haeri highlight the tensions between legal and erotic discourses. In fact, as Haeri states:

> I believe that historically there has been tension, ebbing and flowing, between the legal discourse that restricts gender relations and the gaze, *ahkam-i nigah*, and the erotic discourse that subverts the very same regulations by encouraging the opposite, the culturally meaningful play of glances, *nazar bazi*.[16]

Shirin may be considered to activate a different kind of 'play of glances' between the on-screen female viewers that we see and our own gaze that longs to see the 'images' that emanate from the sonic realm. But between such discourses emerges a third, which is the rich legacy of literary, poetic, and mystical traditions that informs many treatments and interpretations of love in Iranian cinema. While such a legacy, as Haeri and others have noted, has the capacity to counter the hegemony of the legal discourse, it does not go so far as subverting the regulations entirely, in part because those literary traditions typically figure love as ambivalent and in metaphorical rather than in literal terms: love is frequently left unrequited, unattainable, or unconsummated, allowing it as Makhmalbaf has suggested to transcend the physical realm. In fact, one of the fundamental characteristics of a form of Persian lyrical love poetry known as the *ghazal* is precisely the 'blurring of the distinction between sacred and profane love.'[17] It is in this sense that the traces of such poetic traditions, particularly those that emphasize the highly ambivalent nature of love, return as counter-memories in post-revolutionary Iranian cinema, and more specifically within the interstitial space between sound and image in *Shirin*.

The influence of classical Persian literature and poetry on cinematic treatments of love in Iranian cinema has a long history, dating back to the silent era which boasted numerous filmic adaptations of classical Persian love stories such as 'Khosrow and Shirin' and 'Leila and Majnun,' many of which were produced in the Parsi-owned studios of India. Indeed, as Pedram Partovi has demonstrated, such 'courtly texts' became templates for the narrative and thematic treatment of love in commercial cinemas across the Persianate world, including Iran, India, and Turkey, which thrived during the veritable 'golden age' of popular film entertainment in the 1950s–1970s. As he argues, the representation of erotic love in these films follows conventional narrative patterns in which the 'seductive appeal and even nobility' of erotic love is eventually 'stifled by or subsumed under familial devotion and obligation'.[18] But despite the narrative drive aimed at eliminating socially transgressive sexuality, as Partovi writes '[m]ore often than not, cinematic appropriations of courtly "texts" and practices concerning erotic love and heroism would also serve as the "pleasure-seeking" and "idolatrous" outside of prohibitive clerical or legalist interpretations of worldly existence.'[19] Thus, the tensions that Haeri and Atwood have identified between legal and erotic discourses in the cinema of the post-revolutionary period cannot be seen merely as a consequence of censorship, but should be considered part of a much longer cultural tradition. We must, therefore, consider Kiarostami's film in conversation with this long tradition. Let's now listen more closely to the film.

Staging for the Ear: Seeking Love in the Interstices

'Your eyes are blindfolded, open up your ears! Just follow our voices!' says one of Shirin's handmaidens. I see neither the source of the sound nor Shirin, the person to whom the words are presumably directed. In the absence of an image, the voice spills forth from what I imagine to be an off-screen diegetic world, a world to which I am blind. This leads me to experience these words as a direct address, a directive for me also to open my ears and follow the voices. This voice that emanates from somewhere beyond the screen functions like the sonic equivalent of a baroque *trompe l'oeil* in which an image seems to spill out from two-dimensional space. But it is not my eye that is being tricked. We might call this a trompe l'oreille, a trick of the ear. This effect of trompe l'oreille means that as I listen, not only do I experience a verbal direct address but my body is also enveloped in a kind of sonic *mise-en-scène*. I perceive the story unfolding in time and situated in space, together with textures, shapes, colors, even tastes all inflected by the volume, pitch, and timbre of sound effects and music. This soundscape provides a fitting stage upon which this turbulent story of love, desire, and loss may unfold. In displacing the love story onto the soundtrack, *Shirin* harkens back to a long tradition of verbal recitation of poetry in Iranian culture. However, the complex sound design goes far beyond this oral tradition and, in doing so, an entire world, a cinematic world, is staged for my ear. Kiarostami's film and Rahmanian's screenplay capitalizes on the dramatic potential embedded in the source text, which is rendered cinematically.[20] Indeed, Peter Chelkowski refers to Nezami's epic poem as a 'closet drama' which bears the artistic and structural 'essentials of any dramatic form' and therefore making it eminently suitable for filmic adaptation.[21]

In order to unpack the various dimensions of the soundtrack and its effects, I engage in a practice of acousmatic listening. The term 'acousmatic' refers to any heard sound whose source remains unseen. This split between seeing and hearing can render sound ambiguous by virtue of the lack of a visual referent that would link it to an object or situate it in time and space. In reference to cinema, the film sound theorist Michel Chion uses the term to refer to off-screen sound; the sounds and voices that emanate from the space beyond the frame, but which may still be a part of the diegetic world. But for him, what is interesting about acousmatic sound is how it might call upon us to engage in different modes of listening. According to Chion there are three main modes of listening: '*causal listening, semantic listening,* and *reduced listening.*'[22] When we hear an acousmatic sound, causal listening might first be activated as we attempt to identify the cause of the sound. Semantic listening refers to how we interpret sounds according to a pre-existing code or language. When undertaking semantic listening, we attempt to determine what sounds 'mean.' In a reduced listening mode, we focus 'on the traits of the sound itself, independent of its cause and its meaning.'[23] This would be similar to adopting a purely formalist approach to film analysis. As Chion highlights, however, it is almost impossible to engage in reduced listening independently of 'a sound's actual content, its source, and its meaning.' For Chion, '[r]educed listening and the acousmatic situation share something in common.' He writes: 'Acousmatic sound draws our attention to sound traits normally hidden from us by the simultaneous sight of the causes – hidden because this sight reinforces the perception of certain elements of the sound and obscures others. The acousmatic truly allows sound to reveal itself in all its dimensions.'[24] To Chion's three modes of listening, I would like to add a fourth that is relevant to *Shirin*. Just as Chion highlights the fact that we hear not only with our ears but also with our minds,[25] inspired by Vivian Sobchack's theorization of cinesthesia, a multi-modal embodied form of spectatorship, I propose that *Shirin*'s use of acousmatic sound encourages a kind of affective listening in which we listen also with our bodies and through which a range of sense perceptions are activated.[26] Let us now, therefore, open our bodies to the richly evocative soundscape of *Shirin*.

Shirin opens with a credit sequence, which is accompanied by a rather melodramatic non-diegetic orchestral score. Already, this seems atypical of a film by Abbas Kiarostami, who rarely used non-diegetic music in his films. The music, however, seems a fitting accompaniment to the images, pages of an illustrated manuscript depicting scenes from the story of Khosrow and Shirin.

These might be familiar to Iranian viewers, but the illustrated scenes of love and war depicted should be fairly legible for most viewers no matter their background. These illustrations serve a double purpose. First, they provide the only actual visualization of the story that will be shown in the film and, second, they carry the credits for the main creative team that worked on the film. The last title card, an image of Shirin lying close beside the slain Khosrow, blood

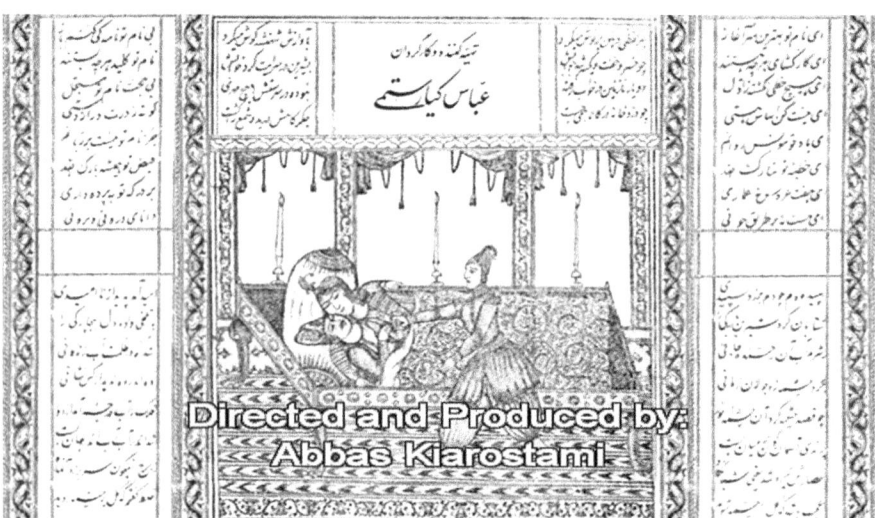

Figure 8.1 Credit sequence depicting scenes from *Khoshrow and Shirin*. (Source: Screen grab from *Shirin*, 2008).

streaming from his belly, announces the name of the director and producer, Abbas Kiarostami. It is this image of Shirin, mourning her lover, their bodies entwined, and on the precipice of her own death, that viewers will take with them into the veritable darkness of the movie theater as the film proper begins.

As the melodramatic music reaches a crescendo, the image suddenly cuts to a shot of two female spectators and the melodramatic music begins to fade away. At this point, I close my eyes so that I may experience the narrative scene as it is offered up to my ears in the sonic equivalent of living color. What do my ears 'see'? The clanking of an old metal lock; a creaking door; the slow and steady click-clack of footsteps on a stone floor; dripping water. Click-clack, click-clack. The footsteps continue, descending into the depths of a dark, cavernous space. The sounds immerse me in this space, language a poor substitute for what I hear. I feel the cold, damp atmosphere on my skin. I smell the bitterness of musty air. I taste the tang of rusting metal, and the strange sweetness of fresh blood. I continue to track the footsteps. In the distance, I hear the faint cries of women wailing, always accompanied by a drip, drip, drip, drip and a click-clack, click-clack. With each step, I am led through the darkness, a single flame perhaps lighting our way. With each step, I am brought closer and closer to the wailing women and, eventually, before my ears I behold Khosrow's bloody and lifeless body, an after-image lingering from the title sequence. It is only now that a female voice begins to speak: 'Listen to me, my sisters. It is time for my story now. Right here, by the lifeless body of Khosrow.'

Mohammad Rahmanian's screenplay for *Shirin*, ostensibly 'inspired' by Nezami's epic poem, was adapted from a version of the story by contemporary Iranian writer Farideh Golbou. However, while both Nezami's tale and Golbou's retelling unfold in chronological order, the film shuffles the temporal sequence of events. *Shirin* begins near the very end of the story, just after Khosrow has been assassinated at the behest of his own son Shiruya. It ends as Shirin takes her own life, finding the loss of her beloved Khosrow and the prospect of a forced marriage to Shiruya unbearable. In between, various episodes from the story occur as flashbacks from Shirin's perspective and we occasionally return to this opening scene from which new episodes of the story are launched in flashback. As the acousmatic soundscape described above suggests, the narrative perspective in the film has been realigned so that Shirin, rather than Khosrow, becomes the focal point. Indeed, one of the innovations of Rahmanian's screenplay is to unfold the story through Shirin's perspective, either from the vantage point of her own immanent death, or as a voice-over explaining events as they unfold in flashback. However, even before she speaks her first words, we closely follow her in an acousmatic tracking shot that already aligns us with her perspective. Although commentators have noted that in Nezami's epic Shirin is depicted as a strong woman capable of resisting Khosrow's tendency towards moral weakness,[27] Nezami's tale takes its dramatic point of departure from the world of

Khosrow's imagination. Early in the story, Khosrow's grandfather (Khosrow Anushirvan) comes to him in a dream to prophesize that Khosrow the younger will achieve four great things in his lifetime: he will ride upon the powerful stallion Shabdiz; he will sit upon the throne of thrones; the great musician Barbad will play for him, and, above all, he will have Shirin, the beautiful princess and heir to the Armenian throne. In Nezami, therefore, the love story gains its drive from Khosrow's libidinal desire, afforded by his patriarchal privilege that has been metaphorically handed down to him by his grandfather, after whom he has been named. The thrust of this libidinal desire drives towards the attainment of power and the 'possession' of a woman, just one among other worldly things.

Most strikingly, *Shirin* begins with Shirin mourning over *her* Khosrow, *her* husband, and in doing so the film adopts a very different narrative logic. Shirin's voice is activated, claiming agency, and inviting us to hear the story from *her* perspective. As she says, this is *her* story now. Amidst the cacophony of wailing women her voice continues: 'a man who was your king and my husband until yesterday. Today he found refuge in death. Look, my sisters, how serene he seems. As calm as the first time I saw him. I was seventeen and the world was still young. How many twilights have passed since then? How may springs turned into autumns, to bring us here, to this bloody sight, my Khosrow. See how your sweet Shirin has become bitter?' At this point Shirin's voice, which has until now been clear and strong begins to falter as though she too is about to weep. 'Oh, my husband, it is not Shirin's fault if the world has become bitter.' In comparing her transformation from being 'sweet' (*shirin*) to 'bitter' (*talkh*) to the passing of the seasons, Shirin's words emphasize the inevitability of the tragic ending that is always already upon us.

I want to argue that by beginning at the penultimate 'scene' of the story, *Shirin* not only draws our attention to what Iranian (and likely many other culturally aware) viewers will recognize as the inevitability of a 'bitter' ending, which is a typical and widely known trope of Persian love stories, it also frames the story to come, presenting it not via Khosrow's libidinal desire, but via Shirin's bitter lamentation. Furthermore, the acousmatic *mise-en-scène*, as I have described above, helps to immerse us fully in this world that has become bitter. This steady and constant sound of water dripping not only echoes the weeping voices, but also invests this acousmatic image with what Walter Benjamin might describe as 'petrified unrest,' a dialectical image that describes a kind of contradictory temporality in which the transitory and eternal coexist.[28] Similarly, *Shirin* seems to acknowledge the eternal and unchanging tropes of prototypical Persian love stories like Khosrow and Shirin, which commonly tend towards the ultimate demise of the couple, precluding any possibility of a 'happily-ever-after' coupling. I emphasize the acousmatic sound of the dripping of water, for according to Chion sound has the capacity not only to invest the two-dimensional film image with something akin to three dimensions, surrounding us in ways that the image never can, but sound can also serve to 'vectorize' an image, that is, to invest an image that may have no particular temporality in and of itself with a temporal dimension.[29] In terms of narrative structure, *Shirin* unfolds as a series of flashbacks that are launched from this opening moment of lamentation, and to which we intermittently return. Each time we return to this moment, we are signaled by the eternal but transitory sound of drip, drip, drip, drip. The world is weeping at the lovers' demise. Drip, drip, drip, drip. Through the acousmatic effect of trompe l'oreille, I feel a drop of water upon my cheek, perhaps I too am weeping. Such is the effect of affective listening to acousmatic sound.

As mentioned above, in the scholarly literature on *Shirin* much has been made of the importance of the play of gazes (*nazar bāzi*) between the female spectators that we see on screen while the story unfolds and our own gaze. Saljoughi argues that with its unrelenting focus on the image of women looking, Kiarostami's film boldly resists the censorship rules that emphasize '*not* looking at women' and 'avoiding the spectator-image relationship' that emerge from the Islamic regime's presumption of a heterosexual male viewer. In other words, the censorship rules pertaining to the modest representation of women mandate the effacement of what Laura Mulvey called a woman's 'to-be-looked-at-ness.'[30] However, despite the post-revolutionary mandate to construct a new and ostensibly Islamic subject-spectator to counter the 'dominant cinema's formal systems of looking,' this subject-spectator was still constructed as male, excluding the female gaze.[31] According to Saljoughi, Kiarostami's emphasis on female spectatorship mounts a direct challenge to the virtual obliteration of the female gaze in post-revolutionary Iranian cinema and, in doing so, he performs a decidedly counter-hegemonic gesture. Noting the fact that in the background, some male colleagues of the women are given prominence in the image, Saljoughi writes:

> Yet because the spectators in *Shirin* are women foregrounded *amongst* their male spectators/colleagues, the film demands that we consider female spectatorship in the context of the history of Iranian visual arts. By inserting women within the nation's imagined ideal spectator, rather than merely replacing him, Kiarostami uses spectatorship to re-imagine the national community [. . .] The vigor of Kiarostami's critique emerges in this provocation because it claims that women's vision has been lost in the post-revolutionary project.[32]

We might ask whether this argument holds true when we lower our gaze, shift our attention away from the images, and attend to the acousmatic dimensions of the film? Indeed, echoing Saljoughi, I argue that the acousmatic dimensions of the film foreground not just women as spectators, but they emphasize another veritable blind spot of Iranian cinema by foregrounding women's *bodies* among other bodies in ways that far exceed the allowable visual representation of women's bodies and their desires. To paraphrase Saljoughi, Kiarostami's provocative film might also be claiming that women's (erotic) bodies have also been lost in the post-revolutionary project. In one of the rare articles on *Shirin* that attends briefly to the sonic dimensions of the film, Najmeh Moradiyan Rizi has argued that because the women's voices emanate from an invisible off-screen world, they are disembodied.[33] However, I argue that in *Shirin*, women's bodies are very much present, returning as acousmatic counter-memories from another time and place, from the courtly world of romantic poetry.

It was perhaps a canny move on Kiarostami's part, in collaboration with the screenwriter Rahmanian, to finally decide on using the story of Khosrow and Shirin, particularly given its continued significance in Iranian culture. Much like Romeo and Juliet in English-language (and other) contexts, the story of Khosrow and Shirin is widely known throughout the Persiante world and beyond. Even after the revolution, the works of Nezami and other prominent poets of classical Persian literature who have written on matters of love have continued to circulate, despite that fact that many of the works, Khosrow and Shirin included, contain highly suggestive scenes of male-female intimacy, wine-drinking, and other kinds of physical pleasure-seeking that would be impossible to show on film in the post-revolutionary context. Indeed, in 2011, just a few years after the release of *Shirin*, the Iranian literary world was shocked at the announcement that Nezami's 'Khosrow and Shirin' had been denied permission to be republished. According to Blake Atwood, the authorities cited wine-drinking, unchaperoned visits between lovers, and 'the heroine's embrace of a male body' belonging to her deceased husband as problematic.[34] For these same reasons, making a standard live action feature film with this content without serious omissions would have been highly problematic and would have almost certainly faced similar issues with censorship. Given the permissibility of the 'text' at the time of production, its recreation as a sonic performance would have presented far fewer obstacles; however, as I have indicated, this sonic performance with its acousmatic affect goes far beyond the verbal recitation of a written text.

Throughout *Shirin*, there are numerous 'scenes' that make use of acousmatic affect to inscribe the film with the textures of eroticized bodies, although it avoids depicting actual consummation of physical love between man and woman. A series of such scenes occurs immediately after the opening scene of Shirin's lamentation over Khosrow's body as the film-within-the-film launches into a flashback of happier times. In terms of the overall story, the scenes depict Shirin's encounters with a series of portraits of Khosrow as she is frolicking in the countryside with her ladies-in-waiting. Viewers familiar with the story will know that the portraits of the prince that Shirin finds have been strategically placed there by Khosrow's aide Shapur for the express purpose of making Shirin fall madly in love with the prince. Significantly, however, the scene makes use of restricted narration by presenting the scene from Shirin's perspective so that the origin of the images is only revealed later by Shirin in a reflective voice-over. This functions to align the acousmatic listener with the embodied affect generated by Shirin's encounter with Khosrow's portrait. This flashback scene makes a stark contrast from the melancholy bitterness of the opening scene and, as mentioned above, it is here that a voice, spilling out from the soundscape, compels us together with Shirin to 'open our ears,' which, much like the use of the apostrophe in poetic discourse, further reinforces the listener's identification with Shirin.

A non-diegetic musical interlude serves as a transition from the bitterness of Shirin in the present to the sweetness of the past. As the opening scene draws to a close, the music, which is dominated by slow melancholy strings, gradually fades in overlapping briefly with the mournful voices of wailing women, which soon fade out. As the music takes over completely, we might imagine a cross dissolve signaled by a subtle change in the tone of the violins, replacing a feeling of melancholy with one of reflective nostalgia. Significantly, at this point the image track seems to synchronize nicely with the shift from the aging Shirin to her younger, more hopeful counterpart by cutting from a shot of the mature actress, Soraya Ghasemi, to the much more youthful face of Khatereh Asadi, a cut that closely coincides with the slightly more hopeful turn of the music. This constitutes a variation of what Chion calls a 'synch point,' for while the sound of the music still emanates from an off-screen, non-diegetic space, it nonetheless corresponds with the flow of images, which the sound vectorizes, lending the images a kind of temporal order.[35] Soon after this cut, we begin to hear birds twittering and the distant sound of women giggling gradually fades in, suggesting a mobile shot searching a landscape for the happy scene. Correspondingly, the change of setting in the heard space seems to cast a brighter light upon the face of Asadi, which helps us to imagine an idyllic pastoral setting on a bright summer's day. The play of light and sound generates a Kuleshov effect as we imagine that the micro-gestures of Asadi's face are responding to this acousmatic scene. Amidst the giggling and merriment, the women beckon a blindfolded Shirin to open up her ears and follow their voices. Like us, Shirin must navigate the space without the aid of sight, but the world we encounter together with her is still filled with an array of sensations. One of the ladies entices her to enjoy the sweet nectar of flowers. Suddenly, Shirin reaches out and we hear as her fingers come into contact with a mysterious wooden object, brought as another lady suggests 'by the winds.' It is at first through her sense of touch that she encounters the image of Khosrow engraved upon the wood, her fingers tracing the contours of his handsome face. The breathless sighs of the handmaidens confirm for her and us what Shirin's fingers already knew. Vivian Sobchack describes a similar sensation in her discussion of the opening shot of *The Piano* (Jane Campion, 1993). She writes, 'Despite my "almost blindness," the "unrecognizable blur," the resistance of the image to my eyes, *my fingers knew what I was looking at*.'[36] While Sobchack is referring to the cinethesthetic activation of the sense of touch by ambiguous visual stimuli, here, in *Shirin*, it is the tactility of sound that enables my fingers to know what I am hearing and what Shirin is feeling. As the scene continues, Shirin insists that they remove her blindfold at once and at the sight of the portrait, she gasps for breath at the wonderous sight. As the dialogue continues, the breathless voices of Shirin and the other women fall upon my ears and I feel their bodies heaving, so overcome they are at this enticing image, too beautiful to be human. In fact, the image has such a powerful effect on Shirin that they conclude that this 'portrait of an angel (*parya*)' must surely be 'the work of a demon (*div*).'[37] I catch my breath, my own body heaving in synergy with Shirin. As the next scenes unfold, Shirin continues to be haunted by similar portraits of Khosrow. As the mature Shirin recalls in voice-over, this image even came to haunt her in her bedchamber at night. Throughout these scenes, the acousmatic soundscape allows me to feel her oscillating waves of fear and desire.

In contrast to Nezami's telling of the tale – which emphasizes the cunning actions of Shapur to place this and other duplicate portraits in Shirin's path so that she may be entrapped by what she describes as Khosrow's 'grotesque game,' an indirect play of glances – in *Shirin*, the woman's own embodied desire is given direct expression through the acousmatic soundscape that encourages affective listening and brings us into close proximity with the woman's body and desires. Given the emphasis on female spectatorship in the visuals of the film, which as Saljoughi and others have argued opens a space for female spectatorship, the sonic dimensions of the film also arguably reorient the acousmatic spectator towards a tantalizing and ostensibly taboo identification with female desire. This is perhaps nowhere more evident than in *Shirin*'s acousmatic treatment of one of the most famous scenes of the story, in which Khosrow happens upon Shirin bathing in a stream.

As with the earlier scenes already described, the spectator is aligned with Shirin's sonic perspective and is encouraged to engage in affective listening. The scene occurs soon after Shirin, encouraged by Shapur masquerading as a mysterious magus, decides to ride the majestic stallion Shabdiz to Ctesiphon (Tisfun) in search of Khosrow.[38] In the story, Khosrow is coincidentally riding towards Armenia in the hope of taking possession of Shirin, but narration of Khosrow's parallel journey is omitted from *Shirin*. Once again, the gendered agency of the original story is reversed, for it is Shirin's desire that drives the narrative perspective, Khosrow only appearing fleetingly as Shirin senses him spying on her from the long grass on the riverbank.

A bright musical interlude accompanies the rhythmic sound of Shabdiz's galloping hooves carrying Shirin swiftly towards Ctesiphon. My mind embellishes what I hear, giving rise to vivid images, aided by the on-screen spectators whose faces are made to gently map Shirin's adventure. I imagine a montage of shots, connected by lap dissolves, of Shirin on horseback, her robes trailing behind her as she traverses grassy meadows, vast deserts, gentle hills, and deep valleys. As the music begins to fade, Shirin rides into a mid-shot, the sound of her breath clearly audible alongside the neighing and gentle clip-clop of trusty Shabdiz, who also lets out a snort. I hear the rustle of Shirin's robes as she dismounts, her breath as she exhales and her feet as she shuffles in the dry grass. I hear her breathe, haaahhh . . . haaahhh . . . haaahhh as her feet fall gently upon the earth, haaahhh . . . haaahhh . . . haaahhh. I hear as Shirin gracefully slips out of her clothes, bells tinkling as she lets them drop to the ground. I see signs of pleasure awakening upon the faces of the female spectators in the on-screen audience, confirming what my ears already know. I accompany Shirin closely as she approaches the riverbank, the water gently bubbling over the stones that have been worn smooth by time. I listen attentively as the water begins to envelop her naked body, clinging to every contour of her womanly curvature. Her voice aspirates a sigh of pleasure as she invokes the water, personified as a lover: 'Oh, water, water embrace me! Caress me with your droplets, hold me like a lover, take my breath away!' As I experience the eroticized pleasures of Shirin's body, on the image track, Kiarostami's strategic editing provides me with a synch point that reinforces the affects of the acousmatic sound, which allows erotic desire to spill out from the interstices of the off-screen space. I see the face of Iranian voice actress Shahindokht Najafzadeh who adopts a cheeky smile and puts her thumb to her mouth as she too seems to indulge in Shirin's physical pleasure. The splashing continues, and with it, gentle sighs remind us of Shirin's erotic desires which seem to be consummated by the water. 'Immerse me in your kisses, oh water,' she commands. Suddenly, this acousmatic film that is flickering away in my ears seems to cut away from Shirin as we hear the sound of another figure lurking nearby amidst the dry grass, birds twittering and frogs croaking somewhere in the distance. The familiar sound of water rolling over pebbles signals a cut back to Shirin in the water. Tentatively she exhales, asking 'Who's there' in barely more than a whisper. Cut back to the figure lurking in the grass. Shirin asks, 'Who are you?' Now worried, she asks: 'A stranger who like a thief spies on me at night?' The water continues to lap against her body, her modesty veiled by the night. She receives no response to her interrogations. 'Was it he?' she asks, 'Khosrow? The prince of Persia?' The scene ends with Shirin taking a deep breath, exclaiming 'Oh destiny . . .' as the rich, woody sounds of an oboe fade in to herald the next part of her journey. Words are inadequate to fully describe the textures of the acousmatic soundscape in this scene, and while the sound mix is technically quite simple the effect enables the listener to feel the presence of Shirin's body and its coalescence with the water through which her erotic desires are evoked. In contrast, we get but the barest glimpse of Khosrow lurking in the long grass, strengthening our identification with Shirin's perspective as she exposes the presence of a voyeur.

With its suggestions of nudity and female desire, in the context of Iranian cinema this scene is potentially transgressive. However, the provenance of the scene, drawing closely from Nezami's 'closet drama' enables the erotic female body to emerge vividly from the interstices, or, as Haeri might describe, from 'below the surface' and directly out of the Persian poetic traditions from which it is derived. According to Saeed Honarmand, the bathing scene in which a woman appears 'naked in water [. . .] her future lover [. . .] on the hill gazing upon her from above' is a common trope of the medieval Persian romance. In such poetry, including Nezami's 'Khosrow and Shirin,' the woman's body is typically 'described from the man's point of view; thus it is erotic.' However, according to Honarmand, the 'eroticism is not there to serve the readers' desires; it is there to make them ashamed.'[39] Although I am not entirely convinced by Honarmand's account of the shaming effect of eroticism on the reader, nor of the assumption that eroticism derives only from the male gaze, we can still mark a contrast between the presentation of the scene in *Shirin* and its literary ancestor. Although the scene cuts briefly to Khosrow, reminding us that he is spying on Shirin, the effect of presenting the scene acousmatically, rather than visually, effectively takes Khosrow's gaze out of the equation. If, as Saljoughi and others have argued, the visual spectatorial address of *Shirin* is predominantly female, then, as I hope to have demonstrated, the acousmatic spectator is constructed also as decidedly feminine. The enactment of Shirin's desire therefore transcends the kind of objectifying 'visual' pleasure and with it the supposed 'shame' that, according to Honarmand, such scenes traditionally inspire. Importantly, at no point during the scene do Kiarostami's female spectators seem to express any visible signs of shame such as averting their gaze. Instead, they look on attentively, with pleasure on their lips and in their eyes, and it is with a similarly enticing aural 'gaze' that I am encouraged to listen with the attentiveness of a fully embodied spectator, surrounded by a rare scene of female desire in post-revolutionary Iranian cinema.

Inescapable Sorrow

But where does all this desire and the erotic bodies that experience it ultimately lead us? As much as *Shirin* presents us with an acousmatic image of female pleasure, it also reminds us that, in the Persian literary and cinematic tradition, with pleasure must also inevitably come pain and sorrow. Intermittently, we are reminded of the sorrowful opening of the film and ending of the story, and thus of the fact that this pleasure is always already overshadowed by despair. In this telling of the tale, love is viewed from the vantage point of death and it is women that mourn its inevitable demise. Love occurs only in the interstices, in the space between two deaths. In the film's penultimate scene, we return to the cavernous space from where the story was launched by Shirin's voice. We hear Khosrow calling out for his beloved Shirin, echoing in the cavernous dungeon where the blinded king has been banished by his own son, hungry for power. The imminence of death registers on the faces of the female spectators, tears beginning to stream down their cheeks. Shirin tries to calm her beloved Khosrow, 'Be calm, my love. The hour is cruel, but I cherish the fact that you are alive. I will share your last breath.' She implores him to sleep, promising never to leave him. 'Sleep, sleep' she whispers amidst the sound of crickets and as non-diegetic strings signal the coming tragedy. Shirin's voice returns, this time as a voice-over reflecting on the tragic past: 'It was the last time I ever slept.' Suddenly, a horn blows out a series of long, deep, ominous notes foreshadowing Khosrow's impending assassination. Leila Hatami watches on fearfully, her hand tensely pressed against her mouth, her brow furrowing. Crickets continue to chirp, innocent to the mounting tragedy. Footsteps approach. On-screen, Nioosha Zeighami suddenly startles as I hear the shwing of a sword being drawn from its scabbard followed by the grunts of an assassin. A blade sinks into flesh. Shirin begins to wail and sob, her cries ringing out from the off-screen space. As in the scenes of erotic pleasure, the foregrounding of Shirin's voice places me right there beside her. As the assassin re-sheaths his sword, Khosrow feebly utters his final word, 'Shiiiriin. . . .' For just a moment, silence descends upon the scene. I imagine a lap dissolve bringing us full circle as I hear the familiar sound of drip, drip, drip, drip, synchronized perfectly it seems with the tears that stream down Golshifteh Farahani's left cheek. Shirin continues her narration. 'And here we are, me, Khosrow and you, my grieving sisters.' Her direct address and the effect of trompe l'oreille allow her words to spill out, not only to the female spectators that are supposedly watching her story on screen, but also those of us listening in, *falgoosh*-style, to the acousmatic film that has unfolded around us. We become enveloped by her grief and despair. The acoustic *mise-en-scène* weeps: drip, drip, drip, drip. 'You listen to my story and you cry.' Golshifteh wipes the stream of tears from her cheek.

We see a succession of women, young and old, among them Merila Zarei, Juliette Binoche, Nikou Kheradmand, Mahtab Keramati, and, finally, Hamideh Kheirabadi, all weeping synchronous tears of sorrow. Shirin says: 'Through these tears, I see your eyes. Are you shedding these tears for me, Shirin? Or for the Shirin that hides in each one of you?' It seems fitting that it is the aging face of Kheirabadi that bears virtual witness to Shirin's inevitable death at her own hand. Often described as the 'mother of Iranian cinema,' she is also the mother of Soraya Ghasemi, whose image gave way to the film's first flashback described earlier in this chapter. As we hear Shirin press the knife into her own flesh, Kheirabadi wipes the tears from her cheek, tears generated not by this

Figure 8.2 Tears that stream down Golshifteh Farahani's cheek. (Source: Screen grab from *Shirin*, 2008).

story, but by all the stories of lost love experienced over a lifetime. *Shirin* would coincidentally be Kheirabadi's final performance.

But, we might ask, what becomes of all this weeping? Sharon Lin Tay has pointed out that *Shirin* 'bears an uncanny resemblance' to an installation entitled '*Ta'ziyeh*' that Kiarostami exhibited at London's Victoria and Albert Museum in 2005.⁴⁰ In the installation, a television screen displayed scenes from a *ta'ziyeh* performance, while two additional screens showed the emotive faces of Iranian villagers. As in *Shirin*, throughout the installation the faces of the villagers were 'edited so that their reactions would correspond to the drama unfolding on the TV screen.' As the play reaches its climax and 'tragic denouement' '[w]omen sob uncontrollably into their *chador*.'⁴¹ Like Kiarostami's installation, *Shirin* seems to borrow from *ta'ziyeh*. *Ta'ziyeh* is an Iranian form of religious drama, sometimes compared to medieval passion plays, in which the events of the martyrdom of Hussein on the plains of Karbala in 680 CE and other stories of Shi'ite Islam are re-enacted in dramatized form. *Ta'ziyeh* grew out of Shi'a mourning rituals observed during the month of Muharram when vast numbers spill onto the streets to participate in public mourning rituals that involve chest thumping, self-flagellation and weeping. During the performance of *ta'ziyeh*, the audience is encouraged to participate by the *ta'ziyeh gardan*, a kind of on-stage director who directs the audience's reactions and is sometimes referred to as the *mo'in-al-boka*, 'the one who brings tears,' for it is he who induces the audience to weep. As in his

London installation in which Kiarostami used editing to 'synch' facial expression to the unfolding of the drama, so too, in *Shirin*, Kiarostami's careful editing of facial expressions to generate synch points highlights his role as a veritable *moʻin-al-boka*. He brings us tears in the acousmatic world inhabited by Shirin, a world in which even the walls weep. He brings us tears in the visual world, the 'cinema' inhabited by 109 actresses, and arguably all of these tears spill out into the space beyond the screen that I inhabit. As spectators, we are encompassed in an act of collective mourning. But for what, or for whom, do we mourn? Ultimately, we mourn the veritable absence of romantic love from Iran's cinema screens, but between our tears we might also celebrate the fleeting return of erotic love, if only as a counter-memory of older poetic traditions. This counter-memory emerges from the richly allusive interstitial space between sound and image, calling us to reject the hegemony of vision so that we may indulge, if only fleetingly, in the passionate embrace of amorous desire.[42]

Notes

1. Other authors have given the number as 114 actresses, but the names of only 109 appear in the end credits. The non-Iranian actress is Juliette Binoche, who would star in Kiarostami's next film *Certified Copy* (*Copie conforme*, 2010).
2. Sara Saljoughi, 'Seeing, Iranian Style: Women and Collective Vision in Abbas Kiarostami's Shirin,' in *Iranian Studies*, Vol. 45, No. 4 (2012), pp. 519–35.
3. Asbjørn Grønstadt, 'Abbas Kiarostami's *Shirin* and the Aesthetics of Ethical Intimacy,' in *Film Criticism*, Vol. 37, No. 2 (2012/2013), pp. 22–37, p. 25.
4. Khatereh Khodaei, '*Shirin* as Described by Kiarostami,' in *Offscreen*, Vol. 13, No. 1 (2009), online at https://offscreen.com/view/shirin_kiarostami (accessed 15 May 2019).
5. This idea has been inspired by the work of Negar Mottahedeh. See Negar Mottahedeh, *Whisper Tapes: Kate Millett in Iran* (Stanford, CA: Stanford University Press 2019), in which she figures her own research process, listening to the soundscape of Kate Millett's tape recordings made in Iran in 1979, as a kind of *falgoosh*.
6. Michel Chion, *Audio-Vision: Sound on Screen* (New York: Columbia University Press 1994).
7. Shahla Haeri, 'Sacred Canopy: Love and Sex under the Veil,' in *Iranian* Studies, Vol. 42, No. 1 (2009), pp. 113–26, p. 114. The implementation of the guidelines is haphazard and rather fluid. This means that for each rule we commonly find films that appear to transgress them in some way.
8. See for example, Michelle Langford, *Allegory in Iranian Cinema: The Aesthetics of Poetry and Resistance* (London: Bloomsbury 2019), especially chapter 4 'Allegories of Love: The Cinematic *Ghazal*'; Michelle Langford, 'Tales (*Ghesseha*, 2014) and the Cinematic *Divan* of Rakhshan Banietemad,' in *Re-Focus: The Films of Rakhshan Banietemad*, ed. Maryam Ghorbankarimi (Edinburgh: Edinburgh University Press 2021); Michelle Langford, 'Negotiating the Sacred Body

in Iranian Cinema(s): National, Physical and Cinematic Embodiment in Majid Majidi's *Baran* (2002),' in *Negotiating the Sacred II: Blasphemy and Sacrilege in the Arts*, eds. Elizabeth Coleman and Maria Suzette Fernandes-Dias (Canberra: ANU e-Press 2008), pp. 161–71.
9. Haeri, 'Sacred Canopy,' p. 114.
10. See for example, Tahmineh Milani's 'Fereshteh trilogy.' I have previously discussed the use of melodramatic form in these films. Michelle Langford, 'Practical Melodrama: From Recognition to Action in Tahmineh Milani's Fereshteh Trilogy,' in *Screen*, Vol. 51 (2010), pp. 341–64.
11. Blake Atwood, *Reform Cinema in Iran: Film and Political Change in the Islamic Republic* (New York & Chichester: Columbia University Press 2016), p. 30. Atwood cites a *Jomhuri-ye Eslami* editorial that complained of 'cheap love taking the place of higher love at the Fajr Film Festival.'
12. It should be noted that similar concerns about the impact of cinema on viewers' moral health underpinned the establishment of the Motion Picture Production Code (MPPC) in Hollywood in 1930, although in contrast to the Iranian context the MPPC was industry regulated, rather than a system of censorship imposed and regulated by the government.
13. Atwood, *Reform Cinema in Iran*, p. 43.
14. Ibid., pp. 45–6.
15. Ibid., p. 46.
16. Haeri, 'Sacred Canopy,' pp. 114–15.
17. Charles-Henri de Fouchécour, 'Iran viii. Persian Literature (2) Classical,' http://www.iranicaonline.org/articles/iran-viii2-classical-persian-literature (accessed 9 August 2019).
18. Pedram Partovi, 'Constituting Love in Persiante Cinemas,' in *Journal of Persinate Studies*, Vol. 10 (2017), pp. 186–217, p. 188.
19. Partovi, 'Constituting Love,' p. 192.
20. Various critics have described *Shirin*'s soundtrack as a kind of radio play; however, my own close listening reveals that the soundtrack is structured very much like a film with scenes, flashbacks, editing transitions, camera movements, voice-over, sound effects, non-diegetic music, and a variety of shot lengths audible via the relative closeness of particular sounds.
21. Peter Chelkowski, 'Nezami: Master Dramatist,' in *Persian Literature*, ed. Ehsan Yarshate (Albany, NY: Bibliotheca Persica 1998), pp. 179–80.
22. Chion, *Audio-Vision*, p. 25.
23. Ibid., p. 29.
24. Ibid., p. 32.
25. Ibid., p. 33.
26. Vivian Sobchack, 'What My Fingers Knew: The Cinesthetic Subject, or Vision in the Flesh,' in *Senses of Cinema* (2000), http://sensesofcinema.com/2000/conference-special-effects-special-affects/fingers/ (accessed 23 August 2019).
27. Peter Chelkowski, 'Nezami: Master Dramatist,' p. 187.
28. Walter Benjamin, 'Central Park,' trans. Lloyd Spencer, in *New German Critique*, Vol. 34 (1985), pp. 32–58, p. 40.

29. Chion, *Audio-Vision*, p. 13.
30. Laura Mulvey, *Visual and Other Pleasures* (Bloomington: Indiana University Press 1981), pp. 14–28.
31. Negar Mottahedeh, *Displaced Allegories: Post-Revolutionary Iranian Cinema* (Durham, NC and London: Duke University Press 2008), p. 2.
32. Saljoughi, 'Seeing, Iranian Style,' p. 534.
33. Najmeh Moradiyan Rizi, 'The Acoustic Screen: The Dynamics of the Female Look and Voice in Kiarostami's *Shirin*,' in *Synoptique*, Vol. 5, No. 6 (2016), pp. 44–56, p. 53. Moradiyan Rizi argues that 'there is no other information about the voice and its body, which makes Shirin ethereal and mysterious.' In contrast, I argue that the rich soundscape and use of the voice and sound effects invests the sonic image with very well-defined acoustic bodies.
34. Blake Atwood, 'Sense and Censorship in the Islamic Republic of Iran,' in *World Literature Today*, Vol. 86, No. 3 (2012), pp. 38–41, p. 38.
35. Chion, *Audio-Vision*, p. 14.
36. Vivian Sobchack, 'What My Fingers Knew.'
37. In Persian, *parya* is the most beautiful of all angels. There are many *div* in Persian mythology.
38. A magus is a sorcerer or conjuror. Ctesiphon, located about 35 kilometers from present-day Baghdad, served as the capital of the Persian empire for eight centuries.
39. Saeed Honarmand, 'Between the Water and the Wall: The Power of Love in Medieval Persian Romance,' in *The Layered Heart: Essays on Persian Poetry*, ed. A. A. Seyed-Ghorab, (Washington, DC: Mage Publishers 2019), pp. 55–80, p. 77.
40. Sharon Lin Tay, 'Abbas Kiarostami,' in *Fifty Contemporary Film Directors*, ed. Yvonne Tasker (2nd edition) (New York: Routledge 2011), pp. 233–9, p. 237.
41. Amin Sharifi Isaloo, *Power, Legitimacy and the Public Sphere: The Iranian Ta'ziyeh Theatre Ritual* (Abingdon and New York: Routledge 2017), p. 60.
42. I would like to thank Mahsa Salamati, Mazda Moradabbasi, Elham Naeej, and Laetitia Nanquette for their feedback on various aspects of this chapter.

References

Atwood, Blake, *Reform Cinema in Iran: Film and Political Change in the Islamic Republic* (New York and Chichester: Columbia University Press 2016).

Atwood, Blake, 'Sense and Censorship in the Islamic Republic of Iran,' in *World Literature Today*, Vol. 86, No. 3 (2012), pp. 38–41.

Benjamin, Walter, 'Central Park,' trans. Lloyd Spencer, in *New German Critique*, Vol. 34 (1985), pp. 32–58.

Chelkowski, Peter, 'Nezami: Master Dramatist,' in Ehsan Yarshater (ed.), *Persian Literature* (Albany, NY: Bibliotheca Persica 1998), pp. 179–80.

Chion, Michel, *Audio-Vision: Sound on Screen* (New York: Columbia University Press 1994).

Fouchécour, Charles-Henri de, 'Iran viii. Persian Literature (2) Classical,' http://www.iranicaonline.org/articles/iran-viii2-classical-persian-literature (accessed 9 August 2019).

Grønstadt, Asbjørn, 'Abbas Kiarostami's *Shirin* and the Aesthetics of Ethical Intimacy,' in *Film Criticism*, Vol. 37, No. 2 (2012/2013), pp. 22–37.

Haeri, Shahla, 'Sacred Canopy: Love and Sex under the Veil,' in *Iranian Studies*, Vol. 42, No. 1 (2009), pp. 113–26.

Honarmand, Saeed, 'Between the Water and the Wall: The Power of Love in Medieval Persian Romance,' in A. A. Seyed-Ghorab (ed.), *The Layered Heart: Essays on Persian Poetry* (Washington, DC: Mage Publishers 2019), pp. 55–80.

Isaloo, Amin Sharifi, *Power, Legitimacy and the Public Sphere: The Iranian Ta'ziyeh Theatre Ritual* (Abingdon and New York: Routledge 2017).

Khodaei, Khatereh, '*Shirin* as Described by Kiarostami,' in *Offscreen*, Vol. 13, No. 1 (2009), online at https://offscreen.com/view/shirin_kiarostami (accessed 15 May 2019).

Langford, Michelle, *Allegory in Iranian Cinema: The Aesthetics of Poetry and Resistance* (London: Bloomsbury 2019).

Langford, Michelle, 'Negotiating the Sacred Body in Iranian Cinema(s): National, Physical and Cinematic Embodiment in Majid Majidi's *Baran* (2002),' in Elizabeth Coleman and Maria Suzette Fernandes-Dias (eds.), *Negotiating The Sacred II: Blasphemy And Sacrilege In The Arts* (Canberra: ANU e-Press 2008), pp. 161–71.

Langford, Michelle, 'Practical Melodrama: From Recognition to Action in Tahmineh Milani's Fereshteh Trilogy,' in *Screen*, Vol. 51 (2010), pp. 341–64.

Langford, Michelle, 'Tales (*Ghesse-ha*, 2014) and the Cinematic *Divan* of Rakhshan Banietemad,' in Maryam Ghorbankarimi (ed.), *Re-Focus: The Films of Rakhshan Banietemad* (Edinburgh: Edinburgh University Press 2021).

Mottahedeh, Negar, *Displaced Allegories: Post-Revolutionary Iranian Cinema* (Durham, NC and London: Duke University Press 2008).

Mottahedeh, Negar, *Whisper Tapes: Kate Millett in Iran* (Stanford, CA: Stanford University Press 2019).

Mulvey, Laura, *Visual and Other Pleasures* (Bloomington: Indiana University Press 1981), pp. 14–28.

Partovi, Pedram, 'Constituting Love in Persiante Cinemas,' in *Journal of Persinate Studies*, Vol. 10 (2017), pp. 186–217.

Rizi, Najmeh Moradiyan, 'The Acoustic Screen: The Dynamics of the Female Look and Voice in Kiarostami's *Shirin*,' in *Synoptique*, Vol. 5, No. 6 (2016), pp. 44–56.

Saljoughi, Sara, 'Seeing, Iranian Style: Women and Collective Vision in Abbas Kiarostami's Shirin,' in *Iranian Studies*, Vol. 45, No. 4 (2012), pp. 519–35.

Sobchack, Vivian, 'What My Fingers Knew: The Cinesthetic Subject, or Vision in the Flesh,' in *Senses of Cinema* (2000), http://sensesofcinema.com/2000/conference-special-effects-special-affects/fingers/ (accessed 23 August 2019).

Tay, Sharon Lin, 'Abbas Kiarostami,' in Yvonne Tasker (ed.), *Fifty Contemporary Film Directors* (2nd edition) (New York: Routledge 2011), pp. 233–9.

9. SPIRITUAL COUNTER-MEMORIES OF THE WAR: MOHAMMAD ALI AHANGAR'S RECENT CONTRIBUTIONS TO THE SĪNEMĀ-YE DEFĀʿ-YE MOQADDAS

Viktor Ullmann

Sometime in the mid-1980s, at the height of the Iran-Iraq War, an Iranian soldier, the sole survivor of an Iraqi airstrike, is running along a sandbank in the borderland of the Ḥavīzeh marshes. Around him, missiles hit the ground continuously, but the soldier does not deviate from his path. When he hears a shell strike right next to him, he stops, alarmed. The camera pans to a nearby hideout down the sandbank in the shallow water of the marsh, into which he scrambles. Hidden under his helmet, he awaits the explosion, but we hear nothing but a quiet hissing sound. After a few moments, the soldier peeks out from under his helmet, only to see the source of the hissing: a smoking missile stuck in the mud in front of him – it was a blind shell. Tragic music plays and the soldier begins to sob desperately: he has missed the opportunity for martyrdom. After he has cried for a while, a sudden cut ends his regret. The music stops, the scout has stood up and climbed back onto the sandbank. From a distance, we see the young man taking one last look at the blind shell, until he leaves the frame, and the camera stays with the shell.

It is this scene that starts the titular soldier's path in Ebrahim Hatamikia's straightforward propaganda film *Dīdehbān/The Scout* (1990). Two decades later, director Mohammad Ali Ahangar takes it up again in his war drama *Malakeh/The Queen* (2012). In its opening sequence, Seyfollah, a bomb disposal expert in the Iranian military, arrives at an identical sandbank in 1988, during the last days of the war. While he awaits his colleagues, Seyfollah observes scorpions crawling over the rusty bombshells stuck in the mud

Figure 9.1(a) The opening scene of *The Scout* . . . (Source: Screen grab from *The Scout*, 1990).

Figure 9.1(b) . . . referenced at the beginning of *The Queen*. (Source: Screen grab from *The Queen*, 2012).

around him. Soon, a truck with two soldiers arrives and the three men enter the water to recover a blind shell stuck at the bottom of the now refreshed lake. The shell is positioned in the same way as in *The Scout*: under the shore, on the right side of the sandbank. Seyfollah ties a rope around the missile and together with his colleagues carefully pulls it out of the water before carrying it to the truck for disposal.

Opening his film with this intertextual reference to Hatamikia's classic of Iranian war cinema, Ahangar makes several statements at once. Superficially, the director positions his work in the rich tradition of Sacred Defense cinema (*Sīnemā-ye Defāʿ-ye Moqaddas*), under which films about the Iran-Iraq War are subsumed in the IRI. Beyond this alignment with the genre, however, Ahangar points out that *The Queen* intends to dig deeper into the subject matter of the war and its impact on the spiritual lives of the people affected by it. Decades have passed since the end of the war and the context has changed; the lake is filled with water again, but the remains of the war have become somehow more frightening and less glorious than they were in *The Scout* back in 1990: the shells are associated with scorpions, recalling an unpredictable danger, and have to be handled with extreme care. From heaven-sent opportunities for martyrdom, they have transformed into a looming menace that has yet to be processed, haunting the country's soil.

This ethos of re-interrogating the war and its spiritual ramifications for survivors is precisely what motivates Ahangar's movies. Their association with Sacred Defense cinema in combination with a challenge of the genre's discursive boundaries makes them intriguing cases of counter-memories operating from within hegemonic memory culture while at the same time breaking their mnemonic monopoly: Ahangar paints a decidedly different picture of the war than the official state iconography. To examine these different layers of alignment and reinvention of Iranian war cinema in this chapter, I will briefly discuss the tradition of Sacred Defense cinema and Ahangar's relation to it, before taking a closer look at his work. Here, two of his later films, *The Queen* (2012) and *Sarv Zīr-e Āb/Cypress Under Water* (2018), will be of particular interest. Through an analysis of their transgression of established rules and reappropriation of classic Sacred Defense themes, I argue that Ahangar's films work as counter-memories of the war with a spiritual twist.

Sacred Defense as a Mnemonic Tradition Carried by the State

While Hamid Naficy in his seminal *Social History of Iranian Cinema* argues against the Sacred Defense films constituting a genre,[1] I will treat them as a relatively coherent tradition of filmmaking. It is valid that a range of very different film forms covered the war, from Seyyed Morteza Avini's front documentaries produced during the war, to the high-profile action movies and veteran dramas emerging in the 1990s, to the mainstream war comedies of the early 2000s. Yet, even if the Sacred Defense films lack a common approach in structure and aesthetic, they have important commonalities both in topic and institutional history, as I shall briefly address in the following.

The initiation of the genre was very much a governmental project and has to be seen in the context of the mobilization effort that started right after the beginning of the war in 1980. As the consolidating Islamic Republic deemed the conflict with Iraq an 'Imposed War' (*Jang-e Tahmīlī*), the Iranian involvement was framed as a 'Sacred Defense' (*Defā'-ye Moqaddas*), a term that soon encompassed not only military operations, but also all kinds of political and cultural projects serving the war effort. The output of the resulting 'war culture industry'[2] that consolidated in the following years was thus marked by outright pro-war propaganda, commissioned by a state desperate to recruit, or at least persuade, people for the war effort. It was produced by genuinely convinced young documentary filmmakers who often had more experience in fighting than filmmaking. Seyyed Morteza Avini (1947–93) was the most prominent of these soldiers cum directors who pioneered the tradition of Sacred Defense filmmaking – although Agnés Devictor pointedly locates his work closer to 'cinematographic engagement' (*engagement cinémathographique*) than conventional filmmaking.[3] As Sacred Defense directors grew more experienced and the war ended, their films gradually evolved and centered around the sacrifices of the war, in many cases criticizing society's treatment of veterans, a group they associated themselves with.

These cases of careful dissent from within the *Sīnemā-ye Defā'-ye Moqaddas* have been relatively well-researched. Pedram Khosronejad's edited volume on Sacred Defense cinema[4] gives an exemplary overview of the spectrum of prominent critical voices from within the genre that reaches from Mohsen Makhmalbaf (b. 1957), who turned away from the government completely and avoided being associated with the war movies he had directed in the 1980s, to Ebrahim Hatamikia (b. 1961), who tested the boundaries of criticism from within the system of the genre. The overall result was a shift from the straightforward military features of the 1980s to the veteran films of the 1990s, often containing careful criticism but still operating under the official doctrine of not challenging the war effort as a whole and thus reproducing the hegemonic narrative of the Sacred Defense and the Imposed War.

Thematically, the guiding thread that runs through all films of the *Defā'-ye Moqaddas* is the topic of martyrdom. From the front-line propaganda to the veteran dramas to even the more recent comedies, death is usually staged as an integral part of the 'ritual of purification and transcendence'[5] that participating in the war is supposed to be. As the opening scene from *The Scout* has shown earlier, death is often desired to the extent that surviving a missile strike is staged as a tragic event. As such, the protagonist's martyrdom, which regularly serves as the finale of the film, offers a dramaturgic paradox at first sight: it is staged both as a melodramatic moment and as a glorious and cathartic victory. This apparent contradiction has a certain tradition in Shi'ite *ta'ziyeh* performances, which is addressed by Roxanne Varzi in her contribution to Richard Tapper's edited volume on post-revolutionary Iranian cinema as follows:

> The thematic use of Ashura in the war, and again in cinema, is an attempt to make the war itself a performance of *ta'ziyeh*, doubled in the cinema, which re-enacts the re-enactment, bringing many mimetic layers to the ghost-memory of martyrdom in Shi'ite mourning. It is an absent moment that history makes present in the very call to jehad: a call for martyrs.[6]

Yet, although the films' underlying conceptualization of martyrdom calls back deeply into Shi'ite tradition, namely into the seventh-century battle of Karbala and the rich tradition of its theatrical re-enactment, in the discursive context of the Sacred Defense this showcasing of spirituality has a very obvious and limited narrative function: a glorification of death in combat to recruit an audience during the war years and to justify it retrospectively in the aftermath. The elements of spirituality, here, clearly serve to reinforce the state's epistemic hegemony on the war, even in films notorious for their criticism, such as Hatamikia's *The Glass Agency* (*Āzhāns-e Shīsheh-ī*, 1998): after showcasing the struggle of former Basij Kazem to get his fatally ill friend to Europe for medical treatment, the film ends with the latter dying on the plane to London, suggesting that a death on Iranian soil was preferable to seeking help in the West.

Given this transparent and repetitive structure that reliably pushes the narrative into a justification of the war, it should not be surprising that another common factor in Sacred Defense films is their reception. Most of them failed to convince both audiences and critics, apart from some rare box office hits or critical successes. On the other hand, the films remained popular with political hardliners and ultraconservatives, which is why the institutional backing never faded and continues to be organized in different forms: state foundations like the Islamic Ideology Dissemination Organization *(Sāzemān-e Tablīghāt-e Eslāmī)* offer financial support, there are low thresholds for the registration of religious production companies or for military veterans becoming film producers, and the Iranian military sponsors bases and equipment in the filming process. The 2010s even saw an upsurge in the foundation of specialized war film festivals such as the Avini Awards or the Resistance Film Festival *(Jashnvāreh-ye Fīlm-e Moqāvemat)*. It is in the context of these conservative networks and ongoing state support for the *Sīnemā-ye Defā'-ye Moqaddas* that director Mohammad Ali Ahangar (b. 1962) is to be located.

Mohammad Ali Ahangar

At first glance, it might seem irritating to connect the director with counter-hegemonic films challenging the state's epistemic monopoly of memory culture, a notion that is usually associated with outspoken reformists like Jafar Panahi or young dissident filmmakers such as Reza Dormishian. Ahangar, on the other hand, is an inconspicuous man in his fifties, sporting a full beard and mostly wearing plain black clothes and thick glasses. His background further distinguishes him from other Iranian directors, most of whom are Tehran based: he was born in the small town of Dezfoul in the rural south-western province of Khuzestan and spent most of his life in the oil refinery town of Abadan on the Gulf coast.

Being a deeply religious person, Ahangar proved very popular with the state-carried ultraconservative institutions sponsoring Sacred Defense cinema, especially at the beginning of his career. His first feature, *Farzand-e Khāk/Child of the Soil* (2008), was produced with significant support from the Tehran Art Bureau (*Ḥouzeh-ye Honarī-ye Tehrān*) of the Islamic Ideology Dissemination Organization. At that time, in a speech at the Iran Cinema Celebration (*Jashn-e Bozorg-e Sīnemā-ye Īrān*) at *Khāneh-ye Sīnemā*, he openly complained about the 'apathetic reception by the Fajr film organizers,' who run the country's largest mainstream film festival, where Ahangar's debut had been, in his own words, 'completely overlooked.'[7] Instead of Fajr, the director was more closely connected to a network of ultraconservative niche festivals: in 2009, he was a jury member at the Avini Awards, which are handed out to war documentaries 'in spirit of martyr Avini,' and in the following year, his second film, *Bīdārī-ye Rūyā-hā/Awakening Dreams* (2010), won the Resistance Film Festival, a war film festival committed not only to the Sacred Defense tradition but also to current military engagements of the Islamic Republic – so committed, in fact, that the 2010 edition took place in Afghanistan. In 2012, however, Ahangar's popularity within the film industry's ultraconservative networks started to crumble with the premiere of his third film, *The Queen*.

As it was debated widely after its release for its anti-war sentiments and transgressions of the Sacred Defense tradition, I will take a closer look into it in the following. At the beginning of the film, set in late 1980s Abadan, the embattled oil refinery town at the Iraqi border has already largely been destroyed by the war. The Iranian army is looking for ways to defend it against a possible invasion and sends out a group of four relatively inexperienced soldiers to a deserted refinery, where they expect them to find a good spot to watch the Iraqi front line and give them coordinates for airstrikes. One of the soldiers, Siavash, finds a convenient observatory on top of a refinery tower from which he has a wide view. But as he starts using the spot to give the army the coordinates of possible targets, he is soon haunted by the ghost of its previous user, Jamshid, an Iranian soldier who used the tower for the same purpose before his death. Jamshid appears to him repeatedly and points out the moral complexity of his seemingly simple task: the bombardments he is ordered to command will cause counter strikes with civilian victims. But, on the other hand, if he were to start to spare the lives of Iraqi soldiers and concentrate only on targeting their equipment, the surviving soldiers will carry out future attacks.

The moral dilemma of his task begins to drive Siavash crazy. Although he tries to fulfill his duty, he keeps the location of his observatory a secret, which again causes severe conflicts with his fellow soldiers and supervisors. He soon realizes that navigating between his orders, his own moral assumptions, and the ambiguous, almost nihilist, morality offered to him by his predecessor's ghost is pointless, as every action he takes causes more violence. In the end, one of his fellow soldiers is killed in an attack on the refinery, and in the aftermath his grieving father, a weapons' supplier, loses his mind and accidentally drops a grenade, killing himself and many fellow soldiers in the explosion.

Upon losing his colleagues in such a pointless manner, the demoralized Siavash starts to dedicate his job exclusively to saving the lives of Iranian and Iraqi soldiers alike, until he is ultimately killed in a bombardment on his observatory. One of the last scenes shows him receiving the news of a short-lived ceasefire via radio. While the other listeners cheer upon this development, Siavash only shakes his head and leaves the scene. Unlike his cinematic siblings, the war heroes from the classical Sacred Defense films, the death of those around him does not fill him with sympathetic joy for their martyrdom; instead, their loss leaves him devastated and demoralized.

Despite the subversive elements of the film, such as the protagonist's clear desperation and ultimate lack of faith, *The Queen* is clearly embedded in the *Defāʿ-ye Moqaddas* tradition. Ahangar is a strongly religious director and repeatedly identified himself in interviews as a war filmmaker, an alignment that manifests itself in the movie. From the opening quote of Hatamikia's *The Scout* to the melodramatic music and the monochrome cinematography, it constantly references the aesthetics of the genre. Furthermore, in terms of production, the film's setting shows strong military support – a crucial factor in Sacred Defense cinema. Ahangar and his producers have good relations with the military, which supports them with equipment as requisites and also filming locations such as airfields and training grounds.

But despite this active self-identification as a Sacred Defense film, *The Queen* consciously breaks with some of the most crucial cornerstones of the genre. The biggest point of difference, and the one that was discussed most amongst its ultraconservative critics, and led to problems with censorship, is his sympathy with the Iraqi soldiers.

Representation of Friends and Enemies

The representation of the enemy is one of the few cornerstones that connects all Sacred Defense films.[8] While the portrayal of Iraqi soldiers evolved slightly over time, from faceless and evil to incompetent and inferior,[9] their unsympathetic staging as villains remained a constant. Generally, enemy soldiers are rarely shown or addressed in Sacred Defense films, although it is debatable whether their absence is a constant of the genre, an assumption that Mehrzad Karimabadi makes.[10] There are lots of instances where we can see Iraqi soldiers; sometimes they even have script lines. Roxanne Varzi's description is much more accurate in this regard: concerning the Iraqi generals in *Ofoq/The Horizon* (1989), one of the most popular and high-profile war films of the 1980s, she writes: 'They are shown as clean-cut, suave, cigarette-smoking, westernized strategists who sit in their highly technologized war machine – a battleship equipped with massive control panels and surveillance machines – watching and waiting for the Iranians.'[11]

The Queen also shows Iraqi soldiers mostly from afar through Siavash's looking glass, but, beyond that, it radically breaks with tradition by letting the protagonist empathize with the enemy. After every bombardment, his regret and doubts are shown extensively, not only over the circle of violence that he perpetuates, but also over the killing itself. He repeatedly avoids shooting at already wounded Iraqis and makes a point of only destroying military equipment instead of aiming at people. His comparatively empathic approach is further mirrored in *The Queen*'s symbolic subtext: the title refers to a bee queen, since Siavash is taking care of a beehive in the deserted refinery. The comparison of the Iraqis with his bees underlines his responsibility towards them; analogous to a beekeeper who is well aware of the danger posed by the animals but at the same time works hard not to harm them while keeping them at bay. This equation of people with insects might seem degrading at first sight but given the director's religious background and the role of bees in the Quran, which gives them the status of sacred animals due to their high level of organization,[12] it is actually a charming comparison.

The most striking example of Siavash's compassion towards the enemy plays out near the end of the film, when he actively saves the life of an Iraqi general on the verge of committing suicide. Through his looking glass, Siavash observes the crying and desperate general walking away from his base into a field. When he stops and dramatically holds a gun to his temple, Siavash calls his colleagues and orders a missile strike on coordinates right next to the general. When the shell strikes and the explosion deliberately misses, the general falls to his knees and thanks God for what he interprets as a divine signal not to take his own life. Siavash's prevention of the suicide is the peak of his compassion towards the Iraqis that is central to *The Queen*. This point is further underlined by the scene's meta-filmic elements: the Iraqi general is portrayed by none other than Homayoun Ershadi (b. 1947), who started his acting career by playing the lead role in *Ṭa'm-e Gīlās/Taste of Cherry* (1997). Considering that Kiarostami's film was criticized harshly by religious hardliners in Iran for the fact that Ershadi's protagonist intends to take his own life, the scene becomes a remarkable intertextual commentary. On the one hand, Ahangar offers possible ways out of suicide that *Taste of Cherry* refused his protagonist, namely empathy between strangers and faith in divine salvation. But, more importantly, it immediately gives audiences a point of reference for the Iraqi general, who affectively becomes much more than a bit role that could have been played by an extra: an ambiguous character with complex emotions and hints of a backstory that reflects his death wish. Even for audiences unfamiliar with Kiarostami's film, at the very least the casting of arguably one of the biggest and most recognizable film stars in Iran in a role that neither involves a speaking part nor is shown up close evokes another level of audience empathy.

Siavash's treatment strongly highlights empathy with Iraqi soldiers and even their generals. Meanwhile, the Iranian military in *The Queen* is no shining example for 'the official pro-war ideology of heroic martyrdom' as Sacred Defense films normally promote it.[13] Rather than faithful young men certain of Iranian victory, the soldiers are terrified and doubt their actions at every turn. Their display of fear is another transgression of the Sacred Defense tradition, because frightened soldiers do not appear in hegemonic memory culture: 'One who believes they are being taken to a better place does not have fear,' Roxanne Varzi points out in her book on martyrdom in Iranian popular culture.[14]

The Queen's rather un-heroic portrayal of Iranians also applies to the military as a whole. While films like *The Scout* had underlined companionship and coherence with a score that resembled the cacophony of the footsteps of a marching army present even in scenes where the protagonist is running on his own, the military in *The Queen* is not presented as a unified body. Instead, it is torn apart by internal conflicts: the superior officers seem as demoralized and clueless as the protagonist, leading to heated arguments about possible strategies between themselves. Siavash distrusts them and his fellow soldiers so much that at one point he lies to them about a target to spare the life of a wounded Iraqi. This is a harsh contrast to the picture of the Iranian military most other Sacred Defense films are aiming to broadcast: a coherent body strengthened and unified by its faith in victory, acknowledging tragedy only when mourning its martyrs.

Absence and Martyrdom

In addition to the portrayal of military individuals on both sides of the conflict as complex and ambiguous, *The Queen* transgresses two other taboos of the hegemonic memory culture of the war, namely the staging of absence and martyrdom.

While the paradigm of martyrdom is central in Sacred Defense culture, the notion of absence is less obvious, although it is a prominent theme in Shi'ite culture in general[15] and in *Defā'-ye Moqaddas* films in particular, especially in prisoner-of-war films that deal with the uncertain fate of missing soldiers. Probably the most prolific example of this subgenre of Sacred Defense cinema is Ebrahim Hatamikia's *Bū-ye Pīrāhan-e Yūsef/The Scent of Yusef's Shirt* (1995). With regard to that film, Roxanne Varzi argues that through the staging of the absence of soldiers missing in action, cinema gives audiences – many of whom have lost family members themselves – a safe space to mourn: 'Like a manifesto or a proclamation of death, cinema provides an image to be mourned, a ghostly presence: a hauntology of the after-war films that are created in the wake of the now-dead martyrs.'[16] Michaël Abecassis doubles down on the potential of films to make absent soldiers visible again for a traumatized audience when he states that 'through a profusion of light, sound, taste and feeling, it allows us to see and almost to touch those who have gone.'[17]

In *The Queen*, it is the body of Jamshid, the previous soldier using the observatory, that is absent, which is stressed through an arrangement of his empty clothes when Siavash finds his place. But in contrast to the official glorification of missing soldiers, the ghost of Jamshid is portrayed as a highly ambiguous figure. The knowledge he obtained after death is not at all in line with the state-carried narrative of the war: he questions the moral aspect of killing and constantly points out the dilemmas that follow along with it to the degree that he seems to enjoy the misery of his successor's resulting moral crisis.

The film not only questions the glorification of fallen soldiers by portraying a ghost as a demoralized nihilist, it also challenges the concept of martyrdom itself. None of the protagonists in *The Queen* dies in a meaningful way necessary for the war effort. Siavash finds death in a surprise bombardment of his tower, realizing that his experiment to keep the Iraqi army at bay while sparing as many lives as possible has failed. Through his demise, nothing is won. In the classics of Sacred Defense cinema, the death of a soldier at the very least motivates his comrades to revenge him and fight the enemy with even more commitment. In *The Queen*, on the other hand, half of the protagonists die in an accident caused by an Iranian weapons' smuggler who lost his mind mourning his dead son. His son's death doesn't ignite a motivation for revenge but rather a madness that causes even more death. Given that the glorification of martyrdom is the very cornerstone of Sacred Defense cinema, this challenge from within the genre is remarkable.

Apart from *The Queen*, all of Ahangar's films belong to the prisoner-of-war subgenre and play with the notion of absence and death in a way that counters the state's reading of the war. His 2018 drama *Cypress Under Water* is the most recent example for this, as it tests the boundaries of possible statements in the highly restricted discourse on mourning for missing or deceased soldiers.

Like *The Queen*, *Cypress Under Water* is set in the final year of the war at the Iraqi border and focuses on the efforts of the Ahwaz chapter of the Martyr Organization (*Bonyād-e Shahīd*) to recover bodies of Iranian soldiers, identify them, and send them back to their relatives. Responsible for these operations are the brothers Jahanbakhsh and Jahangir. In particular, Jahanbakhsh doubts the prevalent cult around martyrs, which celebrates the passing of deceased spirits into paradise, and instead prioritizes the surviving families' wish to receive physical remains, and with them a proof of death and a material anchor for their grief. These beliefs even lead Jahanbakhsh to occasionally hand out unidentifiable bodies to families whose relatives remain missing.

When a Zoroastrian family claims the body of their son, Jahanbakhsh is forced to reflect on this practice, as they identify their son in pictures of a corpse that has already been given away to a grieving mullah in Lorestan, the rural province north of Ahwaz. For clarification, the brothers travel to Lorestan to exhume the body against the strong resistance of the mullah and his family, who fear for the closure they had regained with the burial of their son. Most of the film revolves around the conflict between the two families and the Martyr Organization, which negotiates the significance of the materiality of the physical remains in opposition to the absence of the martyred spirit in the realm of the living. The resolution of the conflict is told ambiguously: after the Lori family has seemingly averted the exhumation of the body in question, the film closes with a Zoroastrian burial ceremony, implying that the family has ultimately found something – the body or a placeholder – to bury and grieve for. While the fog from the frankincense obscures their grief, which can only be heard in the screams of the relatives, it stresses the importance of the ceremonial closure.

That this closure can only be found along with the physical remains of the deceased is a point *Cypress Under Water* makes repeatedly through graphic pictures of the corpses that the *Bonyād-e Shahīd* recovers. A particularly conspicuous shot in the beginning of the film shows five recently reclaimed bodies in an open truck photographed against a strong light, which gives them a large halo, surrounded by dozens of praying morgue workers. This celebration of the martyred is nothing new in the tradition of Sacred Defense cinema. Its focus on the physical corpses, instead of the immortal soul, however, offers a slight variation. The line between cheering for the dead's ascension into paradise and focusing on the needs of the survivors is crossed explicitly in an argument between Jahanbakhsh and an especially religious colleague early in the film. After the latter has noticed that Jahanbakhsh illegally handed out unidentifiable body parts to a grieving family, he reminds him that lying about a martyr's remains is an offense to his immortal soul, to which Jahanbakhsh replies angrily: 'Actually, my God rather considers the living!'[18]

The prioritization of the concerns of the living over those of the martyred is clearly not in line with the hegemonic discourse on martyrdom reflected in other Sacred Defense films. It is further notable that it comes from a member of the *Bonyād-e Shahīd*, a state-carried foundation, and is delivered as a spiritual argument: instead of personal conviction or empathy with the grieving, Jahanbakhsh claims to act out of religious dedication – it is, after all, his God who commands him to care for the living. This dedication later leads him to openly criticize the Iranian army's lack of tags, which makes the identification of bodies much harder, while noticing that this is in fact a purposeful omission. *Cypress Under Water* here establishes that during the war the army actively let soldiers die namelessly and questions this practice through a focus on relatives craving for closure and confirmation of death. Its criticism of the army and the war effort as a whole even reaches the point where Jahanbakhsh's brother Jahangir complains about his working conditions to a visiting general from Tehran and yells at him that he wished the Iranians had never entered Iraqi territory in the first place.

A Zoroastrian Perspective on the War

Apart from questioning the Iranian army and the state's discourse on martyrdom, which was already central to *The Queen*, *Cypress Under Water* adds a further dimension to Ahangar's recollection of the war: the role of non-Muslim soldiers and the conceptualization of Iran as a religiously pluralist nation state. From the titular cypress, the paradisiac tree which has a crucial role in Zoroastrian cosmology, to the burial ceremony in its finale, the film focuses on the particularities of the Zoroastrian experience in the war, especially with regard to their different assumptions on the afterlife. While the belief in martyrdom leads the mullah's family to celebrate their son's ascension into paradise, the Zoroastrian parents need the missing body for completely different reasons: first, they seek confirmation to bury their hope for their son to be alive and well, and, second, in case he is actually dead, they need to lay him to rest properly according to Zoroastrian rituals. This conflict, which is at the core of the drama, underlines the difficulties that come with living as a marginalized community inside a Muslim majority country whose public administration is organized along the lines of different religious practices. Jahanbakhsh and Jahangir, whose religious affiliation is never confirmed but whose ancient names indicate a non-Muslim background, play the role of the rare public officials who make exceptions and actively champion these minorities, often against the resistance of the institution they represent.

In terms of character development, the Zoroastrian family and the brothers working for the Martyr Organization are the emotional protagonists of the film. The Zoroastrian father is played again by Homayoun Ershadi, the prominent actor who was already used as an anchor into a previously underrepresented perspective in *The Queen*, where he portrayed the suicidal Iraqi general, while the mother serves as a Zoroastrian priest. Her figure represents an element of

Zoroastrian tradition that is presented as particularly progressive, namely their ability to accept women in high-ranking religious positions. In contrast, the Muslim family, whose patriarch is a Lori village mullah, is portrayed as vile and driven by ulterior motives: during the course of the conflict, it is revealed that they plan to remarry the deceased soldier's widow to his brother, which is part of the reason that they desperately need a buried body that proves that their son is actually dead.

According to Ahangar, this focus on Zoroastrian characters and their particular needs in the context of the war and its aftermath is no mere plot device. In a press conference after the premiere of *Cypress Under Water* in February 2018, the director underlined that his central concern in the film was to highlight the previously underserved Zoroastrian experience of the war and to bring their perspective into the mnemonic discourse, as their sacrifice was much greater than is usually remembered in official accounts: 'In comparison to other religions, Zoroastrians had a higher share of martyrs in their community.'[19]

It is important to note, however, that this criticism of official memory culture is by no means challenging the Iranian state as a whole. On the contrary, the film finds an outspokenly nationalist way to resolve the sectarian conflict at its core by pointing to the imagination of Iran as a religiously pluralist state. Visually, this manifests in different scenes that stage the Iranian flag prominently. The coffins which carry unidentified or disputed bodies are usually wrapped in large flags, an overt symbolism which states that even if their individual identity is unclear, the deceased are all Iranians. At one point, Jahangir finds a large flag in the mud and hangs it out to dry near a campfire, accompanied by music as melodramatic and blatant as the scene's symbolism. In the following sequence, his brother talks about the countless neglected Zoroastrian, Jewish, and Armenian sacrifices for the war effort in a conversation with the sister of the missing soldier – not without mentioning that these communities were present in Iran before the emergence of Islam and thus represented the ancient backbone of the nation. These unambiguous nationalist overtones again highlight that Ahangar is in no way speaking in opposition to the Iranian state and even actively identifies himself as a member of the ultraconservative spectrum. It is precisely this position within the Sacred Defense discourse that makes his counter-readings of the war all the more intriguing.

Spiritual Criticism

When it comes to criticism and breaking taboos from within the tradition of Sacred Defense cinema, one could now easily point towards directors like Ebrahim Hatamikia. His films, too, belong to the *Sīnemā-ye Defāʿ-ye*

Moqaddas, and some of them are very outspoken in criticizing the treatment of veterans, like *The Glass Agency*, his most popular film, or the consequences of living with guilt, like his 2006 drama *Beh Nām-e Pedar/In the Name of the Father*. In contrast to Ahangar, however, Hatamikia's and others' criticism comes from psychological drama, and thus from a rational place: veteran Kazem is taking hostages to save his dying friend and make a political point; the father struggles with guilt over being responsible for putting his daughter in danger; and in *Az Karkheh Tā Rayn/From Karkheh to Rhine* (1993), wounded veteran Saeed has to go to Germany to receive proper treatment. Consequently, when the plot is resolved and the rational goals are achieved or the psychological drama is put to rest in one way or another, all of these films find reconciliation with the state's epistemic hegemony on the war as inevitable and its actions necessary.

In *The Queen* and *Cypress Under Water*, on the other hand, the criticism is coming from a spiritual place, which is compelling, because this is actually the perspective of the official state historiography of the Sacred Defense. The whole project of framing the war with Iraq as a 'sacred' operation is religiously motivated by design, and one of the main imperatives behind the genre of the *Sīnemā-ye Defā'-ye Moqaddas* is to distinguish itself from Western war cinema by underlining 'the war's spiritual dimensions,' as Hamid Naficy points out.[20] In her work on martyrdom and media culture, Roxanne Varzi elaborates that this manifests in filmmaking that 'uses less action and more narrative in order to promote the spiritual aspects of the war rather than show it as a series of cold-blooded strategic maneuvers.'[21] Religion, thus, became central to the films' legitimation of the war: 'This move from action to narrative films is marked by the presence of Islam, which serves to promote the war as Sacred Defence.'[22]

Considering that one of the defining traits of Sacred Defense cinema is its use of religious imagery and narrative to stage the war as a necessary and often glorious affair, it is notable that Ahangar's films come to very different interpretations despite speaking the same language. Not only that, but his films often derive their counter-readings of the war precisely from their spiritual perspective. *The Queen* illustrates this point best: like in many Sacred Defense films, the plot is very much organized as a spiritual path for the protagonist. When Siavash finds his tower, he has to climb up a dark shaft towards the light of the observatory, from which he can supposedly help the war effort. But in classics of the genre, most strikingly in *The Scout*, this path never deviates from the route preordained by official military strategy and the presumed necessities of war. Siavash's journey in *The Queen*, on the other hand, is very much one of transgressing orders and official policy, and is a constant negotiation between the notions of strategy, morality, and the righteousness of his superiors, Jamshid's ghost, and his own presumptions of God's will. After he has found the observatory and the ghost that haunts it, he desperately tries to keep it secret from his superiors, which clearly illustrates that this is his very own spiritual path, independent from the military and the bigger picture of the nation's war effort. In *Cypress Under Water*, this is mirrored by Jahangir's independent effort to help grieving relatives and to transgress the rules of the Martyr Organization out of a religious imperative that prioritizes the living over the dead. Both work with decidedly spiritual plot points and images, which is common in Sacred Defense cinema, but end up in positions that strongly challenge its prevalent mnemonic discourses.

The Current State of Sacred Defense Cinema in Iranian Media Discourse

Being a religious filmmaker well established in the ultraconservative networks of the film industry did not save Ahangar from being attacked and *The Queen* causing heated debates after its premiere at the Fajr Film Festival in 2012. The strongest criticism of the film came from the ultraconservative camp itself, who accused Ahangar of sympathizing with the Iraqi side. The film's depiction of the Iranian military as a quarreling bunch of terrified and clueless men was also seen as an affront, as was its refusal to promote martyrdom. The debate heated up to a point where Ahangar himself felt the need to step in and defend his reading of the war, quoting personal experiences as a soldier to qualify his claim to truth.[23]

The problems that the film faced did not end with these debates. It remained in the state of examination by the Ministry of Culture and Islamic Guidance for a long time and it took over fourteen months from its premiere at Fajr to its theatrical release. When *The Queen* was finally approved, the screening council released it suddenly in May 2013 without notifying the distribution company in advance. Surprised by the film being pulled forward on short notice, no advertising material was prepared in time and the film played only in selected theaters.[24] These forms of soft restrictions, in combination with the debates in 2012, which made its release highly anticipated, show that the film's reading of the war was not particularly popular with the authorities, given its strong disagreement with official state historiography. In a personal interview, one of Ahangar's colleagues even claimed that since *The Queen*, his films were surveyed and restricted even more closely than the works of many of his more popular liberal colleagues.

Such suggestions of ultraconservatives being more restricted in their criticism than liberal filmmakers surely should not be taken at face value. Yet they illustrate that in terms of public reception, Ahangar exists in a bipartisan limbo: while young and liberal moviegoers dismiss his films as examples of a new wave of religiously bloated Sacred Defense cinema, conservative audiences are affronted because their portrayal of the war and its aftermath transgresses the boundaries of the mnemonic discourse on the *Defā'-ye Moqaddas*. In current academic examinations of subversive tendencies in Iranian war cinema, this position to date is quite under-researched. Recent contributions concentrate either on the box office hits dealing with the war, such as the trauma-induced dramas of the 1990s[25] or the ongoing resurgence of the genre since the 2000s through comedies[26] and action blockbusters,[27] or the more critically acclaimed subversive films.[28] More thorough analyses of films from this niche in Sacred Defense cinema, which challenges its basic notions from a spiritual perspective, will complete the picture of the genre's current state, which is a continuously evolving and influential part of the Iranian film industry, as shown by the success and lively debates around *Ekhrājī-hā/The Outcasts* (2007), *Beh Vaqt-e Shām/Damascus Time* (2018), or *The Queen*. In this way, taking Ahangar's films into consideration can help studies of the current state of Iranian war cinema to avoid the mistakes of research on the classics of the genre, which usually adopt a binary analysis that assumes Sacred Defense films in a spectrum between propaganda and liberal criticism instead of looking at the particularities of the films that often classify in neither of these categories.[29]

Ahangar's Films as Spiritual Counter-Memories of the War

It remains to take note that the case of Mohammad Ali Ahangar shows that counter-memories of the war do not only originate in liberal circles or from rational perspectives. There is also criticism by religious and conservative filmmakers who must navigate the same minefield of taboos and doctrines that rule the hegemonic discourse on memory culture. In Ahangar's case, an analysis of his recent films shows exactly how he derives his interrogation of hegemonic memory culture from spiritual standpoints. On the surface, his films very much align with prevalent Sacred Defense discourse: told from the perspective of deeply religious military insiders, they move well within the circle of those who are allowed to speak about the war according to the discursive power structures of the Islamic Republic. However, their spiritual beliefs in particular lead these protagonists to positions differing strongly from official state historiography. It is the religious dogma of the equal worth of all human beings that leads Siavash to take the Iraqi perspective into account and that motivates Jahanbakhsh's commitment to the grieving Zoroastrians. Accordingly, the protagonists' attitude to the paramount value of life, in opposition to death and afterlife, shapes their worldview and actions. This leads to the neglect of martyrdom in *The Queen* and the prioritization of the needs of the living over those of the dead in *Cypress Under Water*. Both films start out from the perspective of the classics of the *Sīnemā-ye Defā'-ye Moqaddas*, but after decidedly spiritual detours they end up in a refusal to glorify the war, challenging the genre's very right to exist.

Notes

1. Naficy, Hamid, *A Social History of Iranian Cinema. Vol. 4: The Globalizing Era, 1984–2010* (Durham, NC: Duke University Press 2012), p. 26.
2. Ibid., p. 8.
3. Devictor, Agnés, 'Shahid Morteza Avini, cinéaste et martyr,' in *L'Iran, derrière le miroir*, ed. Christian Bromberger (Arles: Actes sud 2009), p. 55.
4. Khosronejad, Pedram (ed.), *Iranian Sacred Defence Cinema: Religion, Martyrdom and National Identity* (Canon Pyon: Sean Kingston Publishing 2012).
5. Esfandiary, Shahab, *Iranian Cinema and Globalization: National, Transnational, and Islamic Dimensions* (Bristol: Intellect Books 2012), p. 151.
6. Varzi, Roxanne, 'A Ghost in the Machine: The Cinema of the Iranian Sacred Defence,' in *The New Iranian Cinema: Politics, Representation and Identity*, ed. Richard Tapper (London and New York: I. B. Tauris 2002), p. 159.
7. '"Child of the Earth" Receives Much Attention at Iran Cinema Celebration,' in *Tehran Times*, 18 September 2008, https://www.tehrantimes.com/news/178232/Child-of-the-Earth-receives-much-attention-at-Iran-Cinema-Celebration (last accessed 15 September 2020).
8. Naficy, *A Social History of Iranian Cinema*, p. 24.
9. Givian, Abdollah and Zohreh Tavakoli, 'Tasvīr-e ʿArāqī-hā dar Sīnemā-ye Defāʿ-ye Moqaddas,' in *Taḥqīqāt-e Farhangī-ye Īrān*, Vol. 4, No. 2 (2012), pp. 87–107.
10. Karimabadi, Mehrzad, 'Manifesto of Martyrdom: Similarities and Differences between Aviniʿs Ravāyat-e Fath [Chronicles of Victory] and More Traditional Manifestoes,' in *Iranian Studies*, Vol. 44, No. 3 (2011), p. 386.
11. Varzi, 'A Ghost in the Machine,' p. 158.
12. Viré, Francois, 'Naḥl,' in *The Encyclopaedia of Islam, Second Edition* (Leiden: Brill 1986).
13. Naficy, *A Social History of Iranian Cinema*, p. 24.
14. Varzi, Roxanne, *Warring Souls: Youth, Media, and Martyrdom in Post-Revolution Iran* (Durham, NC: Duke University Press 2006), p. 97.
15. This is evident in the centrality of the concept of the 'great absence' (*al-Ghayba al-Kubrā*), which describes the anticipation of the 'guided one' (*Mahdī*), the twelfth Imam expected to appear on the Day of Judgment.
16. Varzi, 'A Ghost in the Machine,' pp. 162f.
17. Abecassis, Michaël, 'Iranian War Cinema: Between Reality and Fiction,' in *Iranian Studies*, Vol. 44, No. 3 (2011), p. 389.
18. 'Etefāqan, khodā-ye man bishtar beh fekr-e zendeh ast!' min. 16:30.
19. 'Zartoshtyān nesbat beh jamʿyateshān shahedā-ī bīshtarī az dīgar-e edyān dārand': 'Neshast-e Khabarī-ye Fīlm-e Sarv Zīr-e Āb – Bāsheh Āhangar: "Zartoshtyān nesbat beh jamʿyateshān shahedā-ī bīshtarī az dīgar-e edyān dārand,"' in *Khabargozārī-ye Tasnīm*, 7 February 2018, https://www.tasnimnews.com/fa/news/1396/11/18/1650961/نشست-خبری-فیلم-سرو-زیر-آب-باشه-آهنگر- دارند-ادیان-دیگر-از-بیشتری-شهدای-جمعیتشان-به-نسبت-زرتشتیان) (last accessed 15 September 2020).
20. Naficy, *A Social History of Iranian Cinema*, p. 21.

183

21. Varzi, *Warring Souls*, p. 98.
22. Varzi, 'A Ghost in the Machine', p. 157.
23. 'Moḥammad ʿAlī Bāsheh Āhangar: Man Khod Sanad Zendeh Jang Hastam,' in *Bāshgāh-e Khabarnegārān-e Javān*, 29 December 2013, https://www.yjc.ir/fa/news/4365651/ قبلی-هستم عوامل-جنگ-زنده-سند-خود-آهنگر من-باشه-محمدعلی داشتند-مهمی-نقش-فیلم-این-تخریب-در-هفت-برنامه (last accessed 15 September 2020).
24. '"The Queen" Coming to Iranian Theaters,' in *Mehr News Agency*, 1 May 2013, https://en.mehrnews.com/news/55075/The-Queen-coming-to-Iranian-theaters (last accessed 15 September 2020).
25. Ebrahim Hatamikia's veteran films are surely the most prolific contributions to this subgenre and have been featured heavily in academic literature. For example: Esfandiary, *Iranian Cinema and Globalization*, pp. 141–76; Khosronejad, *Iranian Sacred Defence Cinema*, pp. 59–110.
26. The trend of hugely popular comedies on the war, like Kamal Tabrizi's *Leyli is With Me* (*Leylī bā Man Ast*, 1996) or Masoud Dehnamaki's *The Outcasts* (*Ekhrājī-hā*, 2007) and their relation to Sacred Defense cinema is well covered in: Partovi, Pedram, 'Martyrdom and the "Good Life" in the Iranian Cinema of Sacred Defense,' in *Comparative Studies of South Asia, Africa and the Middle East*, Vol. 28, No. 3 (2008), pp. 513–32.
27. The most influential recent examples for this phenomenon are Ebrahim Hatamikia's *Damascus Time* (*Beh Vaqt-e Sham*, 2018) and Bahram Tavakoli's *The Lost Strait* (*Tangeh-ye Abū Qrayb*, 2018), two expensive action movies which heavily rely on the aesthetics of Sacred Defense cinema. Abbasian, Kaveh, 'Damascus Time: The Resurgence of Iranian "Sacred Defence" Cinema,' in *The Middle East in London*, Vol. 15, No. 2 (2019), pp. 15–18.
28. In this regard, the interest focuses most strongly on Mohsen Makhmalbaf who, as a former Sacred Defense filmmaker whose films started to turn against hegemonic state discourse, continues to amaze academic researchers. See for example: Dabashi, Hamid, *Close Up: Iranian Cinema, Past, Present, and Future* (London and New York: Verso 2001), pp. 156–212.
29. Laudable exceptions to this rule, i.e. analyses looking closely at the classics of the genre and their aesthetics instead of dismissing them as outright propaganda, are the respective works of Roxanne Varzi and Agnés Devictor: Varzi, *Warring Souls*; Devictor, 'Shahid Morteza Avini, cinéaste et martyr,' pp. 54–60.

References

Abbasian, Kaveh, 'Damascus Time: The Resurgence of Iranian "Sacred Defence" Cinema,' in *The Middle East in London*, Vol. 15, No. 2 (2019), pp. 15–18.
Abecassis, Michaël, 'Iranian War Cinema: Between Reality and Fiction,' in *Iranian Studies*, Vol. 44, No. 3 (2011), pp. 387–94.
'"Child of the Earth" Receives Much Attention at Iran Cinema Celebration,' in *Tehran Times*, 18 September 2008, https://www.tehrantimes.com/news/178232/Child-of-the-

Earth-receives-much-attention-at-Iran-Cinema-Celebration (last accessed 15 September 2020).

Dabashi, Hamid, *Close Up: Iranian Cinema, Past, Present, and Future* (London and New York: Verso 2001).

Devictor, Agnés, 'Shahid Morteza Avini, cinéaste et martyr,' in Christian Bromberger (ed.), *L'Iran, derrière le miroir* (Arles: Actes sud 2009), pp. 54–60.

Esfandiary, Shahab, *Iranian Cinema and Globalization: National, Transnational, and Islamic Dimensions* (Bristol: Intellect Books 2012).

Givian, Abdollah and Zohreh Tavakoli, 'Tasvīr-e ʿArāqī-hā dar Sīnemā-ye Defāʿ-ye Moqaddas,' in *Tahqīqāt-e Farhangī-ye Īrān*, Vol. 4, No. 2 (2012), pp. 87–107.

Karimabadi, Mehrzad, 'Manifesto of Martyrdom: Similarities and Differences between Avini's Ravāyat-e Fath [Chronicles of Victory] and More Traditional Manifestoes,' in *Iranian Studies*, Vol. 44, No. 3 (2011), pp. 381–86.

Khosronejad, Pedram, *Iranian Sacred Defence Cinema: Religion, Martyrdom and National Identity* (Canon Pyon: Sean Kingston Publishing 2012).

'Mohammad ʿAlī Bāsheh Āhangar: Man Khod Sanad Zendeh Jang Hastam,' in *Bāshgāh-e Khabarnegārān-e Javān*, 29 December 2013, https://www.yjc.ir/fa/news/4365651/ قبلی-هستم-عوامل-جنگ-زنده-سند-خود-سند-آهنگر-من-باشه-محمدعلی داشتند-مهمی-نقش-فیلم-این-تخریب-در-هفت-برنامه (last accessed 15 September 2020).

Naficy, Hamid, *A Social History of Iranian Cinema. Vol. 4: The Globalizing Era, 1984–2010* (Durham, NC: Duke University Press 2012).

'Neshast-e Khabarī-ye Fīlm-e Sarv Zīr-e Āb – Bāsheh Āhangar: "Zartoshtyān nesbat beh jamʿyateshān shahedā-ī bīshtarī az dīgar-e edyān dārand,"' in *Khabargozārī-ye Tasnīm*, 7 February 2018, https://www.tasnimnews.com/fa/news/1396/11/18/1650961/ شهدای-جمعیتشان-به-نسبت-زرتشتیان-آهنگر-باشه-زیر-سرو-فیلم-خبری-نشست دارند-ادیان-دیگر-از-بیشتری (last accessed 15 September 2020).

Partovi, Pedram, 'Martyrdom and the "Good Life" in the Iranian Cinema of Sacred Defense,' in *Comparative Studies of South Asia, Africa and the Middle East*, Vol. 28, No. 3 (2008), pp. 513–32.

'"The Queen" Coming to Iranian Theaters,' in *Mehr News Agency*, 1 May 2013, https://en.mehrnews.com/news/55075/The-Queen-coming-to-Iranian-theaters (last accessed 15 September 2020).

Varzi, Roxanne, 'A Ghost in the Machine: The Cinema of the Iranian Sacred Defence,' in Richard Tapper (ed.), *The New Iranian Cinema: Politics, Representation and Identity* (London and New York: I. B. Tauris 2002), pp. 154–66.

Varzi, Roxanne, *Warring Souls: Youth, Media, and Martyrdom in Post-Revolution Iran* (Durham, NC: Duke University Press 2006).

Viré, Francois, 'Naḥl,' in *The Encyclopaedia of Islam, Second Edition* (Leiden: Brill 1986).

PART IV

TRANSGENERATIONAL GAPS AND TRANSMISSIONS

'I want to go see where the stream ends. You know, Mother, I've been wondering where the end of the stream is . . . I haven't been able to think about anything else. I didn't sleep a wink all night. At last, I decided to go and find where the stream ends. I want to know what's happening in other places.'

The mother laughed –'When I was a child, I used to think a lot like that. But, my dear, a stream has no beginning and no end. That's the way it is. The stream just flows and never goes anywhere.'

'But mother dear, isn't it true that everything comes to an end? Nights end, days end, weeks, months, years . . .'

Samad Behrangi, The Little Black Fish
(Māhī-ye Sīyāh-e Kūchūlū, 1967)

10. *FILMFARSI* AS COUNTER-MEMORY

Pedram Partovi

I argue in this essay that *filmfarsi* ('Persian-film'),[1] a long-standing term of abuse for the popular commercial cinema of the late Pahlavi era, has functioned as a 'counter-memory,' an absent presence that has problematized official ideas of Iranian cinema and national culture both before and after the Islamic Revolution of 1978–9. I pay particular attention to cultural and political elites' demonization and suppression of *filmfarsi* under the Islamic Republic, taken to be a prominent symbol of Pahlavi modernism and its sins. Yet, this official post-revolutionary memory of *filmfarsi* obscures Pahlavi-era modernists' own dismissal and marginalization of the commercial cinema during its heyday. In fact, *filmfarsi* as counter-memory would seem to highlight the contrasting claims that intellectuals and politicians have made about entertainment in modern Iranian life: at once culturally irrelevant and politically dangerous. Correspondingly, the continuing circulation in Iran of banned *filmfarsi* titles and official concerns about the supposedly contaminating presence of themes, images, sounds, and individuals from the pre-revolutionary commercial cinema in more recent film and television productions do not necessarily indicate an upsurge of mass nostalgia. Their predominantly youthful audiences likely do not have a prior memory of these films to relive. Rather, *filmfarsi* revivals and survivals may point to the Pahlavi-era cinema's current reconfiguration as an alternative account of the Islamic Revolution and its cultural effects. *Filmfarsi*, both as a catalog of films and as a style of filmmaking, has thus consolidated a formidable presence in the minds of millions that decades of imposed forgetting has not managed to extinguish.

By the same token, *filmfarsi* has not simply revealed the hidden and authentic thoughts and wishes of the Iranian masses. To be sure, the masses have consumed these films, but they have not authored them. Rather the authors of *filmfarsi* and its more recent traces have themselves belonged to the 'exemplary' classes if not to the elite stratum themselves, as the post-revolutionary case study presented below demonstrates. Filmmakers have thus repeatedly embraced the narrative conventions and stylistic elements of *filmfarsi* to challenge the 'official' memory that (rival) elites have produced. The viewing public in turn has continued to endorse this model of entertainment, whose persistence (or metastasis) I address in the final section of the chapter.

Faulty Memories

On 25 May 2018, Nasir Malik Muti'i, one of the biggest male stars of the pre-revolutionary commercial cinema, passed away in Tehran.[2] The mass outpouring of grief on social media networks and at various public memorials was noteworthy for a number of reasons. For one, Malik Muti'i had not starred in a film in thirty-six years. Young ideologues had pressured officials to halt screenings of that film, *Barzakhiha/The In-betweeners*,[3] after only two weeks for insulting what they believed to be the revolution's goals and principles.[4] The narrative centered on a group of ne'er-do-wells who escape prison in the chaos that followed the end of Pahlavi rule and then head for the border to flee the country. However, in their last stop before freedom, they stumble across a secret Iraqi plot to invade Iran. The prisoners are thus stuck in no man's land: between self and national interest, past and future, life and death, and heaven and hell – hence, the title of the film. Ultimately, the Iraqi plot stirs their patriotism, and they remain to fight to the death alongside a badly outgunned border guard (played by Malik Muti'i) and local villagers. In the minds of the film's critics, the revolution had explicitly rejected the 'vulgarity' of Pahlavi-era popular cinema, filled as it were with gratuitous sex, violence, and immorality. Thus, its symbols had no place in a new era of 'Islamic' filmmaking, an ill-defined concept at the time but one that such critics anticipated would be a clean break from the supposed obscenities of the Pahlavi past and representative of the true message of Islam to the world.[5] Nevertheless, during those two weeks, *The In-betweeners* drew massive audiences and smashed a number of box office records.[6] Malik Muti'i was afterwards banned informally from all state-run media, which undoubtedly frustrated any acting comeback.[7] Only in death was this ban lifted, with television and some newspaper reports celebrating the life of a star now decades removed from the spotlight.[8] In turn, legions of adoring fans, many of whom were either too young to have ever attended legal screenings of his films or born after his career had essentially ended, honored him virtually and in real life in spite (or perhaps because) of his associations with the era of 'idolatry' (*ṭāghūt*).

A similar public reaction had followed the death of another *filmfarsi* star, Muhammad ʿAli Fardin, in 2000.[9] Fardin, Malik Mutiʿi's fellow headliner in *The In-betweeners*, was also the target of a public and private campaign after its release that effectively made him *mamnūʿ al-taṣvīr*, or banned from any television and film appearances.[10] Again, only in death was the ban lifted so that the media could cover his funeral, which attracted substantial crowds. In fact, the mass gathering for his burial prompted family members of other prominent figures of the pre-revolutionary cinema, like Iraj Qadiri and Furuzan (Parvin Khayrbakhsh), who would pass away in subsequent years, to keep silent about their deaths under rumored official pressure.[11]

The 'official' handling of each of these deaths also led to a cycle of accusations and recriminations involving current and past industry figures, intellectuals, politicians, and the judiciary. The disputes surrounding Malik Mutiʿi's passing were especially intense and emblematic of the political divisions between elites that have grown more public in recent years, with society at large invited to choose sides. Celebrities often associated with liberal democratic or reformist (*iṣlāḥ ṭalab*) currents in Iran like actor Parviz Parastuʾi blasted what they claimed to be the hypocrisy of state media heads who had seemingly boycotted *filmfarsi* stars during their lives but now exploited them in death.[12] Interestingly, some prominent religious conservatives and authoritarian populists, often grouped together under the principlist (*uṣūlgarā*) label, also criticized the state media and cultural organizations for their role in seemingly blackballing Malik Mutiʿi, but for different reasons. A day after the death of Malik Mutiʿi, the director Masʿud Dihnamaki posted a picture (Figure 10.1) on his Instagram account of Malik Mutiʿi in prayer from *The In-betweeners*. In the caption, he asked whether someone like him who gave up his career to remain in Iran, mimicking the self-sacrificing, pure-hearted street tough or *lūṭī* that he often played in his films, was truer to the revolution's principles than the now-exiled 'pseudo-intellectual' (*rawshanfikr namā*) Mohsen Makhmalbaf – unsubtly pointing to Makhmalbaf's alleged role in the 1982 campaign against the film and the purge of its two biggest stars from the industry.[13] The judiciary, dominated by religious conservatives, adopted a more orthodox position and claimed that recent attempts to rehabilitate the stars and popular films of the Pahlavi era were part of yet another foreign-led plot to corrupt the moral fabric of society – a plot that must be frustrated.[14] One editorial in *Kayhan*, the organ press observers have claimed to be most representative of the views of Ayatollah Khomeini's office, had argued that the complaints from some corners about the banning of certain figures of the pre-revolutionary cinema were themselves acts against the revolution.[15]

Figure 10.1 Mas'ud Dihnamaki's salute to Malik Muti'i. (Source: Instagram).

Interestingly, the same *Kayhan* article noted that even during the Pahlavi era, state-run television did not give airtime to popular *filmfarsi* titles, in support of its argument for their banning under the Islamic Republic.[16] To be sure, the writer did not absolve then-political and cultural elites for the 'stain' of *filmfarsi*. Even if they officially disavowed this cinema, it was in any case a product of the permissive, Westernizing culture of the time that they had cultivated. Nevertheless, the editorial highlighted a historical detail often neglected in the heated debates over the propriety or impropriety of *filmfarsi* traces in Iranian cinema since the revolution. Dismissive, even hostile, attitudes on the part of officials and intellectuals towards popular commercial features in Iran have stretched back to the very origins of the film industry after World War II. Moreover, Pahlavi officials did very little to encourage a more creative or dynamic domestic industry, with high tax rates and import costs topping the list of producers' complaints throughout the post-war period.[17] Neither did the general relegation of home-grown productions to government-designated second- and third-class cinemas, while Western films dumped in the Iranian market enjoyed access to the first-class theater halls with their higher ticket prices, help to improve local production quality relative to Western imports.[18] This quality gap in turn became another stick for critics to beat the home-grown industry with.[19] Censoring, rather than cultivating, film production was always the primary objective of Pahlavi-era elites.[20] Policymakers instead gave precedence to other mass communications technologies like radio and television in their cultural vision.[21] Even when some modernist zealots close to the royal court made an effort in the 1960s and 1970s to cultivate an 'art' cinema after prevailing European models, but also in opposition to the narrative and stylistic conventions associated with *filmfarsi*, their work was in many ways personal and lacked any inter-ministerial coordination. Consequently, some of these 'New-Wave' projects after their completion never received a public screening, even on state television networks.[22]

'Professional' critics, for their part, had employed the term *filmfarsi* ironically in disparaging reviews of domestic productions as far back as the early 1950s. While its precise meaning has to this day remained a matter of debate, a consensus would emerge around the supposed cultural inauthenticity of the vast majority of the domestic industry's output.[23] In fact, *filmfarsi* became a shorthand reference for a set of filmmaking conventions in these home-grown features that the critics took to be wholly plagiarized. They were thus little more than second- and third-rate versions of foreign hits, filled with lewd characters and behavior, whose only seeming concession to their home environment was the use of Persian in the recording of dialogue and songs. To be sure, a good number of *filmfarsi* titles did bear a familial resemblance to the popular Egyptian, Indian, and Turkish cinemas of the same period. The dominant regional cinematic 'genre' in the post-war years was the contemporary social drama, often centered on an antagonistic relationship between two or more (overlapping) circles of friends or family, punctuated by violence (otherwise known as action sequences), heightened emotion (especially in musical interludes), and occasionally relieved by comic moments.[24] I have in fact argued elsewhere for the deep historical roots of this 'shared' filmmaking style.[25] Regardless, reviewers in the press and even some industry people generally took Hollywood cinema to be the model for *filmfarsi* but, to add insult to injury, without Hollywood's modernist values surviving the transfer process. Their press counterparts in Egypt, India, and Turkey had also associated their own home-grown features primarily with Hollywood cinema and what they believed to be its worst excesses.[26] In the case of *filmfarsi*, critics often pointed to filmmakers' reliance on sexual themes and images to market their productions as a vital link between the local and US-based industries.[27]

Commentators in the 1970s would increasingly adopt a political interpretation of popular cinema, including *filmfarsi*, by consciously or unconsciously drawing on Marxist critiques to highlight its supposedly propagandistic content.[28] They claimed that such features were more than just simple-minded diversions but had, along with some other modern cultural imports, inculcated their predominantly youthful viewers in a gross materialism and moral decadence that ultimately served the interests of ruling elites and especially their Western patrons.[29] Among religious circles, critiques of the cinema dated back to the very introduction of the medium in Iran but primarily on moral and aesthetic grounds.[30] During the revolution and its aftermath, radical reformist clerics and their supporters also built upon and extended the political criticism of leftist secular intellectuals about Pahlavi-era film and filmgoing culture, stressing the part that cinema played in 'conspiracies' to undermine the Islamic world.[31] Arson attacks on cinema halls nationwide were physical manifestations of these political critiques, drawing into question the very place of film in national life.[32] Even the officials who eventually took charge of the film industry's reorganization and revival under the Islamic Republic characterized the first four years after the revolution as a period of policy paralysis and uncertainty about cinema's future.[33] Of course, what policymakers did finally cultivate was from their perspective the very antithesis of *filmfarsi* in its narrative themes and aesthetic choices.[34]

Thus, a surprising consensus of opinion among Pahlavi modernists, leftist intellectuals, Shi'ite clerics, and lay religious radicals had come together about *filmfarsi* by the 1970s. The domestic features of the time served for all, albeit for different reasons, as a constant reminder of the failures, not triumphs, of Iranian cinema.[35] The immense popularity that some *filmfarsi* productions and actors enjoyed only underlined these failures. Those critical of the Pahlavi-era popular cinema in turn sought to distance themselves from its purported audience, who were often maligned for their lack of intelligence, taste, decency, and faith alongside the figures responsible for the films.

In this atmosphere of near universal opprobrium, *filmfarsi* productions could take on a scandalous, even forbidden appeal for filmgoers. The exemplars of Pahlavi modernization, the newly educated middle class, stood out in their repudiations of *filmfarsi* and claimed it to be far more suited to the tastes of the working and lower classes (especially the traditionally minded among them). Ironically, the middle class figured heavily in the making of such home-grown features and likely made up the bulk of their viewers too.[36] Of course, popular entertainments have long had a controversial character in Iran, with practices like storytelling, dance, music, theater, and buffoonery historically relegated in elite accounts to groups and individuals on the social margins.[37] Such entertainments, which included the Shi'ite *ta'ziyih* passion plays, invariably took romance and heroism as their subjects and involved the adaptation or, from a more hostile perspective, debasement of texts and tropes from courtly and religious 'high culture.' In fact, these stories and their various performative modes could not only invite the condemnation of political figures and clerics but also arouse anxieties about their supposed hangover effects – namely social disruption and religious defilement. Interestingly, scholars have linked entertainers from at least the early modern era to criminality and criminal gangs.[38] This social 'deviance' could even extend to sexual behaviors, including prostitution.[39] As the cinema, radio, cabaret, and other modern leisure activities gradually eclipsed older ones over the past century, the performers responsible for these new entertainment forms in turn became associated with the same immorality and licentiousness that had tainted their predecessors.[40] Nevertheless, that social marginality had in the past also freed such performers from behavioral norms otherwise binding audience members and provided opportunities for pointed criticism and commentary as part of their entertainment.[41] Yet, since elites often patronized such entertainments, their seemingly subversive content could ultimately give way to validations of the dominant ideology of society.[42] *Filmfarsi* titles, rooted in some of the same themes and images of heroism and romance as earlier entertainments, were likewise condemned by both the filmgoing and non-filmgoing public as 'mindless' and 'vulgar' entertainment but were also deeply implicated in modern society's understanding of itself (even if negatively). Moreover, the best loved (and often best remembered) of these films largely endorsed the Pahlavi modernization project even as they offered viewers different exemplars of it and objectives for it. Borrowing from R. G. Collingwood's categories of modern 'art' as representation, *filmfarsi* from its beginnings seemingly operated as both 'amusement' and 'magic': arousing certain emotions to be discharged in the course of its consumption, but also inviting others to be channeled into real life.[43] Thus, *filmfarsi* titles could before the show titillate would-be audiences as a taboo. They could animate audiences during their unspooling by ignoring or critiquing political and cultural elites' ideas of what Iranian society and national cinema should be. However, the films did not necessarily seek to incite popular revolt, rather to bring about a recognition of the potential dangers, moral and material, of modernization decoupled from the interests of the (middle-class) family as its chief subject. The condemnations that *filmfarsi* productions would draw at once overestimated and underestimated their political charge and cultural relevance.

Filmfarsi during the late Pahlavi era operated as a foil for a national cinema and even culture whose existence was largely a matter of speculation. The appeal, at least in part, of the more than 1,000 productions associated with this style of filmmaking lay in their ability to highlight the contradictions and hypocrisies that characterized the utopian vision of Pahlavi modernists. In doing so, such films followed an established pattern in Iranian popular entertainments that despite or perhaps because of their social marginalization have remained important venues for self-criticism and commentary. The efforts of Pahlavi elites, as well as of their ideologically diverse opponents, to alienate *filmfarsi* from its audiences have thus been part of a long-term push by such groups to keep their own fantasies of Iranian society and culture alive. To be sure, the (less than successful) efforts of post-revolutionary elites to rewrite or suppress the memory of *filmfarsi* also fit into this pattern.[44]

Counter-memories

The survival of *filmfarsi* features, icons, and themes in the Islamic Republic has operated as a counter-memory, a term adapted from Michel Foucault's work, disturbing hegemonic narratives of revolutionary and post-revolutionary history.[45] The fretting of media critics and political figures about the 'contaminating' presence of *filmfarsi* on screens has, then, sprung from a conviction that such Pahlavi-era features and their generic traces not only pander to their audience's basest instincts but actively undermine the cultural vision that state-run media, educational organs, charitable foundations, and other local and national institutions had formulated and disseminated since the revolution.

Nevertheless, the revolutionary leadership's official line was that the *filmfarsi* era had come to a definitive end, even if early on bureaucrats and industry members could hardly agree on what that 'end' meant.[46] Answers to questions about who and what from the film culture of the *ancien régime* could be rehabilitated in a new cinematic order were less straightforward than in other institutional transitions of the time, partly because the hostility of revolutionaries to *filmfarsi* and its principals was neither uniform nor unanimous.[47] Even seemingly unambiguous acts of violence against *filmfarsi* and other symbols of 'decadent' Pahlavi culture, like the destruction of movie houses, could on closer inspection be more complex in their motivations.[48] Ayatollah Khomeini and other leaders may have promised an apocalyptic break with the cinematic past but the lower ranks were not entirely convinced.

The available histories have identified the Iran-Iraq War (1980–8) as a pivotal event in the development of a truly 'revolutionary cinema,' a genre of authentic and Islamically sanctioned films that supposedly represented a total rejection of the commercial features of the previous era.[49] Scholars have noted that the emergence of a war film genre, now commonly known as the Cinema of Sacred Defense (*Sinamā-yi Difā'-i Muqaddas*), coincided with the emergence of a new generation of 'committed' filmmakers, many of whom had received a practical field training at the war front.[50] Ironically, the 'hysterical campaign' against the release of *The In-betweeners*, which had caught many policymakers at the time by surprise, as well as the various bans that followed it, necessitated the infusion of new talent to prop up a now increasingly government-controlled industry, with the Cinema of Sacred Defense perhaps its most prominent beneficiary.[51] In fact, Cinema of Sacred Defense productions would come to make up roughly 25 percent of all feature films produced in the first decade and a half after the revolution.[52] Even though critics and academics have generally labeled the post-1982 Cinema of Sacred Defense as state propaganda, they have also asserted the novelty of its narrative themes and techniques, with its focus on what the war documentarian and film theorist Murtaza Avini called 'frontline mysticism.'[53] Thus, features associated with this 'movement' did not necessarily celebrate victory on the battlefield but in the spiritual realm over their 'godless' Iraqi foes. They highlighted the religious zeal of war volunteers, often from humble backgrounds, who willingly sacrificed themselves to prove the righteousness of the revolutionary cause.[54]

However, such claims of authenticity have typically ignored the prominence of martyrdom and self-sacrifice by lumpen heroes on the social margins as a narrative trope in many *filmfarsi* features.[55] To be sure, the on-screen heroes of the Pahlavi-era popular cinema were not martyrs for Islam or for an Islamic republic. Still, filmmakers often did portray their sacrifices as furthering another righteous cause – namely the well-being of family and friends, of one's social circle rather than of the atomized individual, as the true objective of Pahlavi modernization. Moreover, declarations of the novelty of Cinema of Sacred Defense productions have ignored the war films' own depiction of relationships with friends and family that frequently explain or complicate the war volunteers' on-screen actions for God and revolutionary principles.[56] If not the aesthetic then at least the moral dimensions of *filmfarsi* as a genre may shed light on the seeming lack of unanimity after the revolution about the fate of its productions and their principals, as well as on its mostly unacknowledged imprint on the Cinema of Sacred Defense. Indeed, despite the claims that officials, industry people, and critics have made about the Cinema of Sacred Defense, its features have neither been solely tools of propaganda nor the fulfillment of an 'Islamic cinema' seemingly unrelated to all that had come before. Rather, such films may also function as counter-memories of the Iran-Iraq War, of the revolution, and of Iranian film history.

One war feature whose release nearly matched the controversy of *The In-betweeners* was Mas'ud Dihnamaki's *Ikhrajiha/The Outcasts*,[57] a comedy set in the final year of the conflict. Audiences flocked to theaters to see it, which made it then the highest-grossing film of all time.[58] Critics, though, generally panned *The Outcasts* as a vulgar attempt to revive the Sacred Defense genre through cheap entertainment, with the clear insinuation that aspects of it resembled the discredited popular cinema of an earlier era. At particular issue for commentators was the supposed lampooning of the post-revolutionary heroic ideal through its conflation with comic and seemingly 'anti-heroic' characters.[59] Yet, I would argue this to be an ahistorical critique that fails to recognize the problematic conceptions of heroism and masculinity long rooted in Iranian entertainments at work in the film. The virtuous and ignoble have existed in uncomfortable proximity to one another, both in performances of heroism and in their performers.

Dihnamaki forces the viewer to confront these historical connections in the opening scene, where small-time gangster Majid 'Suzuki' (played by Kambiz Dirbaz), adorned in the symbols of past lumpen anti-heroes, violently avenges with his motorcycle's chain lock what he views to be a violation of his neighbor's daughter's honor. His motorcycle itself alerts viewers to his working-class character, as the most common conveyance for young men in poorer Tehran neighborhoods. The scene also focuses on Majid's clothing, including those accessories especially associated in films past and present with *lūṭī* street toughs, such as his canvas *gīvih* slippers and the Yazdi or Kashani kerchief around his hand. In the following scene, the audience encounters Majid finishing a prison term for his thuggery. Majid's explanation to family and neighbors for his long absence was a pilgrimage to Mecca but an ex-convict buddy unwittingly reveals the truth soon after his return. In these early scenes, the film fleshes out a character in Majid potentially familiar to audiences – one that closely resembles the loutish heroes of the cinematic (and pre-cinematic) past who were often equal parts brawn and guile. Much of the rest of the film concerns Majid's scheming to win the hand of Nargis (Niyusha Zayghami), his neighbor's daughter, by fraudulently gaining war veteran status. His idle friends eagerly join him in this scam, which also conveniently keeps the potential lovers a morally appropriate distance of several hundred kilometers apart. However, Majid and his gang's plan goes awry as their experiences at the front ultimately turn them into war heroes. Dihnamaki certainly makes concessions in the film to the revolutionary clergy's moral and political critique of *filmfarsi* that had supposedly necessitated the Cinema of Sacred Defense genre. Still, themes and images that formerly characterized popular cinema manage to infiltrate *The Outcasts*, even if in diluted form. Reviewers, for their part, may well have accepted the considerations of romantic love and homosociality within as complementary (or even competing) motivations for war volunteerism but the association of war heroism with thugs, petty thieves, and drug addicts was perhaps a bridge too far. Dihnamaki's heroization of streetwise rogues made a mockery of the incorruptible and self-abnegating Basij (Mobilization) militia volunteer at the center of more conventional Sacred Defense titles while aligning the film with literally hundreds of *filmfarsi* features.

Of course, this break with generic conventions was itself a source of comedy in the film, whose title alone alerts audiences to Majid and his corrupted sidekicks' seeming lack of suitability for the war, the war film genre, and even post-revolutionary reality. Moreover, other characters repeatedly affirm the gang's outcast status; the most notable example being the puritanical and narrow-minded registrar Hajj Salih (Muhammad Sharifi Niya) who initially rejects their applications to volunteer for the Basij militia on the grounds that their presence will desecrate the 'spiritual atmosphere' (*fażā-yi ma'navī*) of the war front. The outcasts, for their part, maintain a blasphemous attitude towards the war effort once they arrive at the front – never dressing in their fatigues, sleeping through communal prayer, singing bawdy songs, gambling, and smoking opium. However, Dihnamaki ultimately portrays his heroes as undergoing a moral transformation wherein they become devoted believers and patriots.

The Outcasts does incorporate into the plot a 'standard' Sacred Defense hero in drill sergeant Murtaza (Javad Hashimi), who functions as Majid's foil. Appropriately enough, Majid is hostile to this fellow neighborhood son, believing him to be a rival suitor for Nargis. Murtaza, on the other hand, embraces Majid and his friends and seeks to convince them that their salty language, posturing, and transgressive behaviors do not add up to true manliness, or *mardānagī*. Selfless acts of devotion and bravery, he claims, are the markers of masculine virtue at the front. Despite Murtaza's efforts, the gang is eventually cast out of the war front for its inappropriate conduct. In response, the noble and self-effacing Murtaza takes responsibility for their failures and performs drill exercises as penance. Soon his unit members, including the now seemingly converted outcasts, join in the exercise. Such communal acts of devotion (to God, the nation, and/or one's brothers in arms) have often figured in Sacred Defense features, especially as a prelude to martyrdom.[60] True to form, what follows is the climactic battle scene, during which Majid demonstrates his profound personal reformation by sacrificing his life (and love) to save a field hospital from Iraqi tank attack. The film ends with Majid dying in the arms of his new and old friends.

If policymakers and filmmakers had in fact wholly rejected the early and so-called unpersuasive attempts at war features rooted in the conventions of *filmfarsi*, to instead favor an approach that better embodied revolutionary goals and principles, then *The Outcasts* does appear to revive this 'decadent' past for its audiences. In fact, audiences may well have interpreted both the title and plot of *The Outcasts* to be a rather transparent homage to *The In-betweeners*, the film whose release had so enraged some revolutionaries that historians have credited it for the policy changes that paved the way for the Sacred Defense film movement. For Dihnamaki, and likely for some audience members, *The Outcasts* operates as a counter-memory of Iranian film history and its customary representations of the Sacred Defense cinema as generic innovation. The audiovisual argument at the heart of the film resolves that social marginality, alongside martyrdom and self-sacrifice, has always been central to Iranian popular cinema's depictions of male heroism even as it underlines the authenticity of the Sacred Defense film. Dihnamaki's defense of Malik Muti'i in death makes more sense in light of Dihnamaki's own filmmaking career.

The director has stated that *The Outcasts* was an autobiographical film. In an April 2007 television interview with Riza Rashidpur, Dihnamaki tearfully admitted that he himself was once a Murtaza to a young Majid martyred in the war. He did not allow for those like Majid, of which in his experience there were many, to be outcasts at the front. According to him, the film sets up an opposition between those who may be a rogue (*lāt*) on the outside but possess an inner purity, like Majid, and those who may be outwardly pious (*dīndār*) but ignoble (*lāt*) in spirit, like Hajj Salih. The film draws this contrast most explicitly in the battle scene where a terrified Hajj Salih runs for cover while a fearless Majid faces down a tank. The observant Hajj Salih may dutifully perform his religious obligations in the mold of the ideal citizen that the radical reformist clergy had envisioned for their utopian society, but it is the impious Majid who ultimately proves to be more dedicated to the revolutionary project, despite his willful ignorance or rejection of his religious duties. In highlighting the tensions underlying masculinity in and male obligation to the Islamic Republic, the film also operates as a counter-memory upsetting the official and sanitized narratives of the Iran-Iraq War (including the Cinema of Sacred Defense) that have taken Iranian soldiers' morale and *esprit de corps* to be proof of the realization of a Muslim utopia as a revolutionary objective.[61] In doing so, the film perhaps also draws viewers more skeptical of the achievements and consequences of that era.

The Outcasts was Dihnamaki's first feature-length film. He had previously directed two social realist documentaries in 2004 and 2006. The documentaries also had the same setting as *The Outcasts*: those poor and working-class neighborhoods of Tehran that had played such a crucial role in the revolution and its aftermath. Given his relatively short career in film, some critics derided *The Outcasts* as the work of a non-professional.[62] Yet, his lack of experience was no different from that of many others already in the industry who had launched their careers via the war and war documentary. Dihnamaki himself has claimed that the once architecture student turned filmmaker Murtaza Avini was the greatest inspiration for his move to film. Like Avini before him, his revolutionary and war credentials undoubtedly aided this professional transition. Before his filmmaker days, many Iranians knew Dihnamaki for his role as the self-appointed leader of the Ansar-i Hizb Allah (Followers of the Party of God). This group, with many former Basijis and war veterans as its members, often resorted to violence and intimidation to protect revolutionary ideals as they and their ultraconservative patrons in government or clerical circles understood them. Its semi-official thuggery included the infamous attacks on the University of Tehran dormitories during the student uprising of 1999.[63] Newspaper and magazine articles reporting on the audience reception of *The Outcasts* rarely failed to note the director's violent and controversial past, presumably as an explanation for the intense public interest in the film. Dihnamaki may have aligned himself with the character of Murtaza but his more youthful exploits were seemingly closer in temperament to the hot-headed Majid. In fact, his career would appear to be a modern parallel to those of the mercenaries, outlaws, and neighborhood toughs who once claimed to defend the honor of society while simultaneously engaging in violations of it.

In the early modern era these hooligans had built both their martial and moral reputations in youth against and among the brethren of their 'order' to later earn positions of leadership in promoting the controversial principles of masculine virtue or *javānmardī* (literally 'young-manhood') to a new generation of disciples.⁶⁴ From a transhistorical perspective, Dihnamaki's turn to cinema takes on added layers of significance – not only because cinema has come to supersede earlier practices (including pre-cinematic entertainments) that 'masters' could employ to instill a masculine ethic of social justice in the next generation but, for Dihnamaki at least, cinema was already performing this function during the *filmfarsi* era. Of course, *The Outcasts* also focuses on the contemporization of the *javānmardī* ethos, and so it forces audiences to consider the camaraderie of the street and its code of ethics in the mobilization of the Ansar-i Hizb Allah, Basij, and other groups alongside or imbricated in official revolutionary and war ideology. The radical reformist clergy did not simply impose its social and political vision on especially poor and working-class male youth, as many scholarly accounts have until recently assumed. Rather, these young men were often crucial to both the formulation and wider imposition of that vision during and after the revolution.⁶⁵ Dihnamaki's life and career achievements, including *The Outcasts*, present a counter-memory of the post-revolutionary era that argues for the Islamic Republic as less a gerontocracy of clerics than a juvenilocracy of militants.

Critics who have accused Dihnamaki of rehabilitating *filmfarsi* tropes in *The Outcasts* have also leveled similar criticisms at other filmmakers and films. Ironically, those journalists, policymakers, and industry people who have complained about the romanticization of a bygone film era have done much the same themselves. However, these alarmist voices have turned their wistful gaze to the 1980s as a 'golden age' (*dawrān-i ṭalāyi*) of formal and stylistic advances and ideological purity that policy shifts and cultural developments since have gradually compromised.⁶⁶ Significantly, the aesthetic and political 'confusion' and even 'decline' of cinema in the 1990s and beyond coincided for these voices with a partial loosening of the official stranglehold over the film industry. To be sure, heavy-handed government involvement in and oversight of cinema continued in the post-war era. In fact, it was during the 1990s that Western cineastes came to paradoxically champion an Iranian art cinema, which they viewed to be a 'challenge' to official representations of Iranian society and culture, even as many of its exemplars were very much the products of government censorship and financing.⁶⁷ This art film movement was itself a revival of sorts of Pahlavi-era cinema; specifically, the semi-official attempts to counter *filmfarsi* through the embrace of a film aesthetic largely European in origin. The post-revolutionary version of the New Wave included at least one major adjustment, namely the elimination or metaphorization of romance (read 'sexuality') to deflect any opposition from clerics and censors.⁶⁸ Even so, this art cinema has enjoyed an increasingly controversial existence in Iran. Consequently, its European promoters have in more recent years taken on greater financial responsibility for it and its auteurs too have moved offshore or underground to make their films now often quite explicitly for foreign audiences.[69] At the same time, the more commercially oriented film industry enjoyed an inward-looking expansion. Post-war reconstruction planning had invited the private sector to play a larger role in the economy, in line with a policy of 'economic liberalization' that international financing organizations had encouraged political leaders to adopt.[70] Private interests also deepened their engagement in cinema, with an eye towards profiting from a then-growing middle class with disposable income. The idea of film as entertainment enjoyed a comeback in the post-war years and coincided with a shift towards more entertainment programming on state television networks. Schedulers now made more room for popular films and television series, both foreign and domestically produced, in a bid to keep viewers at home as well as to counter the new threat of foreign-based Persian-language satellite broadcasting.[71]

This resurgence of commercial filmmaking, though, would by the end of the 1990s and early 2000s prompt ever more frantic warnings in newspaper editorials and television talk shows about the reappearance of *filmfarsi* formulas on Iranian screens.[72] There certainly were producers, writers, directors, and stars who in rather explicit ways drew on the collective memory of *filmfarsi* in their work, including storylines, characters, gags, and even titles. One prominent example was *Gul-i yakh/Ice Flower*,[73] featuring one of the current heart-throbs of the Iranian cinema, Muhammad Riza Gulzar, that contemporized the plot and characters of the much-loved and remembered *Sultan-i qalbha/King of Hearts*[74] to win the 2005 box office title. Muhammad 'Ali Fardin, the biggest male star of the 1960s, directed this earlier version and played the same role as Gulzar of the pop singer ultimately reunited with his long-lost wife and son (Figure 10.2).

Figure 10.2 Muhammad 'Ali Fardin (left) in *King of Hearts* and Muhammad Riza Gulzar (right) in *Ice Flower* playing the same role. (Source: Screen grab from Pars Video/TDH Home Entertainment).

The concern of cultural but also political elites with the 'return' of Pahlavi-era popular cinema and the continuing reverence for film icons like Malik Muti'i are undoubtedly related to the failure of official national culture to effectively socialize the masses in the Islamic Republic. The now exiled and officially discredited filmmaker Muhsin Makhmalbaf represents an exemplary case of this failure. Moreover, the call-backs and references to *filmfarsi* would appear to be evidence of a broader reconsideration of the revolution and its consequences. A series of recent events, including the 2009 election crisis, the nuclear file and fears of growing international isolation, regional wars, corruption and mismanagement trials, explosive new revelations of past government misdeeds, and the fortieth anniversary of the Islamic Republic, have all intensified public reappraisals of the post-revolutionary era. What some commentators have problematically identified as a wave of 'nostalgia' (*nustālzhī*) in Iranian media consumption habits[75] is, from my perspective, more accurately the operation of counter-memory. These counter-memories conflict with an official past, both national and personal, that state-run media outlets and educational venues have encouraged ordinary Iranians to internalize. Privately financed though officially permitted media productions like the direct-to-video series *Shahrzad*,[76] that recontextualizes the Mosaddeq era,[77] or the hit film *Nahang-i anbar/Sperm Whale*,[78] that relives the 1980s from the perspective of the first post-revolutionary generation,[79] but also foreign-based satellite television programs like Manoto TV's re-litigation of the Pahlavi era in its documentary series *Tunil-i zaman/Time Tunnel*[80] make up examples of the counter-programming that has amplified and shaped these alternative histories in recent years. Indeed, the operation of counter-memory contributes to the very entertainment of such films and programs, which stand alongside or actively engage with *filmfarsi* traces.

Entertainment and the Persistence of *Filmfarsi*

Despite the massive odds stacked against it in both the Pahlavi and the Islamic Republican eras, *filmfarsi* has survived. Indeed, it has survived even as the Hollywood titles that supposedly served as its source material have long escaped audience memories. Neither the cultural projects of secular Pahlavi modernists nor the Islamic Republic's radical reformist Shi'ites would accommodate *filmfarsi*. Its persistence as a discursive object provides a unique view of the parallels in official attitudes towards popular film that standard histories have altogether ignored as inconsequential. Paradoxically, even the filmgoing masses have engaged in this campaign of vilification and erasure of *filmfarsi*, as classist disavowals of viewing interest in it demonstrate. Elites and masses have alienated *filmfarsi* socially via its performers, culturally and morally via its performances, physically via its purported foreign origins, and historically via its relegation to an 'irrelevant' past.

The positioning of *filmfarsi* as alien and thus seemingly not integral to public or private life has undoubtedly contributed to its potentially subversive appeal. Yet, what has constituted many *filmfarsi* titles' entertainment is a native aesthetic experience, at least partly rooted in pre-cinematic ideas and practices of (male) heroism and romance, that officially sanctioned national culture has lacked. Before the revolution, proponents of an official national culture, such as it was, endorsed a modernist (read 'Western') aesthetic in place of native but now supposedly obsolescent models – a 'policy' position which the *filmfarsi* genre by its very presence would unsettle. Since the revolution, political and intellectual elites have emphasized the moral edification and uplift of the masses and rejected aesthetic concerns altogether as decadent. Ironically, the only coherent aesthetic sensibility that post-revolutionary officials at least tolerated has belonged to the art cinema movement, which adopted the erstwhile New Wave's modernist aesthetic with some adjustments. Nevertheless, the *filmfarsi* aesthetic has survived to problematize as well as shape official national culture and official and unofficial ideas of the nation in the Islamic Republic precisely because its entertainment has had its own moral dimensions. Following Collingwood, modern entertainments in Iran have functioned as art and magic, with widespread negative attitudes blunting their revolutionary effects as well as contributing to their critical heft.

To be sure, *filmfarsi* is a historical phenomenon and not some eternal cultural essence that different state ideologies have foolishly targeted for suppression. Its themes and images do not appear in the same way as they once did or in criticism of the same moral and social order. *Filmfarsi* has persisted in different forms, or metastasized as its critics might claim, for the very reason that it is an experience. Thus, its 'practitioners' have received a training in it and have transformed it in their own right. Unlike the overly intellectualized and heavily subsidized clerical Islam that, as the officially declared source of moral edification in the Islamic Republic, has insinuated itself into much of the content on official media outlets, *filmfarsi* has received communal support and remained independent of the state – a fact that also surely explains its long-term survival. The watching of these films and their later traces in today's Iran is a social, often familial, activity. The private exposure of youth to especially the older films via a variety of home video formats has differed from that of their parents' or grandparents' generation, who likely first experienced them in the cinema hall.[81] These older viewers have nevertheless played a key role in acculturating the younger generation in *filmfarsi* as an aesthetic experience, often through aestheticized descriptions to compensate for the degraded audio and video appearing on their television screens. Undoubtedly, the links between more recent features and old favorites from the *filmfarsi* era are also most apparent to such seasoned intermediaries who then explain them to novices in their household. The old 'masters,' like the *filmfarsi* heroes and their pre-cinematic predecessors, thus immerse their 'acolytes' in a moral and aesthetic tradition that the new generation ultimately carries forward in forging their own counter-memories.

NOTES

1. According to the transliteration scheme adopted by Edinburgh University Press for Persian technical terms with no recognized English equivalent, *filmfarsi* should be represented as follows: *filmfārsī*. However, considering its frequent appearance, I have not in this case followed the rule in order to minimize diacritical marks in the chapter.
2. Bardia Afshin, 'Naser Malek Motiee: Actor from Iran's Golden Age of Cinema Whose Career Stopped When the Ayatollah Arrived,' in *The Independent*, 31 May 2018, https://www.independent.co.uk/news/obituaries/naser-malek-motiee-dead-iran-actor-cinema-ayatollah-revolution-a8377106.html (last accessed 19 December 2018).
3. *Barzakhiha*, film, directed by Iraj Qadiri. Iran: Bunyad-i Farhangi-i Huda 1982.
4. The film's title derives from Islamic cosmology and thus is difficult to translate since there is no ready English equivalent. The *barzakh* refers to a liminal state in human existence after death and before the Day of Judgment. See Christian Lange, 'Barzakh,' in *Encyclopaedia of Islam*, 3rd edition, ed. Kate Fleet et al. (Leiden: E. J. Brill 2011), https://referenceworks.brillonline.com/entries/encyclopaedia-of-islam-3/barzakh-COM_23704 (last accessed 10 July 2019).
5. Jamal Umid has highlighted the role of the Council of Islamic Art and Thought (Hawzih-yi Andishah va Hunar-i Islami) in this public campaign against *The In-betweeners*, which ultimately led to the resignation of the Minister of Culture and Islamic Guidance. See *Tarikh-i sinama-yi Iran: 1358–1369* (Tehran: Intisharat-i Rawzaneh 2004), pp. 115–16.
6. Ibid., p. 119.
7. Political and cultural elites' commitment to the ban's enforcement was apparent as recently as 2017 when news broke of Malek Muti'i's upcoming appearance on comedian Mihran Mudiri's variety show *Dawr-i hami/Get-together* (television series; Iran: Avval 2016–). A *Kayhan* editorial, 'Talash-i mashkuk bara-yi bih sahnih avurdan-i 'avamil-i hunar-i shahanshahi,' 23 December 2017, http://kayhan.ir/fa/news/121803 (last accessed 5 July 2019), and behind-the-scenes pressure forced the pre-emption of the episode.
8. Malik Muti'i's only film role since *The In-betweeners* was a cameo in *Naqsh-i Nigar/Nigar's Role* (directed by 'Ali 'Atshani. Iran: Bita Film 2014). Officials suspended its theatrical release for two years, with press commentary later linking the suspension to Malik Muti'i's participation. Despite his relatively small role, the film's publicity featured him heavily.
9. 'Va hala ruhat bih Khuda bispar . . .,' in *Film*, Vol. 251 (April–May 2000), pp. 34–5.
10. Fardin claimed to have received acting offers after *The In-betweeners* but refused them because of his conviction that those opposed to his acting career would ultimately not allow for the projects to reach an audience. See *Sinama-yi Fardin bih rivayat-i Muhammad 'Ali Fardin*, ed. 'Abbas Baharlu (Tehran: Nashr-i Qatrih 2001), p. 392.

11. See Aram Muvahhid, 'Qadiri, filmsaz-i mardum-i kuchih va bazar,' *BBC Persian*, 6 May 2012, https://www.bbc.com/persian/arts/2012/05/120506_l44_ghaderi_iraj_filmmaker (last accessed 11 November 2018).
12. 'Marasim-i tashiyʻ-i Nasir Malik Mutiʻi: Intiqad az Sida va Sima va pakhsh-i payam-i Bihruz Vusuqi,' *BBC Persian*, 27 May 2018, http://www.bbc.com/persian/arts-44271007 (last accessed 15 November 2018).
13. Masoud Dihnamaki (@masoudDihnamaki), 'Luti va rawshanfikr nama,' Instagram photo, 26 May 2018, https://www.instagram.com/p/BjP1KYgnuCq/ (last accessed 15 June 2019). Umid has documented Makhmalbaf's ideological interventions as a member of the Council of Islamic Art and Thought in *Tarikh-i sinama-yi Iran*, p. 115.
14. Malik Mutiʻi's death in this regard was connected with the rumored request of another Pahlavi-era star, Bihruz Vusuqi, to return to Iran and restart his frustrated acting career. See 'Mukhalifat-i Quvvih-i Qazaiyih va *Kayhan* ba bazgasht-i Bihruz Vusuqi,' *BBC Persian*, 5 June 2018, http://www.bbc.com/persian/arts-44371811 (last accessed 5 July 2019).
15. 'Dalil-i israr bih bargashtan-i sharik-i Ashraf Pahlavi,' in *Kayhan*, 30 May 2018, http://kayhan.ir/fa/news/133875 (last accessed 5 July 2019).
16. Ibid.
17. See 'Man bih film farsi iman daram,' in *Film va hunar*, Vol. 200 (21 August 1968), pp. 16–17, 38. In August 1978, the 'governing' *Rastakhiz* (Resurgence) Party introduced a proposal to alleviate the tax burden on film producers, along with a raft of other industry-boosting reforms. However, the production and exhibition sectors had all but collapsed by then, with the events of the revolution only exacerbating their crisis state. See Muhammad Tahami Nizhad, *Sinama-yi Iran* (Tehran: Daftar-i Pazhuhishha-yi Farhangi 2001), p. 70.
18. Behrad Najafi, *Film in Iran, 1900–1979: A Political and Cultural Analysis*, PhD dissertation (Universitet Stockholms 1986), pp. 100–1.
19. See 'Mizgird-i sinama-yi Iran (1),' in *Farhang va zindagi*, Vol. 18 (1975), pp. 59–66, 69–71.
20. See M. Ali Issari, *Cinema in Iran: 1900–1979* (Metuchen, NJ: The Scarecrow Press 1989), pp. 199–201.
21. Djamchid Behnam has laid out the case for Pahlavi elites' focus on radio and television, then government monopolies, in *Cultural Policy in Iran* (Paris: UNESCO 1973). In fact, the monies allotted to the development of radio and television networks in just the fourth Five-Year Plan (1968–72) were more than double the entire budget for the Ministry of Culture and Art (p. 22). He has also noted the comparatively limited official investment in cinema in the late 1960s and early 1970s (p. 28).
22. Hamid Naficy, *A Social History of Iranian Cinema: The Industrializing Years, 1941–1978* (Durham, NC: Duke University Press 2011), pp. 327–32.
23. See Muhammad ʻAbdi, 'Muntaqidan-i dahihha-yi si va chihil va mubarizih ba padidihʼi bih nam-i filmfarsi,' in *Filmfarsi chist?*, ed. Husayn Muʻazzizi Niya (Tehran: Nashr-i Saqi 1999), pp. 171–82.
24. On the Pahlavi-era cinema's generic conventions and film critics' and officials' negative perceptions of them, see Pedram Partovi, *Popular Iranian Cinema*

before the Revolution: Family and Nation in Fīlmfārsī (New York: Routledge 2017), pp. 4–10.
25. See Pedram Partovi, 'Constituting Love in Persianate Cinemas,' in *Journal of Persianate Studies*, Vol. 10, No. 2 (2017), pp. 186–217.
26. See Savaş Arslan, *Cinema in Turkey: A New Critical History* (New York: Oxford University Press 2011), pp. 18–19.
27. See 'Vaqti kih labha bih ham nazdik mishavand!' in *Sitarih-i sinama*, Vol. 276 (30 October 1960), pp. 8–9.
28. See Isma'il Nuri 'Ala', 'Dar justuju-yi sinama-yi milli,' in *Darbarih-'i sinama va ti'atr*, ed. Bahman Maqsudlu (Tehran: Intisharat-i Babak 1973), pp. 39–47. To be sure, earlier criticisms had occasionally questioned the patriotism of industry figures for their supposedly derivative work ('Abdi, 'Muntaqidan-i dahihha-yi si va chihil . . .,' p. 175) but they rarely if ever accused the films' content of being political in character.
29. As Annabelle Sreberny-Mohammadi and Ali Mohammadi have argued, political critiques of mass culture even infiltrated some domestically produced films, especially those linked to the aforementioned art cinema initiative that government-linked cultural organs had funded during the 1970s (*Small Media, Big Revolution: Communication Culture, and the Iranian Revolution* (Minneapolis: University of Minnesota Press 1994), pp. 96–7.
30. See Shaykh Fazl Allah Nuri's famous objections to the public exhibition of films in 1906 ('Abbas Baharlu, *Ruzshumar-i sinama-yi Iran az aghaz ta inqiraz-i Qajariyih* (Tehran: Mu'assassah-'i Ta'lif, Tarjumih, va Nashr-i Asar-i Hunari 2011), pp. 37–8).
31. Tahami Nizhad has described the ideologically inspired paranoia that colored the early efforts of revolutionaries empowered with oversight of the production, distribution, and exhibition sectors (*Sinama-yi Iran*, pp. 71–2). For at least one newly installed official, a key responsibility was warding off 'the dirty hand of Zionism' from the film business in Iran (Umid, *Tarikh-i sinama-yi Iran*, p. 115). The claim that *filmfarsi* was part of an international plot to corrupt the faith of Iranian youth would appear to still hold currency among ideologues some forty years after the revolution. See Sa'id Mustaqasi, 'Raqs va kabarih anasur-i lazim-i filmfarsi va mawj-i naw,' in *Kayhan*, 18 September 2016, http://kayhan.ir/fa/news/85846 (last accessed 6 July 2019).
32. Revolutionary violence destroyed as many as 200 theaters out of roughly 470 nationwide (Susan Siavoshi, 'Cultural Policies and the Islamic Republic: Cinema and Book Publication,' in *International Journal of Middle East Studies*, Vol. 29, No. 4 (1997), p. 515). This destruction of cinema halls only intensified after Ayatollah Khomeini's return to Iran in February 1979, despite his multiple public statements in support of a morally sound and edifying cinema (Umid, *Tarikh-i sinama-yi Iran*, p. 3).
33. See Sayyid Muhammad Bihishti, *Guftiguha-yi sinamayi-i Sayyid Muhammad Bihishti (dahah-'i shast)*, ed. Mahmud Arzhmand and Muhammad 'Ali Haydari (Tehran: Intisharat-i Rawzanih 2014), pp. 223–4, p. 301.
34. Ibid., pp. 227–33.

35. For a contemporaneous sourcebook of complaints and criticisms from nearly all segments of society about *filmfarsi*, see Mustafa Izadi Najafabadi, *Tamasha-yi manfiha* (Tabriz: Saʻdi 1974).
36. These middle-class disavowals would even filter down to the scholarly literature on *filmfarsi*, with historians and sociologists turning to distortions of urban demographics and filmgoing data, overly simplistic theories of audience identification, and even personal anecdotes to claim that such films primarily appealed to the 'tradition-bound' lower classes who were drawn to their native settings, lumpen heroes, and familiar (read 'reactionary') themes while the modern, educated middle class flocked to more 'sophisticated' European or American fare. See Parviz Ijlali, *Digarguni-i ijtimaʻi va filmha-yi sinamayi dar Iran: Jamiʻihshinasi-i filmha-yi ʻammihpasand-i Irani (1309–1357)* (Tehran: Farhang va Andishih 2004). I have argued elsewhere that Ijlali's evidence makes a better case for the modernizing middle class as the primary audience for *filmfarsi* (as well as for European and American films). See Pedram Partovi, 'Reconsidering Popular Iranian Cinema and its Audiences,' in *Iranian Studies*, Vol. 45, No. 3 (2012), pp. 439–47.
37. See Willem Floor, 'The Lūṭīs: A Social Phenomenon in Qājār Persia: A Reappraisal,' in *Die Welt des Islams* (n.s.), No. 13 (1971), pp. 103–20.
38. Willem Floor, 'The Political Role of the Lutis in Iran,' in *Modern Iran: The Dialectics of Continuity and Change*, eds. Michael Bonine and Nikki Keddie (Albany: State University of New York Press 1981), pp. 83–95. Floor has insisted on a distinction between *lūṭī* 'entertainers' and 'social bandits' in the Qajar era but has also conceded that the lines between these groups quickly broke down upon closer inspection, with entertainer wrestlers also belonging to gangs of street thugs.
39. See the essays by Rudi Matthee ('Prostitutes, Courtesans and Dancing Girls: Women Entertainers in Safavid Iran') and Houchang Chehabi ('Voices Unveiled: Women Singers in Iran') in *Iran and Beyond: Essays in Middle Eastern History in Honor of Nikki R. Keddie*, eds. Rudi Matthee and Beth Baron (Costa Mesa, CA: Mazda Publishers 2000), pp. 121–50 and 151–66.
40. The almost immediate stigmatization of cinema meant that filmmakers had to find on-screen talent quite literally from marginal social communities. The first female actors were non-Muslim minorities from the Armenian Christian community (Hamid Naficy, *A Social History of Iranian Cinema: The Artisanal Era, 1897–1941* (Durham, NC: Duke University Press 2010), pp. 210–13). The Armenian community had also played an outsized role in then-popular musical traditions (*muṭribī*) (Sasan Fatemi, 'Music, Festivity, and Gender in Iran from the Qajar to the Early Pahlavi Period,' in *Iranian Studies*, Vol. 38, No. 3 (2006), p. 401) and the negative associations of *muṭribī*, along with their performers, were then insinuated in the cinema.
41. See Shiva Masʻudi, *Karnamih-yi talkhakan: Bazshinakht-i atvar-i talkhaki va dalqaki ba nigahi bih mutun-i namayishi-i imruzi, miyangahi, va kuhan* (Tehran: Nashr-i Nay 2016), pp. 389–95.
42. One example of elite patronage of potentially subversive entertainments was the Qajar courtʻs funding of the Shi'ite passion plays. Kamran Scot Aghaie has written in *The Martyrs of Karbala: Shiʻi Symbols and Rituals in Modern Iran* (Seattle: University of

Washington Press 2004) about the monarch's vast financial obligations to the *ta'ziyih* performances (pp. 20–1), even as many prominent clerics boycotted this rough public spectacle (pp. 18–19) in favor of 'more dignified' and intellectualized private commemorations of the martydom of the Shi'ite Imams.

43. *The Principles of Art* (London: Oxford University Press 1958), pp. 57–104.
44. Elitist denials of *filmfarsi* have continued in exile regardless of the equally hostile attitudes of cultural policymakers in the Islamic Republic to Pahlavi-era commercial productions. See Yusif Latifpur, 'Nigahi dubarih bih filmfarsi,' *BBC Persian*, 26 September 2015, http://www.bbc.com/persian/blogs/2015/09/150925_144_nazeran_iran_cinema (last accessed 5 July 2019), in which the writer has rejected *filmfarsi* as Iranian cinema, describing it instead as its *hamzād*, or dark twin.
45. In his essay, 'Nietzsche, Genealogy, History,' Foucault has laid out his understanding of counter-memory in comparing Nietzschean genealogy with 'traditional history,' which he rejects. See *Language, Counter-Memory, Practice: Selected Interviews*, ed. Donald Bouchard, trans. Donald Bouchard and Sherry Simon (Ithaca, NY: Cornell University Press 1977), pp. 139–64. In traditional history, '. . . events are reduced to accentuate their essential traits, their final meaning, or their initial and final value.' But '. . . the true historical sense confirms our existence among countless lost events, without a landmark or a point of reference' (p. 155). Genealogy thus implies '. . . a use of history that severs its connection to memory, its metaphysical and anthropological model, and constructs a counter-memory – a transformation of history into a totally different form of time' (p. 160).
46. See Riza 'Allamihzadih, *Sarab-i sinama-yi Islami-i Iran* (Saarbrücken: Nawid Verlag 1991), pp. 15–36.
47. 'Allamihzadih has drawn attention to bureaucratic rivalries, rather than ideological imperatives, that contributed to early cinema policies (ibid., esp. pp. 26–36). Consequently, those with *filmfarsi* associations could receive permission to work or to screen their films only for such approvals to be revoked at another level of bureaucracy or after a change in leadership. Riza Safa'i's experiences illustrate the professional uncertainty that figures linked to the Pahlavi-era cinema faced in this new order (Hamid Naficy, *A Social History of Iranian Cinema: The Islamicate Period, 1978–1984* (Durham, NC: Duke University Press 2012), pp. 44–6).
48. Bihruz Vusuqi has provided an (admittedly self-serving) anecdote that presents a far messier relationship between revolutionaries and *filmfarsi* than either official or scholarly narratives have generally claimed. He has explained in his memoirs that what motivated him to sell the Silver City Cinema in Tehran during the last days of the Shah's reign was an anonymous phone call from a fan. The fan informed him of his intention to bomb the theater but did not want his favorite star to take a financial loss and decided that he would give Vusuqi a chance to sell it before he did so! (*Bihruz Vusuqi: zindaginamih* (San Francisco, CA: Araan 2004), pp. 332–4).
49. Hamid Reza Sadr has written about the conceptualization of a highly politicized 'revolutionary cinema' in the 1980s that extended the struggle for political and cultural independence from the West to the silver screen. The ideologues of this new cinema

renounced not only Hollywood films but pre-revolutionary 'Hollywood-style' Iranian films and filmmakers. Sadr has listed the different but related subgenres of 1980s revolutionary cinema, which included the war film, in *Iranian Cinema: A Political History* (London: I. B. Tauris 2006), pp. 172–99.
50. Agnès Devictor, *Images, combattants et martyrs: La guerre Iran-Irak vue par le cinéma iranien* (Paris: Éditions Karthala 2015), pp. 123–6.
51. Sadr has directly linked the hysteria surrounding the release of *The In-betweeners* with the emergence of a more focused government-led project to reorient the film industry in *Iranian Cinema*, pp. 178–81.
52. Hamid Naficy, *A Social History of Iranian Cinema: The Globalizing Era, 1984–2010* (Durham, NC: Duke University Press 2012), p. 7.
53. See Roxanne Varzi, 'A Ghost in the Machine: The Cinema of the Iranian Sacred Defence,' in *The New Iranian Cinema: Politics, Representation, and Identity*, ed. Richard Tapper (New York: I. B. Tauris 2002), pp. 154–66. Mohamad Tavakoli-Targhi has argued that Avini and other revolutionary thinkers envisioned front-line mysticism as simultaneously an aesthetic and practical approach to the Iran-Iraq War in 'Frontline Mysticism and Eastern Spirituality,' in *ISIM Newsletter*, Vol. 9 (January 2002), pp. 13, 38.
54. Akbar Muhammadabadi, 'Sinama-yi jang va sinama-yi Difaʿ-i muqaddas,' in *Dunya-yi tasvir*, Vol. 32 (May 1996), pp. 54–5.
55. See Partovi, *Popular Iranian Cinema before the Revolution*, pp. 97–138.
56. On narrative 'complications' in the Cinema of Sacred Defense and their links to *filmfarsi*, see ibid., pp. 204–5.
57. *Ikhrajiha*, film, directed by Masʿud Dihnamaki. Iran: Habib Allah Kasihsaz 2007.
58. *The Outcasts* generated the equivalent of more than twenty million dollars in box office receipts. See 'Gishih-i chahar miliyard tumani,' in *I'timad*, 26 September 2007.
59. Husayn Muʿazzizi Niya, 'Film-i jangi-i Iran va tamashagarish: Aya Sinama-yi Difaʿ-i muqaddas mukhatibash ra payda kardih ast?' in *Dunya-yi tasvir*, Vol. 174 (September 2007), pp. 49–51.
60. See, for example, Varzi, 'A Ghost in the Machine,' p. 159.
61. I have written at greater length about the role of the Cinema of Sacred Defense in the official project to create a revolutionary Muslim society in Pedram Partovi, 'Martyrdom and the "Good Life" in the Iranian Cinema of Sacred Defense,' in *Comparative Studies of South Asia, Africa and the Middle East*, Vol. 28, No. 3 (2008), pp. 513–32.
62. See Mihrzad Danish, 'Khashm va khandih va faryad,' in *Film*, Vol. 360 (April–May 2007), pp. 33–4.
63. Nazila Fathi, 'A Revolutionary Channels his Inner Michael Moore,' in *The New York Times*, 26 November 2005.
64. Floor, 'The Lūṭīs.'
65. Said Amir Arjomand's *The Turban for the Crown: The Islamic Revolution in Iran* (New York: Oxford University Press 1988) is a particularly interesting example of clergy 'bias' in the historical narratives of the revolution and the Islamic Republic precisely because he has also included occasional references to

the underlying tensions between youth-dominated groups or institutions and the clerical elite over the political direction of the revolution (pp. 170–3).
66. See 'Sayyid Muhammad Bihishti: Dunbal-i dawlati kardan-i sinama nabudim,' in *Bani Film*, 4 August 2013.
67. Azadeh Farahmand, 'Perspectives on Recent (International Acclaim for) Iranian Cinema,' in *The New Iranian Cinema*, pp. 86–108.
68. On the metaphorization of romantic love primarily in post-revolutionary art cinema, see Blake Atwood, *Reform Cinema in Iran: Film and Political Change in the Islamic Republic* (New York: Columbia University Press 2016), pp. 27–60.
69. Shahab Esfandiary has traced this historical trajectory in the film career of Muhsin Makhmalbaf from self-styled 'Quranic' filmmaker in the 1980s and early 1990s to 'transnational' auteur of a universal humanism in the mid-1990s and beyond. See *Iranian Cinema and Globalization: National, Transnational and Islamic Dimensions* (Bristol: Intellect Ltd 2012), pp. 83–112.
70. Sohrab Behdad, 'From Populism to Economic Liberalism: The Iranian Predicament,' in *The Economy of Iran: The Dilemma of an Islamic State*, ed. Parvin Alizadeh (London: I. B. Tauris 2000), pp. 100–41.
71. For a brief history of the entry of satellite television into Iran and its cultural after-effects, see Pedram Partovi, 'Televisual Representations of Iran's Isolation: Turkish Melodrama and Homegrown Comedy in the Sanctions Era,' in *Review of Middle East Studies*, Vol. 52, No. 1 (2018), pp. 117–20.
72. See 'Mushkil in ast: Man Iraj Qadiri hastam,' in *Sharq*, 27 December 2004.
73. *Gul-i yakh*, film, directed by Kiyumars Pur Ahmad. Iran: Bita Film 2005.
74. *Sultan-i qalbha*, film, directed by M. Fardin. Iran: Mahdi Misaqiyih 1968.
75. Farhad Kuhradani and Zahra Tizraw, 'Nustalzhi dar Iran-i muʿasir,' *BBC Persian*, 19 October 2018, http://www.bbc.com/persian/blog-viewpoints-45901553 (last accessed 16 June 2019).
76. *Shahrzad*, television series, directed by Hasan Fathi. Iran: Sayyid Muhammad Imami 2014–18.
77. Saeed Kamali Dehghan, 'Iran TV Series Set in 1950s Draws Big Audiences with Echoes in Politics Today,' in *The Guardian*, 19 April 2016, https://www.theguardian.com/world/2016/apr/19/iran-tv-series-set-1950s-draws-big-audiences-echoes-politics-today (last accessed 16 June 2019).
78. *Nahang-i Anbar*, film, directed by Saman Muqaddam. Iran: Saman Muqaddam 2015.
79. Maryam Jaʿfari Hissarlu, 'Naqdi bar film-i "Nahang-i anbar" sakhtih-i Saman Muqaddam,' in *Iran*, 25 July 2015, http://www.iran-newspaper.com/newspaper/item/73967 (last accessed 18 June 2019).
80. *Tunil-i Zaman*, television series. UK: Manoto TV, 2011–. See Narges Bajoghli, 'A London Television Station has Convinced Iran that the Shah was Great,' in *Foreign Policy*, 12 January 2018, https://foreignpolicy.com/2018/01/12/a-london-television-station-has-convinced-iran-the-shah-was-great/ (last accessed 1 July 2019).
81. The filmmaker Ehsan Khoshbakht has narrated in the recent documentary *Filmfarsi* (2019) his own youthful post-revolutionary introduction on bootlegged VHS tapes in the company of family to the Pahlavi-era popular cinema.

References

ʿAbdi, Muhammad, 'Muntaqidan-i dahihha-yi si va chihil va mubarizih ba padidihʾi bih nam-i filmfarsi,' in Husayn Muʿazzizi Niya (ed.), *Filmfarsi chist?* (Tehran: Nashr-i Saqi 1999), pp. 171–82.

Afshin, Bardia, 'Naser Malek Motiee: Actor from Iran's Golden Age of Cinema Whose Career Stopped When the Ayatollah Arrived,' in *The Independent*, 31 May 2018, https://www.independent.co.uk/news/obituaries/naser-malek-motiee-dead-iran-actor-cinema-ayatollah-revolution-a8377106.htm (last accessed 19 December 2018).

Aghaie, Kamran Scot, *The Martyrs of Karbala: Shiʿi Symbols and Rituals in Modern Iran* (Seattle: University of Washington Press 2004).

ʿAllamihzadih, Riza, *Sarab-i sinama-yi Islami-i Iran* (Saarbrücken: Nawid Verlag 1991).

Arjomand, Said Amir, *The Turban for the Crown: The Islamic Revolution in Iran* (New York: Oxford University Press 1988).

Arslan, Savaş, *Cinema in Turkey: A New Critical History* (New York: Oxford University Press 2011).

Atwood, Blake, *Reform Cinema in Iran: Film and Political Change in the Islamic Republic* (New York: Columbia University Press 2016).

Baharlu, ʿAbbas, *Ruzshumar-i sinama-yi Iran az aghaz ta inqiraz-i Qajariyih* (Tehran: Muʾassassah-ʾi Taʾlif, Tarjumih, va Nashr-i Asar-i Hunari 2011).

Bajoghli, Narges, 'A London Television Station has Convinced Iran that the Shah was Great,' *Foreign Policy*, 12 January, https://foreignpolicy.com/2018/01/12/a-london-television-station-has-convinced-iran-the-shah-was-great/ (last accessed 1 July 2019).

Behdad, Sohrab, 'From Populism to Economic Liberalism: The Iranian Predicament,' in Parvin Alizadeh (ed.), *The Economy of Iran: The Dilemma of an Islamic State* (London: I. B. Tauris 2000), pp. 100–41.

Behnam, Djamchid, *Cultural Policy in Iran* (Paris: UNESCO 1973).

Bihishti, Sayyid Muhammad, *Guftiguha-yi sinamayi-i Sayyid Muhammad Bihishti (dahah-ʾi shast)*, ed. Mahmud Arzhmand and Muhammad ʿAli Haydari (Tehran: Intisharat-i Rawzanih 2014).

Chehabi, Houchang, 'Voices Unveiled: Women Singers in Iran,' in Rudi Matthee and Beth Baron (eds.), *Iran and Beyond: Essays in Middle Eastern History in Honor of Nikki R. Keddie* (Costa Mesa, CA: Mazda Publishers 2000), pp. 151–66.

Collingwood, R. G., *The Principles of Art* (London: Oxford University Press 1958).

'Dalil-i israr bih bargashtan-i sharik-i Ashraf Pahlavi,' *Kayhan*, 30 May 2018, http://kayhan.ir/fa/news/133875 (last accessed 5 July 2019).

Danish, Mihrzad, 'Khashm va khandih va faryad,' in *Film*, Vol. 360, April–May 2007, pp. 33–4.

Dehghan, Saeed Kamali, 'Iran TV Series Set in 1950s Draws Big Audiences with Echoes in Politics Today,' in *The Guardian*, 19 April 2016, https://www.theguardian.com/world/2016/apr/19/iran-tv-series-set-1950s-draws-big-audiences-echoes-politics-today (last accessed 16 June 2019).

Devictor, Agnès, *Images, combattants et martyrs: La guerre Iran-Irak vue par le cinéma Iranien* (Paris: Éditions Karthala 2015).

Esfandiary, Shahab, *Iranian Cinema and Globalization: National, Transnational and Dimensions* (Bristol: Intellect Ltd 2012).

Farahmand, Azadeh, 'Perspectives on Recent (International Acclaim for) Iranian Cinema,' in Richard Tapper (ed.), *The New Iranian Cinema: Politics, Representation, and Identity* (New York: I. B. Tauris 2002), pp. 86–108.

Fardin, Muhammad ʿAli, *Sinama-yi Fardin bih rivayat-i Muhammad ʿAli Fardin*, ed. ʿAbbas Baharlu (Tehran: Nashr-i Qatrih 2001).

Fatemi, Sasan, 'Music, Festivity, and Gender in Iran from the Qajar to the Early Pahlavi Period,' in *Iranian Studies*, Vol. 38, No. 3 (2006), pp. 399–416.

Fathi, Nazila, 'A Revolutionary Channels his Inner Michael Moore,' *The New York Times*, 26 November 2005.

Floor, Willem, 'The Lūṭīs: A Social Phenomenon in Qājār Persia: A Reappraisal,' *Die Welt des Islams* (n.s.), No. 13 (1971), pp. 103–20.

Floor, Willem, 'The Political Role of the Lutis in Iran,' in Michael Bonine and Nikki Keddie (eds.), *Modern Iran: The Dialectics of Continuity and Change* (Albany: State University of New York Press 1981), pp. 83–95.

Foucault, Michel, 'Nietzsche, Genealogy, History,' in *Language, Counter-Memory, Practice: Selected Interviews*, ed. Donald Bouchard, trans. Donald Bouchard and Sherry Simon (Ithaca, NY: Cornell University Press 1977), pp. 139–64.

'Gishih-i chahar miliyard tumani,' *Iʿtimad*, 26 September 2007.

Hissarlu, Maryam Jaʿfari, 'Naqdi bar film-i "Nahang-i anbar" sakhtih-i Saman Muqaddam,' in *Iran*, 25 July 2015, http://www.iran-newspaper.com/newspaper/item/73967 (last accessed 18 June 2019).

Ijlali, Parviz, *Digarguni-i ijtimaʿi va filmha-yi sinamayi dar Iran: Jamiʿihshinasi-i filmha-yi ʿammihpasand-i Irani (1309–1357)* (Tehran: Farhang va Andishih 2004)

Issari, M. Ali, *Cinema in Iran: 1900–1979* (Metuchen, NJ: The Scarecrow Press 1989).

Kuhradani, Farhad and Zahra Tizraw, 'Nustalzhi dar Iran-i muʿasir,' *BBC Persian*, 19 October 20018, http://www.bbc.com/persian/blog-viewpoints-45901553 (last accessed 16 June 2019).

Lange, Christian, 'Barzakh,' in Kate Fleet et al. (eds.), *Encyclopaedia of Islam* (3rd edition) (Leiden: E. J. Brill 2011), https://referenceworks.brillonline.com/entries/encyclopaedia-of-islam-3/barzakh-COM_23704 (last accessed 10 July 2019).

Latifpur, Yusif, 'Nigahi dubarih bih filmfarsi,' *BBC Persian*, 26 September 2015, http://www.bbc.com/persian/blogs/2015/09/150925_l44_nazeran_iran_cinema (last accessed 5 July 2019).

'Man bih film farsi iman daram,' in *Film va hunar*, Vol. 200, 21 August 1968, pp. 16–17, 38.

'Marasim-i tashiyʿ-i Nasir Malik Mutiʿi: Intiqad az Sida va Sima va pakhsh-i payam-i Bihruz Vusuqi,' *BBC Persian*, 27 May 2018, http://www.bbc.com/persian/arts-44271007 (last accessed 15 November 2018).

Masʿudi, Shiva, *Karnamih-yi talkhakan: Bazshinakht-i atvar-i talkhaki va dalqaki ba nigahi bih mutun-i namayishi-i imruzi, miyangahi, va kuhan* (Tehran: Nashr-i Nay 2016).

Matthee, Rudi, 'Prostitutes, Courtesans and Dancing Girls: Women Entertainers in Safavid Iran,' in Rudi Matthee and Beth Baron (eds.), *Iran and Beyond: Essays in Middle Eastern History in Honor of Nikki R. Keddie* (Costa Mesa, CA: Mazda Publishers 2000), pp. 121–50.

'Mizgird-i sinama-yi Iran (1),' *Farhang va zindagi*, Vol. 18 (1975), pp. 59–66, 69–71.

Muʿazzizi Niya, Husayn, 'Film-i jangi-i Iran va tamashagarish: Aya Sinama-yi Difaʿ-i muqaddas mukhatibash ra payda kardih ast?' in *Dunya-yi tasvir*, Vol. 174 (September 2007), pp. 49–51.

Muhammadabadi, Akbar, 'Sinama-yi jang va sinama-yi Difaʿ-i muqaddas,' in *Dunya-yi tasvir*, Vol. 32 (May 1996), pp. 54–5.

'Mukhalifat-i Quvvih-i Qazaiyih va *Kayhan* ba bazgasht-i Bihruz Vusuqi,' *BBC Persian*, 5 June 2018, http://www.bbc.com/persian/arts-44371811 (last accessed 5 July 2019).

'Mushkil in ast: Man Iraj Qadiri hastam,' in *Sharq*, 27 December 2004.

Mustaqasi, Saʿid, 'Raqs va kabarih anasur-i lazim-i filmfarsi va mawj-i naw,' in *Kayhan*, 18 September 2016, http://kayhan.ir/fa/news/85846 (last accessed 6 July 2019).

Muvahhid, Aram, 'Qadiri, filmsaz-i mardum-i kuchih va bazar,' *BBC Persian*, 6 May 2012, https://www.bbc.com/persian/arts/2012/05/120506_l44_ghaderi_iraj_filmmaker (last accessed 11 November 2018).

Naficy, Hamid, *A Social History of Iranian Cinema: The Artisanal Era, 1897–1941* (Durham, NC: Duke University Press 2010).

Naficy, Hamid, *A Social History of Iranian Cinema: The Industrializing Years, 1941–1978* (Durham, NC: Duke University Press 2011).

Naficy, Hamid, *A Social History of Iranian Cinema: The Islamicate Period, 1978–1984* (Durham, NC: Duke University Press 2012).

Naficy, Hamid, *A Social History of Iranian Cinema: The Globalizing Era, 1984–2010* (Durham, NC: Duke University Press 2012).

Najafabadi, Mustafa Izadi, *Tamasha-yi manfiha* (Tabriz: Saʿdi 1974).

Najafi, Behrad, *Film in Iran, 1900–1979: A Political and Cultural Analysis*, PhD dissertation (Universitet Stockholms 1986).

Nuri ʿAlaʾ, Ismaʿil, 'Dar justuju-yi sinama-yi milli,' in Bahman Maqsudlu (ed.), *Darbarih-ʾi sinama va tiʾatr* (Tehran: Intisharat-i Babak 1973), pp. 39–47.

Partovi, Pedram, 'Constituting Love in Persianate Cinemas,' in *Journal of Persianate Studies*, Vol. 10, No. 2 (2017), pp. 186–217.

Partovi, Pedram, 'Martyrdom and the "Good Life" in the Iranian Cinema of Sacred Defense,' in *Comparative Studies of South Asia, Africa and the Middle East*, Vol. 28, No. 3 (2008), pp. 513–32.

Partovi, Pedram, *Popular Iranian Cinema before the Revolution: Family and Nation in Fīlmfārsī* (New York: Routledge 2017).

Partovi, Pedram, 'Reconsidering Popular Iranian Cinema and its Audiences,' in *Iranian Studies*, Vol. 45, No. 3 (2012), pp. 439–47.

Partovi, Pedram, 'Televisual Representations of Iran's Isolation: Turkish Melodrama and Homegrown Comedy in the Sanctions Era,' in *Review of Middle East Studies*, Vol. 52, No. 1 (2018), pp. 115–34.

Sadr, Hamid Reza, *Iranian Cinema: A Political History* (London: I. B. Tauris 2006).

'Sayyid Muhammad Bihishti: Dunbal-i dawlati kardan-i sinama nabudim,' *Bani Film*, 4 August 2013.

Siavoshi, Susan, 'Cultural Policies and the Islamic Republic: Cinema and Book Publication,' *International Journal of Middle East Studies*, Vol. 29, No. 4 (1997), pp. 509–30.

Sreberny-Mohammadi, Annabelle and Ali Mohammadi, *Small Media, Big Revolution: Communication Culture, and the Iranian Revolution* (Minneapolis: University of Minnesota Press 1994).

Tahami Nizhad, Muhammad, *Sinama-yi Iran* (Tehran: Daftar-i Pazhuhishha-yi Farhangi 2001).

'Talash-i mashkuk bara-yi bih sahnih avurdan-i 'avamil-i hunar-i shahanshahi,' in *Kayhan*, 23 December 2017, http://kayhan.ir/fa/news/121803 (last accessed 5 July 2019).

Tavakoli-Targhi, Mohamad, 'Frontline Mysticism and Eastern Spirituality,' *ISIM Newsletter*, Vol. 9 (September 2002), pp. 13, 38.

Umid, Jamal, *Tarikh-i sinama-yi Iran: 1358–1369* (Tehran: Intisharat-i Rawzaneh 2004).

'Va hala ruhat bih Khuda bispar . . . ,' in *Film*, Vol. 251 (April–May 2000), pp. 34–5.

'Vaqti kih labha bih ham nazdik mishavand!' in *Sitarih-i sinama*, Vol. 276 (30 October 1960), pp. 8–9.

Varzi, Roxanne, 'A Ghost in the Machine: The Cinema of the Iranian Sacred Defence,' in Richard Tapper (ed.), *The New Iranian Cinema: Politics, Representation, and Identity* (New York: I. B. Tauris 2002), pp. 154–66.

Vusuqi, Bihruz, *Bihruz Vusuqi: zindaginamih* (San Francisco, CA: Araan 2004).

11. A SHADOW FOR INVISIBLE FILMS: A WAY TO BREAK THE MONOPOLY OF IMAGE PRODUCTION IN IRAN

Shahram Mokri

In this chapter, I try to discuss the reasons behind the emergence of a new generation of filmmakers in Iran and the generation that is known as the 'sixth generation'[1] of Iranian filmmakers. I start with the presence of video cameras and their vital role in the various modes of film production in Iran and will expand on Iranian cinema's social and economic settings. The main part focuses on the years after 2000 (1379) and is about the roots and practices of the filmmakers who joined the film industry in Iran. But to shed light on the reasons why a new generation of filmmakers emerged out of the digital revolution in Iran, I will start a bit earlier and briefly discuss film production between 1980 and 2000 in Iran.

The Bureaucratic System: State Control of Film Equipment

Between the years 1980 and 2000, Iranian cinema was conducted through various bureaucratic forms. In order for filmmakers to exhibit their films in cinemas, they first had to gain the Ministry of Culture's approval for their script. This would mean that the film would have to pass censorship monitoring and be accepted for professional film production procedures in Iran.

During the years after the 1979 Revolution (and already from 1977) the Iranian film market belonged exclusively to Iranian films and produced fifty to sixty films per year. All these films passed the above-mentioned procedure carried out by the Ministry of Culture. The council that accepts and admits the film scripts, and is still active to this date, has one main job and that is to enforce various forms of censorship to the script. The script is read by a committee that mainly consists of state officials as well as a couple of filmmakers at times, and the changes that are supposed to happen are announced to the scriptwriter, producer, and filmmaker. The council follows no clear procedure or instructions. There are a few issues that are mentioned in the council's handouts such as hijab regulations, no singing for women, no touching between women and men, no exhibition of drug use, no exhibition of erotic or sexual scenes. Still, it is ultimately the members of the council that decide on various script issues. For example, one year for one council hijab may mean the full religious hijab, and in another year for another council this can mean the common practice of hijab in the society, which is not as strict as the religious one. To give another example, when touching is forbidden among men and women, in many Iranian films we see that beating is allowed and is not categorized as a form of touching, so it ultimately falls to the council to determine if beating as a form of touching is forbidden or not. Thus, clarification of the details of Ministry of Culture's restrictions is one of the main demands of Iranian filmmakers, especially when it comes to censorship that does not concern outfits and visible issues but instead deals with the content of films. Such as what did the filmmaker mean by this scene? What is the idea that the filmmaker is trying to convey? And other similar questions, which form the most complicated element of dealing with censorship and film production in Iran.

But as mentioned above, a film also has to go through the professional production procedures inside the country. To understand that, consider the union limits for those who look for work. In various countries and in the film industry, a union outlines certain measures and standards for its members. Before the formation of the union organization House of Cinema in October 1993, three different semi-governmental organizations overlooked film production. The first organization that was in charge of film production was National Television, and the supreme leader selected its head. The second organization was Hozeh Honari (Art Center), which is one of the main trusts in the state economy, and its head was also selected by the supreme leader. Finally, the third organization was the Farabi Cinema Foundation, which was partially governmental and functioned under the presidential offices. In addition to these three, the Institute for the Intellectual Development of Children and Young Adults (Kanoon) and a few other institutes also produced film in the country. Still, most authority lay in the hands of the first three organizations. In other words, in Iran's state-directed economy, all production companies had to function under the state, and all cameras, tripods, light equipment, film negatives, prints, and labs were accessible under the state's bureaucratic system. Obviously, in order to rent a camera or film or to work in the labs after shooting the film, you had to correspond with the state, and nothing of this was possible unless the Ministry of Culture had previously granted you a permit to make your film. Thus, it is clear that complicated conditions were imposed on filmmakers in the first twenty years after the 1979 Revolution. For example, if an Iranian film was going to be screened in a festival outside the country, prior to arrival at the airport a copy of the film had to be exhibited in the Ministry of Culture. After viewing the film, the members would seal the film prints. In order to prevent any screening of unapproved footage outside the country, the airport was only allowed to ship prints that were sealed by the Ministry of Culture. Perhaps the readers of this text do not know that when Abbas Kiarostami's *Taste of Cherry* was screened at the Cannes Film Festival in 1997, the film print was delayed, and without the personal intervention of Iran's Minister of Foreign Affairs at the time, Ali Akbar Velayati, the film would not have made it to the Festival.

The Visual Memory of a Generation

In 1997, something else also happened in Iran. Sayyid Mohammad Khatami was elected as the president and was in office until 2005. The period of his presidency, which is known as the reform era, led to major cultural changes in Iran. Interestingly, before this and between 1982 and 1992, Khatami himself was the head of the Ministry of Culture. During his presidency, Khatami contributed to significant changes such as structural reforms in the Ministry of Culture. One of these changes was to let various private companies compete with state-run film production companies. Simultaneously, video camera technology was developing around the world. The Betacam SP which was highly popular in the 1990s in other countries' television production, was first imported into Iran one year after Khatami's presidency, and for the first time it became possible to think about making films using video. But why were these video cameras so popular in Iran, when using them meant lower-quality production and more technical problems?

Iran's exclusive market for filmmaking and exhibiting film created a unique condition for Iranian filmmakers, which they called the greenhouse atmosphere (*faza-ye golkhāneh-ī*). In this greenhouse, there was no possibility of comparing Iranian cinema with contemporary world cinema. Since that time, the screening of non-Iranian films, whether American or non-American, is prohibited in Iran. But before the year 2000, it was hard to access non-Iranian movies even in the underground markets. Therefore, the visual memory of the generation that was born in the first twenty years after the revolution was empty of the foreign cinema of the time. All the films which were accessible in the underground film market, which were either on Betamax tapes or projectible on 8 mm projectors, belonged to the pre-revolutionary era. These films were either *filmfarsi*, which was the pre-revolutionary Iranian cinema (with actors such as Fardin and Behrouz Vossoughi who were the heroes of the previous generation), or they were Hollywood movies that were screened in Iran before the revolution (featuring John Wayne, James Dean, and Alain Delon). Therefore, anything that was screened in cinemas in the first post-revolutionary decades would be compared with these pre-revolutionary films. It may come as a surprise to hear that after the Iranian Revolution, certain things were prohibited in the country (a prohibition that was lifted later on, without anyone understanding why it was ever imposed or lifted) – for example, fax machines or the act of playing a game of chess were forbidden. But what is important for us is that the video player was banned as a piece of equipment until 1994. Even when the Iranian parliament approved of its use in 1994, stores still did not sell them, fearing unforeseeable trouble. It might interest you to know that accessing and installing satellite television equipment is also illegal in Iran. It was only after 1997, when video players started to feature in Iranian households, that it was possible to compare Iranian cinema with world cinema. In making this comparison, the Iranian audience encountered new dynamics in films. One was that contemporary foreign films were comprised of more shots, a faster pace, and much more advanced special effects. Thus, gradually the Iranian audience's level of expectation rose, while nothing had changed for the filmmakers. At that time, if you wanted to buy raw film from Farabi Cinema Foundation, you had to deal with a limited quota for a film. You would usually only receive 300 minutes worth of film for your project, although if the filmmaker was renowned, they could potentially receive 400 or 500 minutes worth of film.[2] It is clear that under such circumstances it was not possible to explore various angles while shooting. Therefore, Iranian cinema of the time, which was mainly action and comedy, had a much slower pace than its foreign competitors. Another issue was the quality of images projected on screens as well as the quality of the videos screened on television. Since the film's raw material was provided by the state, and its budget was determined by parliament, the purchase of film would happen only once per year. This meant that the three companies that provided the country's film purchased a large amount of film material. That material was then stored in conditions that were less than ideal, and due to a shortage of developing chemicals, the film was used in substandard conditions. Thus, audiences who had access to videotapes were bored by these old magnetic tape films with their fading and low-quality soundtracks.

In 1999, when I went to university, the film industry was still operating under the same circumstances. I remember that I started a student job working on a trailer for an Iranian film. I made the trailer based on film prints and sent the negatives to the lab for editing. The lab contacted me instantly and asked two main questions: (1) 'Are you a student?'; to which I answered yes, and (2) 'Do you watch a lot of American films?' These questions clarified that what I wanted could not be achieved easily. When the lab told me about its technical limitations, I realized that I could not make a trailer similar to the ones I had seen before.[3]

When I look at the films that were made in those years, it seems like they are much older than they really are, and they have not aged well. It is as if those films were made at the beginning of the invention of cinema. In 2000, Dariush Mehrjui, the renowned Iranian filmmaker, made a film called *Mix* that discusses the technical difficulties of making film in Iran. The film depicts a filmmaker who has to wrestle with various obstacles such as technical problems, labs, festivals, complicated production, and the country's distribution companies.

Two Modes of Film Production (the Hitchcock/ Tarkovsky Dichotomy)

Perhaps I should give a brief description of the two modes of film production after the revolution in Iran.

After the Islamic Revolution the main question regarding cultural change was whether it was possible to continue filmmaking in a country ruled by Islamic laws. In this regard, two famous quotes by Ayatollah Khomeini were crucial. When Ayatollah Khomeini saw Mehrjui's 1969 film, *Gāv/ The Cow*, he said that if this is cinema, then he would have no problem with it. On another occasion, he said that he has no problem with cinema, but he disagrees with the exhibition of corruption and prostitution in films. These two sentences opened up a chance for cinema's survival after the revolution.

The Cow (1969) is an important New Wave film from the pre-revolutionary era, and is without any erotic or violent scenes, with a story that deals with the lower classes in Iran, similar to other New Wave Iranian films. Therefore, almost all the pre-revolutionary New Wave filmmakers were granted a permit to make films after the revolution, from Masoud Kimiai to Nasser Taghvai to Bahram Beyzaie and Dariush Mehrjui. However, the main body of cinema before the revolution, which is known as *filmfarsi*, was identified as corrupt and was discontinued. *Filmfarsi* is an expression that is comprised of the words film and Farsi, and it was coined by the Iranian film critic Houshang Kavousi. The two words combine to divorce the words from their initial meanings. *Filmfarsi* was an unfit addition, and all those who worked with it had to abandon their career after the revolution. The majority emigrated and those who stayed never worked within the film industry again. At the same time, the Farabi Cinema Foundation supported the New Wave filmmakers after the revolution, while the Art Council tried to initiate a cinema based on Islamic revolutionary thoughts. According to some of the theoreticians in the Art Council, Hollywood cinema was the best model for film production if it could be copied and adapted to Islamic laws. Based on this idea many Iranian directors were born that were more skilled in making 'Islamic Hitchcock' films than in Iranian New Wave style. These filmmakers include Ebrahim Hatamikia, Behrouz Afkhami, and Mohsen Makhmalbaf (back when he was making film at the beginning of the revolution).

This dichotomy in filmmaking styles in Iran – with New Wave filmmakers on the one hand and Iranian Hollywood filmmakers on the other hand – is known as the 'Hitchcock-Tarkovsky' dichotomy, and is still addressed in various film journals and articles in Farsi.

A Two-class Film System: 'The Cinematic Division' and the 'Digital Division'

I leapfrog the twenty years of the rise and fall of these two styles of filmmaking to discuss the year 2000. This is the year in which it was possible to compare Iranian cinema and Hollywood cinema for the first time. Obviously, Iranian Hollywood cinema was mainly interested in Hollywood's rhythm, innovation, and quality, and therefore the first examples of making films with video were made in this style. The films *Par-e Parvāz*, made by Khosro Masumi in 1999, and *Moje Mordeh/Dead Wave*, made by Ebrahim Hatamikia in 2001, were the first serious attempts to make film with Betacam SP cameras. But these attempts soon failed , and the Iranian Hitchcock cinema had to revert to the old styles of filmmaking due to management problems, which I will explain.

Previously I have written about the power of bureaucratic managers in Iranian cinema. The power of these bureaucrats was so great that it was not possible to think about the private sector for film production or funding. The money was in the state's hands; the producers and distributers were all state employees. To make a film you needed to have a permit, in order to shoot in the city you needed even more permissions, and in order to make new copies of your film, you needed various letters. And at the end, since filmmakers may have circumvented the approved script, the finished film had to be exhibited at the Ministry of Culture to pass the final censors. Therefore, before the start of digital filmmaking in Iran, bureaucrats were in full charge of the Iranian film industry. The beginning of this new cinema alarmed the bureaucrats and their monitored mode of filmmaking. If filmmakers could make works with cameras other than those provided by the Farabi Cinema Foundation, then how could their content be supervised and controlled? The solution that the bureaucrats came up with was to attribute higher value to works that were shot with analog camera rather than digital. Luckily for these bureaucrats, the general idea of 'valuable' film around the world was also the same. Numerous filmmakers had previously spoken about the importance of shooting on film to achieve the proper depth of field, and to benefit from lens potentials and light division. In brief, this was what they meant by 'the soul of film,' and, consequently, the Iranian bureaucrats used the same statements to prove their point about the privileges of analog film over video. This way, they would justify their ideas about the advantage and value of film by borrowing words from Scorsese, Fincher, and Coppola. These years marked the root of this division between analog and video in Iran. Just as the Cannes Film Festival would ask for a film print due to projection limitations in the main cinema, the Iranian Fajr Film Festival also looked for positive copies for screenings, although for different reasons. After all, the quality of screening in Iran was not high anyway. Therefore, in these years if European and American filmmakers could make print out of their videos for the sake of the screening, Iranian filmmakers had to come up with innovative solutions to create such positives. Films such as *Par-e Parvāz* and the *Dead Wave* and *Rāy-e Bāz/Parole* which were made by Mehdi Nourbakhsh in 2002, or even a short film made by me, *Toofān-e Sanjāghak/ The Dragonfly Storm*, were made with this inventive technique. The films were shot with video cameras and then instead of being printed in the lab, they were screened on a television screen while a film camera would shoot the television screen, and, ultimately, the lab would process the film footage. In this way, the bureaucrats at the Ministry of Culture could still control the screening of films in Iran. The long process of paperwork that films were subjected to in these years was to meticulously control film production, and ultimately it led to the foundation of a new section at the Ministry of Culture to oversee the scripts of digital films, but when the permit was issued the producer had to sign an agreement to confirm that a screening permit would not be requested for these digital films. Today, although 35 mm film cameras have been replaced with digital film cameras all over the world, still these two different offices that inspect film and digital scripts are active in the Ministry of Culture. An old tradition that has remained in place, and no one bothers to ask about its original root. Even today, these two separate offices are called 'the cinematic division' and the 'digital division.'

In the Labyrinth of Permits and Instrumentalizations

As mentioned above, when with major political change the country gradually embraced privatization, the Iranian Alliance of Motion Picture Guilds (Khaneh Cinema), which was an alliance of filmmaker's unions, started to operate more actively. In the first few years, these operations mainly focused on the relationship between the film industry and state institutions. With the use of digital cameras, Khaneh Cinema had to deal with a new generation of young filmmakers who did not submit to the complicated dynamics and hierarchies that were set before. The castle of old filmmakers was threatened by young filmmakers who could use a light digital camera, edit films at home, and with only a small film production team. Therefore, a new alliance was formed among the filmmakers who shot on film and the state institutions that controlled them. This alliance was based on their common benefits. They all considered film as a product that had to be produced through the state bureaucratic procedure. For example, as a solution, like other unions, Khaneh Cinema also organized award ceremonies once a year. In the beginning, only those films which were publicly screened in cinemas were eligible for this competition. But later on, after several digital works were granted screening permits, Khaneh Cinema announced that in order for films to enter the competition they had to receive additional permission from the Cinematic Film Council and, a little while after that, they announced that in addition to these permits, the films must have a further license that proved the film's termination. This close relationship between the cinematic unions and the state institutions hinged on the fact that the unions were more supportive of state monitoring rather than defending filmmakers' rights. Now, think of the filmmakers who were born after the revolution and who started making films between 2000 and 2010. They did their best to ignore and bypass all the regulations mentioned above. For example, to shoot a film on the streets in Iran you have to have a permit that can only be issued by the police, and this is after the censorship department has already given you your approval letters, therefore some filmmakers decided not to bother with acquiring shooting permits anymore. They decided to make their films in their small private studios, in the hope that the film's festival presence and that its international market would be large enough to return the expenditure. Abbas Kiarostami's successful film, *Dah/Ten*, 2002, which was shot digitally, inspired a new generation of filmmakers to forget about exhibiting their films inside the Iranian film market and aim directly for foreign audiences and venues. The Iranian film critics call these filmmakers 'festival filmmakers' (*filmsāzān-e-festivāl-ī*). These are the filmmakers who do not play any role inside the dynamics of Iranian cinema and do not even join Khaneh Cinema unions, and their relationship to the state is reduced to applying for shooting permits. These filmmakers make low-cost films, and their filmmaking life depends on international film festivals and markets. This same market though works as an Achilles' heel for these filmmakers since the word 'censor,' which was previously an enemy to film production, could now be used as a positive element for a film's box office trade mark. Censorship was a double-edged sword that exposed the reason behind some of the problems in filmmaking, and at the same time, since the international market was interested in the idea of censored cinema, this type of filmmaking gradually prevailed. The cinema of this period would get as close as possible to censorship lines because its filmmakers tried to depict exotic aspects of Iranian life for foreign viewers. This continued to the extent that some of the filmmakers who made such films were sentenced to prison and were banned from filmmaking. Soon, new orders were established to disallow any collaboration with filmmakers who did not follow the old state-imposed production procedures. (These rules are still in place today.) This created a complicated situation that still persists: if you criticized festival filmmakers, you would be aligned with the state and its censor machine, and if you questioned the state and its monitoring system, you would be blamed for having a touristic and exotic perspective towards Iranian cinema. Along the same lines, my personal experience in the international film festivals has always been disappointing. In some of the question and answer sessions after the film, an audience member would ask the filmmaker why certain parts of their film are disjointed? And the filmmaker would simply say that it is due to censorship – that if s/he wanted to depict things more clearly s/he would be censored. I knew that this was just an excuse that did not stem from reality. In direct response to these opportunistic filmmakers, Kiarostami always asserted that his cinema was never influenced by censorship, but at the same time the state bureaucrats used Kiarostami's words against those who criticized the censorship apparatus. Thus, the censor was on the one hand destructive and on the other hand constructive for opportunists who managed it to submit their work to festivals. Ultimately, these divisions magnified the distance between young filmmakers on the one hand, and union heads and state bureaucrats on the other.

Generation Matters

In recent decades, Iran's population has grown enormously. After the revolution, the Iranian government was hoping for a population of 150 million. Many families had five children, and the young generation that was born in the 1980s and 1990s was so numerous that soon Iran turned into one of the youngest-populated countries in the world. Therefore, youth politics was an essential part of state propaganda, especially since the state needed this young population to invest in the country and participate in elections, so ultimately the older generation was neglected. Now, if we take a moment to look at this abandoned older generation, we will see that the majority of Iranian filmmakers had already made their main career progress before they turned forty, and afterwards their films faced more and more negative reviews and harsh criticism. The international film festivals, which always searched for new young Iranian talent, gradually stopped paying attention to them as they aged, and also society did not have much more to offer and inspire these filmmakers. The speed of technological development, the internet, cell phones, and smart televisions made them feel behind the times and their ideas appeared outdated. But instead of society's dismissal of the older generation being blamed, it was the filmmakers themselves who were condemned. The older generation, therefore, used the traditional connection with the authorities to sustain their former powers, but this did not change anything since the population of filmmakers under the age of thirty was much greater. As I write this chapter, about 70 percent of Iran's population was born after the revolution, but they still have to cope with the old mechanisms at work. Digital developments also deepened the gap between generations.[4] The end result was that young people had to complete harder to get new jobs, and the older generation would create bothersome obstacles to resist the wave of newcomers.

I mentioned above that after 2010, Iran was a filmmaker's heaven. For the first time, young filmmakers found the chance to screen their films. They knew the concerns of their generation well and were willing to work under any circumstances, which meant that they worked either for a meager income or for free. When these films found appreciation in the West, their producers could claim that they were patrons of youth cinema and in this way could attract further funding. Even renowned actors who previously were interested only in prominent directors started showing interest in the work of newcomers. Thus, a young audience could connect better with these new films, which were very energetic, with low costs, and starring famous actors, and this led to the marginalization of older filmmakers. In the past ten years in Iran the highest box office success and the most festival awards have belonged to filmmakers making their first or second films. Nowhere else in the world was a new filmmaker able to work with the best technicians and actors to make a debut. The same actors who appeared in the films of Kimiai and Mehrjui also appeared in the debuts of unknown filmmakers. But the young filmmakers of the 2000s are also now entering their forties and fifties and since they were not able to change the dynamics of society, they are gradually experiencing the same things that the generation before them did. These days there are numerous critical texts published in Iran that demand an improvement in film production conditions, and many of these texts point to the fact that it is easy and cheap to direct a first and second film in Iran, but after that, for the third and fourth films, when filmmakers have to establish their work, the director can no longer find funding. This means that an experienced filmmaker cannot secure funds, payment, union privileges, and social benefits when new filmmakers are willing to work without any of these. Iranian critics explain this situation as follows: a young cinema that ages very fast.

Khosoulati

These days Iran's economy is in the worst shape ever. For years the sanctions imposed by the United States have left Iran's economy breathless, and it is hard to access basic material such as medicine on the market. On the other hand, the Iranian government's lack of interest in joining the international banking system has created a complicated situation for all production industries including the film industry. The state-dependent economy is so shapeless that several bureaucrats from high-end institutions have been arrested and convicted on corruption charges. Some escape the country with vast sums of embezzled and stolen wealth, and the rest create a wealthy class with deep connections to power which simply ressembles an oligarchy. In this chaotic situation, to stay away from power and money is an unwritten virtue for filmmakers. So when Iranian filmmakers say that they are independent, they mean that they are not connected to any of the above-mentioned economic groups. After several failures, in 2004 the state-run economy was supposed to be handed to the private sector. This was something at which other countries in the world had already succeeded. But what occurred in Iran was the distribution of the state's industry into the hands of newly formed state-related branches of the military and politicians. As if, in the absence of a real private sector and foreign investors, the state bought parts of its own body. Thus, a new term formed in Farsi which was similar to *filmfarsi*. 'Khosoulati industry' was a combination of two words: private (*khosousi*) and state (*dowlaty*). *Khosoulati* agencies also formed in the film industry. They claimed to be independent while being funded by the state, and therefore any time they entered a film market they created chaos. For example, if the bureaucrats of these *khosoulati* agencies preferred to get festival exposure they made films that copied independent cinema's aesthetics, and if they wanted films to win in the internal market they made the costliest productions, without worrying about funding. These films destroyed the balances and divisions that already existed in the film market and created a mixture of theoretical arguments that evolved around the division of independent cinema, the new generation, mainstream cinema, and ideologic films. On the other hand, the above-mentioned new wealthy class did not have much experience with art but felt the need to get in touch with art and discuss it at its parties. This new class nurtured a form of extravagant art in Iran. This new extravagant art manifested in new artistic productions, and although cinema was not touched by it as much as painting, sculpture and photography were, it created a corrupt economy in Iranian cinema that changed the path of the film industry. Perhaps the following example will be helpful. Today, a famous actor in Iran can get close to the investors of *khosoulati* agencies, can go to their parties and restaurants. In return they can receive significant funds to invest in filmmaking. A large portion of these funds stays in their personal bank account, and the rest of the money is given to a first-time filmmaker (as explained above) who would make a cheaper film and cast the same actor in the leading role. To fund a film, an investor simply looks for actors who participate in their parties, and, ironically, Iranian cinema hopes to create good cinema from this dynamic. In reality, this ruins all the film industry's balances in the country.

World cinema is changing. Big companies are using technological developments to create even more glamorous and grandiose film projects to be screened on large screens, and, on the other hand, technical limitations are forcing us to make more personal films to be screened in more private settings. This binary is creating an ever-growing gap. Now festivals have no choice but to give foremost exposure on red carpets and in front of camera to the major film industries in order to survive, marginalizing art cinema. Although, superficially, the films are focusing on topics that are popular at both ends of this binary, and the division between a superhero movie and a film about immigration is not that visible – and although festivals such as Cannes, Berlin, and Venice are screening films that have mixed some facets of everyday life problems with the ideals of Hollywood cinema – in practice something else is happening. Technology is removing the filmmaker's opportunity to make decisions. If you want to be a good cameraman, you do not need to make significant decisions anymore. Technology gives you the option not to worry about color and light during shooting, knowing that you can fix them later. Soon we will all probably be able to use high-quality cameras and capture excellent images easily. Editing equipment will be smarter and a simple algorithm rather than an editor will determine a film's pace. Soon it will be so easy to gain various consultations on a film script that the script's primary writer will not matter, and soon there will come a day when filmmaking only means having good ideas. Our presence may not be needed after the idea has been generated. On the other hand, the world of filmmaking is changing quickly. Netflix and other streaming platforms are serious competitors for cinemas, and at the same time private YouTube channels, Instagram, and other similar spaces are competing with these streaming platforms. When you can make films at home in the world of virtual reality, but the product looks similar to high-budget films, we have to accept that we are facing a new definition of filmmaking. Iran is also a part of the same circumstances, although currently it is mainly the consumer of such products. Since Iran cannot continue to remain an isolated island for ever, it too will have opportunities for production in this new industrial space. This path will be paved by future generations.

Hopefully this chapter has been able to provide an image of contemporary Iranian cinema and the reasons behind the formation of a new generation of Iranian filmmakers. Maybe there are only a few differences between this generation and those before it, but I believe that the world today is constructed based on these small differences. The sixth generation of Iranian filmmakers has more awareness of contemporaneous cinema around the world, and one can easily find a critic, a book, or a course on the majority of foreign filmmakers in Iran. Film criticism programs broadcast on television are highly popular, despite the usual paradoxes. This means that although it is illegal to screen foreign films in Iranian cinemas – and the underground film markets are essentially illegitimate – it is still possible to discuss and criticize the same films on television, without anyone even mentioning this paradox. On the other hand, every year scores of different film schools teach filmmaking to their students in Tehran, Isfahan, Mashhad, and Tabriz. Iranian cinema has a museum which contains Oscar, Palme d'Or, Golden Lion, and Golden Bear awards on display. It is possible to say that there are not many festivals at which Iranians have not received awards. But what seems to be the most drastic difference of this new generation is its urge to break its limitations. This generation has at once successfully survived the old and useless rules that were imposed on it and created a new identity for itself despite the shapeless and ever-changing economy in place. This is what makes this generation hopeful that it can break those limitations once again. Young Iranian filmmakers know that the planetarium atmosphere of filmmaking in Iran has created a safe bubble that will not last long. Afterwards, this young generation will have to learn the language of cinema to compete with world cinema, and I believe that the small but significant difference for the sixth generation of Iranian filmmakers is that it yearns to learn the language of cinema, beyond the environment of Iranian cinema.

Notes

1. Before the Iranian Revolution, there were three generations of filmmakers: the first generation is called 'the pioneers of Iranian cinema,' those who worked up to the 1940s (e.g. Ovanes Ohanian-Khan, Baba Motazedi). The filmmakers between 1940 and 1960 (Esmail Koushan, Samuel Khachikian, Hoshang Kavosi, amongst others) are called the second generation. Especially in the period from the 1960s into the 1980s (and beyond), the third generation was active, with the directors of the so-called 'New Wave' essentially co-constituting this generation (Bahram Beyzaie, Abbas Kiarostami, Amir Naderi, and many more). The generation that began making films after the revolution – Rakhshan Banietemad, Mohsen Makhmalbaf, Ebrahim Hatamikia, Abolfazl Jalili, etc. – is called the fourth generation. If you are looking for a time period during which their filmmaking was particularly interlaced, the 1980s until 1995 (and sometimes beyond) can be specified. This was followed by the fifth generation (1995–2010) which included filmmakers such as Mohamad Shirvani, Majid Barzegar, Samira Makhmalbaf, Bahman Ghobadi, Mohamad Rasoolof, Massoud Bakhshi. Needless to say, there are many overlappings, and up to 1979 this demarcation is easier to make. Today's young filmmakers (directors such as Ayda Panahandeh, Sahar Salahshoori, Saeed Roustayi and Reza Dormishian) form the sixth generation of Iranian filmmakers.
2. An assistant director who was active in these years explains that once he was working with a filmmaker who managed to make a 90-minute film out of 200-minutes worth of film negative, and he received the rest of the film negative as an award for his future film.
3. For example, it was impossible to have an 8-frame fade-in. It was not possible to inscribe the title letter by letter, and superimposing colorful letters on moving images was a difficult task.
4. Imagine the amount of time that an old editor needs to learn new editing programs such as Apple Final Cut and Adobe Premiere; by the time they learn how to use such software new versions will be out in the market.

12. 'AT THE END OF A CENTURY' (1996)

Bahram Beyzaie. Translation by Amir Roshan[1]

This article was first published in the Persian language original in: *Iran Nameh*, Vol. 14, No. 3: *Special Issue on Iranian Cinema*.

You all know that illustration had been long forbidden in our society. Even during the pre-Islamic era, our illustrations represented a covered culture contrary to its contemporary Greece illustrations that displayed a culture of nudity. In my opinion, this reflects an essential difference between these two cultures. One culture tends to cover up and conceal, while the other one unveils and reveals.

At the peak of the Greek thought and philosophy, attempts were made to abandon ambiguities. Philosophy, history, performing arts, and free dialogue were sought to unravel the laws and complexities of the life. Whereas, in the Middle East and Iran, even during its golden eras, everything was brought into practice in order to conceal and complicate the laws of the life. Greeks were not ashamed of the human body and rationalism. So, they admired and used them in their illustration, drama, philosophy, and in all aspects of life. In contrast, it seems that we were ashamed of the human body, and that is why we had to cover that from head to toe, as it is the case with our ancient illustration. Of course, along with that we had to cover rationalism and individualism as well.

It has been truly said that what led to the existing differences between these two cultures were, on one hand, products of the Greeks' human-like gods and goddesses, democracy and rationalism, and, on the other hand, long-lasting religious and military despotism in Iran. Exactly at the same time when the

Greek gods and goddesses became worldly and more human characteristics were attached to them, or, as is said, philosophy descended from sky to the earth, in Iran the opposite direction was taken. That is to say, God, who in early religions was supposed to be an integral part of human being, was detached from the people and was taken to the sky. Of course, the golden era in Greece ceased to exist by the dawn of military despotism and Christian culture. But, we are now dealing with ourselves and our own problems.

In the monotheistic religions of Iran's pre-Islamic era illustration was limited but not forbidden. We still do not know whether it was *Mani*[2] himself who used illustration along with his poems in order to get his messages across, or whether his followers illustrated his religious poems. Either case shows that illustration existed and was widely practiced in those days. Mani even has a verse which seems to be an explanation to or a caption on a religious image. We have lost all the murals of those eras except for a few which have survived outside of Iran's present geographical boundaries, and the one which has been gradually ruined in Kuh-e Khajeh, Mount Khawaj.[3]

In the story of Siavash,[4] Ferdowsi refers to a mural illustrating Siavash's death. This indicates that the remnants of the only mural depicting Siavash's death are also nowadays outside of Iran's present geographical boundaries. However, the murals, which were only available in the houses of a few privileged during Ferdowsi's time, i.e. four centuries before the dawn of Islam, could survive only because they were hidden indoors, thus, were not subject to outside scrutiny.

Mas'ud of Ghazni[5] is said to have furtively made murals which he later destroyed out of fear of his father, as reported by Abul-Fazl Bayhaqī.[6] Also, some full- and half-size statues from pre-Islamic eras have survived. Regardless of their quality, this shows that we were not unable to create, although they, like everywhere else in those days, might only deal with such mundane issues as a story of hunting and victory, the unity between the king and the Mobed,[7] Ahura Mazdā,[8] or human-like goddess of Mehr and Nahid. In addition, they are actually accessible evidences on the lifestyle of the people of those days, revealing to us different military and non-military uniforms, make-up, musical instruments, weapons and laws of war, the status of prisoners of war, the decoration of horses, the tradition of gift presentation, and some little details about the ordinary life of previous centuries. Only God knows what precious visual documents we later lost in the absence of sculpture. Human-like gods and goddesses had images, and of course they were associated with myths too.

The images of gods and goddesses disappeared as the human-like gods and goddesses were shunned in favor of monotheism. What remained as a result of such iconoclasm was that the only truth worth to seek is an absolute God, who is of course imageless. Sculpture was forbidden because it was a reminder of pre-Islamic idolatry and because the artists who created it were being accused of infidelity and of bringing God's absolute sovereignty under question. A similar problem occurred with portrait painting. It took us centuries to develop the pre-Islamic tradition of the *Arzhang-i*[9] style of painting into Iranianized Manichaeistic paintings of the Islamic period, which remained available only in the bookshelves of a privileged few, not accessible to all, and which were, during the previous century, sold to foreigners by money-mined uncultured people. And we, the helpless researchers of our domestic visual culture, have seen only the duplicated versions of them in this century, thanks to mechanical reproduction.

The fact is that both the pre-Islamic *Arzhang-i* paintings, examples of which are excavated in north-eastern Iran, and Manichaeistic paintings of the Islamic period were influenced by Chinese traditional painting. This shows that our traditional domestic painting was absent for centuries.

However, we have outstanding examples of pottery paintings of this period which can be found in Ray, Kashan, Save-h, and Neishabour, and which are now kept in the world's museums, displayed under such falsified titles as 'Middle Eastern art' or 'Art of the Arabic world or Islamic world,' only with the aim of removing Iran from history and geography. As far as I know, only two magazines *Iran-Nameh* and *Iran-Shenasi* have objected and protested against that. Why should someone protest at all when others have recovered such pieces of art in our wreckage after we buried them as a consequence of centuries of visual embargo and repression?

Let us return to our main topic. Since we are talking about filmmaking, it makes sense to define the image in its broader sense, i.e. any image emerging from writing or painting. Then one can see that both writing and illustration have been gaged with similar forces throughout history. This means, notwithstanding the artist's ability or disability, his knowledge and personal worldview, him having or not having access to technical facilities, there are external and internal control mechanisms going hand in hand with each other in order to bring an artist into a state of repentance. In fact, these control mechanisms actually decide upon the ultimate fate of an image, morphing it into an entirely different appearance than what the artist had in mind initially. Such a contradiction has become part of the real identity of our images. That is to say, an image, which is essentially transparent and revealing by nature, has to constantly battle with various forces attempting to tarnish its clarity. Why?

We have a little problem which is becoming bigger day by day, and it is the disharmony between our traditional absolutist thoughts and the structure of real life. We all know that image emerges from real life and that control mechanism has to do with traditional absolutism. By absolutism I mean our ancient black and white dichotomy in which realism is abandoned in favor of religious and moral allegories and in which the human being is believed to be the battlefield of good and bad forces. Such a worldview does not consider human as human per se, as one who is dealing with his earthly needs and deficiencies. Rather, man is considered an arena in which *Ahura* and *Ahriman*, the forces of light and darkness, fight, and is split into two irreconcilable parts of soul and body. The soul belongs to goodness and light and the body is associated with darkness and wickedness, and human is ultimately left helpless in this endless battle.

We know that real life doesn't occur unless the soul and body are reconciled. In my opinion, Chinese ancient philosophy, with its opposing but at the same time, complementary forces of yin and yang, which represent the dichotomy of femininity and masculinity, light and darkness, and soul and body, is closer to real life.

Rationalism and human-driven renaissance are unlikely to occur in our country as long as we are overshadowed by this traditional absolutism. Instead, religious and military despotism has created a sort of culture in which no social movement is likely to happen as long as it is not driven by religion. It is strange that the same absolutism is incorporated in all faiths and the so-called reform movements as well. According to this absolutism, which resembles a multi-act drama, everything assumes its right position in the cosmos. Soldiers are arrayed and the stage battles will happen one after another. Goodness and badness, light and darkness, the forces of *Ahura* and *Ahriman* will fight with one another, and undoubtedly the forces of *Ahura* will ultimately win the battle. We have no role in making meanings for this world. We are granted with rationalism only to conveniently identify and understand the pre-arranged meanings of this play, and to figure out where we stand between these two opposing forces and to ultimately admire the grandness of the writer of this play.

Certainly, with its hell and heaven dichotomy and its promise of resurrection, Islam fits in well with this black-and-white world. The point is that it is man who has fallen victim to such an endless divinity and demonic battle. Man is called the little world which is an example of the bigger world. We are reduced to a tiny little fraction in a holistic discourse. At the same time, this battle is going on within us as well. We think that the entire cosmos has turned into an eye to see which side of these bad and good forces we are going to stand with, so that we can be rewarded or punished accordingly. Of course, in the latest version of this divine-written playwright, we are even stripped of the right to stand with either side. Ironically, our good deeds may even not be rewarded if divine providence is unwilling to do so. No way is envisaged in this play for mankind to escape this world. The man's hapless destiny can neither be doubted nor can it be objected. Everything is predetermined and all the answers are given in advance, and if someone doubts them he is to be deemed a demon thus subject to hell. For a long time, our hidden question has been whether the writer of this play was not really aware of the shortcomings and intrinsic power of His creatures' instincts? Will the soul and body, whose everlasting enmity has brought mankind into the state of paralysis, ever be reconciled?

And if the lofty sky could not endure the load of deposit, why were the dice of the work cast in the name of a helpless me?[10] Even the most ascetic of humankind is fearful of his devotion,[11] and his real wish is to rend the roof of sky,[12] and to find out a new way.

What is absolutely clear is that unlike the control system which accepts and encourages domination and intimidation of providence, an artist is a paragon of rejecting it. For centuries, intellectuals have been deliberating about and corroborating such a divine-driven scheme. The legacies it has left behind are war among seventy-two nations, different schools of mysticism, and an ambiguous language crammed with verses, proverbs, anecdotes, and ayahs with no clarity and palpable responsibility.

Over several centuries we have been able to create one of the most complicated cultures wherein no answer is given for the most essential questions of humankind. In this increasing complexity, we were not only able to execute Mansur Al-Hallaj,[13] to refuse a grave to Ferdowsi, and to behead Hasanak Mikali,[14] but we were also able to turn Alexander the Great into a Muslim prophet of the pre-Islamic era and to attribute a saintly role to Genghis Khan who we believed was sent as a result of our sins. Why did we have such an immense sense of sinfulness that we could even justify Genghis Khan's massacre? Because we have a body, and for the absolutist thought, whether we like it or not, the body is the place in which the demonic instincts dwell and is susceptible to sin.

In this way, in a dreadful mental destruction, we were born, have grown up, and died with a sense of sin, with no hope in sight for the reconciliation of body and soul. How can mankind accept such a black and white dichotomy when it knows that there is a plethora of colors between black and white?

Probably, the human inner desire for life, happiness, and creativity as well as the remnants of the ancient nature-worshiping and fertility rites, with their allegoric languages and rituals that have coexisted with every newly arrived belief system, will to some extent water down domination of this absolutism. Without repeating the same absolutism, one can claim that the artist and all those who believe in creativity and construction are the paragon of rejecting providence, while control and supervision emanates from traditional despotic absolutism. Our traditional morality taught us to abandon the mundane world, and we, ashamed of loving this life, sought refuge in cynicism and masochism, hoping that an early death would help us escape from the limbo that the life-loving dogma held for us. Traditional absolutism may never acknowledge that the disharmony of its orders with the reality of day-to-day life is responsible for our perpetual hypocrisy and demagogy. That is why while we gaudily act in a religious manner, we indeed have a penchant for mundane life.

This traditional absolutism is also responsible for our serious historical failures. Instead of giving us a motivation for discovering the world and overcoming its difficulties, this culture has taught us to rely on God and shy away from responsibility by laying everything on God's providence. It tells us that understanding does not come through science or knowledge but through intuition which would be revealed to the ones God chooses while our endeavor would lead nowhere. In such a worldview, natural science is considered meaningless and is associated with the world of forms and meanings. Therefore, it must be discarded because the world of forms and meanings has nothing to do with truth. It tells us that the material world is worthless and fallacious, and we are unable to understand the truth behind everything that happens unless we open our inner eyes towards the occult. But how can one imagine an imageless occult?

As a result, we lagged behind in our scientific progress, and our entire historical writings aim to teach us that the world is worthless, and a powerful hand is behind every event. Spatial and temporal concepts have no place in our stories and allegories. In our stories we have seen *Sahrāye-Mahshar* (Armageddon) and have traveled to the land of *Gog* and *Magog*. We have explained a world which can be explained and imagined in whichever way you want because nobody has ever experienced it to substantiate what you claim. With only few exceptions, we have traveled to the places which have nothing to do with the real life. We have gone through *Haft Shahr*-e *Eshgh*,[15] the Seven Valleys of Spirituality, we have reached *Kūh-e Qāf*,[16] to catch the *Sīmorgh*,[17] we have built the City of Heart, we have gone after *Ābe Hayāt*,[18] the Water of Life, in darkness. But, we have been unable to make a simple description of an alley, to describe a simple social relationship, or interpret man's place in the world.

Nevertheless, these are the only available visual documents; literature and Manichaeistic paintings, with all their shortcomings and merits.

What do we find in our literary and historic writings? We can find strong language and strong description, but [they are] poor in characterization, except for few examples in Shāhnāmeh, weak in employing languages of different social classes, weak in crafting dialogue and dramatic situations, and poor in making direct references to real social life. We also find strong historical and mythological images, and abundant texts teaching us about politics, morality, and emperorship, all of which reveal a true absolutist sprit.

What can we find of our visual arts? No statues, even no Islamic ones. We have scrapped hundreds of architectural masterpieces from every era in favor of a jerry-building culture in the past few decades. This means that we have destroyed the imagery culture of almost all eras including Qajar, Safavid, Mongul, Sassanid, and the Parthian. While in the West architecture and even ecclesiastical statues vivaciously take you to the imagery culture of previous centuries, an Iranian illustrator finds little visual evidence about the customs, dressing habits, and lifestyle of previous centuries except for duplicated versions of small segments of original works that have transpired Iran and Manichaeistic paintings of the Islamic period. However, Manichaeistic paintings are truth-evading as they tend to encapsulate the whole world in a piece of paper. Therefore, they ignore distances, and the images look alike no matter how far or close they are located. Nonetheless, they are much ahead of their time as they employ image and color in the black and white world of paper and ink. They are a treasure of evidences about everything, and in the later eras they get closer to the details of the daily and ordinary life of people, though their drawing method would fail to respond to the pure reality of the future time. Nonetheless, the best of them has to be magnified to allow for understanding the miracle behind it. Under such a magnifying glass one can discover even the color of the warp and weft of a turban. Had it not been for Manichaeistic and pottery paintings, we would have plunged into an abysmal ignorance about our ancestors' visual worldview. Manichaeistic paintings prove once again that we had been able to see and represent the real world, though we had to conceal everything due to the fear for the control mechanism of traditional absolutism.

However, unless for their documentary aspects and for learning their unbelievably detailed descriptive methods, Manichaeistic paintings, which depict a real event with an unrealistic appearance, seem to be of little use in today's world of rationalism and realism.

What happened to the pre-Islamic murals which were hidden indoors?

Living examples of them can be found both in a couple of murals in Safavid Court as well as in teahouse paintings which represent a more popular version. Unfortunately, the original Safavid versions were later detached from the walls and are no longer available.

Owing to the ambiguous use of the term 'Naghsh' – motif and paint – in our ancestor's writings, we still don't know what exactly this term refers to in the old manuscripts. For example, in the book entitled *Ketab-e Al-Naghz*, written in the ninth century, we read 'Like the girls who make up, Rafida decorates and paints the necropolis.' We still don't know if such paintings and decorations refer only to botanical motifs or if they also include portrait paintings. Why not? It is particularly important to note that such a tradition – of portrait painting – is still widely practiced in many known and unknown religious places and some *takias* (mourning halls), the walls of which are decorated with religious portrait paintings, though many of which are sheathed nowadays.

The tradition of religious image reading, which also exists in Mani's works, remained in the hands of practitioners of this custom. I believe this tradition, which simultaneously represents several different religious and moral stories, later provided a significant visual base for *ta'ziyeh*. The imagery examples of the past two or three centuries, be it in the form of murals or teahouse and book paintings, show that illustration has been quicker than literature in keeping pace with the developments of time. In them, one can see an increasing tendency for naturalism and realism, and for breaking the limitations, though they may not represent similar level of expertise.

I really doubt if there are many filmmakers who have happened to take a glance at the old writings and at the Manichaeistic paintings in particular. But I am sure there are many filmmakers who have grown up face to face with those of teahouse paintings with all their religious functions. However, the question is whether we can reconstruct a single scene of all such visual heritages. The answer is no owing to the financial and technical shortcomings of Iranian cinema and the constraint imposed by monitoring. Apparently, we lack the freedom which we had a thousand years ago because at that time it was possible to re-enact the story of Sheikh Sanan[19] in love, who used to drink while strapping a Zunar. Can we do the same today? We don't have even the freedom of *ta'ziyeh*. In *ta'ziyeh*, aniconism does not exist and the sentient beings are shown with a face. Is it possible to practice the same in today's Iranian cinema? Is it possible to organize Chehel Sotoun[20] (Forty Columns) revelry in which women dance to music? No. Watchdogs authorize revelry only if it is not shown. They also authorize you to enact the story of Sheikh Sanan but of course without showing the Christian girl, drinking, and the Zunar. Monitoring negates the real and natural images, and it favors abstracts. You know that abstracts have no image. Truth cannot be depicted, morality cannot be painted, and virtue cannot be illustrated. They cannot be created, unless they are put in a proper framework of a story. Truth against mendacity, morality against immorality, and virtue against vice! All the imagery cultures have understood such a simple fact but watchdogs fail to understand it today. When you explain that a good man is recognized because of his good deeds and a bad man is recognized because he commits vices, how can you represent it without properly showing the vices?

He,[21] who always haughtily talks about cultural invasion, says: 'That is your problem.' What does this mean? You have created this problem, not us. You cannot forsake us in the middle of an ocean and tell us reaching the shore is our problem. We will not reach the shore and you know that, and you are responsible for putting us up there.

Iranian cinema and theater have been stuck in the middle of this ocean for years, and what is to be blamed for is the disharmony between the traditional absolutists' code of conduct and the day-to-day reality of life. Instead of thinking how to open the window to let more light in, they further seal the doors and close the windows. An important point is that Iran has neither experienced the Golden Age of Greek culture, nor it has experienced Europe's Renaissance following the medieval period. What happened in our country during the past few centuries was not a deep-seated and pervasive movement. Here, knowledge still implies satanic pride, laughter means lack of wisdom, and philosophy is blasphemy. The human being is deemed a sinner intrinsically, love is equated with corruption, and people are looked at as if they are born a sinner. Happiness is bad, while suffering, suicide, and masochism are good. There are still many who think they are superior to others, and, thus, have the right to instruct and punish the inferiors, and such cruelty is even worse when it comes to women. It is reminiscent of the West's church culture adorned with the weapon of the Inquisition and anti-wisdom. Thanks to major scientific discoveries, traditional absolutism was overturned in the West and replaced with a zealous scientific curiosity for a better understanding of the world. Then, it became clear that thinking and knowing don't belong to any particular social class, and wisdom is a benediction bestowed upon everyone equally, and everyone can understand and explain the world in his/her own terms. At the same time when we were busy with our mean struggle for power and our imaginary Alexander was about to convert others to Islam, the Westerners began globetrotting, discovered new continents, wrote precise travelogues, and re-measured everything. They trod on terra incognita, collected customs, beliefs, dressing habits, and the housing construction methods of other cultures, and put them under a magnifying glass. They surveyed our land and discovered its potentials, and not only extracted oil and gold from our lands, but also unearthed ancient civilizations and decrypted the unknown writing systems of forgotten languages and read that for us to the extent that we began to understand our own country via the travelogues and studies conducted by the foreigners and not by our own. I believe that foreigners' photography of us was more effective than their writings in making us face our real image. Before that we were seeing ourselves in mirrors, perhaps the oldest camera invented by humankind. The Cup of Jamshid[22] didn't reveal the truth despite the fact that it was believed to be a source of divination. Accordingly, our image in a mirror was transient and unsustainable, only delivering a sign that we would not last too. For centuries, our eyes' camera had been addicted to not seeing and our mind was wont to forgetting. Our illustration, crammed with afterlife beliefs and images, was in no way reflecting our real life. Therefore, the only real images from us were those taken by the Westerners. They were images that could not be interpreted differently than what they were: a poor child working as a brazier, a poor child being punished at school, a death-row convict in the face of a firing squad, poor men holding their heads down, no sign of spirituality or mysticism.

In my opinion, the first photos taken by the Westerners from us marked a turning point in the history of our thought. After centuries of denial, we had to look at our real selves. Unlike a mirror, photos did not change the image after one hour, a day, a week. It was what it was, and it showed what it was intended to show, and we had no option but to accept it. Photos brought down the curtain, and they revealed the very situation in which we lived, and that situation contradicted our perennial anthropocentric beliefs. What we were seeing was not consistent with the fate the Almighty had envisaged for the best of His creatures. They shook our beliefs entirely, and what remained was not what we liked it to be. Therefore, we killed a photographer, and some of us described such photos as insulting and imaginary. If they were insulting, why did we live like that. Wasn't there a need for change?

Over the last few decades of the past century and the first decades following the invention of cinema, the time when Ebrahim Khan[23] the photographer purchased a camera during a trip abroad and showed a film to a constitutional feast arranged by Roussie Khan,[24] a leaflet, whose author's name I don't remember, was distributed in Tehran and Isfahan. In this leaflet, the author organizes an imaginary Q&A session with an imaginary personage, who is of course himself, and attacks all the modern concepts, inter alia, human rights, individualism, and freedom. He describes modern inventions such as the monograph, cinema, and photography as the means intended only to destroy our morality. What else can be expected from such a conspiracy-driven mind? He invented a new language to utter the same long-lasting enmity of traditional absolutism with visual arts and developments.

Many Iranian filmmakers have learnt cinema directly from photos and photography, and later on from watching and re-watching films, and they have no background in literature or the visual arts. In a country with such a low literacy rate, cinema and photography gradually and within a span of a few decades permeated a sort of cultural renaissance among the urbanite populace. That is exactly the reason behind the aforementioned enmity.

Photography is more candid than complicated writings which favor hypocrisy. The clarity of a photo outpaces the complex writings, even the good ones, in changing human behavior.

In spite of years of imagery embargoes, political inquisitions, administrative humiliations, and lack of technical and financial resources, there are many candidates who want to learn visual and performing arts. A large number of video experiments, photography and painting exhibitions, and a growing body of books published on cinema, photography, and painting show that the language of the image is gradually replacing the literary language in our country. The image is the language of ordinary people while words belong to intelligentsia and elites. Many filmmakers adhere to the 8 mm cinema of previous decades, to the so-called free cinema (sinamy-e azad),[25] youth cinema, and the likes. Many come from documentary, though the government-sponsored ones. Many filmmakers are born out of television with all its painful results. Some come even from prison and some have been war photographers and reporters. Some filmmakers come from theater, the visual arts, and from universities, a major base of intellectualism. Some have learnt cinema in the West, the epitome of individualism and rationalism. How can they think traditionally? But this justifies nothing. One can only be judged based on what one produces.

'AT THE END OF A CENTURY' (1996)

There are filmmakers with a traditional absolutist attitude and they are fully supported. There are also filmmakers who try to reconcile traditions and modernity and they are supported conditionally. They are optimistic and they regularly make films. Their optimism is very well justified. There are filmmakers who are struggling with their 1000-year-old culture, and they try to create their own meanings and understand their cultural past with today's knowledge, but of course without freedom. It happens that they also fall prey to the same complicated language, and they are prone to losing their job by posing a simple question to the traditional absolutists. There are also filmmakers who got to know cinema after the 1979 Islamic Revolution and found it their own language. They became filmmakers with the support of the ruling class, and as it is the nature of image, they were changed and took steps towards development and progress, but faced with the iron fist of traditional absolutists as they never accept change. They lost the support of the ruling people after they posed a question, and in the next step they were added to the list of banned filmmakers. There are also filmmakers who were born out of the same monitoring system and are completely fine with it. There are also filmmakers who do the monitoring and censorship themselves. In advance they exclude women, half of the population, so that their film would not be faced with any problems. There are also filmmakers who have learnt cinema on their own. Cut out from their historical past, they accept the status quo with resignation and try to maneuver within the boundaries drawn for them. There are also filmmakers among Iranian diasporas, who are still furious about the situation that forced them to flee their country. Although they might probably have been able to cope with the problem of being a stranger in their own country, they have to deal with the problem of being a stranger in foreign countries. Yet, it is not clear which one is more painful. Also, a new generation of filmmakers is emerging among Iranian expatriates, who don't understand the root base of Iran's complexities today. A generation considering itself not responsible for the events of previous millennia and believing that all the social and intellectual catastrophes had been created in its absence, wondering why it should be held responsible. A generation willing to live, think, and work freely is not ready to shoulder such a heavy burden if being Iranian entails so many complications. This generation does not know where exactly it stands, but knows that it has to strengthen its foothold. It looks at Iran and it looks straight ahead. In the so-called free world, it thinks directly through images and knows that it has to develop a new language for its new conditions. It will create the image it thinks of as long as it does not experience an identity crisis.

What has happened to us during the past 100 years that has made any significant change in our cinema impossible? I believe that what is to be blamed for is our attempt to dichotomize art both as something flawless and virtuous, and sinful and corrupt at the same time. It is painful that even the so-called neo-intellectualism falls prey to the same absolutist dogma. Nonetheless, in a society wherein the same traditional language of loyalty and betrayal is even used for social and political campaigns, and wherein the weapon of slander can take the place of dialogue and trust, the so-called neo-intellectualism would inevitably follow the same route.

No doubt such intellectualism supports the progress of art. That is why it employs pleasant suffixes like committed art, social cinema, moral cinema, thought-stimulating theater, educational theater, political theater, family cinema, progressive cinema, and the likes only in an attempt to defend the arts against centuries of contempt leveled against drama, acting, and image by our hypocritical morality. A kind of morality that tells us entertaining people means corruption and prostitution. This shows the same intellectual apology towards an absolutist culture.

It also shows that the so-called intellectualism has not reached the level of maturity to recognize the essential nature of art, theater, and cinema. That is probably the reason why it uses certain intellectual expressions only to achieve social acceptability.

It is this admission of guilt on the part of filmmakers and intellectuals that the monitoring is taking advantage of and that emboldens everyone in every position to attack cinema and the filmmakers. Cinematic affairs are decided upon by all but not those who have worked and suffered for cinema, and the filmmakers should be accredited by every little office worker, who even doesn't know how to spell out his or her name correctly.

The pre-revolutionary cinema has of course left enough vulgarity to make the cinema indefensible. But, can you punish someone for a crime committed by others? Moreover, didn't the intellectual cinema, which was well recognized by the world, emerge from the same cinema in spite of all difficulties?

Cinema, theater, arts, and culture are left with no option but to undertake such an inexorable repentance, if they want to attain honor and integrity. Our cinema and theater cannot be shoddier than what they are today, and the traditional absolutist control mechanism knows that very well. In addition to monopolizing the industry, which enables the control mechanism to keep the filmmakers in a constant apologetic state, the control mechanism has also employed every possible means in order to bring the filmmakers under its control. In a country where being an artist or intellectual is vilified, filmmakers are actually taken hostage as they can be traumatized in every moment of their career by control mechanisms. Stopping a film halfway means the bankruptcy of its investors, blocking a film's distribution process means taking upon yourself heavy debts, and under this circumstance resistance means putting at stake your future career.

Every day a new official or unofficial list of blacklisted people is released, and one can never anticipate whether or not one's name is or will be in the list. Who can think of deepening and developing his artistic language in such circumstances? How can you think of the essence of an image when you will have to work hard only to maintain your balance like a trapeze artist on a trembling string? Still, not everything should be blamed on the control mechanism. Our painful historic experience, itself the victim of control and supervision, is equally responsible. After centuries of elimination of individuality and individual identity we have today become a nation left with no identity. Throughout history many have got longevity through absence. After centuries of internal and external de-imagization, there are very few people left who have a clear image of themselves and are ready to maintain that under all circumstances. By contrast, there are many opportunists who are ready to adjust themselves with the rules of the age and with whatever they think can bring them success. That is a character trait that the control mechanism is fully taking advantage of. Elimination of individuality, independence, and character, and scrapping dialogue in favor of pure and blindfold obedience are what looked for by the control mechanism. Under such circumstances, our discussion about our abstract and hypothetic identity is of no meaning. If we think of our image as negatively stereotyped it is because the identity of a nation is what it makes. In a society where every precious masterpiece of art is being destroyed in favor of jerry-builders, and nothing but duplication is produced in return, its cinema becomes duplication too. By the same token, its identity becomes the same.

Why should a low-echelon office worker, whose type is being mushroomed by a million every day, be able to trouble a filmmaker, a writer, or an actor? The answer to this question reveals our cultural identity. Let me not make you despondent. The limited and rootless renaissance of the past century has been able to take a few steps forwards. The traditional absolutism has at least practically accepted the very concept of image.

Video screening is now recognized by government-sponsored channels, which seemed a chimera fifteen years ago. Popular movies are now immediately dispatched to the most prestigious international film festivals, which was unfeasible fifteen years ago. While the removal of subsidies from filmmaking and the increasing inflation rate has made it impossible for the private sector to invest in filmmaking and to compete with the government, which enjoys unlimited resources, there are still a few filmmakers who can stand on their own feet with the support of foreign investors, who see Iranians as no more than a cheap workforce. And it is completely convincing that their interest is the priority that must be met in the movies.

Yes, the traditional absolutism has now accepted the image, but more than anything else it has accepted the image of its own victory. While an image is essentially transparent and revealing, the monitoring, which is the executive wing of traditional absolutism, favors an image that is suppressed and manipulated.

As a result, the identity of our cinematic images driven by centuries-old ambiguous language has become duplicitous and hypocritical in nature. How to say something which at the same time sounds like you have not said anything? How to say something which, while it is perceived that you have not said anything, people understand that you have indeed said something?

Many of our filmmakers live with such imagery hypocrisy as they observe the rules and regulations set by the supervision and control mechanism without even believing them. The control mechanism knows that too. So, even if you make a simple image of a bed and a blanket the control mechanism does not believe that it is what it is, and a great number of paid staff is employed to decipher the imaginary codes purportedly concealed in a film. Even if nothing is found by them, the spectators, both intellectuals and pressure groups, would sift through a film in search of hidden meanings. The latter without even watching the movie.

Such complicated and multifaceted language is of use neither to cinema nor to the society which more than anything else needs a clear and straightforward language and dialogue. Like a chariot whose wheels go in different directions, a crumbled society will go nowhere.

While different countries have found their suitable way into cinema 100 years after its invention, we have been able to create one of the most complicated and pervasive control mechanisms, which has incorporated all the negative and cleansing characteristics of despotic regimes. We have created such an elaborate system which, instead of being at cinema's disposal, thinks that filmmakers have to be at its service. As a consequence, filmmakers are obliged to invest all their material and non-material assets and to bear with all the administrative humiliations only to appease that system, even if no one can guarantee their services will be appreciated at the end of the day.

Instead of helping to increase cultural productions and to promote cinema, the office workers of the control system, who in the manner of the Shah currently use the plural pronoun of 'we' for referring to themselves, are only engrossed in excluding everyone who they think is rebellious and defiant.

Every day new orders and a new booklet of rules and regulations are issued. This system constantly tries to prove itself and its presence. That is why its footprint is left on every stage of filmmaking from supervision of the screenplay, which has to be compatible with traditional rules, to what a film should or should not contain. It should not be complex, not bitter, and not even too sweet, not pessimistic and not too optimistic, not display tension; everything is on the right place and if a little misunderstanding occurs accidentally it can be solved by sacrifice. That is how it goes on. You will be presented with the examples of successful movies and those which are banned.

Criticism? At a time when the enemies await an opportunity? No – it will end happily. Why don't you want people to be happy? If you make your movie in such and such a way it will be even bought by the state TV, by airlines, etc.

That is how the supervision, which is rather an imposition of style, sneaks into every single stage of a film. Who should act and who should not, who should be the sound engineer, who should be director and who should not, who should act out the role of a bad character and who should impersonate the good ones, whose name should appear first, who should hold the camera and who should be denied that, who is eligible to take loans even gratuitously and who should be denied them, who can take raw materials and for whom it is his own problem?

Do you remember that the good character should not smoke a cigar and in the case of a bad character permission should be acquired in advance?

Do you mean Islamic dress code? You are not serious. How can you close your eyes on such a social reality which even the world has come to terms with and has found it suitable for us?

I just want to understand, with all due respect for such a social reality, if you are talking about reality, how can you impose such dress codes on people of previous eras and even on pre-Islamic people who were not observing it?

We are happy that we can solve your problems, and you surely know that it is a tradition. Yes, I know but I am asking for more clarification. Why don't we observe the same tradition for men? Why don't we shave their head and make them wear their traditional clothes? They smile. Are you kidding? It seems that you no longer want to make a movie. Such monitoring regulations are there for you not to face any problems while making your film. Have you read the booklet? We can introduce you to an advisor as well.

Such an imposition of style and thought by the monitoring system goes on step by step. Its business is not only what happens on the screen, but what the actors do in their private life also falls under its surveillance. Whether the actors laugh in their homes, whether they go to a party and whether they wear a colorful dress, how the poster must be made, whose name should appear on the poster and where on the poster, everything is subject to its scrutiny.

Men will have no problem in looking colorful, but women should give it a wide berth. They all should look the same, like a dead body, like a corpse. They are even better off not to be seen on the screen and it is even better if they are made to look a bit uglier. Of course, at the end of the day everything depends on who has made the movie.

After undergoing such a maze of bureaucratic mess, the real inspection begins not once or twice but on every stage for everyone. It is then decided whose film must be supported and whose not, whose film must be sold and whose not, whose film can be sent to foreign film festivals and whose not. The inspection does not even end here. After going through such an interminable process, a film can be banned forever by a group of motley hooligans riding on motorcycles, unmindful of the human and material costs invested in it. Indeed, it is the latter which shows that the unofficial control mechanism is far more precarious than the official one. Control and inspection is like a tree of which we can only see the visible parts, not its hidden deep roots. Such a policy, on the one hand, leaves the job-seeking filmmakers with no alternative but to seek refuge in state television and propaganda films, and, on the other hand, forces the thirsty Iranian spectators to desperately seek their favorites through satellite channels.

Under the pretext of fighting vulgarism, which is of course not a matter of concern for intellectuals, the traditional absolutism is thinking of de-intellectualism and of killing every image in which it has no presence. That is why, in 1984, plenty of Iranian and foreign films were confiscated pell-mell, and were later set on fire, without segregating the bad and the good, even by its own criteria and definition, and without thinking that even the bad movies are evidence of a certain era. There was not even any consideration of how many of the world's masterpieces were among the burnt copies.

A hundred years after the invention of cinema, when countries are celebrating and displaying the treasures of their national cinema, our cinema, heedless of its intellectual and glorious past, remains silent to ensure that the past is dead, and its relics are ruined. That is our identity!

Notes (By Translator Amir Roshan)

1. With profound thanks to Sara Landa and Kianoush Amiri who generously assisted me during various phases of the translation.
2. Mani (AD 216–AD 274 or 277), an Iranian prophet and founder of Manichaeism, wrote the book *Arzhang*. What is remarkable is that this book was rich in drawings and paintings.
3. A hill in the middle of Lake Hamun, in the Iranian province of Sistan and Baluchestan.
4. Siavash, a legendary Iranian prince, is a main character in Ferdowsi's epic, the *Shāhnāmeh*, famous for being 'the world's longest piece of epic poetry created by a single poet.'
5. Mas'ud of Ghazni was the third king of the Ghaznavid dynasty which ruled Iran for about two centuries.
6. Abul-Fazl Bayhaqī was a Persian historian and author who wrote the famous work of Persian literature *Tārīkh-e Bayhaqī* aka *Tārīkh-e Mas'oudī (Bayhaqian/ Masoudian History)* in the eleventh century CE.
7. Mobed is a cleric in the Zoroastrian religion.
8. Ahura Mazdā is the supreme creator especially in the religious system of the Iranian prophet Zoroaster.
9. The prevailing method of painting during the Sassanid Empire. The name is associated with the book *Arzhang* (see note 2 above).

10. In the following lines, Beyzaie refers to three *ghazals* from Hafez's Dīwān: 'The load of deposit (of love and of divine knowledge), the lofty sky could not endure; in the name of helpless me, the dice of the work, they cast.'
11. 'For the head of my own faith, I trembled like the willow; for, in the hand of one of bow ex-brow, Kafir in religion, is my heart.'
12. '(O murshid!) Come; so that the rose (of ease and of pleasure) we may scatter, and into the cup (of existence; or of heart), the wine (of love and of divine knowledge) cast; (By our inward strength) The roof of the sky we rend, and (to the height of another heaven) a new way, cast.'
13. Mansur al-Hallaj (244 AH–309 AH) was a revered Persian mystic poet who extensively wrote about and taught Sufism.
14. Hasanak Mikali or Hasanak Vazir, as he is popularly known, was a famous eleventh-century Iranian figure from the Mikalid family, who served as minister in the Ghaznavid Empire. He was executed on a charge of infidelity, which, it is widely believed, was politically motivated. His execution has been documented in Persian literature by Abul-Fazl Bayhaqī.
15. The 'Seven Stages of Spirituality' are described by Farid ud-Din Attar Neishabouri, who is commonly known as Attar of Nishabour, in his book *The Conference of the Birds* (*Manṭeq al-ṭaīr*). The stages are: *The Valley of Quest, The Valley of Love, The Valley of Understanding, The Valley of Independence and Detachment, The Valley of Unity, The Valley of Astonishment and Bewilderment, The Valley of Deprivation and Death.*
16. *Qāf-Kūh* or *Kūh-e Qāf* is a mythological mountain in Iranian tradition and Persian literature, refering to the highest mountain and land of demons. It is also the place where the Sīmorgh's nest is located.
17. *Sīmorgh* is a winged creature in Persian mythology, often depicted 'as a peacock with the head of a dog and the claws of a lion.' Strong and gigantic enough to carry off an elephant, the bird is so old that it had seen the destruction of the world three times over.
18. *Ābe Hayāt* or *Ābe Hayvan* (*Water of Life*) is associated in Persian literature with immortality. If someone drinks a cup of *Ābe-Hayāt* he is to be granted eternal life. Hafiz, for instance, says: 'Water of life has turned dark, where is Glorious Khizr; Flowers are all bleeding, whence the breeze which branches bend.'
19. *Sheikh Sanan*, a verse play written by Huseyn Javid, an Azerbaijani poet, is the story of the Muslim sheikh Sanan, who falls in love with a Georgian-Christian girl.
20. Chehel Sotoun is a Persian pavilion in the city of Isfahan, built by Shah Abbas III. It is especially famous for its murals which depict several revelries during the Safavid era.
21. The author refers to Ali Khamenei, the Supreme Leader of the Islamic Republic, who used the term 'cultural invasion' in the early nineties.
22. In Persian mythology, *Jām-e Jam* or *The Cup of Jamshid* is believed to be a cup of divination and an insignia of power. It has been the subject of many Persian poems and stories, which attributed the success of the Persian Empire to the power of this cup.
23. Mirza Ebrahim Khan Rahmani, also known as Akkas Bashi – who was the royal photographer of Mozaffar ad-Din Shah Qajar – brought photography to Persia after a trip to Europe.

24. Mehdi Ivanov, known as Roussie Khan (1875–1967), was a technician in the royal photography studio during the Qajar dynasty. He played a significant role in promoting cinema in Iran.
25. See Chapter 1 in this volume, by Tara Najd Ahmadi, 'The Incomplete' (p. 23).

INDEX

Page references in *italic text* indicate a figure

8 mm film, 23
35 mm film, 74, 75
400 Blows, The, 25–6

Abdolvahab, Mohsen, 132
Abecassis, Michaël, 176
Abraham, Nicolas, 134
absolutism, 231–2, 233–4, 241
access to film, 73–9, 80
 history of, 64, 66, 73
 underground distribution, 77–8, 204, 218
 world cinema, 218–19
acousmatic listening, 146–7, 151, 154–5, 157
actors, 190–1
Adorno, Theodor, 85
Afkhami, Behrouz, 220
afsordegi see depression
Ahangar, Mohammad Ali, 172–3
 Cypress Under Water, 176–8, 179
 The Queen, 167, 173, 181
 Sacred Defense Cinema, 169, 172, 180, 182
Ahmad Shah Qajar *see* Qajar, Ahmad Shah
Ahura and *Ahriman*, 232
Ahwaz, 23
al-Ahmad, Jalal, 125
alcohol, 156
Alexander the Great, 233, 237
Al-Hallaj, Mansur, 233
allegories, 1, 123, 134
Althusser, Louis, 128
ambiguity in Islamic culture, 3, 127, 134
American cinema *see* Hollywood
analog vs. digital filmmaking, 221–2
Ansar-i Hizb Allah, 200, 201
Antigone, 55, 56
Antigone 88, 9, 52
Anvar, Fakhreddin, 75

INDEX

archaeological perspective of history and memory, 4–5, 7
archaeology and filmmaking, 47–9; see also media archaeology
archaeology of access, 66–7, 79, 80
architecture, 234
archives, 4, 5, 125
art, artists and absolutist control mechanisms, 231, 233, 239–41
Art Center, 217
art cinema, 42, 204
  in the global market, 43, 201–2
Art Council, 220
Arzhang-i paintings, 231
Asadi, Khatereh, 157
Assayas, Olivier, 137
'Aṭṭār, Farīd ad-Dīn-e, 1
Atwood, Blake, 149, 156
audio cassettes, 139
audiovisual distortions, 64–5, 70–1, 72–3, 76
Avini, Morteza, 125–6, 140, 169–70, 196, 200
Avini Awards, 171, 172
Awakening Dreams, 172
awards, film, 137, 171, 172, 222–3
Ayari, Kianoush, 21–2, 23, 26–7, 58
Ayatollah Khomeini see Khomeini, Ruhollah

Banietemad, Rakhshan, 6, 37, 119, 127–8, 132, 133, 134
bāzgasht be khishtan (return to the self), 131
basījī, 122, 126, 139, 200, 201
Bauer, Thomas, 3, 127
Bayat, Asef, 23
Bayhaqī, Abul-Fazl, 230
Bazin, André, 127
bees, 174
Behrangi, Samad, 1, 187
Behrouzan, Orkideh, 123, 125

Benjamin, Walter, 28–9, 57, 61, 85, 129, 139, 154
Betacam SP, 218, 221
Betamax tapes, 218
Beyzaie, Bahram, 122, 125, 220
biopics, 137–8
Bloch, Ernst, 58
body memory, 133–4
Bombay, 67, 68
Bonyād-e Shahīd, 177, 178
Book of the Kings, 55, 234
burning of films, 75, 244

Caesar, 121–2
Cannes Film Festival, 218, 222
celluloid film, 72
Censoring an Iranian Love Story, 121
censorship
  absolutist control mechanisms, 236, 239, 240–1, 242–4
  of film scripts, 216–17, 222
  filmmakers' quiet transgressions, 27, 97
  and the international market, 223–4
  love and eroticism, 148–9, 156
  Michel Foucault's theories, 5
  war films, 181
  women, 155, 243
'Chain Murders of Iran,' 136
Chakrabarty, Dipesh, 1
Channel One, 21–2
chapter summaries, 7–8
  Part I, 8–9
  Part II, 10–11
  Part III, 11–13
  Part IV, 13–15
Chelkowski, Peter, 151
chess, 219
chest-beating, 133–4, 139, 162
Child of the Soil, 172

248

Chinese culture, 231, 232
Chion, Michel, 147, 151–2, 154–5, 157
Chronicles of Victory/Narration of Triumph, 125, 126
cinema, narrative, 106
cinema and absolutist control mechanisms, 239–41, 242–4
cinema and counter-memory theory, 5–8
Cinema Museum, Tehran, 63–4
cinema studies, 43, 67, 80
cinemas, 192, 194, 196
Cinematic Film Council, 223
cinematic memoryscapes, 2–3, 4–5, 6–7, 105, 106–7, 109–11, 113–14
class, social, 128, 139, 194–5, 198, 201
'clerico-engineering,' 126–7
Cold War, 24
collective memory, 66
Collingwood, R. G., 195, 204
Conference of the Birds, The, 1
'context' in cultural studies, 69
control mechanisms over culture, 231, 235, 239–41
Cooley, Claire, 69
coronavirus, 140
counter-memories and heterogeneity, 5–8, 140
    counter-memory theories of Michel Foucault, 3–5, 31, 66, 109–10, 140, 196
Cow, The, 220
crimes against humanity, 50–1
critics, film, 190, 193
crypts, 134–5
crystal simorgh, 137
Cup of Jamshed, 237
Cypress Under Water, 176–8, 178–9, 180, 181, 182

Damascus Time, 182
Damavandi, Reza, 74
Dark Passage, 122
Dead Wave, 221, 222
Deep Breath, 122
depression, 123–4
Derrida, Jacques, 104, 134, 135, 139, 141
destiny of humankind, 232–3, 234
destruction of films, 75, 244
Devictor, Agnés, 170
diegetic music and sound, 91, 93, 150–1
digital filmmaking, 221–2, 223, 227
Dihnamaki, Mas'ud, 191, 192, 199–201
directors, female, 42; *see also* Milani, Tahmineh
disappearances in Iran, 49–51
'displaced allegory', 123
distribution of film, underground, 77–8, 204, 218
docudramas, 137–8
documentaries 52–4, 57, 200; *see also Hitch; May Lady; Newborns, The*
doors, 102–3, 113–14
Dormishian, Reza, 172
Dragonfly Storm, The, 222

earthquake in Iran 1990, 106–7, 111; *see also Life and Nothing More*
Eastman Kodak Institute, 23
economy in Iran, 225–6
editing, 227
editing rooms, 125, 126, 127–8
education, 104
Egyptian film industry, 193
Elena, Alberto, 110
Elsaesser, Thomas, 65–6
emergency rooms, 121–2, 124, 129
enunciation, 85, 87, 95, 97, 110

INDEX

epistolary films, 37–8
eroticism *see* love and eroticism in Iranian cinema
Ershadi, Homayoun, 175, 178
Espinosa, Julio García, 24
Europe, film representations of, 91–2, 95
executions and disappearances, 49–51, 140
exile, 55–6

failure of technology, 72, 79–80
Fajr International Film Festival, 137, 172, 181, 222
falgoosh, 147, 161
Farabi Cinema Foundation, 74, 217, 219, 220, 221
Farahani, Golshifteh, 161, *162*
farang, 91–2, 93
Fardid, Ahmad, 125
Fardin, Muhammad 'Ali, 191, 202
fax machines, 219
faza-ye golkhāneh-ī, 218
Felski, Rita, 69
female bodies and desires, 155–6, 158–160
female directors, 42; *see also* Milani, Tahmineh
female gaze, 146–7, 155, 158, 160
female voice, 147
feminist cinema, 43
feminist historians, 41
Ferdowsi, 230, 233, 234
Ferro, Marc, 6–7
'festival filmmakers', 223–4
festivals *see* film festivals
film archives, 73–4, 76
film awards, 137, 171, 172, 222–3
film critics, 190, 193
film festivals, 137, 171, 172, 223–4, 226–7
film formats, 70, 72, 73, 74

film funding, 202, 226, 241
film industry in Iran
  early cinema, 67, 150
  post-revolution, 123, 127, 148, 194, 196, 201–3, 216
  pre-revolution, 148, 150, 192–3
  young talent, 224–5
film production
  1980–2000, 216–18
  'Hitchcock-Tarkovsky' dichotomy, 220–1
  state control, 217–18, 221–4, 242–4
  technical limitations for filmmakers, 219–20, 221–2
  technological developments, 226–7
  young talent and the generation gap, 224–5
film stars, 190–1
film stock used in film production, 219, 221
film studies *see* cinema studies
film trailers, 219
filmfarsi
  audience and social class, 194–5
  characteristics of the genre, 193
  as counter-memory, 189–90, 196
  critiques of, 190, 193–4, 195
  film stars, 190–1
  martyrdom and sacrifice, 197
  post-revolution attitudes towards, 196, 220
  pre-revolution attitudes towards, 23, 192–3, 195
  revival and legacy, 199, 201, 202–5, 218
filmmakers
  and absolutist control mechanisms, 240–1, 242–4
  'festival', 223–4
  generation gap, 224–5, 239
  imprisonment of, 34

250

and Iranian visual culture, 238–9
sixth generation, 216, 222–4, 224–5, 227–8
filmmaking as archaeology, 47–9
filmsāzān-e-festivāl-ī, 223–4
financing of films, 202, 226, 241
Fish, Laura, 68
Fish and Cat, 134–7, *136*
   crypts, 134–5
   ghosts, 135–7
   mythological structure, 135
   time loops, 134–5
   time is 'out of joint', 135
flashbacks, 38, 113, 135, 153, 155
folk tales *see* Persian poetry and literature
formats of films, 70, 72, 73, 74
Foucault, Michel, 19, 112
   censorship, 5
   counter-memory, 3–5, 31, 66, 109–10, 140, 196
   Iranian Revolution, 3, 59
fourth wall, 111
France, 56
Free Cinema, 23–4, 238
French New Wave, 25–6
French Revolution, 27–8
Freud, Sigmund, 8, 125
Frick, Caroline, 75
From Karkheh to Rhine, 139, 180
Fuller, Sam, 122
funding of films, 202, 226, 241

Gabrys, Jennifer, 80
Ganjavi, Nezami *see* Nezami
Geertz, Clifford, 7
gender norms in film, 69
genealogical perspective of history and memory, 4, 109
generation gap, 224–5
Ghamari-Tabrizi, Behrouz, 35
gharbzadegi, 125

Ghasemi, Soraya, 157, 161
ghazal, 150
Ghobadi, Bahman, 132
ghosts, 135–7, 176
Gilāneh, 132–4
   chest-beating, 133
   screen memory, 132
   'technique of the body', 133
Glass Agency, The, 171, 180
God, 230, 231, 234
gods and goddesses, 229–30
Golbou, Farideh, 153
gramophones, 87, 88, 90–1, 92
graves, 49–50, 52
Greek culture, 229–30
Greek tragedy, 55
greenhouse atmosphere, 218
Grønstadt, Asbjørn, 147
Gulf Wars, 132
Gulzar, Muhammad Riza, 202

Haeri, Shahla, 148, 149, 160
Hamlet, 135
Hatami, Ali, 86, 87, 97–8n
Hatamikia, Ebrahim, 122, 139, 167, 170, 171, 176, 179–80, 220, 221
Heidegger, Martin, 125
heroism in popular entertainment, 194–5, 197, 199–200
heterosexual freedom in the West, 92, 95
Hidden Half, The, 31–44, *32*, *33*
   counter-history and counter-memory, 31, 33, 34–5, 43–4, 125
   female solidarity and temporality of political struggle, 39–42
   Fereshteh's political action, 35–6
   marriage, public and private spheres, 36–9
   scholarly attention, lack of, 42–3
hijab, 217

Hilderbrand, Lucas, 72, 77
historical genre in film, 86
historiography, 1–2, 109
historiography of Iranian cinema, 66
Hitch, 47–59, 54
  archaeology and genealogy, 47–9, 58–9
  counter-investigation, 51
  editing, 57
  post-revolution disappearances, 49–51
  processing trauma, 55–6, 56–7
  scenes with Makaremi and family members, 51–4, 56–7
'Hitchcock-Tarkovsky' dichotomy, 220–1
Hollywood, 86–7, 193, 203, 218–19, 220–1
Honarmand, Saeed, 160
Horizon, The, 174
horror films, 134–7
hospitals, 121–2
House of Cinema 217; *see also* Khaneh Cinema
Hozeh Honari (Art Center), 217
human body in visual culture, 229, 232
human rights, 50–1
humankind's destiny, 232–3, 234

Ice Flower, 202
Identity, 122
illustration, 229–30, 231, 235–6
images in Iranian culture, 231, 237, 241, 241–2
imperfect cinema, 24
Imperial Film Company of Bombay, 68, 69, 74
imprisonment of filmmakers, 34
impure memories, 127, 129, 131
In the Name of the Father, 180

In-betweeners, The, 190, 191, 196, 199
incomplete films and artworks, 22, 27–9
Indian film industry, 68, 193
'injection theory', 149
Instagram, 191, *192*, 227
Institute for the Intellectual Development of Children and Young Adults, 217
intellectualism, 240
International Resistance Film Festival, 137, 171
Iran Tribunal, 51
Irani, Ardeshir, 63
Iranian Alliance of Motion Picture Guilds *see* Khaneh Cinema
Iranian cinema in the international market, 43, 201–2, 218, 223–4, 225, 227–8
Iranian culture, 234, 236–7; *see also* Persian poetry and literature; visual culture in Iran
Iranian economy, 225–6
Iranian Free Cinema *see* Free Cinema
Iranian history, 1–2, 5–6
Iranian Hollywood, 220–1
Iranian music, traditional, 88, 89, 90
Iranian visual culture *see* visual culture in Iran
Iran–Iraq War, 126, 132, 137–8, 140, 170, 196
  war films, 167–9
  see also Sacred Defense Cinema
Iran-Nameh, 231
Iran-Shenasi, 231
Iraq, US invasion, 132
Islam, 232
'Islamic Hitchcock,' 220–1
Islamic Ideology Dissemination Organization, 171, 172

Islamic Republic of Iran (IRI), 2
 national identity, 126–7
 repression of political discourse, 33, 35
 state crimes, 140

Jameson, Frederic, 123
Janet, Pierre, 124
Jetée, La 122
Jetzt der Erkennbarkeit, 139
Johnny Got his Gun, 122
judiciary, 191

Karbala, 126, 127, 162, 171
Karimabadi, Mehrzad, 174
Kavousi, Houshang, 220
Kayhan, 191–2
Ketab-e Al-Naghz, 235
Khan, Ebrahim, 238
Khan, Genghis, 233
Khaneh Cinema, 222–3; *see also* House of Cinema
Khanoom, Zahra, 26
Khatami, Sayyid Mohammad, 5, 34, 218
Kheirabadi, Hamideh, 161–2
Khomeini, Ruhollah, 2, 128, 130, 196, 220–1
khosoulati, 226
Khosronejad, Pedram, 170
Khosrow and Shirin, 156; *see also Shirin*
Kiarostami, Abbas
 censorship, 224
 Koker trilogy, 102, 104, 105–6, 114
 Life and Nothing More, 106–7, 110–11
 Shirin, 146–7, 152–3, 155–6, 162–3
 Taste of Cherry, 175, 218
 Ten, 223
 Through the Olive Trees, 112–13
 Where is the Friend's House? 105

Kimiai, Masoud, 121–2, 122, 220
King of Hearts, 202
Klee, Paul, 28
Koker trilogy
 memory, 100–2, 104, 105–6
 reality and reconstruction, 102, 110, 111
 see also Life and Nothing More; Through the Olive Trees; Where is the Friend's House?
Kūh-e Qāf, 234

land reform program, 22–3
Langford, Michelle, 38, 43, 132–3, 134
Latour, Bruno, 69
leftist marginalization of women's issues, 41
Lévi-Strauss, Claude, 135
Life and Nothing More, 106–11
 gazes and frames, 106, 107–8, 109
 media and memory, 105
 reconstruction, 107, 108, 110
 referenced in *Through the Olive Trees*, 112, 113
 soundtrack, 107, 108, 112
 television, 106, 111
lip-synching, 137
listening, acousmatic, 146–7, 151, 154–5, 157
literacy, 104, 238
literature *see* Persian poetry and literature
Little Black Fish, The, 1, 187
Living Martyr, 122
Lor Girl, The, 63–80, 65, 71
 access to, 73–9
 audiovisual distortions, 64, 66, 70–1, 72–3, 76–7
 critical and scholarly responses, 67–9, 70, 80
 final scene analysis, 70–1

253

Lor Girl, The (cont.)
   formats, 63–4, 65, 74, 76
   history of access, 64, 66–7, 72–3, 76, 78–80
   nationalism, 67–8, 75
   preservation and legacy, 69, 75–6
   production and original release, 63, 66, 68
   sound, 64, 68–9, 71
love and eroticism in Iranian cinema, 147, 158–60
   post-revolution, 37, 148–50, 156
Love Stricken, 85–97, 94, 96
   East/West juxtaposition, 91–2, 95, 97
   enunciation, 85, 87, 95, 97
   national identity, 86–7, 89, 90, 92–3, 95, 97
   plot and context, 87–9
   production as a theme, 87, 90
   resistance of cinematic standardization, 86–7
   scene analysis, 89–90, 91–2, 92–5, 95–7
   sound recording technologies, 86, 87–8, 90
   soundtrack, 93, 97
lūṭīs, 198

McLuhan, Marshall, 126
Mahdavian, Mohammad Hussein, 137
Makaremi, Chowra, 47–59
   counter-investigation, 51
   cultural references, 55, 56, 58
   family genealogy, 58–9
   filmmaking as archaeology, 47–9
   post-revolution disappearances, 49–51
   processing trauma, 55–6, 56–7
   scenes with family members, 51–4, 56–7

Makhmalbaf, Mohsen, 170, 191, 203, 220
Marriage of the Blessed, 122–3, 124–5, 130–2, *130*
A Time for Love, 148–9
male gaze, 155
Mandanipour, Shahriar, 121
Mani, 230, 235
Manichaeistic paintings, 231, 234, 235
Marker, Chris, 114
marriage, 32, 36, 37, 38, 38–9
Marriage of the Blessed, 122–3, 124–5, 130–2, *130*
   bāzgasht be khishtan (return to the self), 131
   emergency room as editing room, 124–5
   'living martyr', 122
   PTSD, 123
   telescoping, 131
   trauma, 123–4
Martyr Organization, 177, 178
martyrdom, 126, 131, 133, 137, 138, 162
   filmfarsi, 197
   'living martyr', 122
   Sacred Defense Cinema, 170–1, 175–6, 199
   shahādat, 131
   shahīd, 138
Marxism, 28, 193
masculinity, 199, 200, 201
masquerades, 112–13
massacres and executions, 47–51
Mas'ud of Ghazni, 230
Masumi, Khosro, 221
Mauss, Marcel, 133
May Lady, 37, 127–8, *128*
   dilemma of ethno-sociography, 128
Maybe Some Other Time, 125

MCIG *see* Ministry of Culture and Islamic Guidance (MCIG)
media and memory, 105–6
media archaeology, 65–6, 66, 72, 79
Medina, José, 34
Mehrjui, Dariush, 220
melodrama, 42–3, 148
memories of war, 131, 132–3, 139
memory
 and the body, 133–4
 loss of, 122
 metaphors of, 99–100, 103–4
 and media, 105–6
 and objects, 51–4, 103
 and power, 34, 38
 and purification, 127, 129–30, 131–2
 and structure, 114
 and trauma, 122–3, 124–5
 see also cinematic memoryscapes
mental health, 123–4
Metz, Christian, 87
Mikali, Hasanak, 233
Milani, Tahmineh, 34, 35, 42–3, 125
Ministry of Culture and Islamic Guidance (MCIG), 75, 77, 148, 181, 216–17, 218, 221–2
mise-en-scène, 41, 42, 91, 92, 93
Mix, 220
mnemo-techniques of memory, 100, 104
modernization of Iran, 28, 67, 68–9
modesty laws, 92
Mograbi, Avi, 52
Mokri, Shahram, 134
Monabat-Kāry, 102–3
monotheistic religion, 230
montage, 123, 125, 129
Montazeri audio tapes, 140
Moqāvemat Film Festival, 172
Mossadegh, Mohammad, 2, 39
Motevaselian, Ahmad, 137

motherhood, 127–8
motorcycles, 198
Mottahedeh, Negar, 123
mourning, 133, 162–3, 171, 176–8, 177
 for film stars, 190–1
Mulvey, Laura, 155
murals, 230, 235
Musavī, Mir-Hosein, 59
Musée d'Art Moderne de la Ville de Paris, 1
music in films, 41, 42, 59, 68, 93
 non-diegetic, 152, 157
mustaz'afin, 128
Muti'i, Malik, 190–1, *192*, 199

Naderi, Amir, 121
Naficy, Hamid, 68, 69, 126, 169, 180
'Naghsh', 235
Nancy, Jean-Luc, 106, 110, 114
narrative cinema, 106
National Film Archives of Iran (NFAI), 73–5, 76–7
national identity, 126–7, 241
national identity explored in film, 89, 90, 92–3, 95
National Television, 217
nationalism in films, 67–8, 69, 179
neo-realism, 42
Netflix, 227
New Wave Iranian cinema, 201, 204, 220–1
Newborns, The, 21–9, 25, 27
 access and formats, 21–2
 influence on other filmmakers, 58
 lack of narration, 26–7
 opening scenes, 24–6
Nezami, 146, 153, 154, 156, 158, 160
NFAI *see* National Film Archives of Iran (NFAI)
Nietzsche, Friedrich, 7, 104, 109, 110
Nochlin, Linda, 27–8

Nooshin, Laudan, 68
nostalgia and counter-memory, 203
Nourbakhsh, Mehdi, 222

objects and memory, 51–4
oil industry, 2
Omid, Jalal, 68–9
Outcasts, The, 182, 197–201

Pahlavi, Mohammad Reza, 2
   filmfarsi, 189, 192
   modernization agenda, 22–3, 28
Pahlavi, Reza Shah, 67, 71, 86
paintings, 231, 235
pāksazi, 127; *see also* purification of cinema; purification of memory
Palestine, 26
Panahi, Jafar, 172
pandemic, 140
Parastu'i, Parviz, 191
Par-e Parvāz, 221, 222
Parikka, Jussi, 65, 79
Paris, 92, 93, 95
Parole, 222
Partovi, Pedram, 127, 133, 150
pathways, 113–14
Pazienza, Claudio, 52
People's Tribunal, 51
Persian language, 56, 63, 64, 124
Persian poetry and literature, 1, 147, 148, 150, 151, 156, 160, 234
photography, 91, 95, 131, 237–8
Piano, The, 158
Plato, 104
poetry, 147, 150, 151, 156, 160, 230
political cinema, 43, 44
political prisoners, 32, 38
   female, 32, 38, 40
popular cinema, 43, 202–3;
   see also filmfarsi
popular entertainment, 194–5, 202–3

portraits, 231, 235
post-revolutionary cinema, 155, 194
   art cinema, 201–2, 204
   banning of *filmfarsi*, 190, 196
   love and eroticism, 148–50
post-revolutionary violence, 47–9, 55, 56–7
   executions and disappearances, 49–51, 58–9
post-traumatic stress disorder (PTSD), 123, 131
pottery, 231, 235
power and memory, 34
Prelinger, Rick, 74
pre-revolution cinema, 148, 150, 192–3; *see also filmfarsi*
preservation of film, 74–6
prisoner-of-war films, 176–7
prisoners, political, 32
private and public spheres, 36–7
private investment in film, 202, 226, 241
production *see* film production
propaganda films, 167, 170, 193
prostitution, 26, 194
Prozāk, 123, 124
psychiatric discourse, 123–4
psychoanalysis, 123–4, 125
PTSD (post-traumatic stress disorder), 123, 131
public and private spheres, 36–7
purification of cinema, 127, 148
purification of memory, 127, 129–30, 131–2

Qadiri, Iraj, 191
Qajar, Ahmad Shah, 86, 88, 89
qatlhā-ye zanjīrehī see 'Chain Murders of Iran'
Queen, The, 168
   anti-war sentiments, 172–3, 175–6
   opening scenes, 167–9

representation of enemy forces, 174–5
spiritual criticism of war, 180–1, 182

Rahmanian, Mohammad, 153, 156
rationalism, 229, 232
reconstruction in cinema, 107, 108, 110
'red line', 56
Rekabtalaei, Golbarg, 67
religion, monotheistic, 230
religious conservatives 191, 193–4
religious minorities, 178–9
Resistance Film Festival, 137, 171
Revolution 1978/9
  historiography, 2, 35
  immediate aftermath, 21, 35–6, 58
  legacy, 122, 130–1, 203
  music, 59
  post-revolutionary violence, 47–51
  representation in film, 21, 43, 58
  women's experiences and role, 26, 31
revolutions, 28–9
Reza Motorcyclist, 122
Rijai, Farhang, 88
Rizi, Najmeh Moradiyan, 156
road accidents, 121–2
romance in popular entertainment, 194–5
Rothberg, Michael, 6
ruptures, 124, 129

Sacred Defense Cinema
  dissent and criticism from within, 170, 172–3, 179–82
  filmmakers, 125, 169–70, 196
  martyrdom, 137, 170–1, 175–6, 177–8, 196–7
  reception by critics and audiences, 171
  representation of enemy forces, 174–5
  see also individual films from the genre
Sadeg, Narmine, 1–2
Safavid Court, 235
Said, Edward, 3
Saljoughi, Sara, 146–7, 155, 156, 158, 160
Saminezhad, Ruhangiz, 74
Sans Soleil, 114
Santayana, George, 56
Scent of Yusef's Shirt, The, 176
scientific knowledge, 234, 237
Scout, The, 167, 168, 175, 180
screen memories, 8, 132, 139;
  see also cinematic memoryscapes
scripts, censorship of, 216–17, 221, 222
sculpture, 230
Sepanta, Abdolhossein, 63
Sepehri, Sohrab, 102
sexuality and censorship, 5
Shabazi, Parviz, 122
shahādat, 131
shahīd, 138
Shāhnāmeh, 55, 234
Shahrzad, 203
shame, 160
Shari'ati, Ali, 131
shell-shock, 122–3
Shi'ism, 55, 126, 127, 162
Shirin, 146–63, *152*, *162*
  bathing scene, 158–60
  ending, 160–3
  listening, 147, 150–1, 152, 154–5, 158
  love and eroticism, 156–8
  music, 152, 157
  opening scenes, 152–3
  Shirin's perspective, 153–4, 158, 160

Shirin (cont.)
  spectatorship, 146–7, 149–50, 155–6
  story structure, 153, 155
Shock Corridor, 122
Simonides of Keos, 100
Sīmorgh, 2, 234, 245
simultaneity, 139, 141
Sinamā-yi Difāʿ-i Muqaddas
  see Sacred Defense Cinema
Sinamā-ye Āzad see free cinema
Sīnemā-ye Defāʿ-ye Moqaddas
  see Sacred Defense Cinema
sixth generation see filmmakers, sixth generation
Sobchack, Vivian, 152, 157–8
soccer, 111
social class, 128, 139, 194–5, 198, 201
social media, 134, 190, 191, 227
Sohrabi, Naghmeh, 35
soldiers
  martyrdom, 122, 126, 167–9, 176–8
  non-Muslim, 178–9
  representation of enemy forces, 172–3, 174–5
  see also Sacred Defense Cinema
Soroush, Abdolkarim, 149
sound in early cinema, 68–9
sound recording technologies, 87–8, 90
soundtracks, 41, 42, 59, 68, 93; see also *Shirin*
South America, 49
spectatorship, 146–7, 149, 155, 158
Sperm Whale, 203
Spirit of Utopia, The, 58
spirituality in war films, 171, 178, 179–81
Standing in the Dust, 137–9, *138*
  'direct cinema'-mimicry, 137
  lip-synching, 137

screen memories, 139
shahīd, 138
state control over film, 73, 75, 77; see also censorship; film production: state control
state media, criticism of, 191
state TV, 243
state violence see post-revolutionary violence
statues, 230, 234
structure and memory, 114
suicide, 174–5
surrealism, 134
Suture, 122

Tabarraee, Babak, 80
Tabrizi, Behrooz-Ghamari, 3
ṭāghūt, 191
Taghvai, Nasser, 220
talkies, 63, 64
Tapper, Richard, 171
tar (musical instrument), 89–90
Taste of Cherry, 175, 218
Tavakoli-Targhi, Mohammad, 126–7
Tay, Sharon Lin, 162
taʾziyeh, 162, 171, 194, 235
teahouse paintings, 235, 236
'technique of the body', 133
technological developments in filmmaking, 226–7
technology failure, 72, 79–80
Tejaratchi, Jafar, 63
telescoping, 129–30, 131, 132, 139, 140
television, 106, 108, 111, 193, 202, 203, 219, 243
temporality of resistance, 31, 33, 35, 39–40, 41–2
theater and absolutist control mechanisms, 240
third cinema, 24
Those Who Said No, 51

Through the Olive Trees, 105, 111–14
Time for Love, A, 148–9
time loops, 134, 135, 137
Time Tunnel, 203
Torok, Maria, 134
toromā see trauma
tragedy, 154, 160–1
trailers, 219
transliteration, 15
trauma, 55, 122–3, 124
Travellers, 122
trompe l'oeil, 151, 155, 161
Trotsky, Leon, 28
Truffaut, François, 25–6
Truth, 125
Turkish film industry, 193
Turtles can Fly, 132

ultraconservative cinema, 171, 172, 173, 179, 181
underground distribution of film, 77–8, 204, 218
unfinished films, 22, 27–9; see also Newborns, The
unions, 217, 222–3
University of Tehran, 200
urbanization and the urban underclass, 22–3
US invasion of Iraq, 132

Varzi, Roxanne, 171, 174, 175, 176, 180
veterans, 170, 180, 200
video cameras, 218, 221, 222
video players, 219
videocassettes, 64, 72–3, 74, 76, 219
underground distribution, 77–8
video-sharing platforms, 63–4, 80
violence, post-revolutionary
atrocities and silence, 47–51, 55, 56–7, 58–9
Virilio, Paul, 223, 129

visual culture in Iran, 229–31, 234–5, 237–8, 239–41, 241–2
Voice and Vision, 126

war films, 167–70, 196–7, 200
anti-war sentiments, 172–3, 175–8, 182
representation of enemy forces, 174–5
spirituality, 171, 178–82
war memories and trauma, 122–3, 131, 132–3, 139
watermarks, 71, 77
Western cultural exploration, 237
Westernization, 2, 24, 67–8, 86, 127
Westoxification, 125
Where is the Friend's House? 100, *101*, 103
media and memory, 105
metaphors of memory, 99–100, 102, 103–4, 104–5
pathways and doors, 102–3, 113–14
referenced in *Life and Nothing More*, 107, 108, 111
women
censorship, 243
in the film industry, 42
gender norms in film, 69
marginalization by leftist groups, 41
and religion, 178–9
repressed history, 31, 39–41
Western, 92, 95
see also female bodies and desires; female gaze
world cinema, 218–19, 226–7; see also Iranian cinema in the international market

Yerushalmi, Yosef Hayim, 123
young population in Iran, 224–5
YouTube, 64, 80, 227

Zoroastrians, 177, 178–9

EU representative:
Easy Access System Europe
Mustamäe tee 50, 10621 Tallinn, Estonia
Gpsr.requests@easproject.com

www.ingramcontent.com/pod-product-compliance
Lightning Source LLC
Chambersburg PA
CBHW071833230426
43671CB00012B/1953